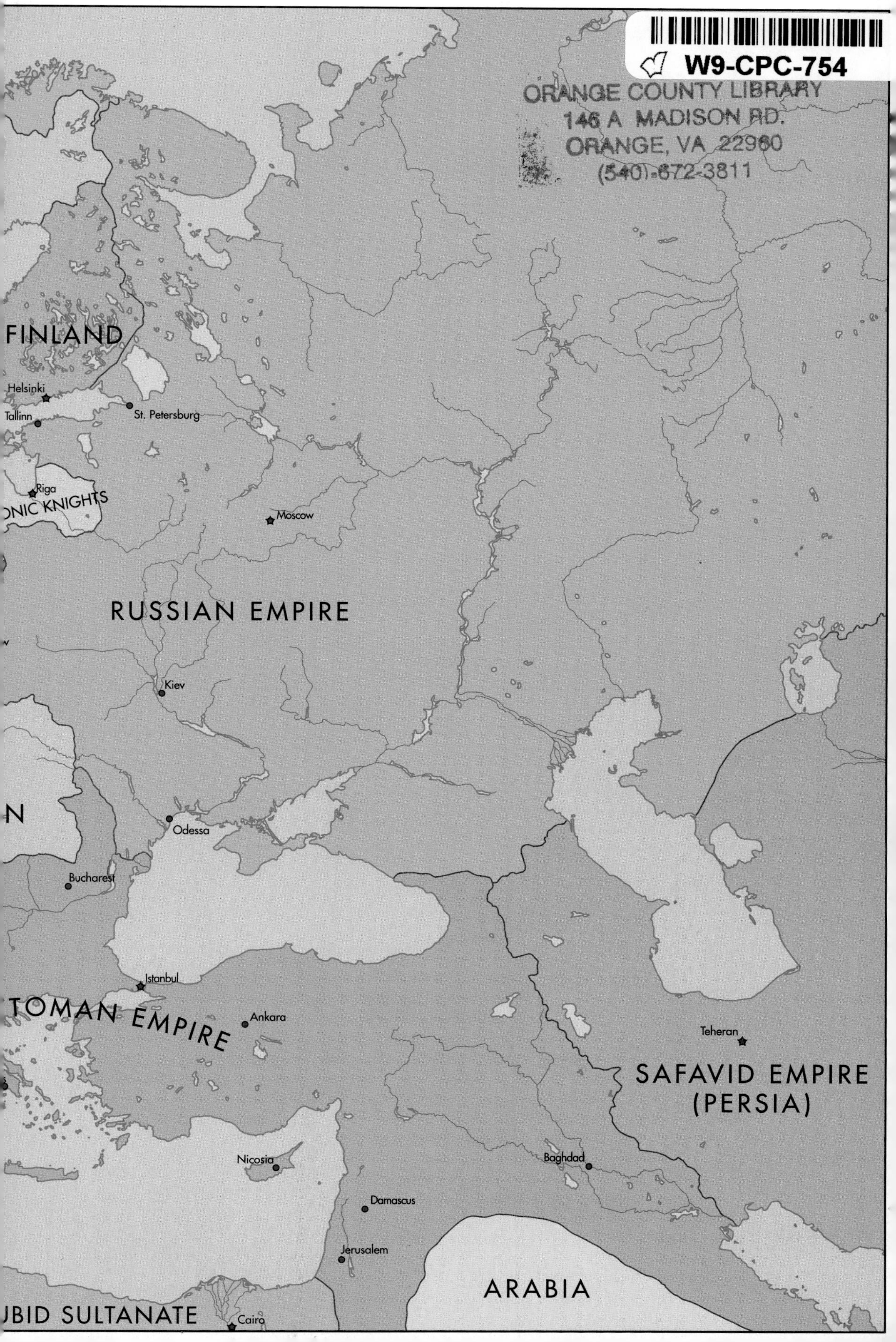
FINLAND
Helsinki
Tallinn
St. Petersburg
Riga
ONIC KNIGHTS
Moscow
RUSSIAN EMPIRE
Kiev
N
Odessa
Bucharest
Istanbul
TOMAN EMPIRE
Ankara
Teheran
SAFAVID EMPIRE
(PERSIA)
Nicosia
Baghdad
Damascus
Jerusalem
ARABIA
UBID SULTANATE
Cairo

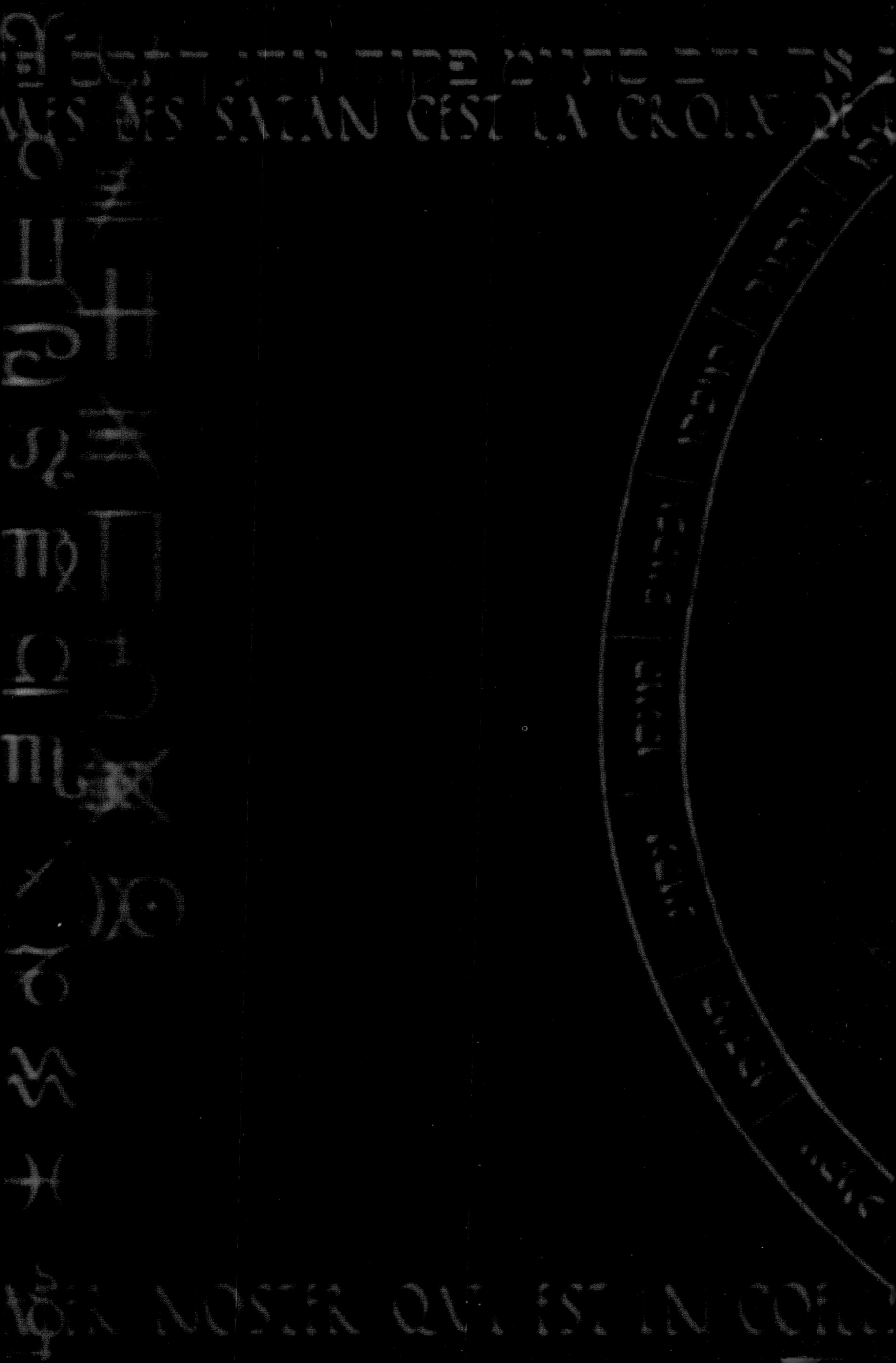
MES DES SATAN CEST LA CROIX
NOSTER QVI EST IN

Rex Mundi

BOOK TWO: THE RIVER UNDERGROUND

REX MUNDI BOOK TWO:

the
RIVER UNDERGROUND

ARVID NELSON
writer letterer layout

ERIC J
artist

JEROMY COX
colorist

❋ ❋ ❋

www.rexmundi.net

REX MUNDI, VOL. 2: THE RIVER UNDER-
GROUND. April 2005. Published by Image
Comics, Inc., Office of publication: 1942
University Avenue, Suite 305, Berkeley,
California 94704. Copyright © 2005 Arvid Nelson
and Eric Johnson. All rights reserved. REX
MUNDI™ (including all prominent characters
featured in this issue), its logo and all character
likenesses are trademarks of Arvid Nelson and
Eric Johnson, unless otherwise noted. Image
Comics® is a trademark of Image Comics, Inc.

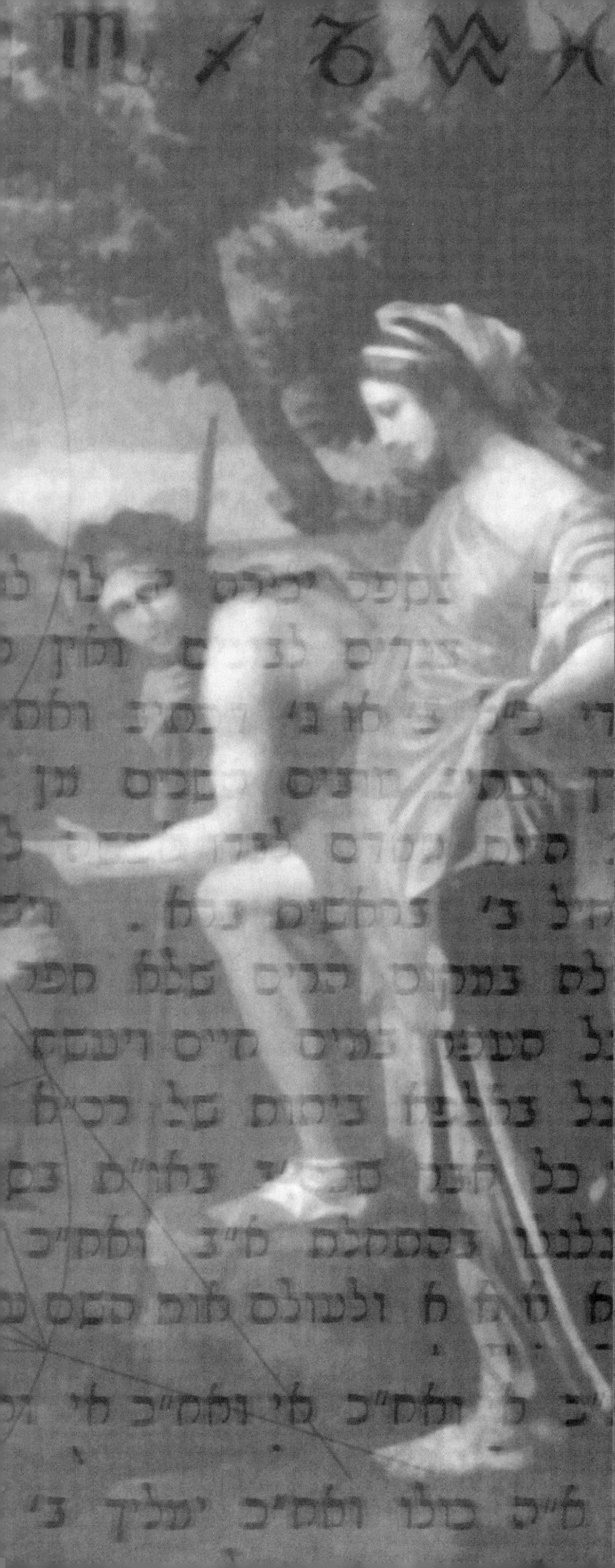

TABLE of CONTENTS

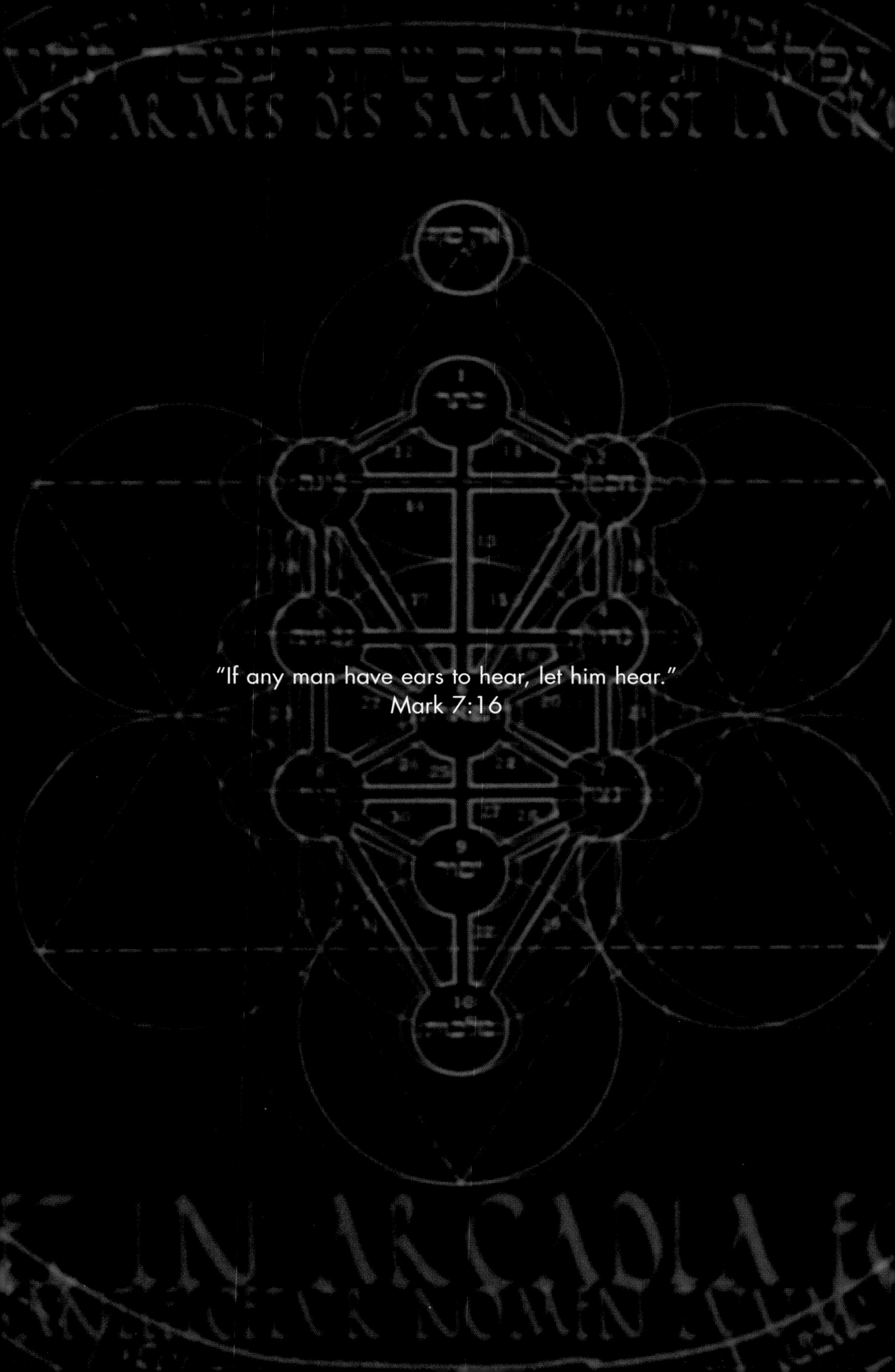

"If any man have ears to hear, let him hear."
Mark 7:16

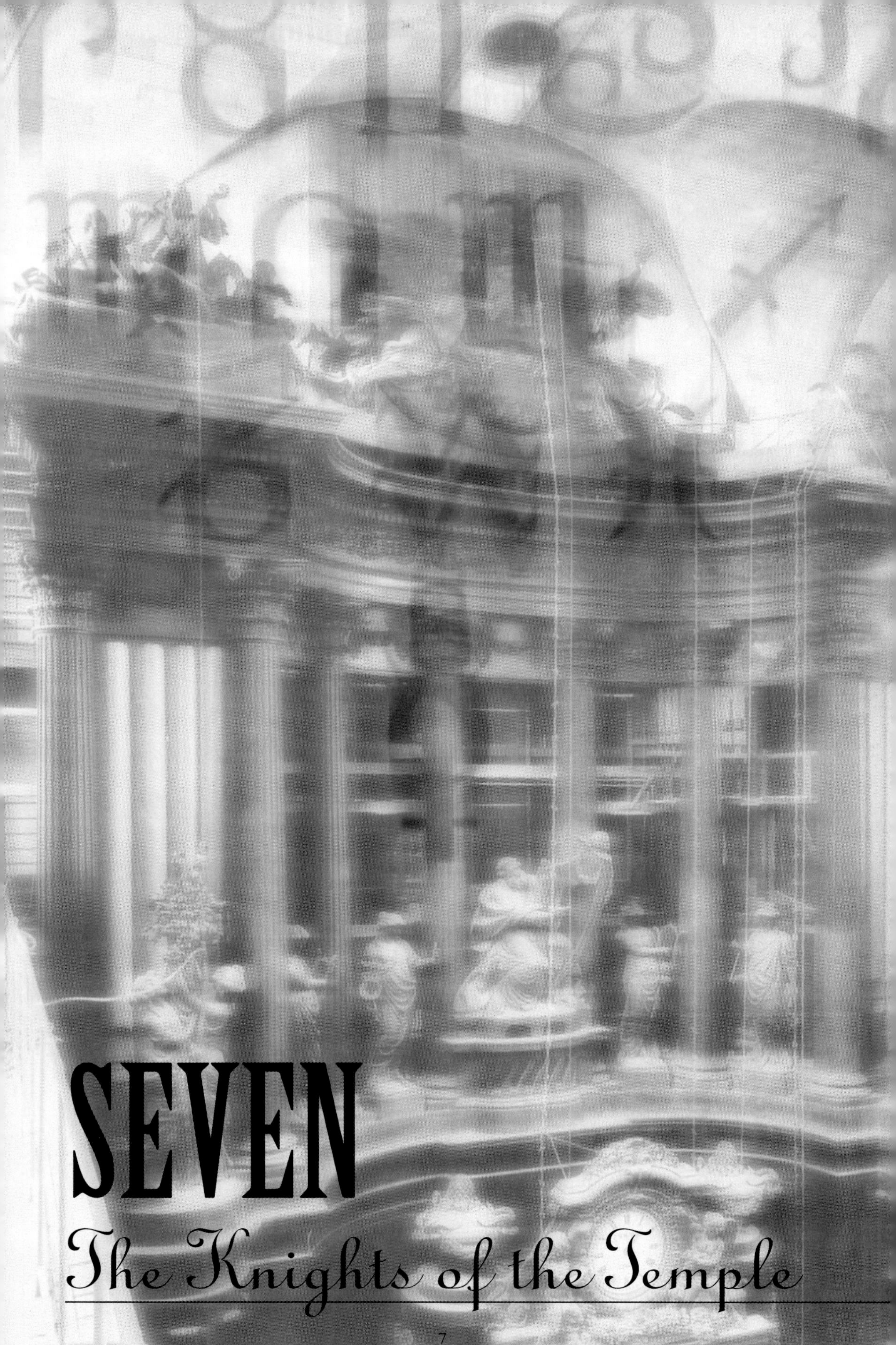

SEVEN

The Knights of the Temple

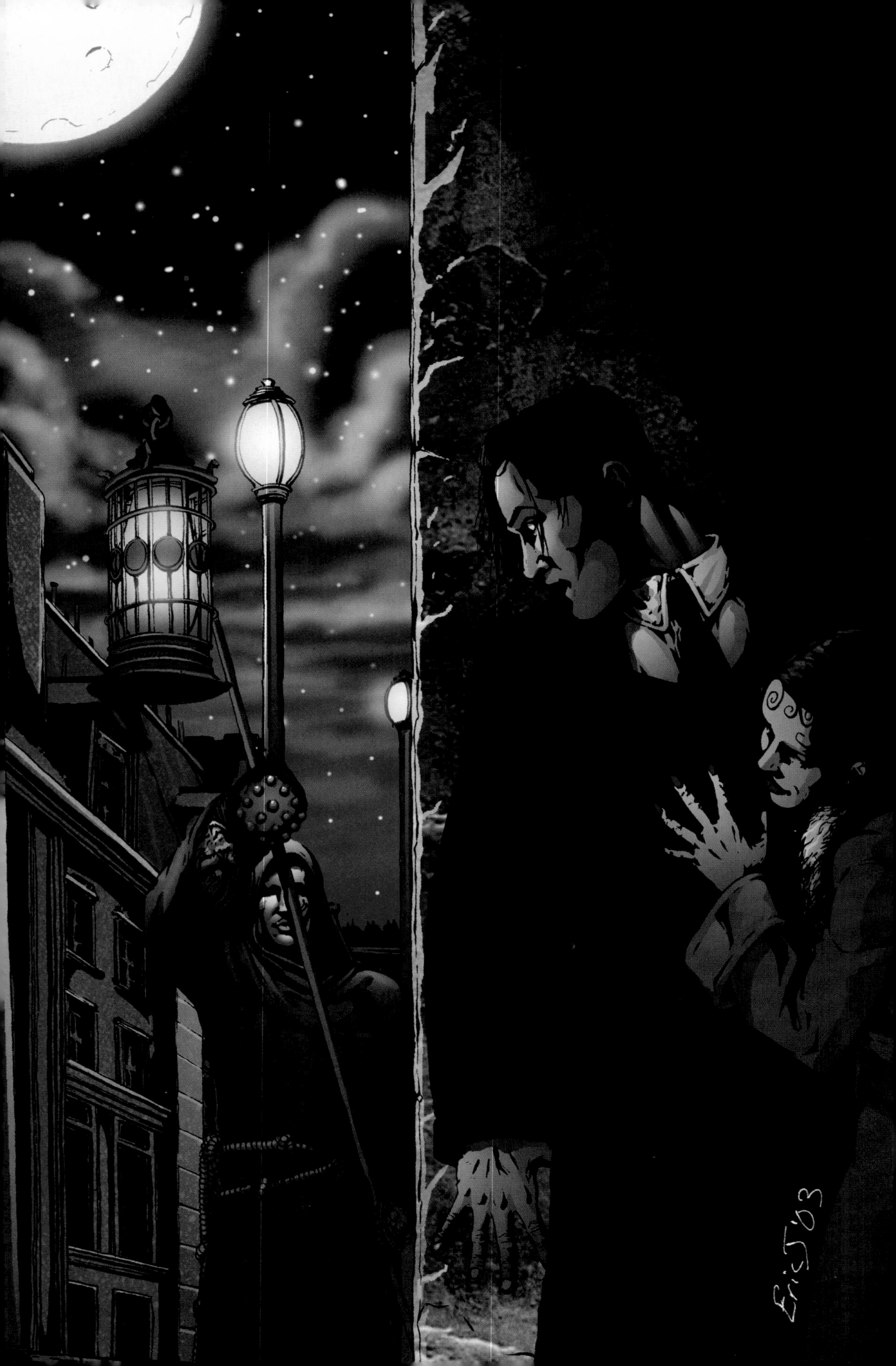
EricJ'03

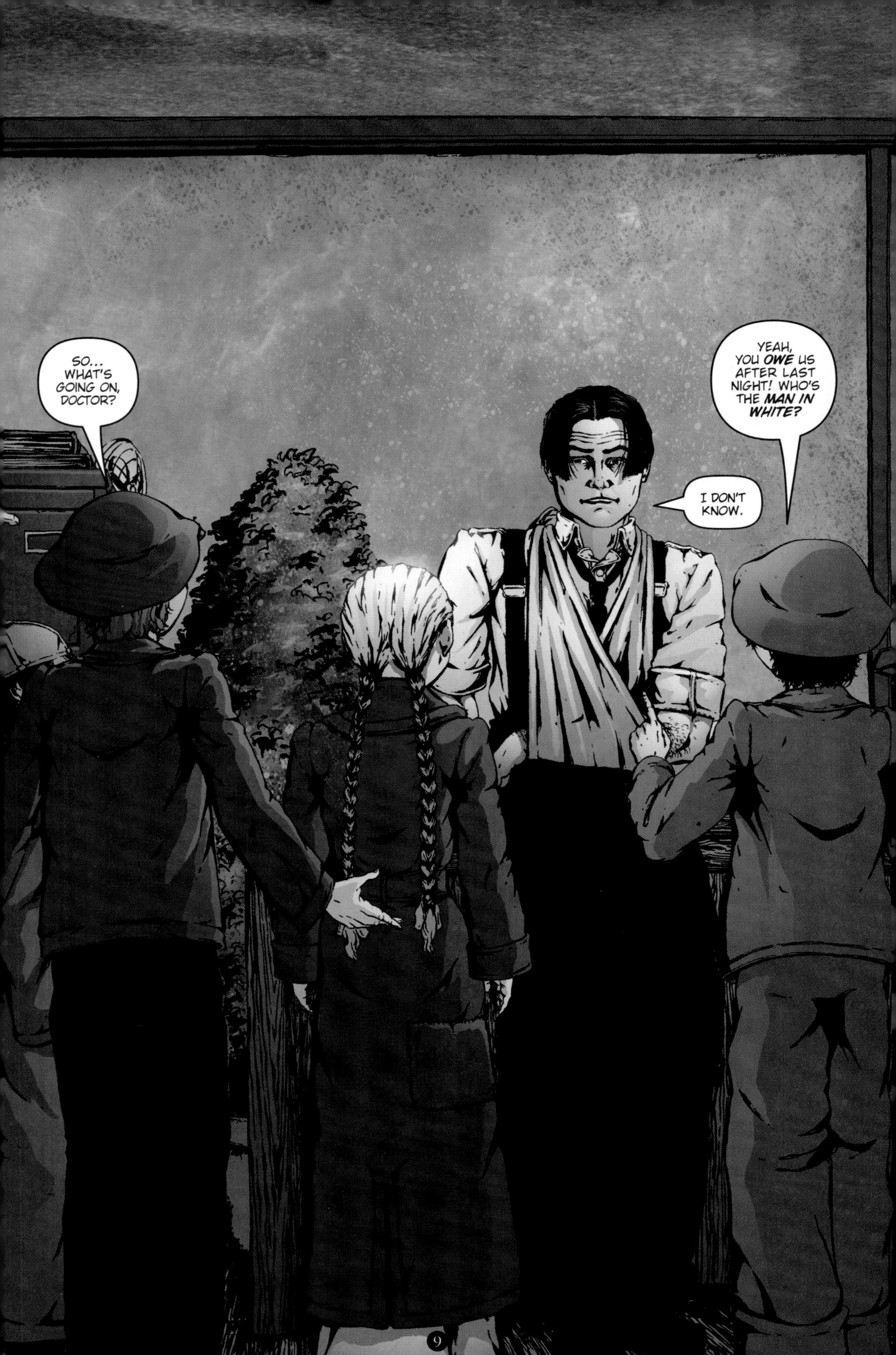
SO... WHAT'S GOING ON, DOCTOR?
YEAH, YOU **OWE** US AFTER LAST NIGHT! WHO'S THE ***MAN IN WHITE?***
I DON'T KNOW.

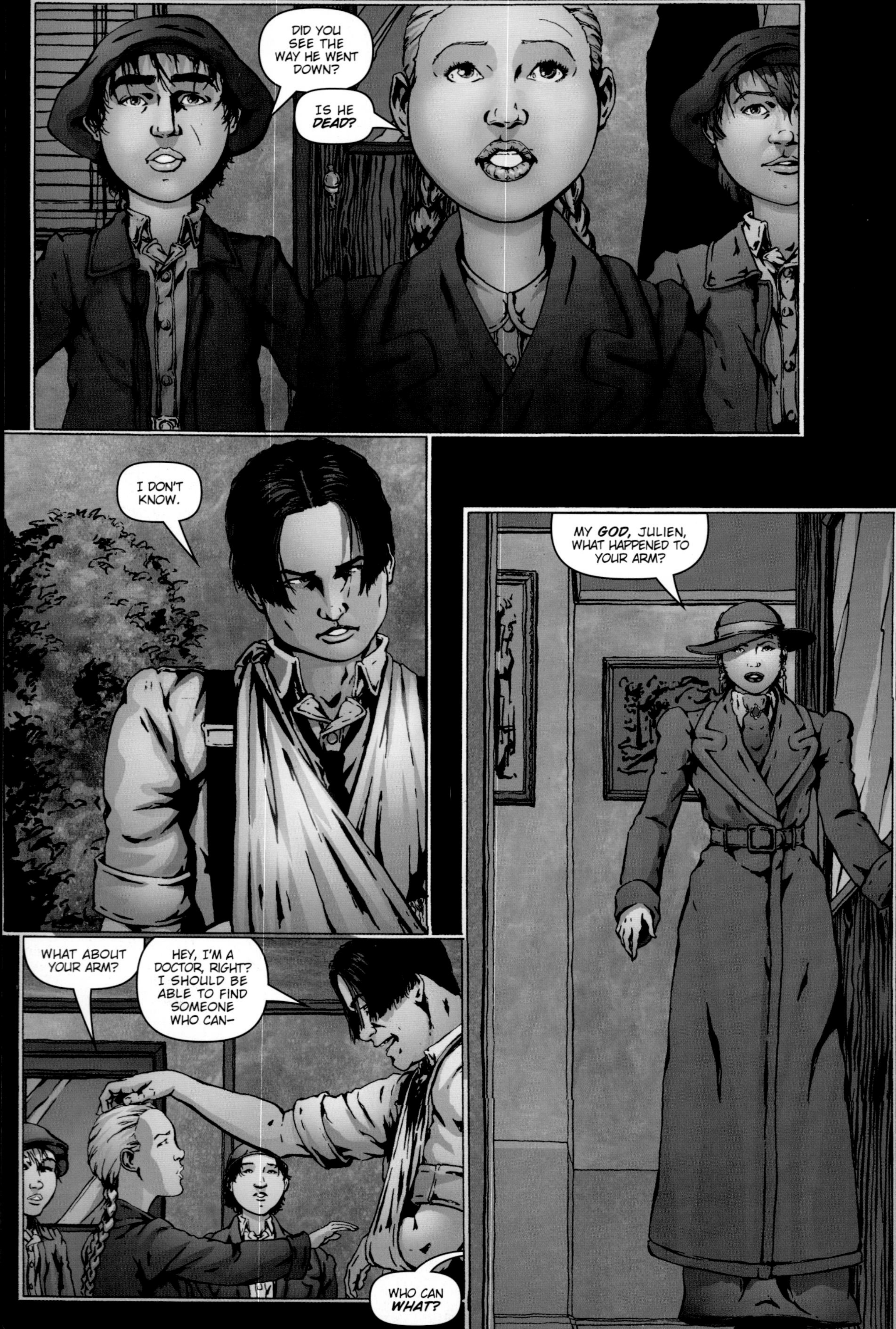
DID YOU SEE THE WAY HE WENT DOWN?
IS HE *DEAD?*
I DON'T KNOW.
WHAT ABOUT YOUR ARM?
HEY, I'M A DOCTOR, RIGHT? I SHOULD BE ABLE TO FIND SOMEONE WHO CAN-
WHO CAN *WHAT?*
MY ***GOD,*** JULIEN, WHAT HAPPENED TO YOUR ARM?

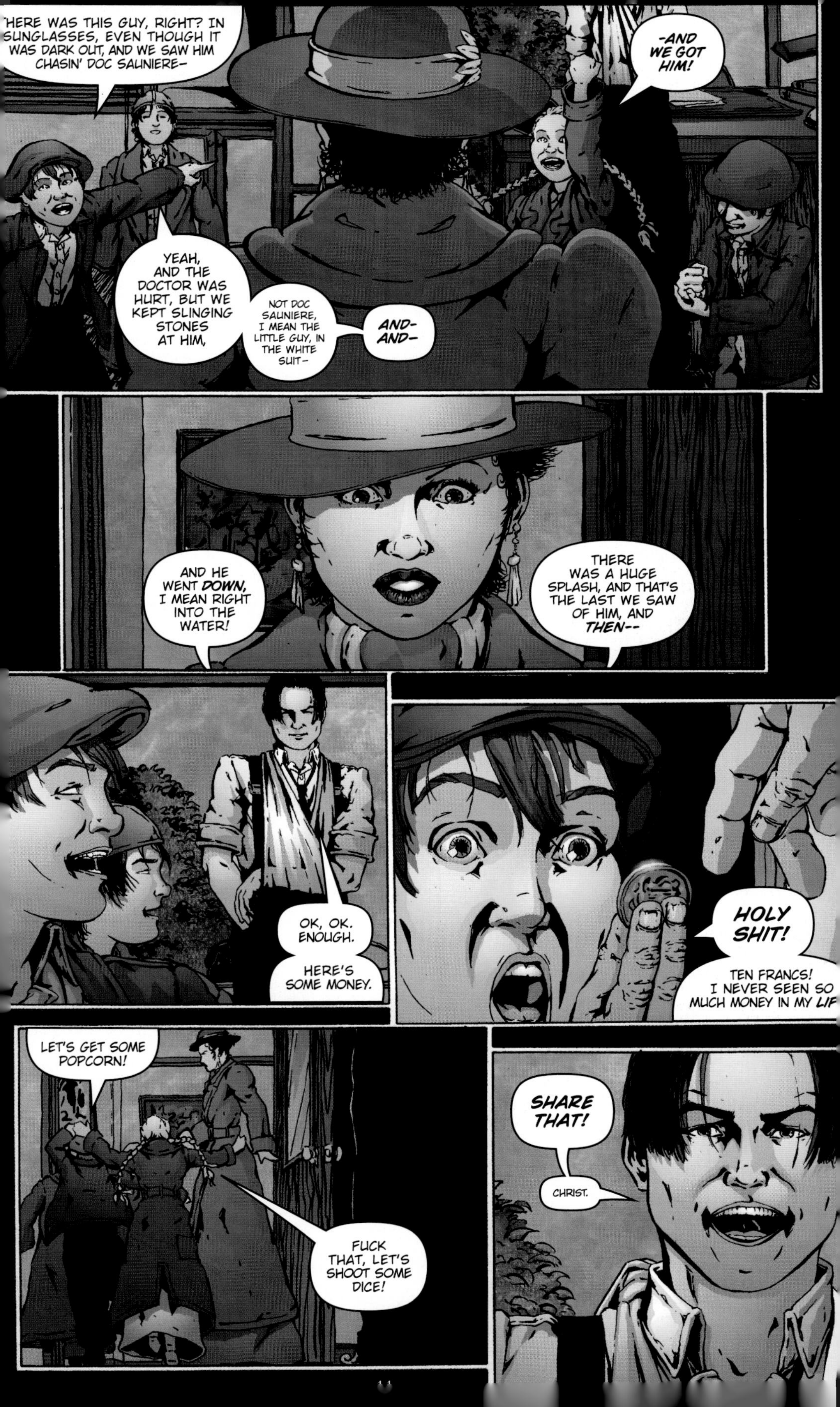
THERE WAS THIS GUY, RIGHT? IN SUNGLASSES, EVEN THOUGH IT WAS DARK OUT, AND WE SAW HIM CHASIN' DOC SAUNIERE–
–AND WE GOT HIM!
YEAH, AND THE DOCTOR WAS HURT, BUT WE KEPT SLINGING STONES AT HIM,
NOT DOC SAUNIERE, I MEAN THE LITTLE GUY, IN THE WHITE SUIT–
AND–AND–
AND HE WENT DOWN, I MEAN RIGHT INTO THE WATER!
THERE WAS A HUGE SPLASH, AND THAT'S THE LAST WE SAW OF HIM, AND THEN--
OK, OK. ENOUGH.
HERE'S SOME MONEY.
HOLY SHIT!
TEN FRANCS! I NEVER SEEN SO MUCH MONEY IN MY LIF
LET'S GET SOME POPCORN!
FUCK THAT, LET'S SHOOT SOME DICE!
SHARE THAT!
CHRIST.

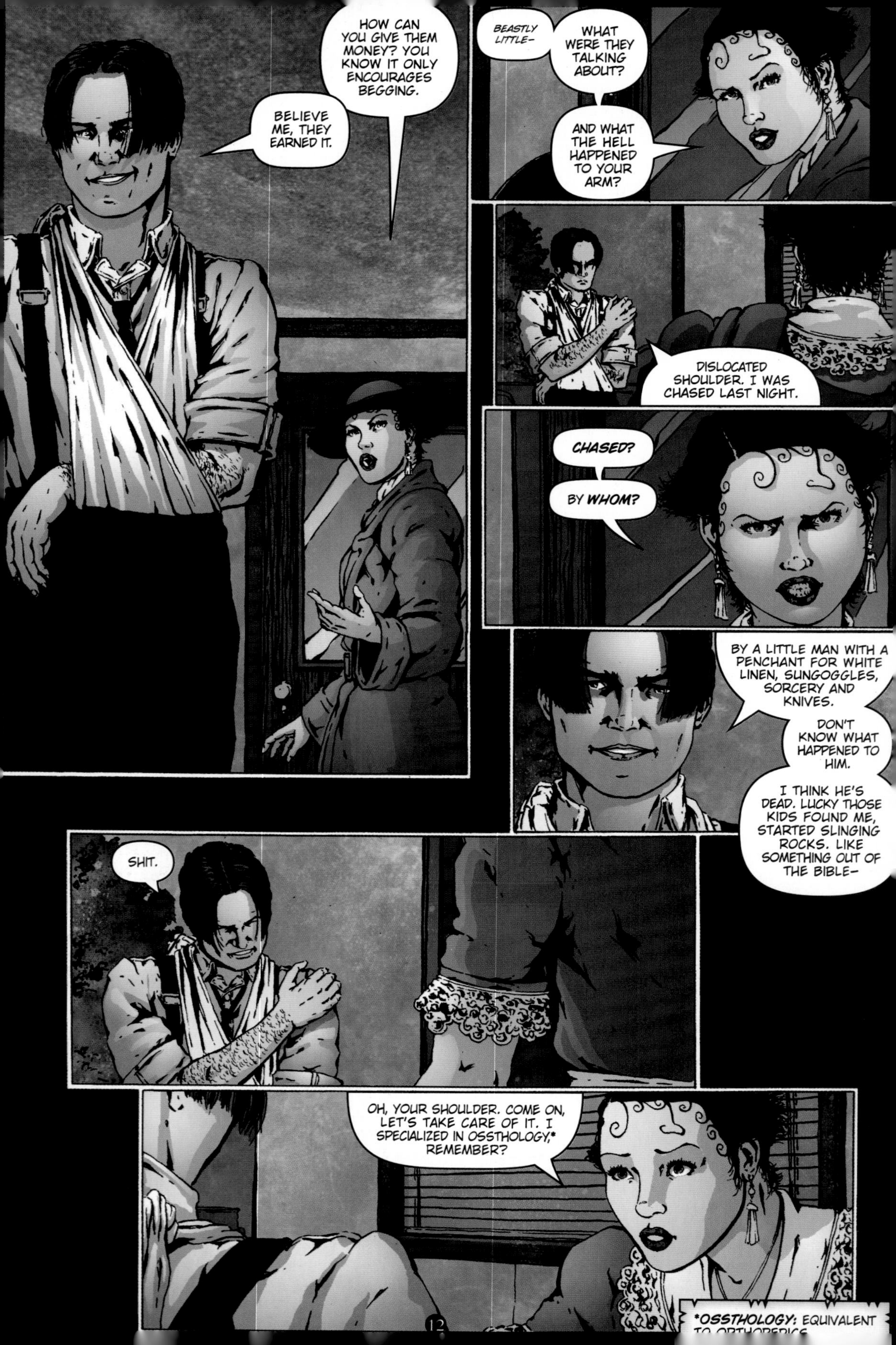
HOW CAN YOU GIVE THEM MONEY? YOU KNOW IT ONLY ENCOURAGES BEGGING.
BELIEVE ME, THEY EARNED IT.
BEASTLY LITTLE–
WHAT WERE THEY TALKING ABOUT?
AND WHAT THE HELL HAPPENED TO YOUR ARM?
DISLOCATED SHOULDER. I WAS CHASED LAST NIGHT.
CHASED?
BY ***WHOM?***
BY A LITTLE MAN WITH A PENCHANT FOR WHITE LINEN, SUNGOGGLES, SORCERY AND KNIVES.
DON'T KNOW WHAT HAPPENED TO HIM.
I THINK HE'S DEAD. LUCKY THOSE KIDS FOUND ME, STARTED SLINGING ROCKS. LIKE SOMETHING OUT OF THE BIBLE–
SHIT.
OH, YOUR SHOULDER. COME ON, LET'S TAKE CARE OF IT. I SPECIALIZED IN OSSTHOLOGY,* REMEMBER?
***OSSTHOLOGY:** EQUIVALENT

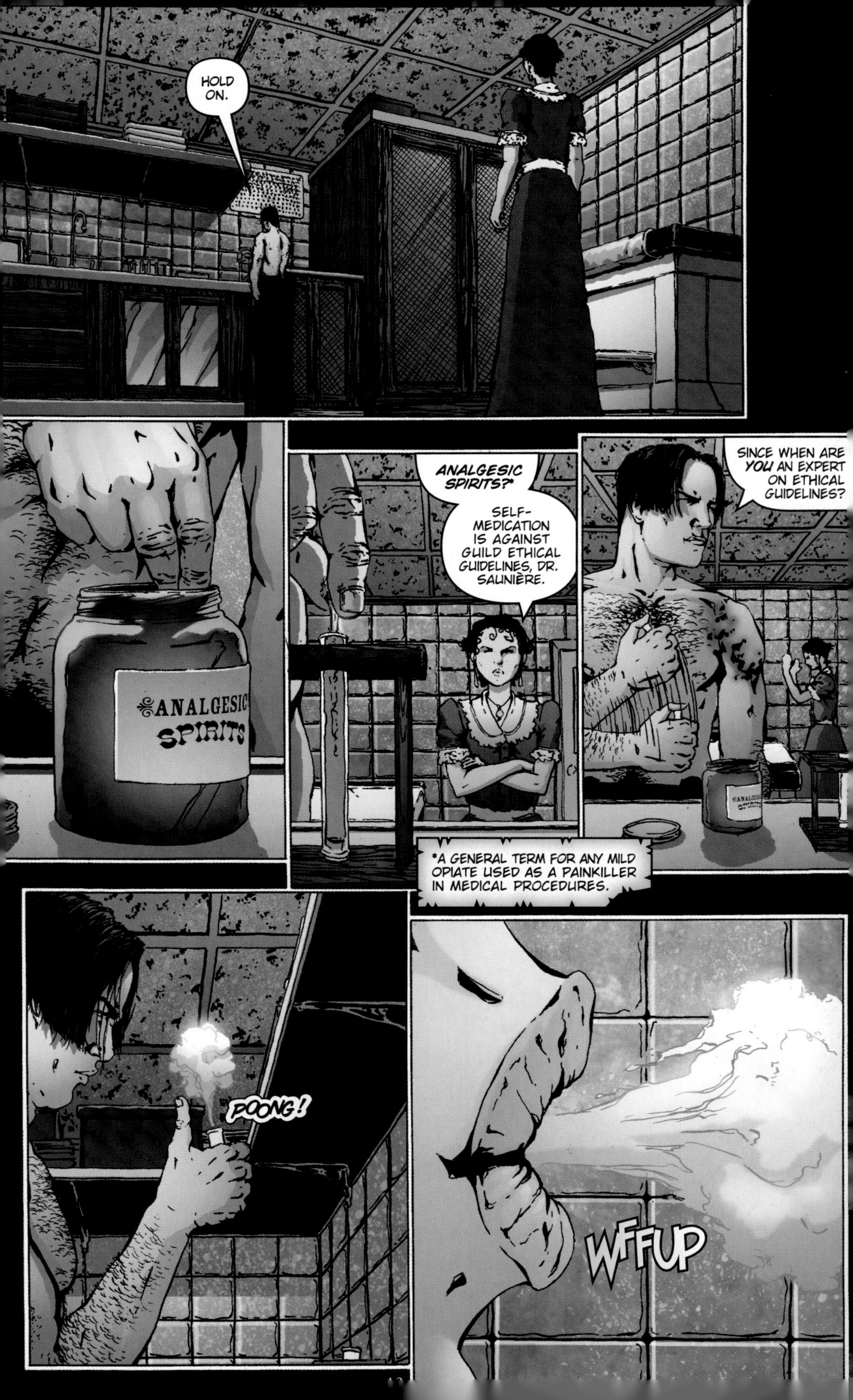
HOLD ON.
ANALGESIC SPIRITS
ANALGESIC SPIRITS?*
SELF-MEDICATION IS AGAINST GUILD ETHICAL GUIDELINES, DR. SAUNIÈRE.
SINCE WHEN ARE YOU AN EXPERT ON ETHICAL GUIDELINES?
ANALGESIC SPIRITS
*A GENERAL TERM FOR ANY MILD OPIATE USED AS A PAINKILLER IN MEDICAL PROCEDURES.
POONG!
WFFUP

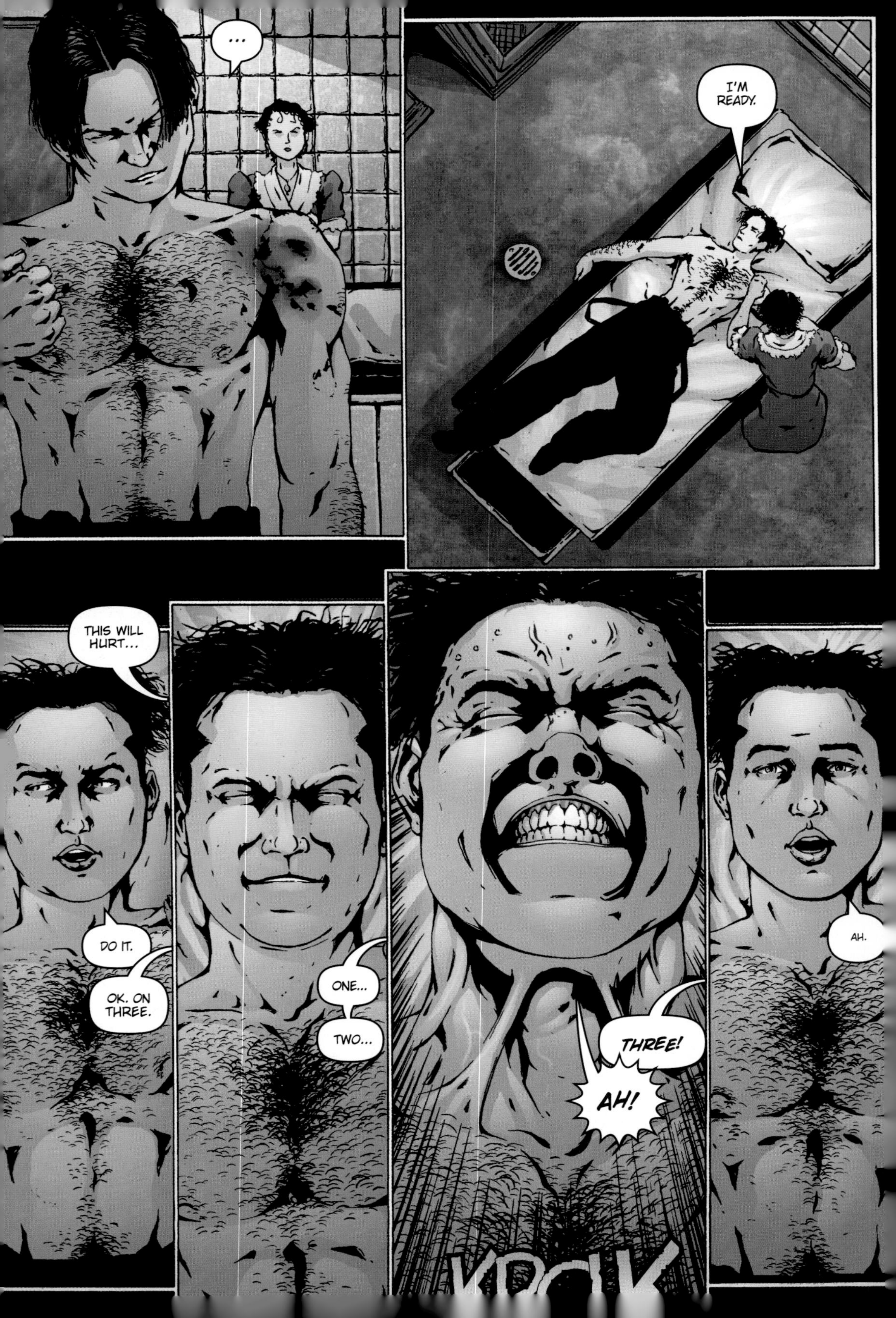
...
I'M READY.
THIS WILL HURT...
DO IT.
OK. ON THREE.
ONE...
TWO...
THREE!
AH!
AH.

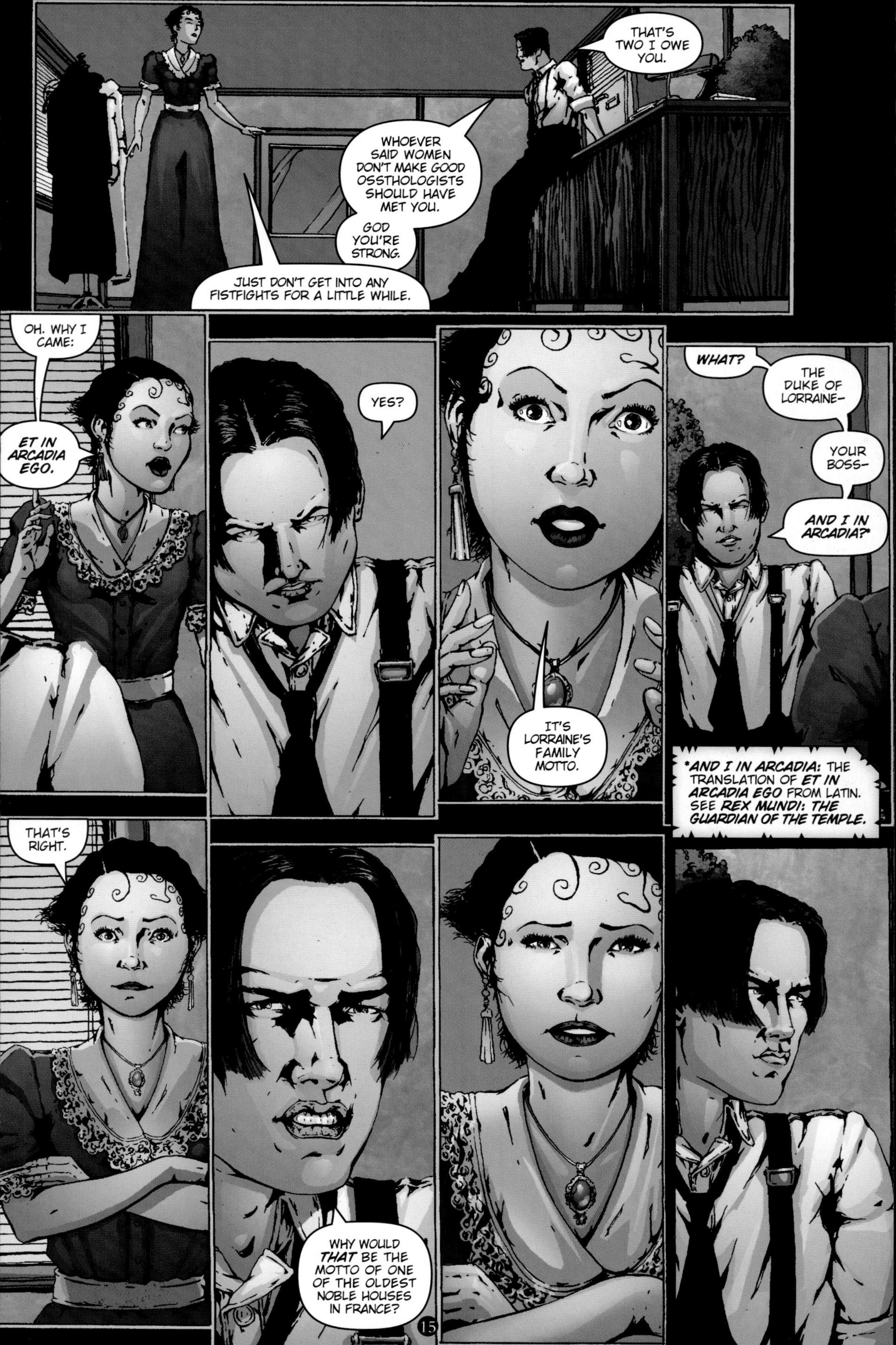
THAT'S TWO I OWE YOU.
WHOEVER SAID WOMEN DON'T MAKE GOOD OSSTHOLOGISTS SHOULD HAVE MET YOU.
GOD YOU'RE STRONG.
JUST DON'T GET INTO ANY FISTFIGHTS FOR A LITTLE WHILE.
OH. WHY I CAME:
ET IN ARCADIA EGO.
YES?
IT'S LORRAINE'S FAMILY MOTTO.
WHAT?
THE DUKE OF LORRAINE-
YOUR BOSS-
AND I IN ARCADIA?*
*AND I IN ARCADIA: THE TRANSLATION OF ET IN ARCADIA EGO FROM LATIN. SEE REX MUNDI: THE GUARDIAN OF THE TEMPLE.
THAT'S RIGHT.
WHY WOULD THAT BE THE MOTTO OF ONE OF THE OLDEST NOBLE HOUSES IN FRANCE?

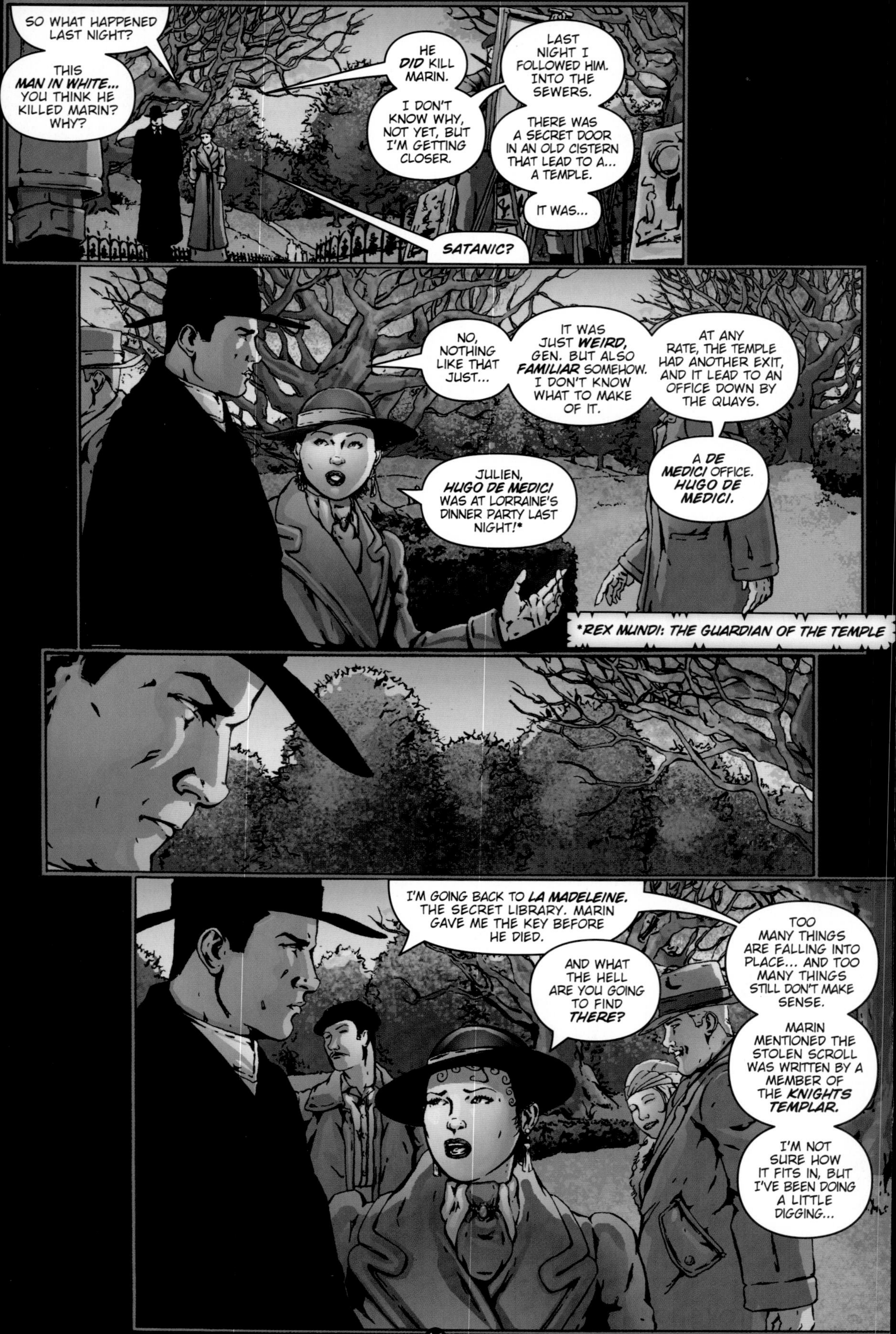

SO WHAT HAPPENED LAST NIGHT?
THIS MAN IN WHITE... YOU THINK HE KILLED MARIN? WHY?
HE DID KILL MARIN.
I DON'T KNOW WHY, NOT YET, BUT I'M GETTING CLOSER.
LAST NIGHT I FOLLOWED HIM. INTO THE SEWERS.
THERE WAS A SECRET DOOR IN AN OLD CISTERN THAT LEAD TO A... A TEMPLE.
IT WAS...
SATANIC?
NO, NOTHING LIKE THAT JUST...
IT WAS JUST WEIRD, GEN. BUT ALSO FAMILIAR SOMEHOW. I DON'T KNOW WHAT TO MAKE OF IT.
AT ANY RATE, THE TEMPLE HAD ANOTHER EXIT, AND IT LEAD TO AN OFFICE DOWN BY THE QUAYS.
A DE MEDICI OFFICE. HUGO DE MEDICI.
JULIEN, HUGO DE MEDICI WAS AT LORRAINE'S DINNER PARTY LAST NIGHT!*
*REX MUNDI: THE GUARDIAN OF THE TEMPLE
I'M GOING BACK TO LA MADELEINE. THE SECRET LIBRARY. MARIN GAVE ME THE KEY BEFORE HE DIED.
AND WHAT THE HELL ARE YOU GOING TO FIND THERE?
TOO MANY THINGS ARE FALLING INTO PLACE... AND TOO MANY THINGS STILL DON'T MAKE SENSE.
MARIN MENTIONED THE STOLEN SCROLL WAS WRITTEN BY A MEMBER OF THE KNIGHTS TEMPLAR.
I'M NOT SURE HOW IT FITS IN, BUT I'VE BEEN DOING A LITTLE DIGGING...

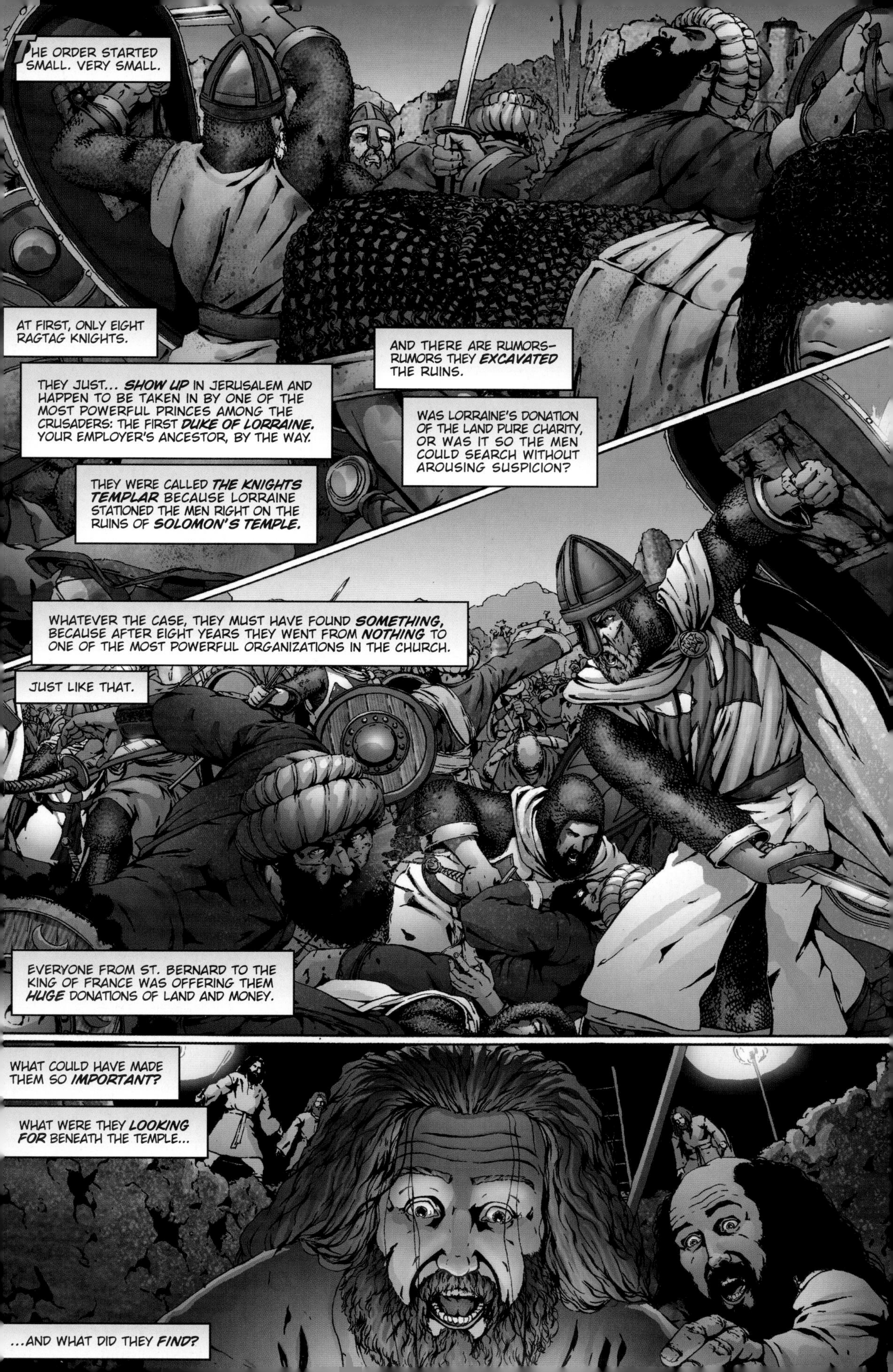
THE ORDER STARTED SMALL. VERY SMALL.
AT FIRST, ONLY EIGHT RAGTAG KNIGHTS.
THEY JUST... SHOW UP IN JERUSALEM AND HAPPEN TO BE TAKEN IN BY ONE OF THE MOST POWERFUL PRINCES AMONG THE CRUSADERS: THE FIRST DUKE OF LORRAINE. YOUR EMPLOYER'S ANCESTOR, BY THE WAY.
THEY WERE CALLED THE KNIGHTS TEMPLAR BECAUSE LORRAINE STATIONED THE MEN RIGHT ON THE RUINS OF SOLOMON'S TEMPLE.
AND THERE ARE RUMORS– RUMORS THEY EXCAVATED THE RUINS.
WAS LORRAINE'S DONATION OF THE LAND PURE CHARITY, OR WAS IT SO THE MEN COULD SEARCH WITHOUT AROUSING SUSPICION?
WHATEVER THE CASE, THEY MUST HAVE FOUND SOMETHING, BECAUSE AFTER EIGHT YEARS THEY WENT FROM NOTHING TO ONE OF THE MOST POWERFUL ORGANIZATIONS IN THE CHURCH.
JUST LIKE THAT.
EVERYONE FROM ST. BERNARD TO THE KING OF FRANCE WAS OFFERING THEM HUGE DONATIONS OF LAND AND MONEY.
WHAT COULD HAVE MADE THEM SO IMPORTANT?
WHAT WERE THEY LOOKING FOR BENEATH THE TEMPLE...
...AND WHAT DID THEY FIND?

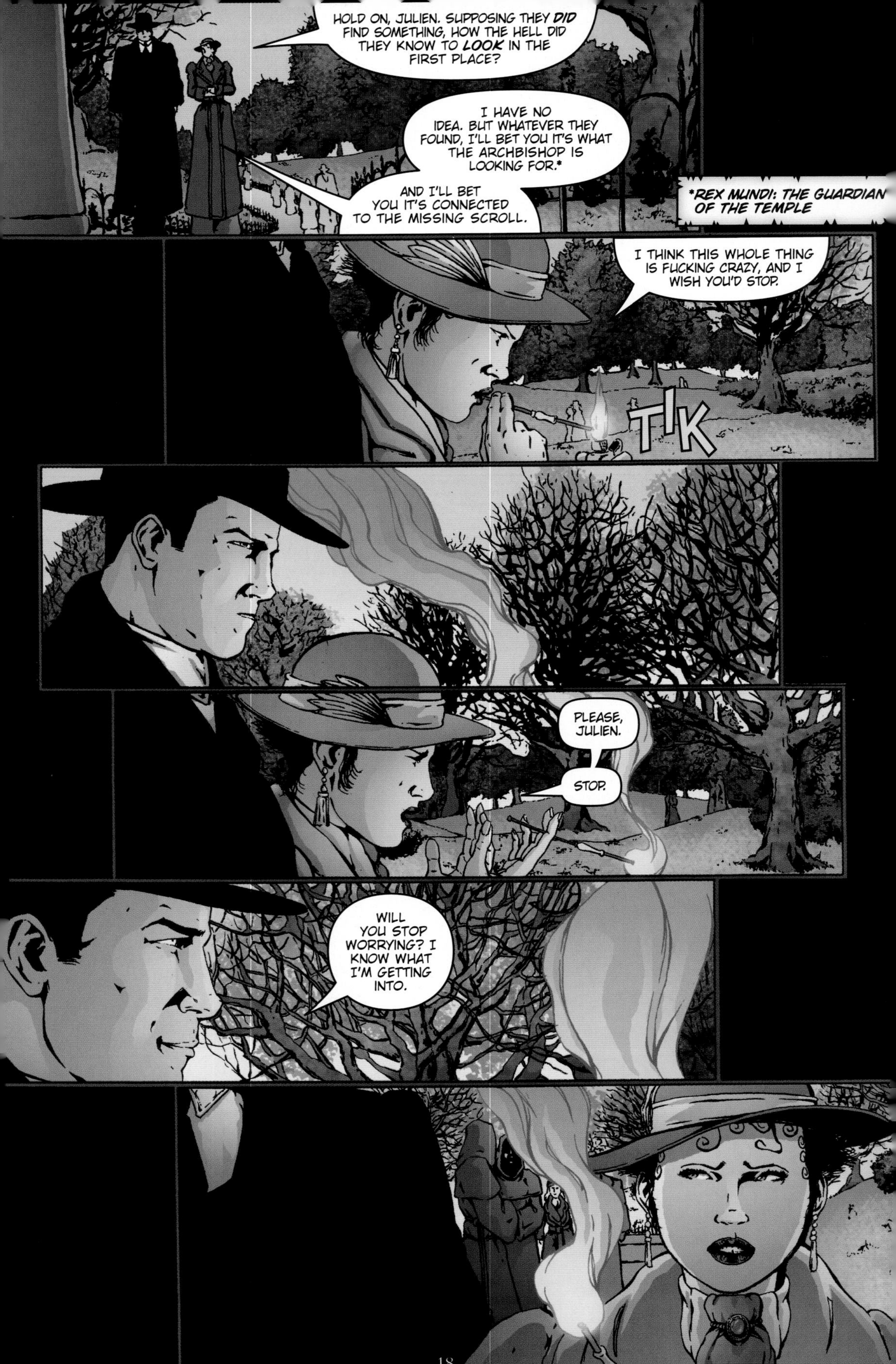
HOLD ON, JULIEN. SUPPOSING THEY DID FIND SOMETHING, HOW THE HELL DID THEY KNOW TO LOOK IN THE FIRST PLACE?
I HAVE NO IDEA. BUT WHATEVER THEY FOUND, I'LL BET YOU IT'S WHAT THE ARCHBISHOP IS LOOKING FOR.*
AND I'LL BET YOU IT'S CONNECTED TO THE MISSING SCROLL.
*REX MUNDI: THE GUARDIAN OF THE TEMPLE
I THINK THIS WHOLE THING IS FUCKING CRAZY, AND I WISH YOU'D STOP.
TIK
PLEASE, JULIEN.
STOP.
WILL YOU STOP WORRYING? I KNOW WHAT I'M GETTING INTO.

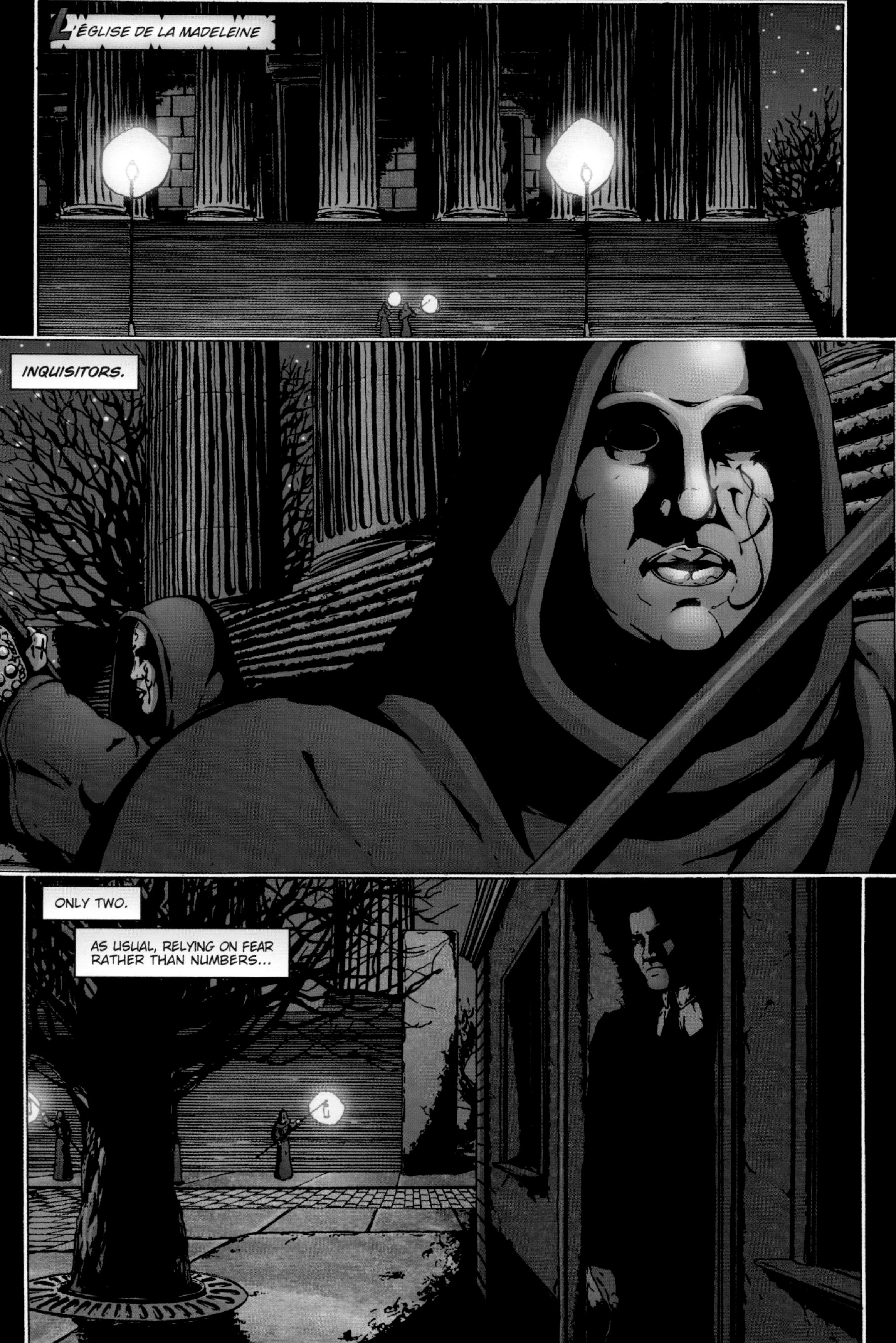
L'ÉGLISE DE LA MADELEINE
INQUISITORS.
ONLY TWO.
AS USUAL, RELYING ON FEAR RATHER THAN NUMBERS...

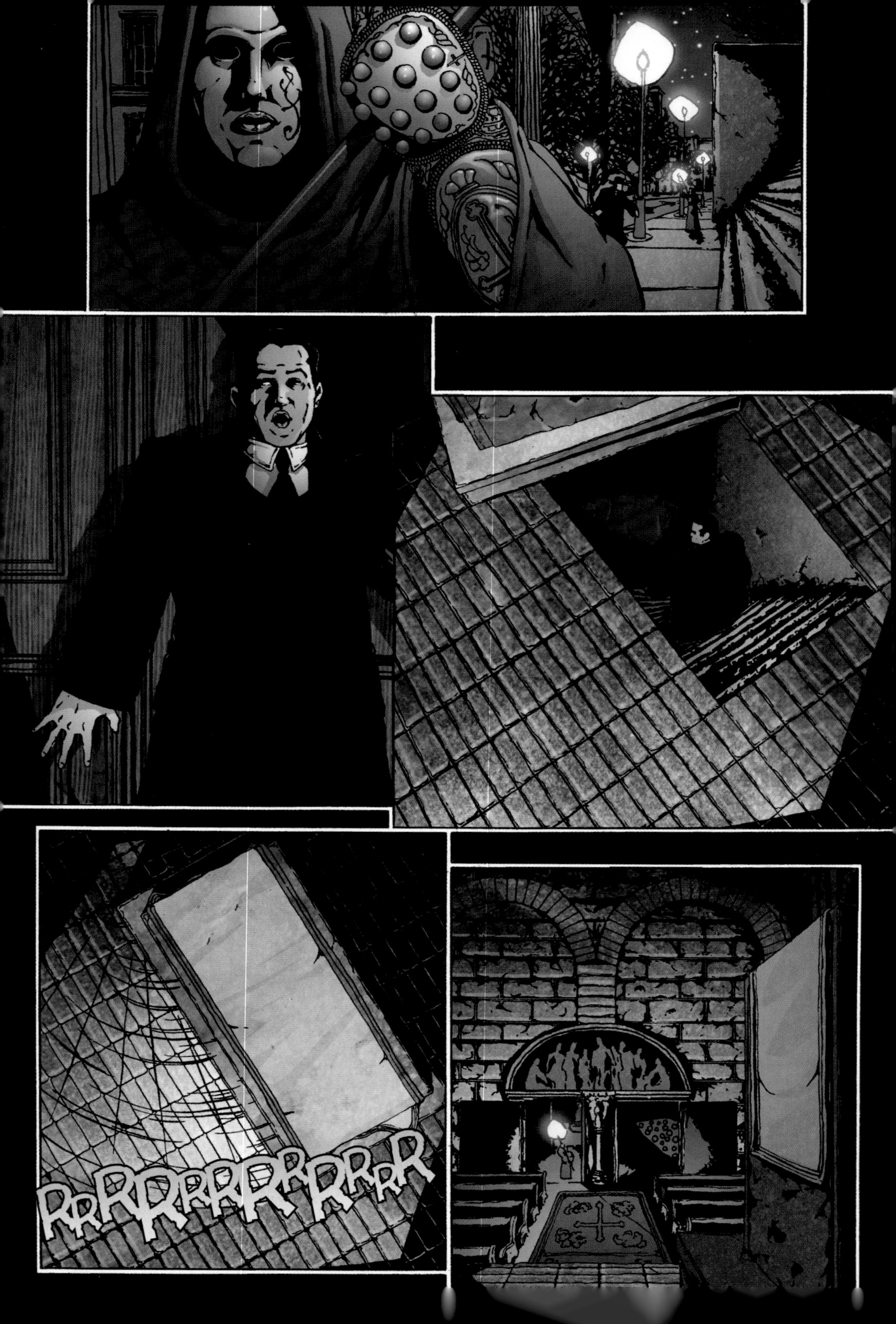
RRRRRRRRRRRRRRR

Official summary of the interrogation of
Jacques De Molay,
last Grand Master of the
Poor Knights Of Christ and the Temple Of Solomon
also known as the
Knights Templar
21 March, 1312
Guillaume de Nogaret
These charges are brought forth under the benign auspices of
h.h. Pope Clement V
h.M. Philip IV of France
God Save the King
UNEXPURGATED AND UNAPPROVED FOR RELEASE TO LAITY. GRAVE PENANCE FOR UNSANCTIONED REMOVAL
Among other things, de Molay
of brand and pliers, to trampling on the
De Molay further confided Templar brethren were required to deny the divinity of our Lord and Saviour Jesus Christ three times and micturate upon a cross before admission into the order. To advance higher, brethren were required to kiss preceptory masters upon the anus and genitals.
Although he relapsed into heresy and eternal damnation by retracting his confession to sodomy, as did many of his Order, de Molay did confirm he and his Templar brethren worshiped the entity known as BAPHOMET. De Molay refused to speak further on the subject, but this humble servant of God can only assume Baphomet is the very DEVIL HIMSELF.
although they declared that the Order had been
approved by the Apostolic See, nevertheless
of the said Order, and at some
by the brothers
BAPHOMET... THE DEVIL?
WHAT IS *BAPHOMET?*
AND WHY SUCH CONTEMPT FOR THE CROSS?

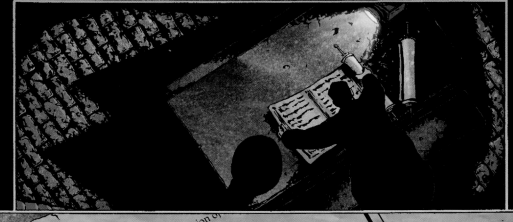

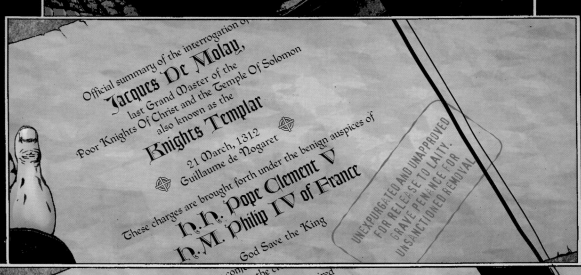

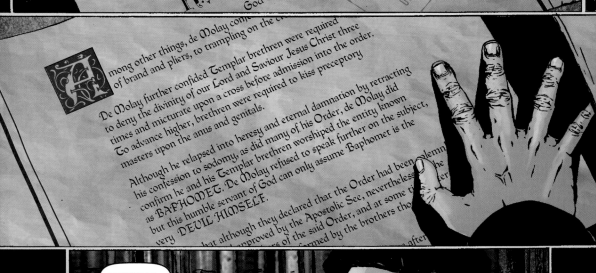

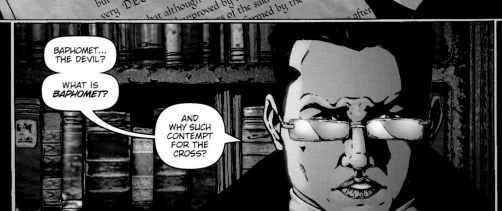

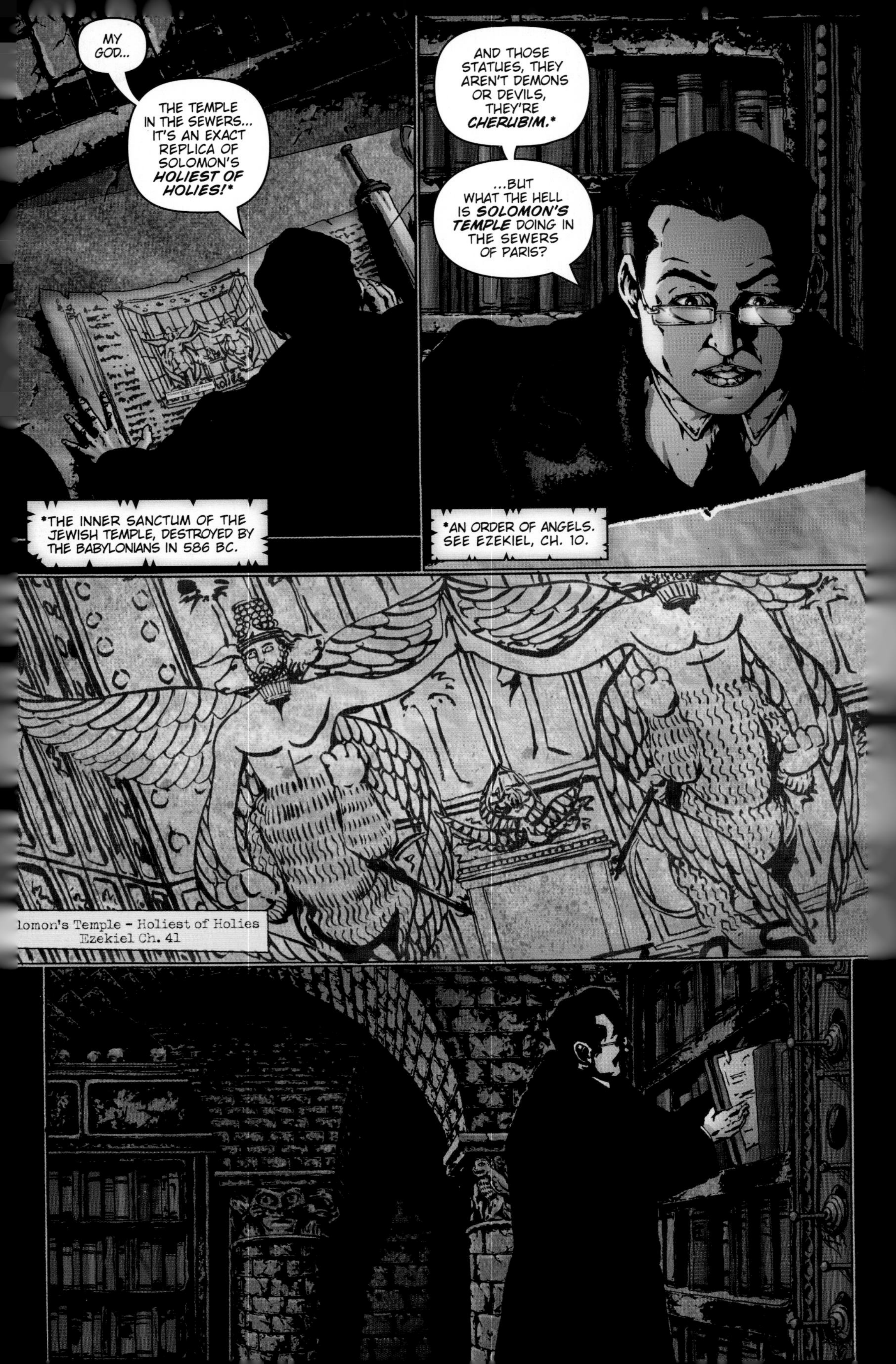
MY GOD...
THE TEMPLE IN THE SEWERS... IT'S AN EXACT REPLICA OF SOLOMON'S HOLIEST OF HOLIES!*
*THE INNER SANCTUM OF THE JEWISH TEMPLE, DESTROYED BY THE BABYLONIANS IN 586 BC.
AND THOSE STATUES, THEY AREN'T DEMONS OR DEVILS, THEY'RE CHERUBIM.*
...BUT WHAT THE HELL IS SOLOMON'S TEMPLE DOING IN THE SEWERS OF PARIS?
*AN ORDER OF ANGELS. SEE EZEKIEL, CH. 10.
lomon's Temple - Holiest of Holies
Ezekiel Ch. 41

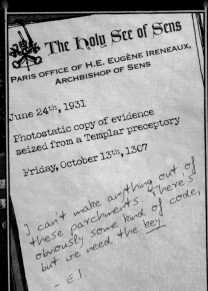

The Holy See of Sens
PARIS OFFICE OF H.E. EUGÈNE IRENEAUX,
ARCHBISHOP OF SENS
June 24th, 1931
Photostatic copy of evidence
seized from a Templar preceptory
Friday, October 13th, 1307
I can't make anything out of these parchments. There's obviously some kind of code, but we need the key.
- E.I.
June 24th, 1931
DO NOT CIRCULATE
JÉSV. MEDÈLA. VVLNÉRVM + SPES. VNA. PŒNITENTIVM.
PER. MAGDALANÆ. LACRYMAS + PECCATA. NOSTRA. DILVAS.
DO NOT CIRCULATE
PS
OULDN'T DECIPHER THE SCROLLS, BUT BOTH
RE SIGNED *PS*. WHAT THE HELL DID IT MEAN?
I WASN'T LETTING GO
UNTIL I FOUND OUT.

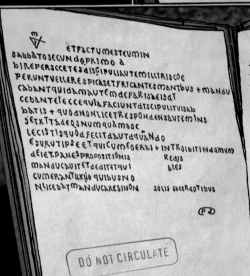

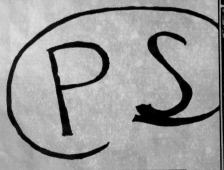

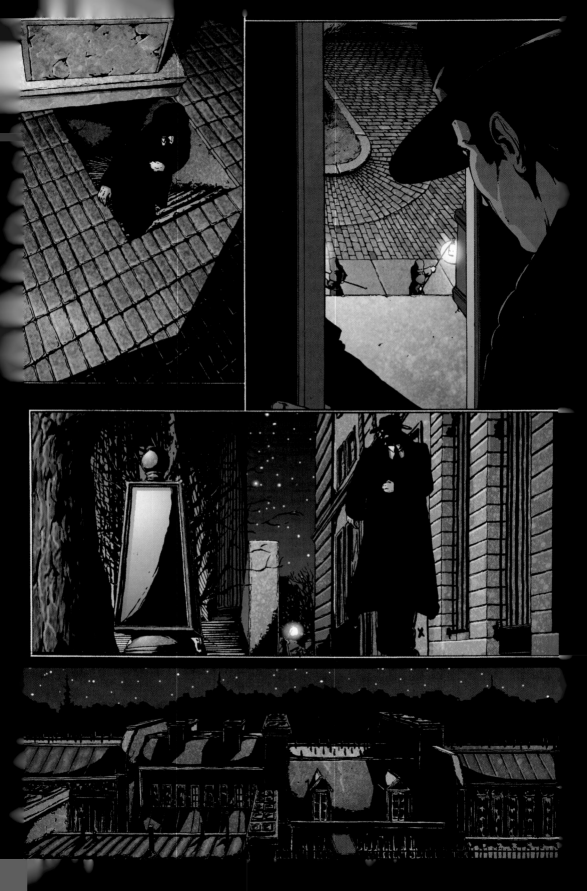

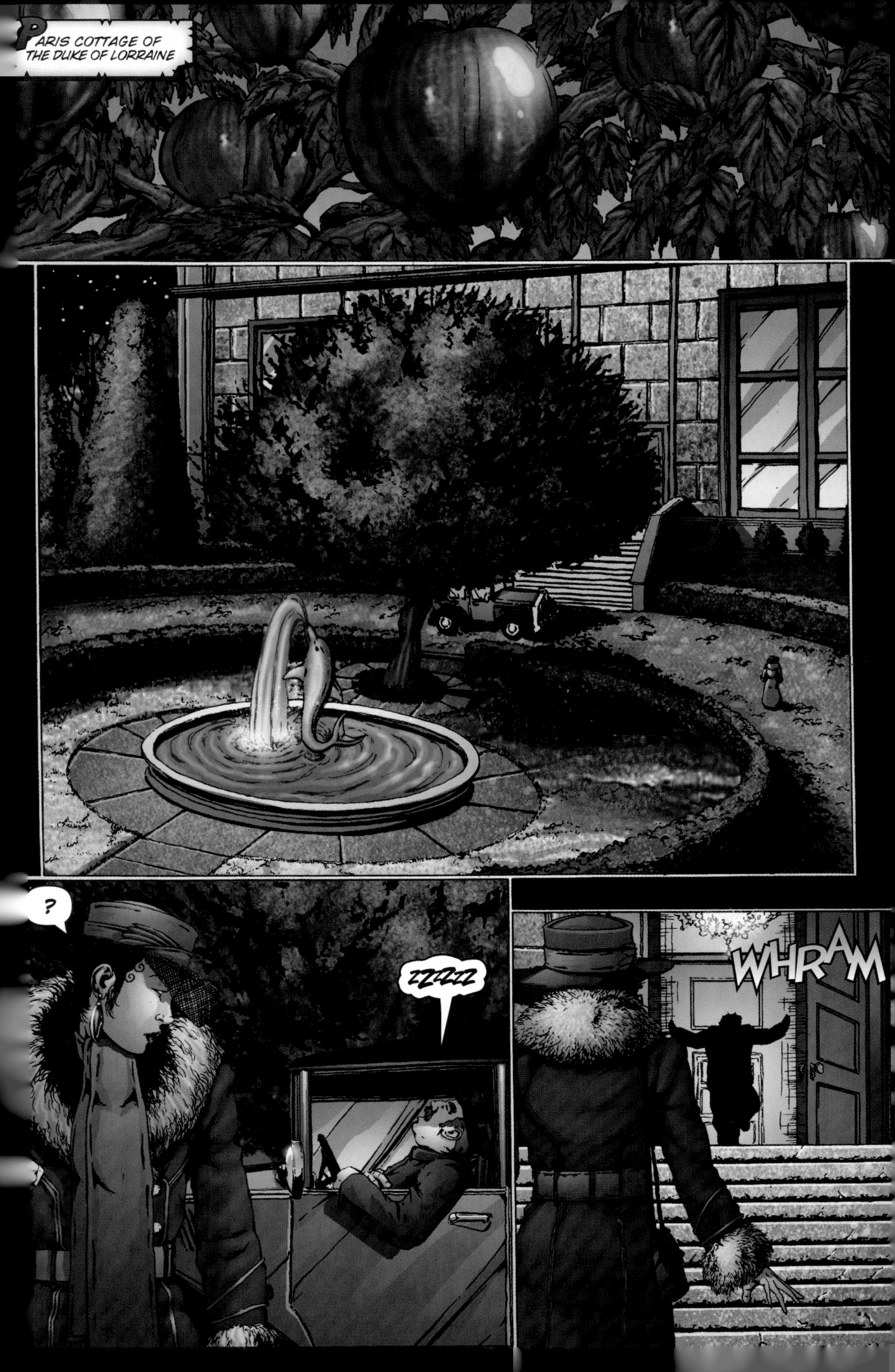
PARIS COTTAGE OF THE DUKE OF LORRAINE
?
ZZZZZZ
WHRAM

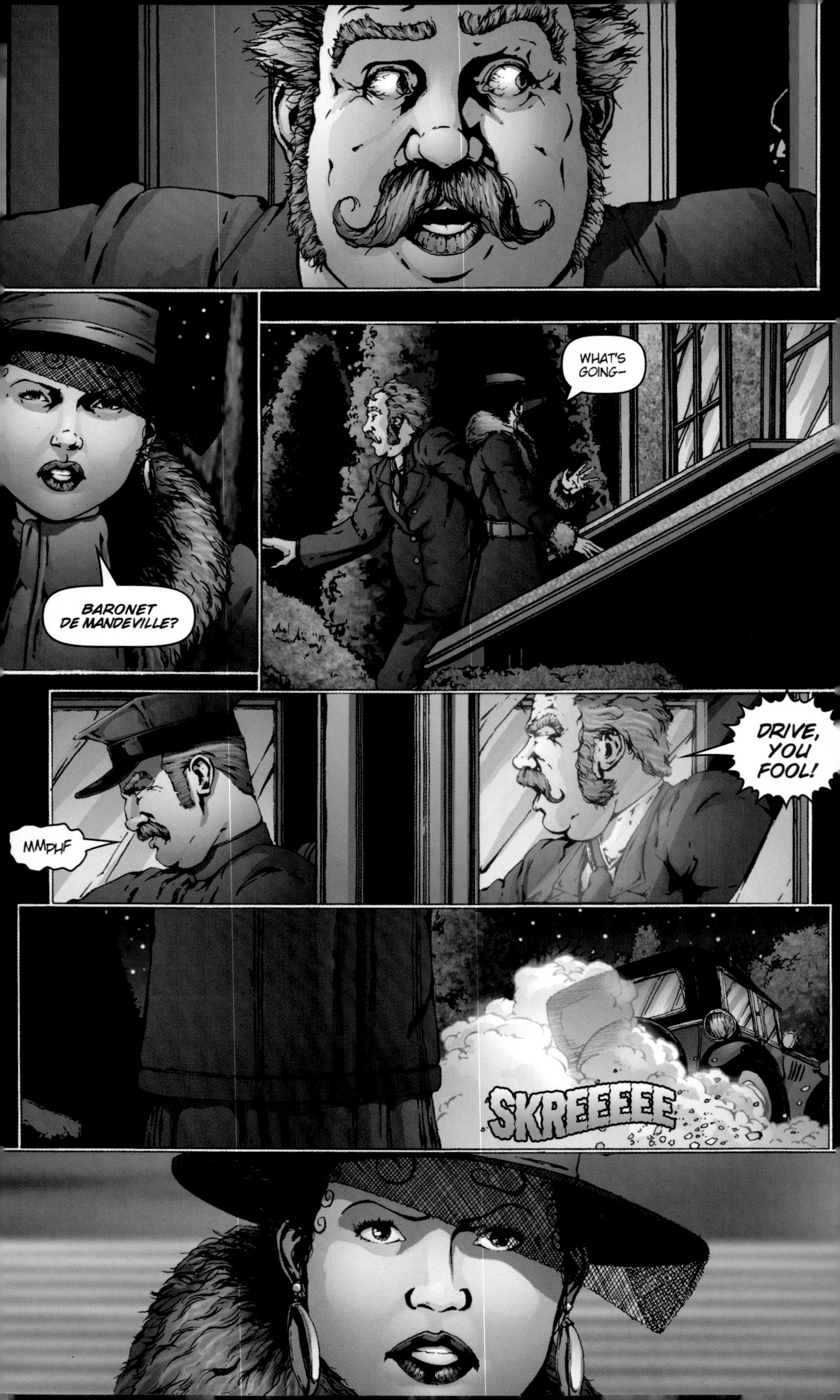
BARONET DE MANDEVILLE?
WHAT'S GOING-
MMPHF
DRIVE, YOU FOOL!
SKREEEEE

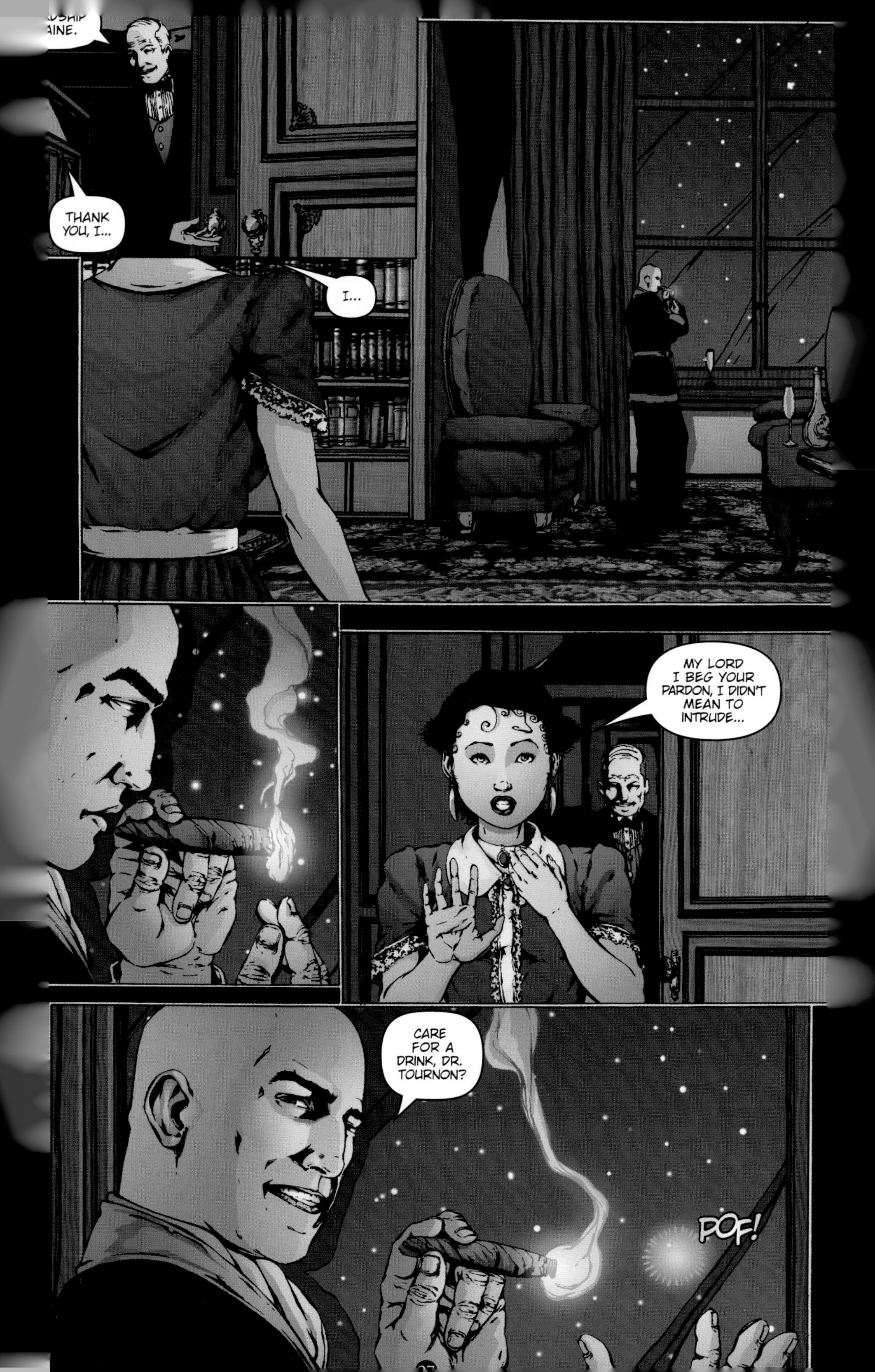
DSHIP
AINE.
THANK YOU, I...
I...
MY LORD I BEG YOUR PARDON, I DIDN'T MEAN TO INTRUDE...
CARE FOR A DRINK, DR. TOURNON?
POF!

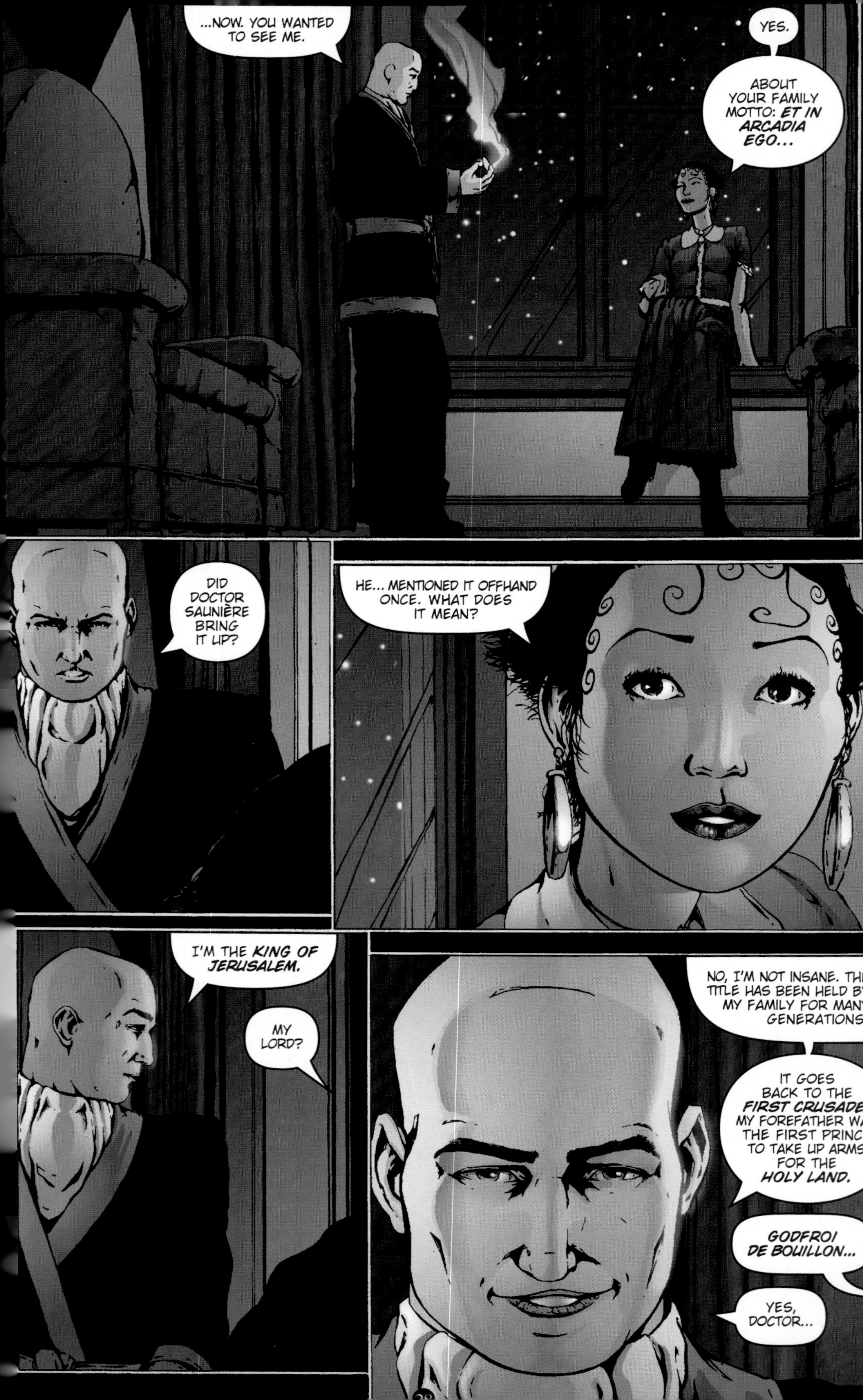
...NOW. YOU WANTED TO SEE ME.
YES.
ABOUT YOUR FAMILY MOTTO: ***ET IN ARCADIA EGO...***
DID DOCTOR SAUNIÈRE BRING IT UP?
HE... MENTIONED IT OFFHAND ONCE. WHAT DOES IT MEAN?
I'M THE ***KING OF JERUSALEM.***
MY LORD?
NO, I'M NOT INSANE. THE TITLE HAS BEEN HELD BY MY FAMILY FOR MANY GENERATIONS.
IT GOES BACK TO THE ***FIRST CRUSADE.*** MY FOREFATHER WAS THE FIRST PRINCE TO TAKE UP ARMS FOR THE ***HOLY LAND.***
GODFROI DE BOUILLON...
YES, DOCTOR...

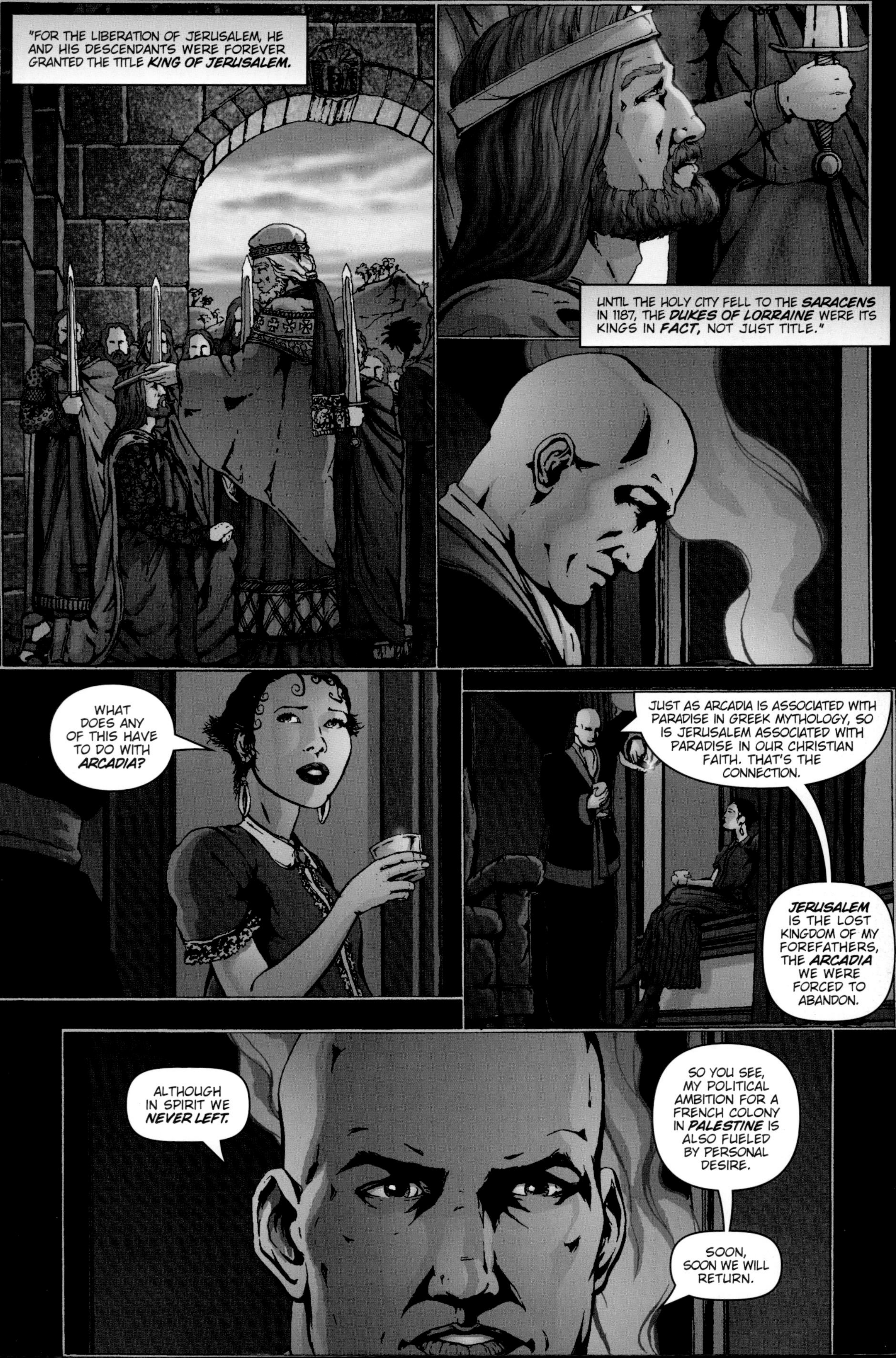
"FOR THE LIBERATION OF JERUSALEM, HE AND HIS DESCENDANTS WERE FOREVER GRANTED THE TITLE *KING OF JERUSALEM.*
UNTIL THE HOLY CITY FELL TO THE *SARACENS* IN 1187, THE *DUKES OF LORRAINE* WERE ITS KINGS IN *FACT,* NOT JUST TITLE."
WHAT DOES ANY OF THIS HAVE TO DO WITH *ARCADIA?*
JUST AS ARCADIA IS ASSOCIATED WITH PARADISE IN GREEK MYTHOLOGY, SO IS JERUSALEM ASSOCIATED WITH PARADISE IN OUR CHRISTIAN FAITH. THAT'S THE CONNECTION.
JERUSALEM IS THE LOST KINGDOM OF MY FOREFATHERS, THE *ARCADIA* WE WERE FORCED TO ABANDON.
ALTHOUGH IN SPIRIT WE *NEVER LEFT.*
SO YOU SEE, MY POLITICAL AMBITION FOR A FRENCH COLONY IN *PALESTINE* IS ALSO FUELED BY PERSONAL DESIRE.
SOON, SOON WE WILL RETURN.

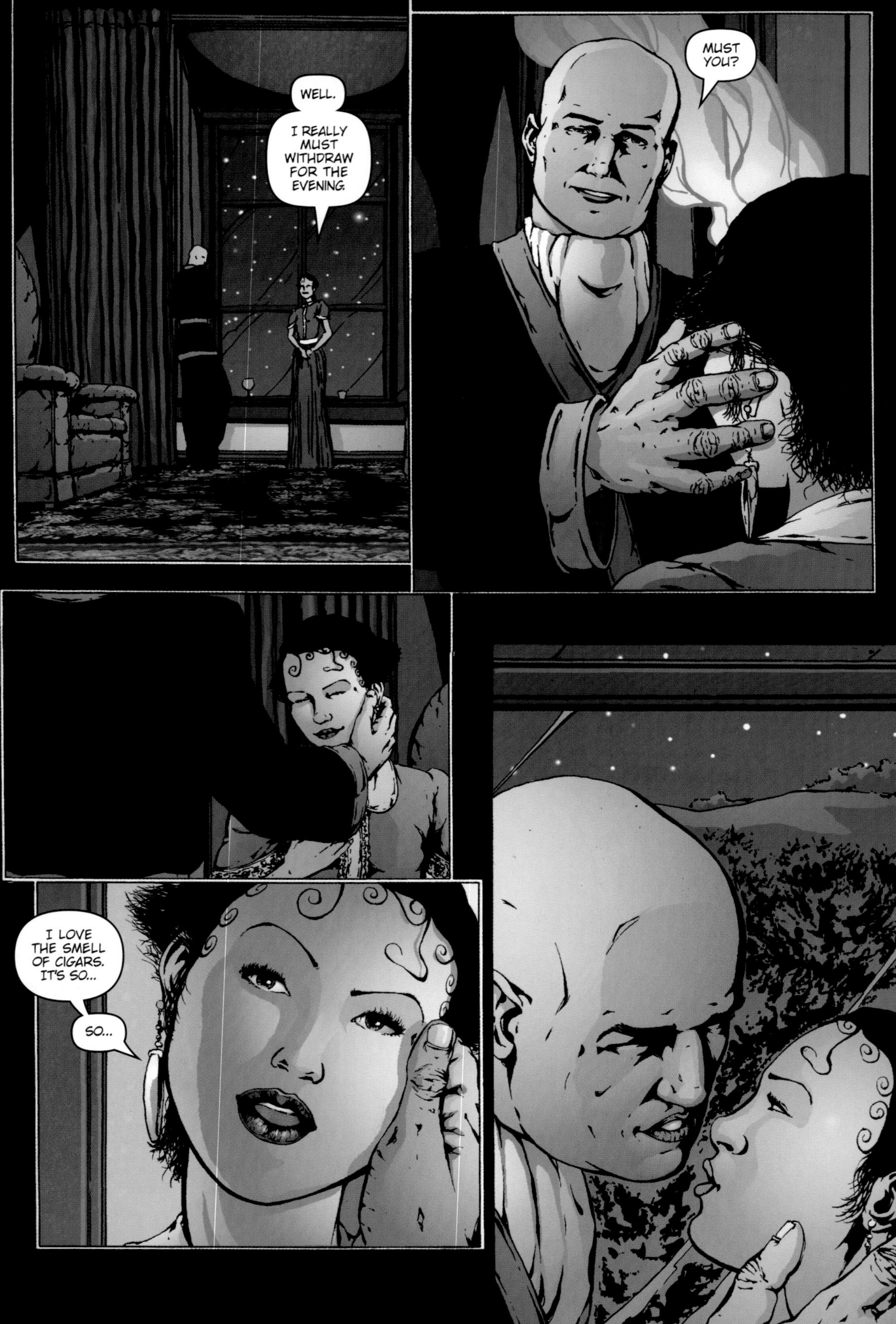
WELL.
I REALLY MUST WITHDRAW FOR THE EVENING.
MUST YOU?
I LOVE THE SMELL OF CIGARS. IT'S SO...
SO...

Le Journal de la Liberté

Paris' leading anglophone newspaper • vol. 205, no. 101 • Oct. 24, MCMXXXIII

Papal Seal

Editors in Chief: M. Tait Bergstrom, M. Matthew Pasteris. **Story Editor:** M. Arvid Nelson. **Art Editors:** M. EricJ, M. Jeromy Cox. **Photography Editor:** M. Alexander Waldman. **Layout Supervisor:** M. William Kartalopoulos. **Editors Emeritus:** M. Clark A. Smith, M. Howard P. Lovecraft, M. Robert E. Howard. Redacted by the Holy Parisian Inquisition under the direction of His Excellency Archbishop Emile-Jean Ireneaux. Le Journal de Liberté is printed under the benign auspices of his most puissant majesty KING LOUIS XXII of FRANCE. GOD SAVE THE KING.

of Approval

KING'S SUPPORTERS BLAST LORRAINE'S PROPOSED COLONIZATION OF THE HOLY LAND

Tough Talk in the Hall of the Robe

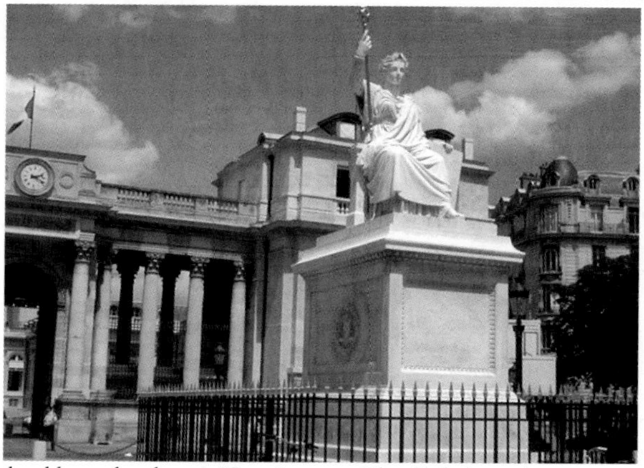

"I know I speak for an overwhelming majority of my colleagues when I say that I have never seen a more rash, a more ill-conceived or a more misguided piece of legislation in my tenure in the Hall of the Robe," Baronet Aristide deMandeville, speaker of the Hall of the Robe, said yesterday.

He spoke before the members of the Robe regarding legislation proposed by the Hall of the Sword to enable French colonization of the Holy Land.

DeMandeville received loud cheers and applause during his speech.

Members of the Robe made it very clear the colonial designs on the Holy Land proposed by the Duke of Lorraine last week would be rejected if it came to a vote in the Hall of the Robe. "Without the support of the Robe, the scheme proposed by the Sword is a dead letter," deMandeville said.

The members of the Robe overwhelmingly proclaimed their support for King Louis XXII's policy of "unstringing the bow," the term political analysts have given to the King's foreign policy strategy aimed at easing tensions in Europe and abroad.

"Christendom can ill afford widespread conflict. We do not advocate a policy of peace because France is weak, but because France is strong," deMandeville said.

"All the monarchies of Europe would be in grave peril should war break out. Now is a time when, for the good of the common man as well as the highest lord, Christian kings should band together to fight the twin hydras of political libertarianism and radical nationalism."

These sentiments are hardly unexpected, since the Robe is entirely made up of Louis XXII's closest political allies.

Charles Martel, the king's mayor of the court, expressed his satisfaction with the proclamations made the other day in the Hall of the Robe.

"The King and the Robe are in complete concurrence on this matter," he said.

The Robe's sentiments were received coolly by members of the Hall of the Sword.

"It is unfortunate we are unable to reach consensus on this issue," Baron Robert Teniers, a spokesman for the Duke of Lorraine, said. "But the members of the Hall of the Sword believe a policy of aggressive colonialism centered on the conquest of the Holy Land is the best course of action for France, given the avowedly aggressive stance of our neighbors."

"Also consider the enormous petrochemical reserves that lie beneath the sands of the Near East,"

continued on page A3

THREE DUTCH MERCHANT VESSELS GUTTED IN CARIBBEAN WATERS

The "Bermuda Triangle" has claimed three more ships.

The gutted hulks of three merchant ships were observed floating adrift about ninety miles East of Eleuthera Island in the Bahamas. All the vessels were Dutch in origin, and all were laden with cotton, sugar and tobacco from the Confederate States of America.

A British naval ship, the *HMS Dauntless*, was alerted to the hulks' presence by plumes of smoke on the horizon.

Immediate suspicion fell on pirates, who are a persistent menace in the region.

"It's quite unsettling to come upon a ship that's been ravaged by pirates," said First Mate Nicholas Englund of the *Dauntless*. "It's like encountering a ghost ship. The most unnerving aspect of this incident was the fact that we didn't find any bodies. Not a one."

Piracy has, of course, evolved since the days of flintlocks and canvas sails.

"Today's pirates use smaller, wood- or metal-hulled vessels with outboard motors. They can subdue a much larger ship with small, high-powered rifles. They're fast and ruthless," Englund said.

In an unusual joint statement,

continued on page E5

Bizarre Nighttime Chase Disturbs Pedestrians; Scraggly Street Urchins Observed Participating in Fracas

Late-night revelers and pedestrians were disturbed last evening in the Fifteenth Arrondissement by an unusual foot chase. By the time Inquisition and Gendarmerie officers arrived at the scene, the parties involved had disappeared.

"We have no more information about this incident than you," Inquisitor Sanival, who was questioning witnesses last night after the incident, said.

Eyewitnesses described the bizarre scene.

"The guy being chased was actually a lot bigger than the guy being chased. Don't know what the problem was, but they were both running hard," Matthieu Carette, who operates a crepe stand in the area, said.

Further reports indicated the pursued man wore a black suit.

"Like a mortician, he was kind of creepy," an eyewitness who spoke on the condition of anonymity said.

But by all accounts, the pursuer was the more peculiar of the pair.

"He was a little guy, looked like he was maybe in his fifties," said Carette. "He was wearing all white. Even his hat and his tie. He was a little bit pudgy, but he sure did run fast."

Several eyewitnesses said the man wore sungoggles, in spite of the darkness.

"The glasses were mirrored, I couldn't see his eyes," said Martha Huguet, who was returning home from the theater when she observed the chase. "There was something about him, something not quite right, if you know what I mean. The kind of person you might avoid on the street."

Perhaps the strangest part of last night's incident was the fact that a band of young street waifs was seen entering into the chase, "close on the heels of the man in white," Huguet said.

"Imagine it. First you see someone in black whip by. Then someone in white. Then a group of noisy children dressed in rags, brandishing slings and screaming

continued on page B11

INSIDE

Plus sanctimonious editorials by eds. A. Nelson and EricJ

THE KEY TO FRANCE: A REPORT ON THE HALL OF THE ROBE

Tensions between the Hall of the Robe and the Hall of the Sword have been boiling over in the past few days, due in large part to a controversial plan for the colonization of the Holy Land submitted by the Duke of Lorraine, Speaker for the Hall of the Sword.

But political conflict in the Assemblée Nationale is nothing new, and neither is the expected outcome of this latest round of strife. Although the endeavor proposed by Lord Lorraine has broad-based support in the Sword, most analysts believe it will never be realized.

This is because the members of the Hall of the Robe have unanimously denounced the measure and made it very clear they do not support its passage into law. As is often the case, the Robe's position perfectly reflects the wishes of the King.

"The Hall of the Robe is the key to France," an official for King Louis XXII who spoke on the condition of anonymity said. "And the key is firmly in the King's hand."

But what makes the Hall of the Robe so pivotal, why does it have so much sway in the affairs of France, and why does His Majesty Louis XXII "hold the key"?

One needs only to understand the origins and workings of our constitutional monarchy to appreciate the Robe's importance.

The Origins of France's Constitutional Monarchy

The foundation of our current government was laid in 1799, when royalist French troops rallied and forced the defeat of the so-called "Republicans," bringing and end to over a decade of brutal mob rule and barbaric disregard for the sanctity of France's ancient and noble institutions.

Indeed, the Monarchy nearly perished—the Dauphin Louis XVII's near capture by a murderous Jacobin mob and his harrowing flight to Luxembourg left a deep scar on the house of Bourbon and the institution of the Monarchy itself.

Therefore in 1801 the Crown, having solely ruled France for over a millennia, finally acquiesced to the demands of the landed aristocracy. A constitutional monarchy was formed, limiting the power of the King with a bicameral diet known as the "National Assembly."

But in many ways the King retained the upper hand.

The Sword and the Robe

The Hall of the Sword derives its name from the ancient oath of martial fealty medieval lords swore to a King. It is exclusively composed of members of ancient noble houses who can trace their lineage back to the time of the First Crusade – almost eight hundred and fifty years ago!

This means the Hall of the Sword is vastly smaller than the Hall of the Robe, and therefore its power is far more concentrated.

In theory, anyways.

"The reality is that the nobles families represented in the Sword often have conflicting viewpoints and are usually at odds with one another due to long-standing feuds and rivalries," Georges Fresnay, a professor of political theology at the Sorbonne, said. "This makes it very difficult for the Sword to coordinate any kind of political strategy."

Fresnay admits the Sword has coalesced as a unified political body over the last few years due to the leadership of the Duke of Lorraine.

"Lorraine's rallying of the Sword is nothing short of a miracle," Fresnay said. "He has taken a very willful group of people and convinced them to work for their collective interests. It's simply unprecedented."

Versailles, court of Louis XXII. Also the nominal center of power for the Hall of the Robe and therefore France itself. Photo: Eugène Atget, staff photographer.

But all this is for naught when the Hall of the Robe is taken into consideration.

Members of the Robe are hand-selected by the King. The term "Robe" therefore refers to the robes of a merchant or a state official.

"The King selects Robe members based on loyalty to the Crown and common political interest. And no one can interfere with the selection process. It's the King's exclusive right," Fresnay said.

Thus, while the Robe is much larger than the Sword, with over 300 members at any given time, it is politically much more cohesive—and fiercely loyal to the Crown.

"The King deliberately cultivates relationships with members of his entourage who demonstrate exemplary loyalty and service for placement into the Hall of the Robe," Fresnay said. "There's no secret about that."

The Crown, the Sword and the Robe each have one vote on proposed legislation. The King casts a vote alone. For either

> ### "The Hall of the Robe is the key to France. And the key is firmly in the King's hand."

house to endorse a proposal, a two-thirds majority vote is required. Two out of three of the Crown, Robe and Sword must endorse a measure for it to be signed into law.

Since the first session of the Assemblée Nationale in 1801, the Robe has never once voted against the King.

Thus the Sword finds itself out-maneuvered time and time again by the King through the agency of the Robe. There is no indication that this latest round of voting—on Lorraine's colonial policy—will be any different.

"The Robe is nothing more than the King's puppet, and our so-called constitutional monarchy exists only on paper," a member of the Hall of the Sword who spoke on the condition of anonymity said.

Members of the Robe deny this characterization. Says Robe member Jean-Michel Modot:

"We simply want what's best for France, and, as loyal subjects, we believe in our King." ⚜

The crest of the House of Bourbon, the reigning kings of France. Because the King reserves the sole power to admit members into the Hall of the Robe, he is assured a virtual monopoly in French politics.

The Hall of the Robe is composed of the King's most loyal supporters. A noble title is also a requirement for entry, but because King Louis XXII has the right to confer titles, this is mere formality.

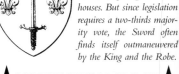

↑ ROYAL VOTING BLOC ↑

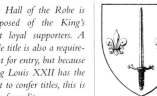

The Hall of the Sword is composed of France's oldest and most prestigious noble houses. But since legislation requires a two-thirds majority vote, the Sword often finds itself outmaneuvered by the King and the Robe.

↑ NOBLE VOTING BLOCK ↑

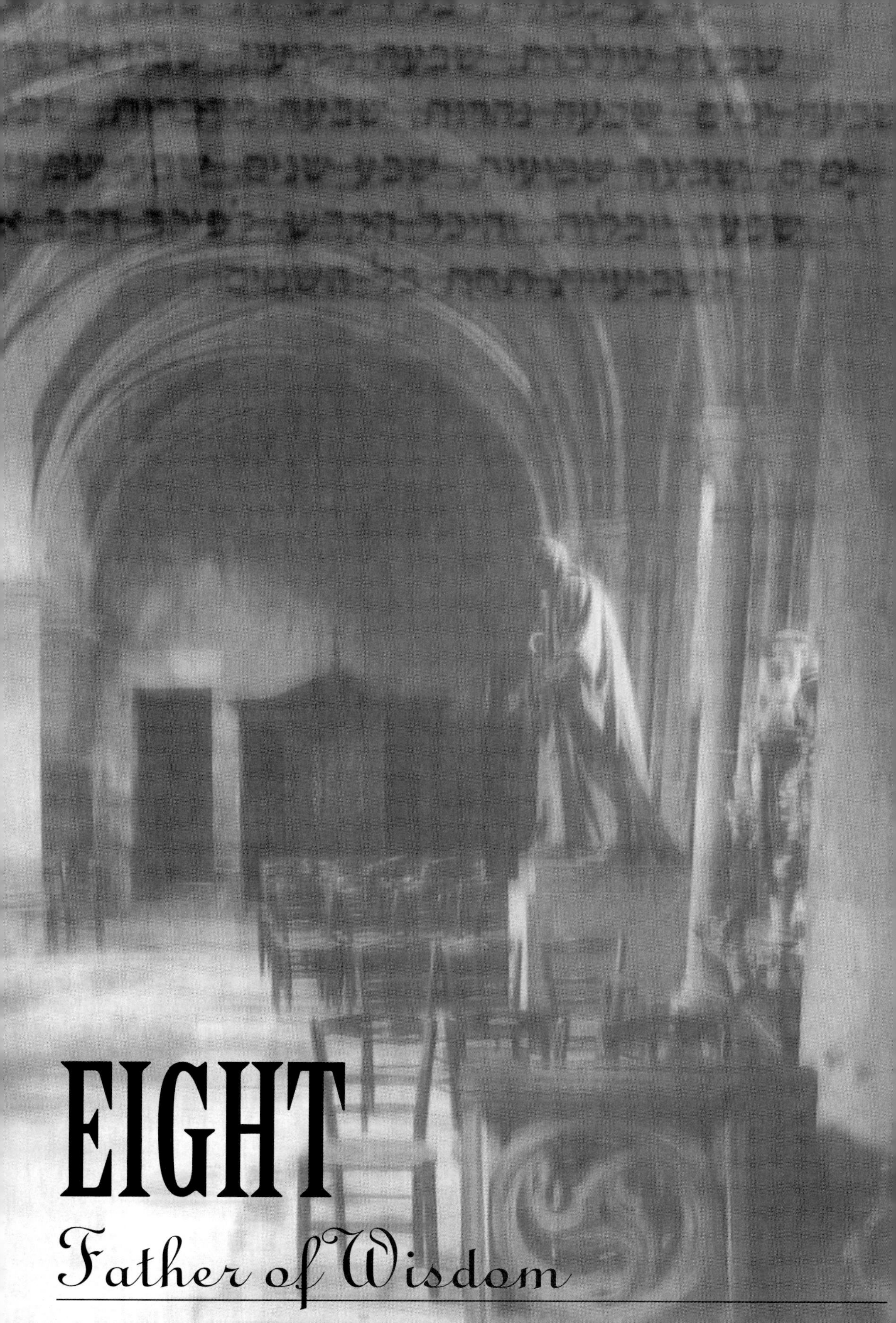

EIGHT

Father of Wisdom

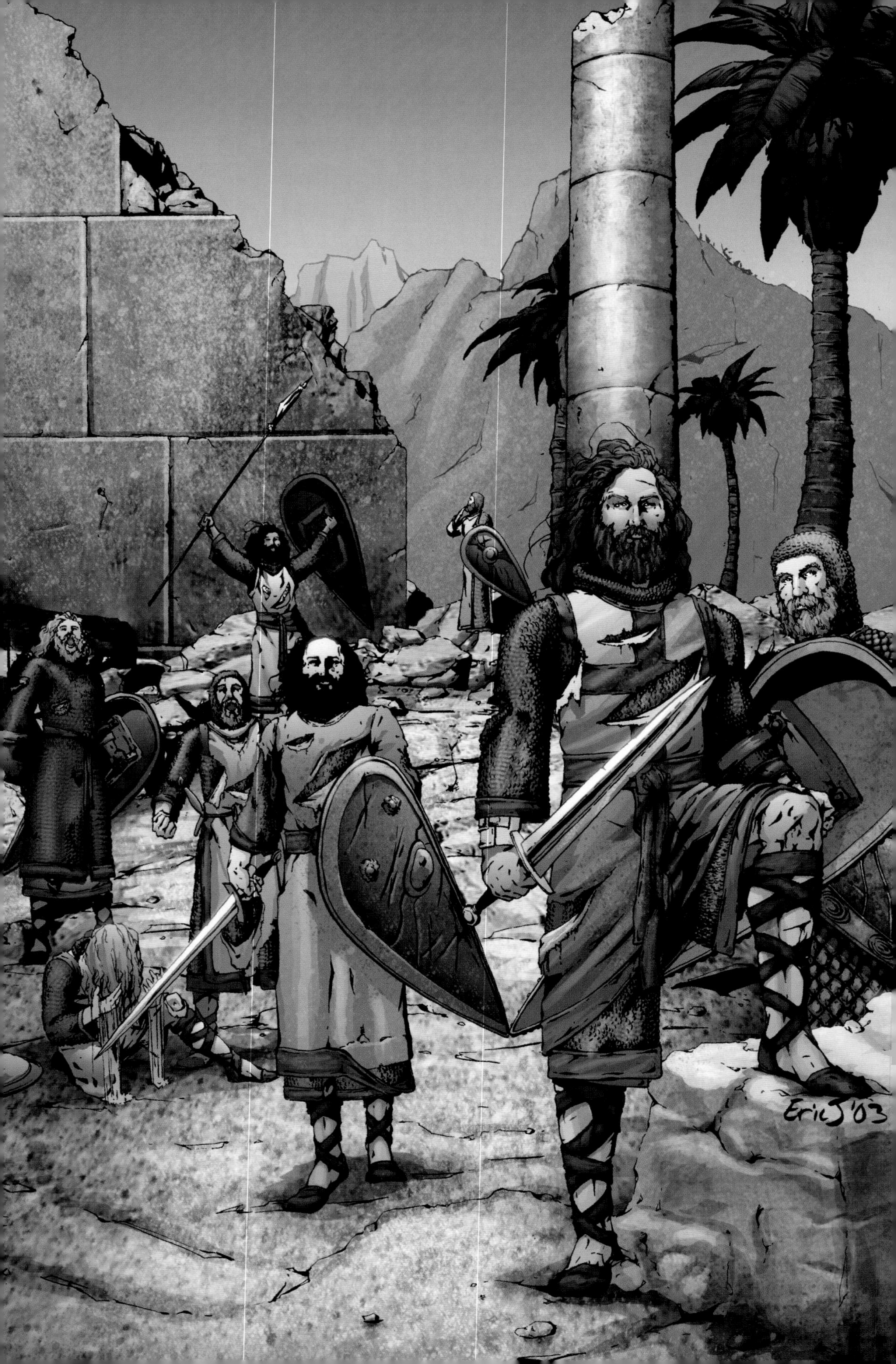
EricJ '03

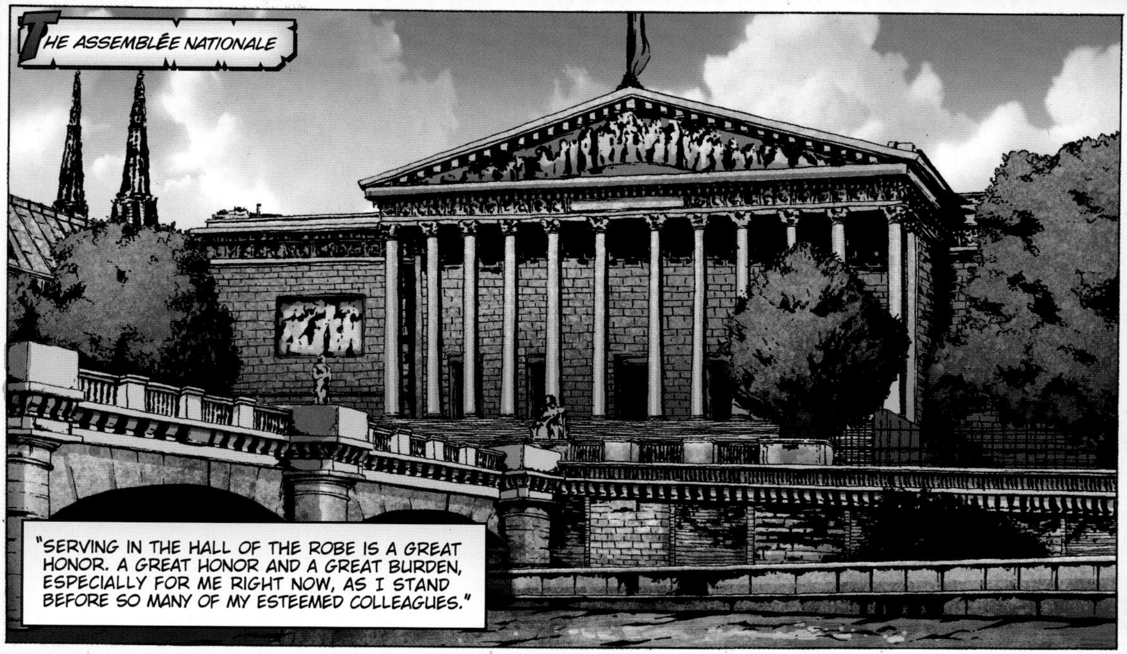
THE ASSEMBLÉE NATIONALE
"SERVING IN THE HALL OF THE ROBE IS A GREAT HONOR. A GREAT HONOR AND A GREAT BURDEN, ESPECIALLY FOR ME RIGHT NOW, AS I STAND BEFORE SO MANY OF MY ESTEEMED COLLEAGUES."

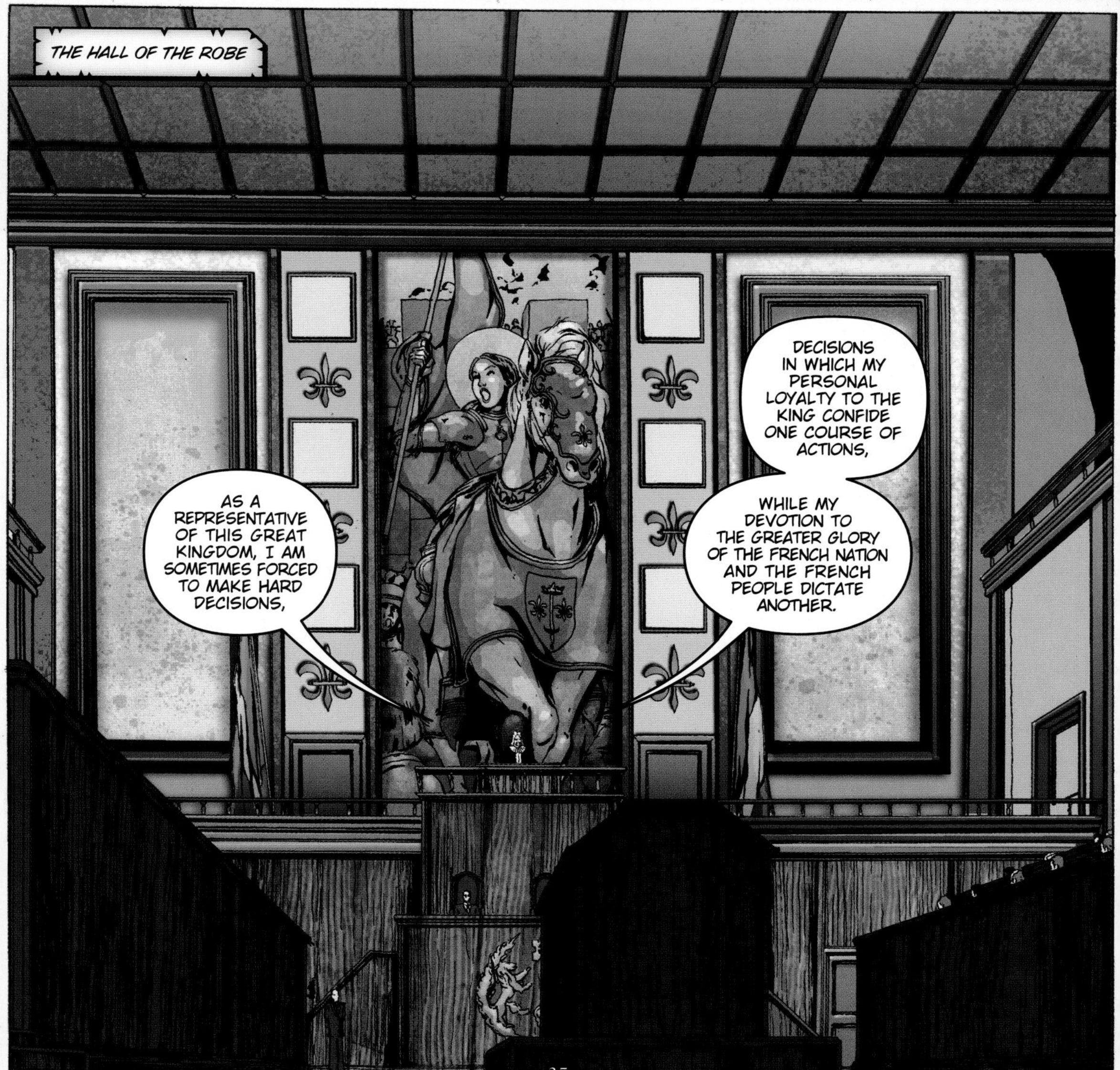
THE HALL OF THE ROBE
AS A REPRESENTATIVE OF THIS GREAT KINGDOM, I AM SOMETIMES FORCED TO MAKE HARD DECISIONS,
DECISIONS IN WHICH MY PERSONAL LOYALTY TO THE KING CONFIDE ONE COURSE OF ACTIONS,
WHILE MY DEVOTION TO THE GREATER GLORY OF THE FRENCH NATION AND THE FRENCH PEOPLE DICTATE ANOTHER.

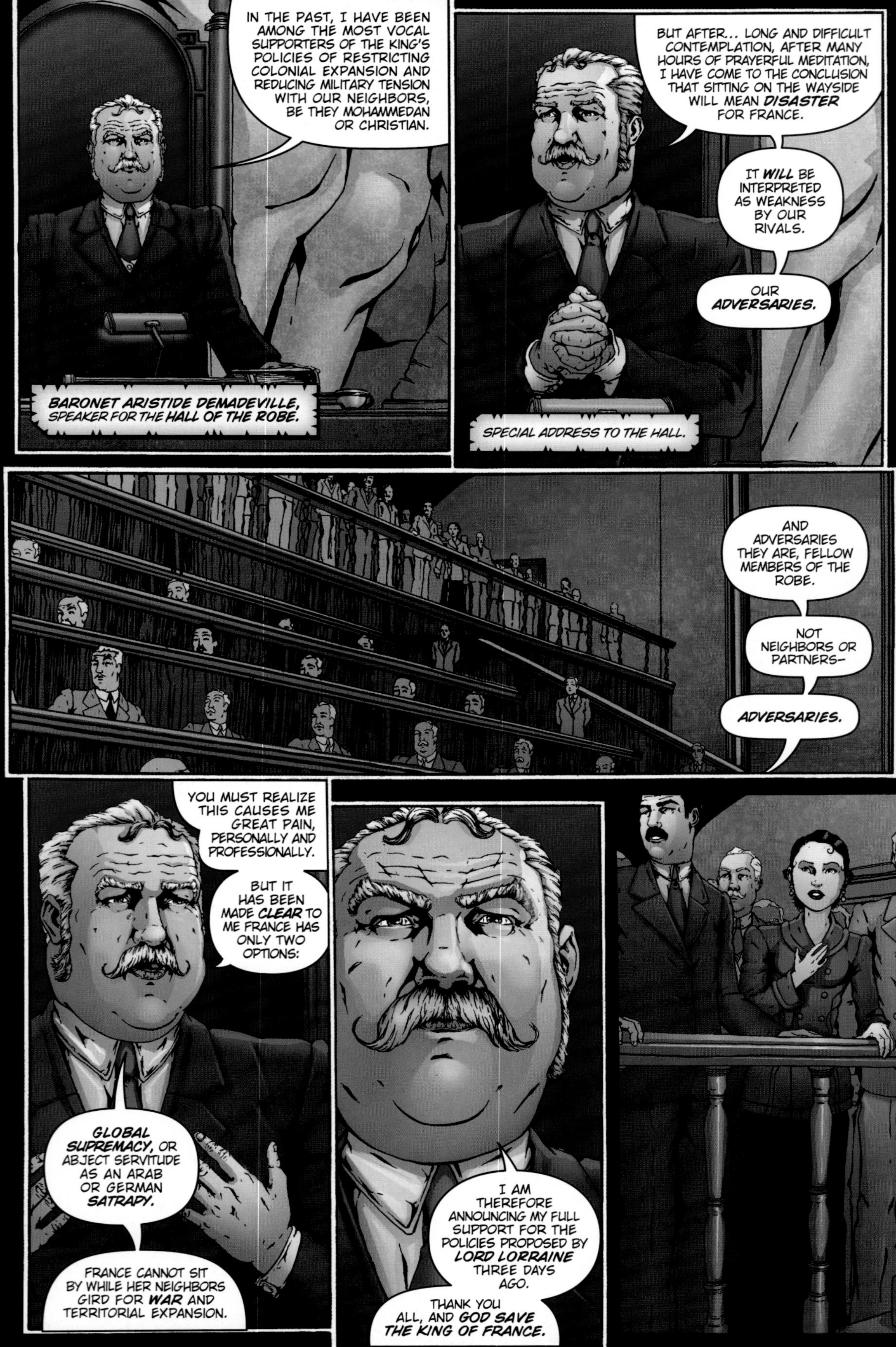
IN THE PAST, I HAVE BEEN AMONG THE MOST VOCAL SUPPORTERS OF THE KING'S POLICIES OF RESTRICTING COLONIAL EXPANSION AND REDUCING MILITARY TENSION WITH OUR NEIGHBORS, BE THEY MOHAMMEDAN OR CHRISTIAN.
BARONET ARISTIDE DEMADEVILLE, SPEAKER FOR THE HALL OF THE ROBE.
BUT AFTER... LONG AND DIFFICULT CONTEMPLATION, AFTER MANY HOURS OF PRAYERFUL MEDITATION, I HAVE COME TO THE CONCLUSION THAT SITTING ON THE WAYSIDE WILL MEAN DISASTER FOR FRANCE.
IT WILL BE INTERPRETED AS WEAKNESS BY OUR RIVALS.
OUR ADVERSARIES.
SPECIAL ADDRESS TO THE HALL.
AND ADVERSARIES THEY ARE, FELLOW MEMBERS OF THE ROBE.
NOT NEIGHBORS OR PARTNERS–
ADVERSARIES.
YOU MUST REALIZE THIS CAUSES ME GREAT PAIN, PERSONALLY AND PROFESSIONALLY.
BUT IT HAS BEEN MADE CLEAR TO ME FRANCE HAS ONLY TWO OPTIONS:
GLOBAL SUPREMACY, OR ABJECT SERVITUDE AS AN ARAB OR GERMAN SATRAPY.
FRANCE CANNOT SIT BY WHILE HER NEIGHBORS GIRD FOR WAR AND TERRITORIAL EXPANSION.
I AM THEREFORE ANNOUNCING MY FULL SUPPORT FOR THE POLICIES PROPOSED BY LORD LORRAINE THREE DAYS AGO.
THANK YOU ALL, AND GOD SAVE THE KING OF FRANCE.

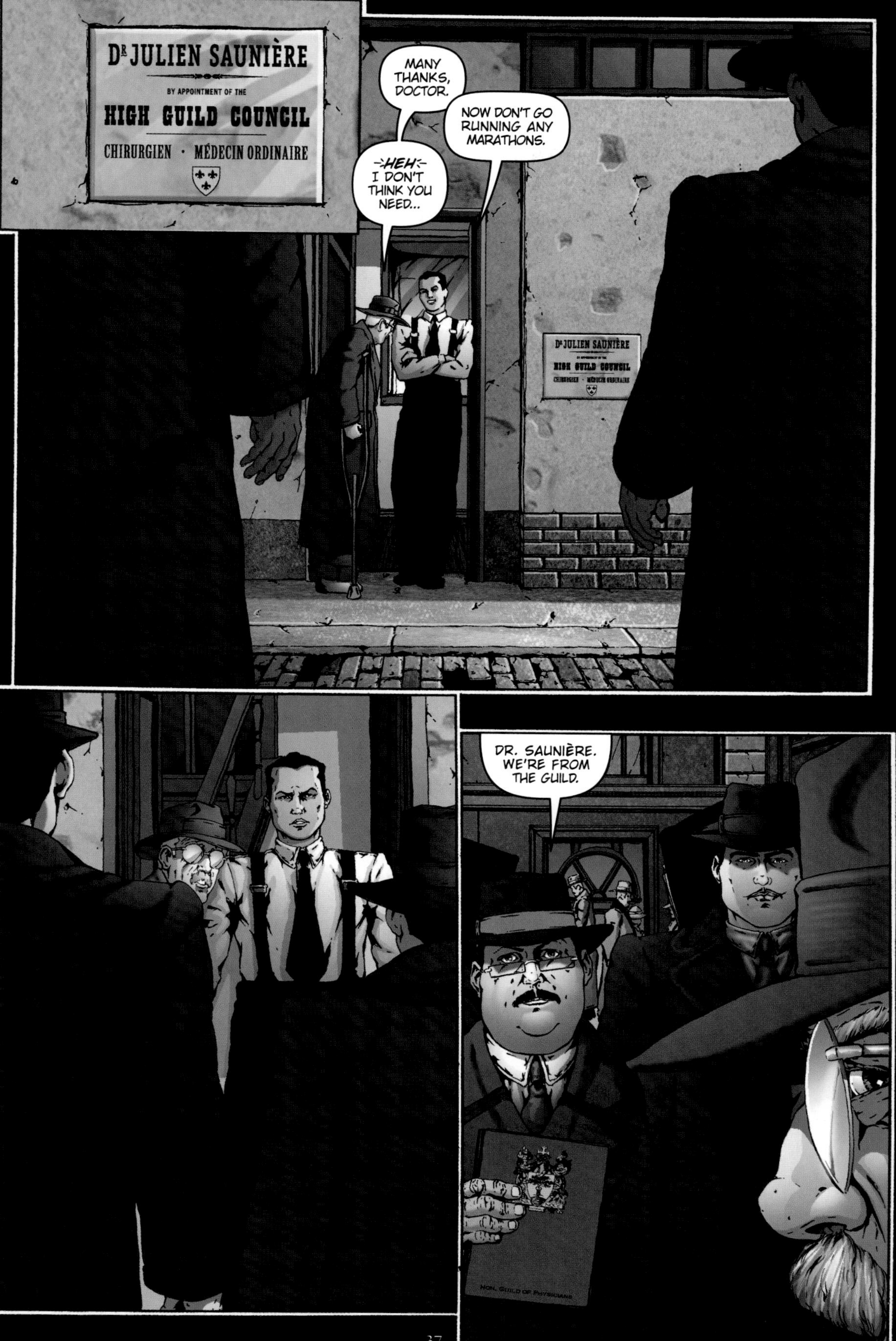
Dr JULIEN SAUNIÈRE
BY APPOINTMENT OF THE
HIGH GUILD COUNCIL
CHIRURGIEN · MÉDECIN ORDINAIRE
MANY THANKS, DOCTOR.
NOW DON'T GO RUNNING ANY MARATHONS.
-HEH- I DON'T THINK YOU NEED...
DR. SAUNIÈRE. WE'RE FROM THE GUILD.
HON. GUILD OF PHYSICIANS

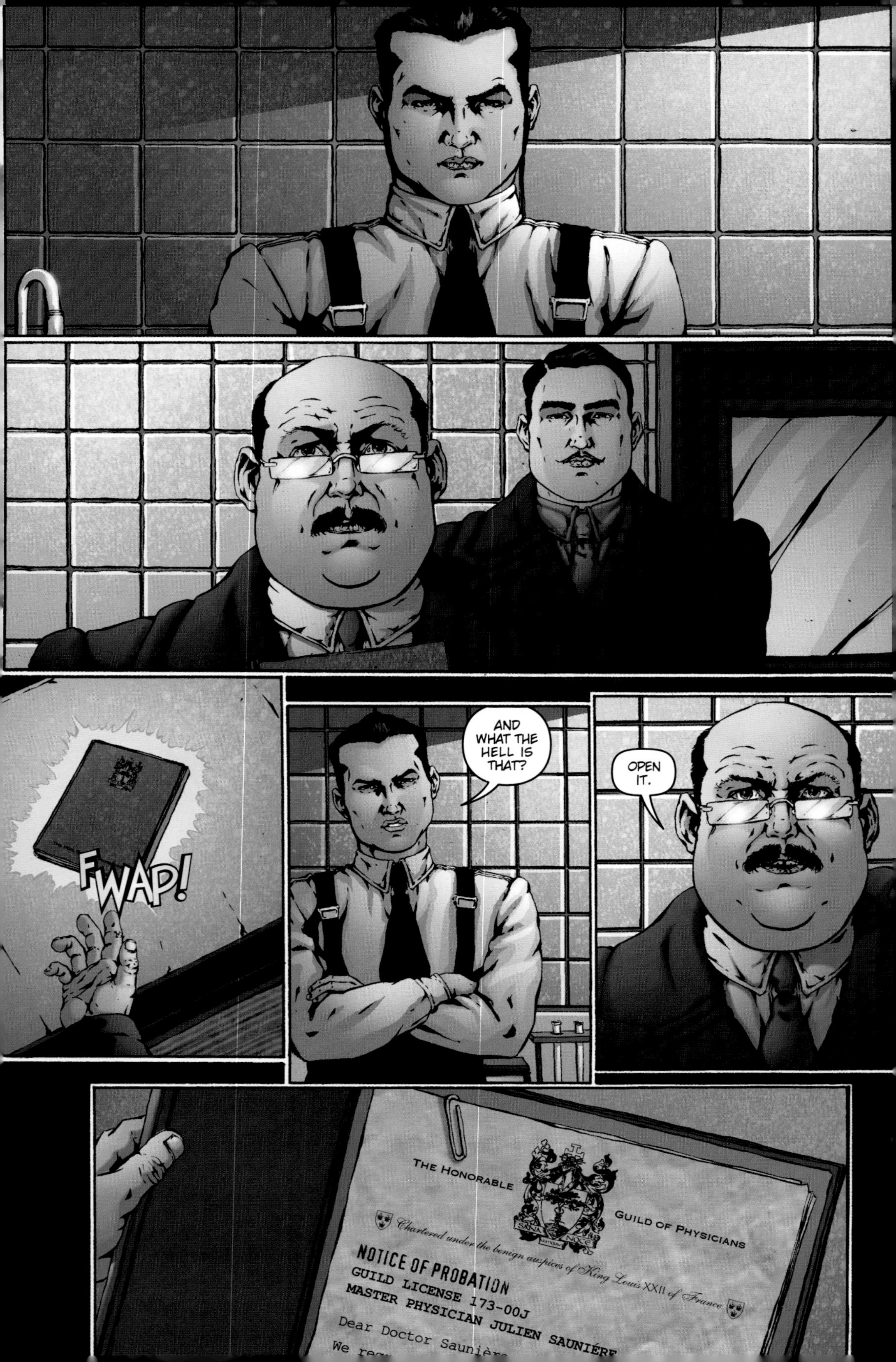
FWAP!
AND WHAT THE HELL IS THAT?
OPEN IT.
THE HONORABLE GUILD OF PHYSICIANS
Chartered under the benign auspices of King Louis XXII of France
NOTICE OF PROBATION
GUILD LICENSE 173-00J
MASTER PHYSICIAN JULIEN SAUNIÉRE
Dear Doctor
We

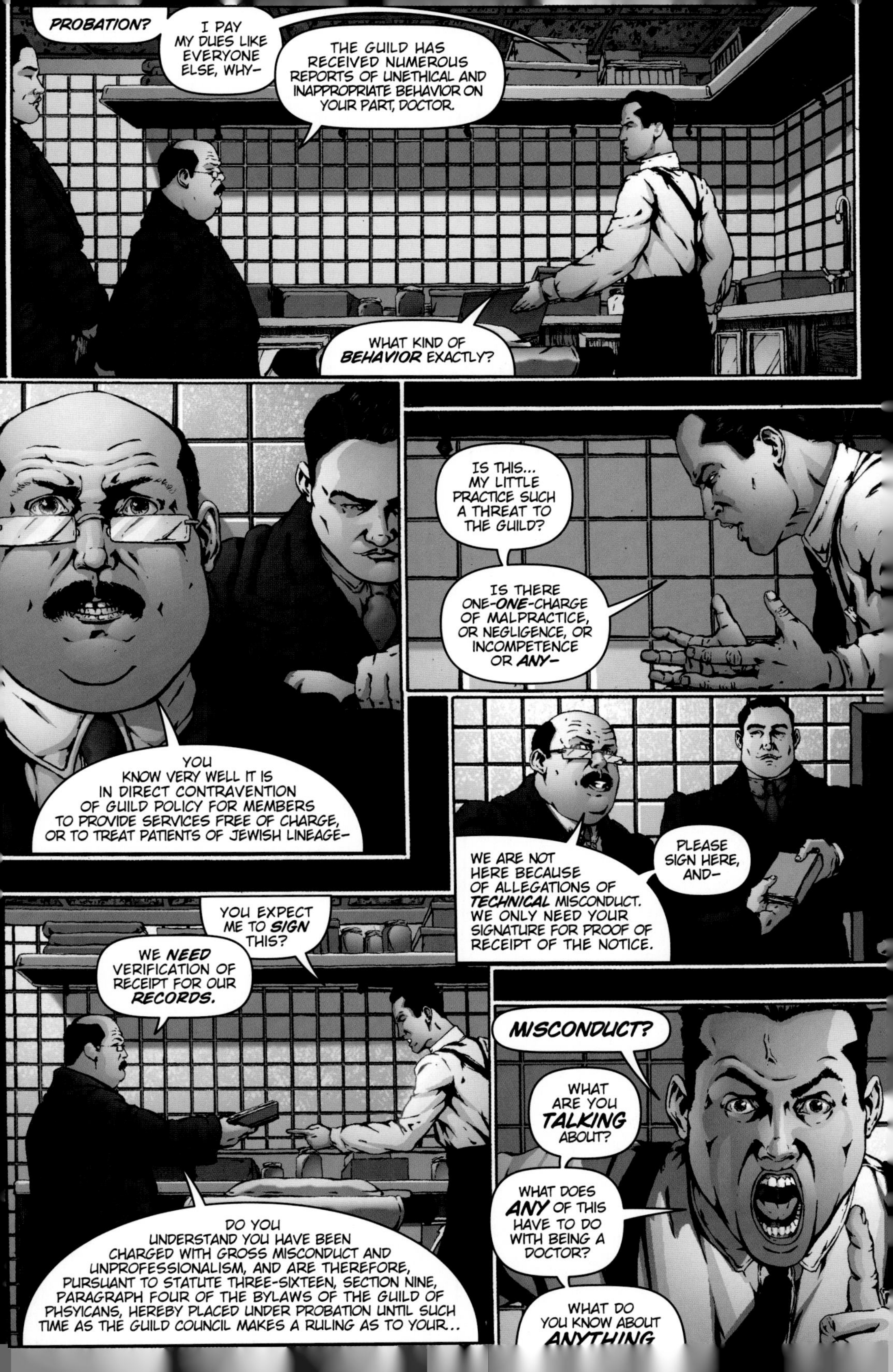
PROBATION?
I PAY MY DUES LIKE EVERYONE ELSE, WHY-
THE GUILD HAS RECEIVED NUMEROUS REPORTS OF UNETHICAL AND INAPPROPRIATE BEHAVIOR ON YOUR PART, DOCTOR.
WHAT KIND OF BEHAVIOR EXACTLY?
YOU KNOW VERY WELL IT IS IN DIRECT CONTRAVENTION OF GUILD POLICY FOR MEMBERS TO PROVIDE SERVICES FREE OF CHARGE, OR TO TREAT PATIENTS OF JEWISH LINEAGE-
IS THIS... MY LITTLE PRACTICE SUCH A THREAT TO THE GUILD?
IS THERE ONE-ONE-CHARGE OF MALPRACTICE, OR NEGLIGENCE, OR INCOMPETENCE OR ANY-
WE ARE NOT HERE BECAUSE OF ALLEGATIONS OF TECHNICAL MISCONDUCT. WE ONLY NEED YOUR SIGNATURE FOR PROOF OF RECEIPT OF THE NOTICE.
PLEASE SIGN HERE, AND-
YOU EXPECT ME TO SIGN THIS?
WE NEED VERIFICATION OF RECEIPT FOR OUR RECORDS.
DO YOU UNDERSTAND YOU HAVE BEEN CHARGED WITH GROSS MISCONDUCT AND UNPROFESSIONALISM, AND ARE THEREFORE, PURSUANT TO STATUTE THREE-SIXTEEN, SECTION NINE, PARAGRAPH FOUR OF THE BYLAWS OF THE GUILD OF PHSYICANS, HEREBY PLACED UNDER PROBATION UNTIL SUCH TIME AS THE GUILD COUNCIL MAKES A RULING AS TO YOUR...
MISCONDUCT?
WHAT ARE YOU TALKING ABOUT?
WHAT DOES ANY OF THIS HAVE TO DO WITH BEING A DOCTOR?
WHAT DO YOU KNOW ABOUT ANYTHING

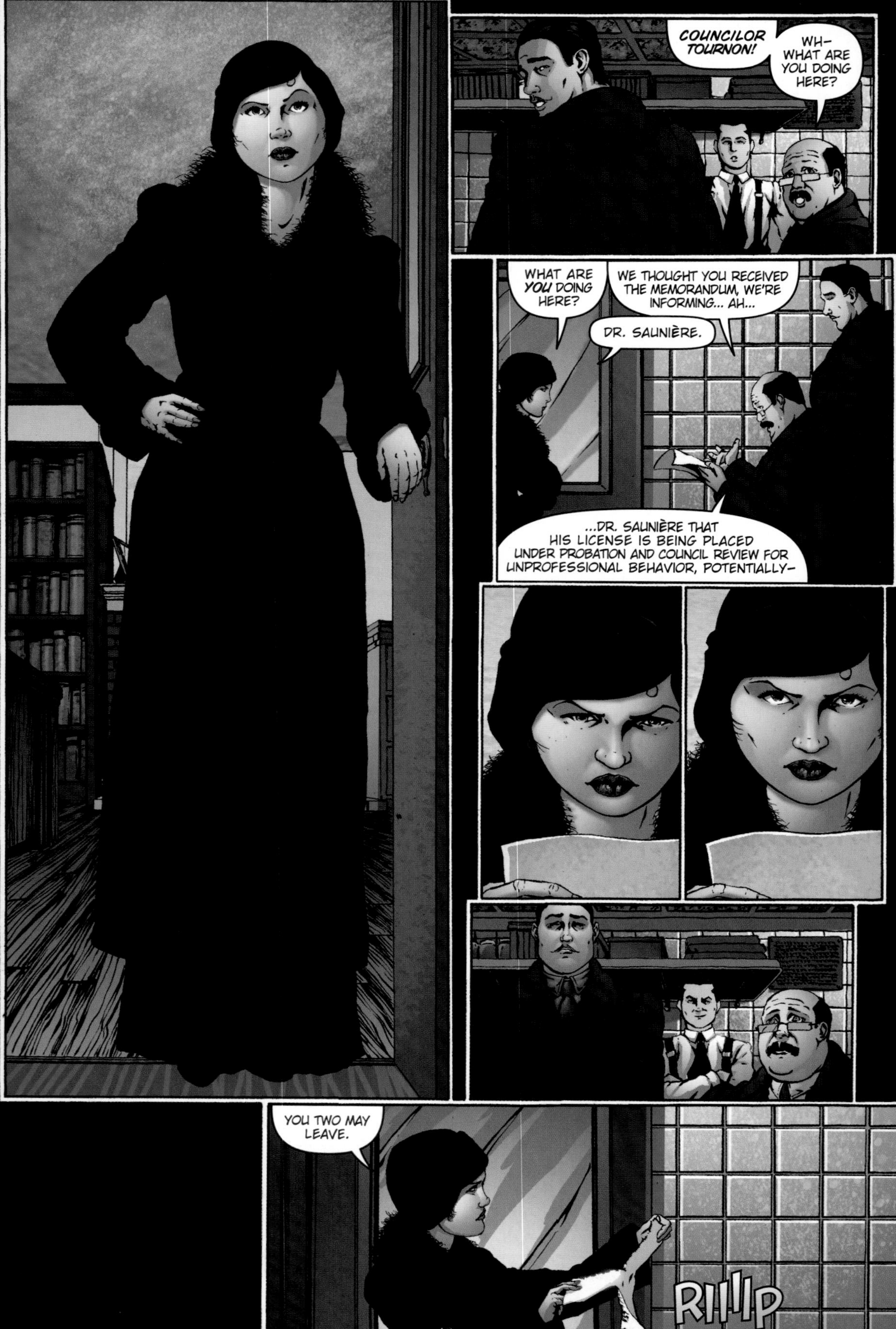
COUNCILOR TOURNON!
WH- WHAT ARE YOU DOING HERE?
WHAT ARE YOU DOING HERE?
WE THOUGHT YOU RECEIVED THE MEMORANDUM, WE'RE INFORMING... AH...
DR. SAUNIÈRE.
...DR. SAUNIÈRE THAT HIS LICENSE IS BEING PLACED UNDER PROBATION AND COUNCIL REVIEW FOR UNPROFESSIONAL BEHAVIOR, POTENTIALLY-
YOU TWO MAY LEAVE.
RIIIIP

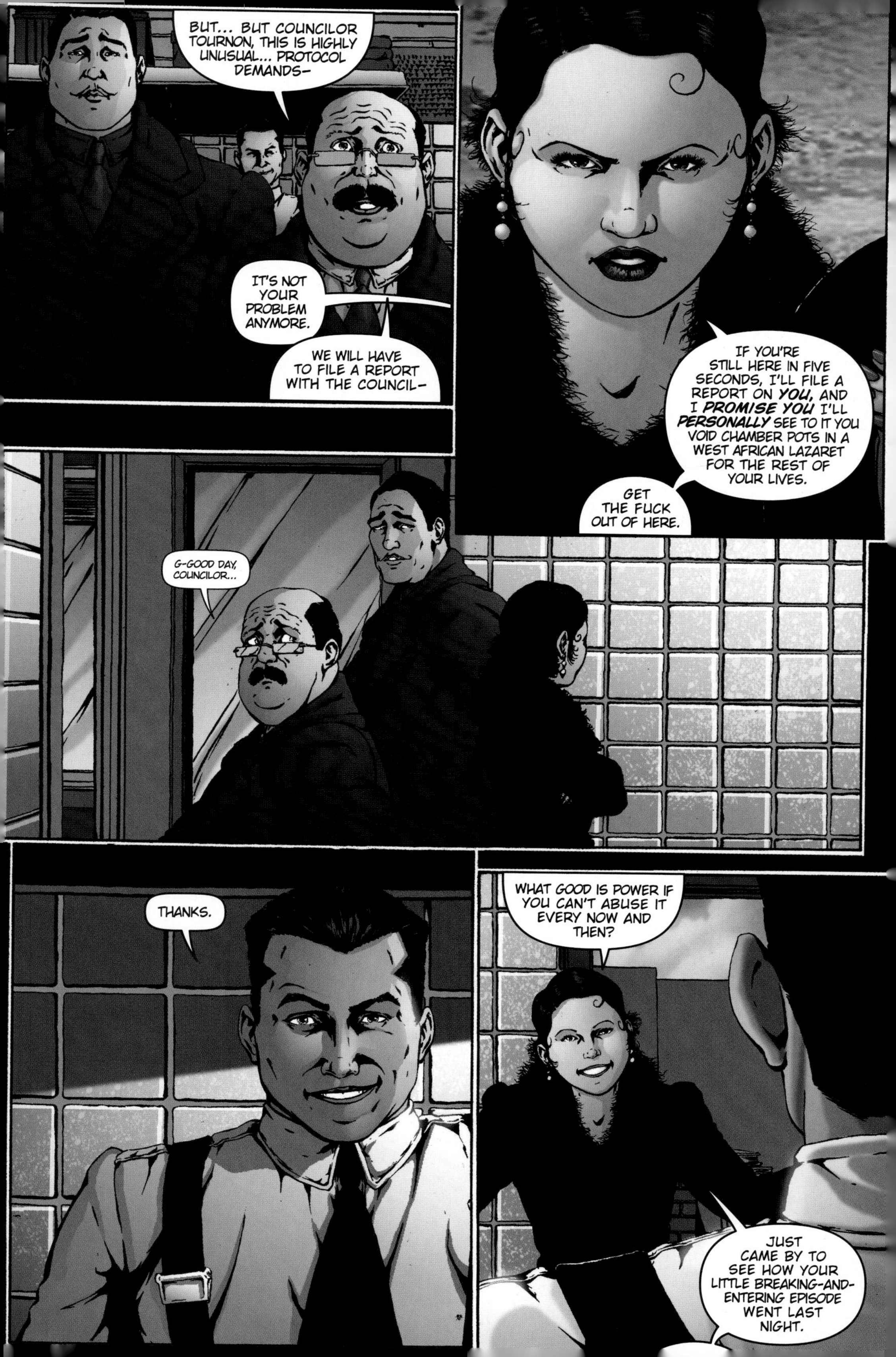
BUT... BUT COUNCILOR TOURNON, THIS IS HIGHLY UNUSUAL... PROTOCOL DEMANDS-
IT'S NOT YOUR PROBLEM ANYMORE.
WE WILL HAVE TO FILE A REPORT WITH THE COUNCIL-
IF YOU'RE STILL HERE IN FIVE SECONDS, I'LL FILE A REPORT ON YOU, AND I PROMISE YOU I'LL PERSONALLY SEE TO IT YOU VOID CHAMBER POTS IN A WEST AFRICAN LAZARET FOR THE REST OF YOUR LIVES.
GET THE FUCK OUT OF HERE.
G-GOOD DAY, COUNCILOR...
THANKS.
WHAT GOOD IS POWER IF YOU CAN'T ABUSE IT EVERY NOW AND THEN?
JUST CAME BY TO SEE HOW YOUR LITTLE BREAKING-AND-ENTERING EPISODE WENT LAST NIGHT.

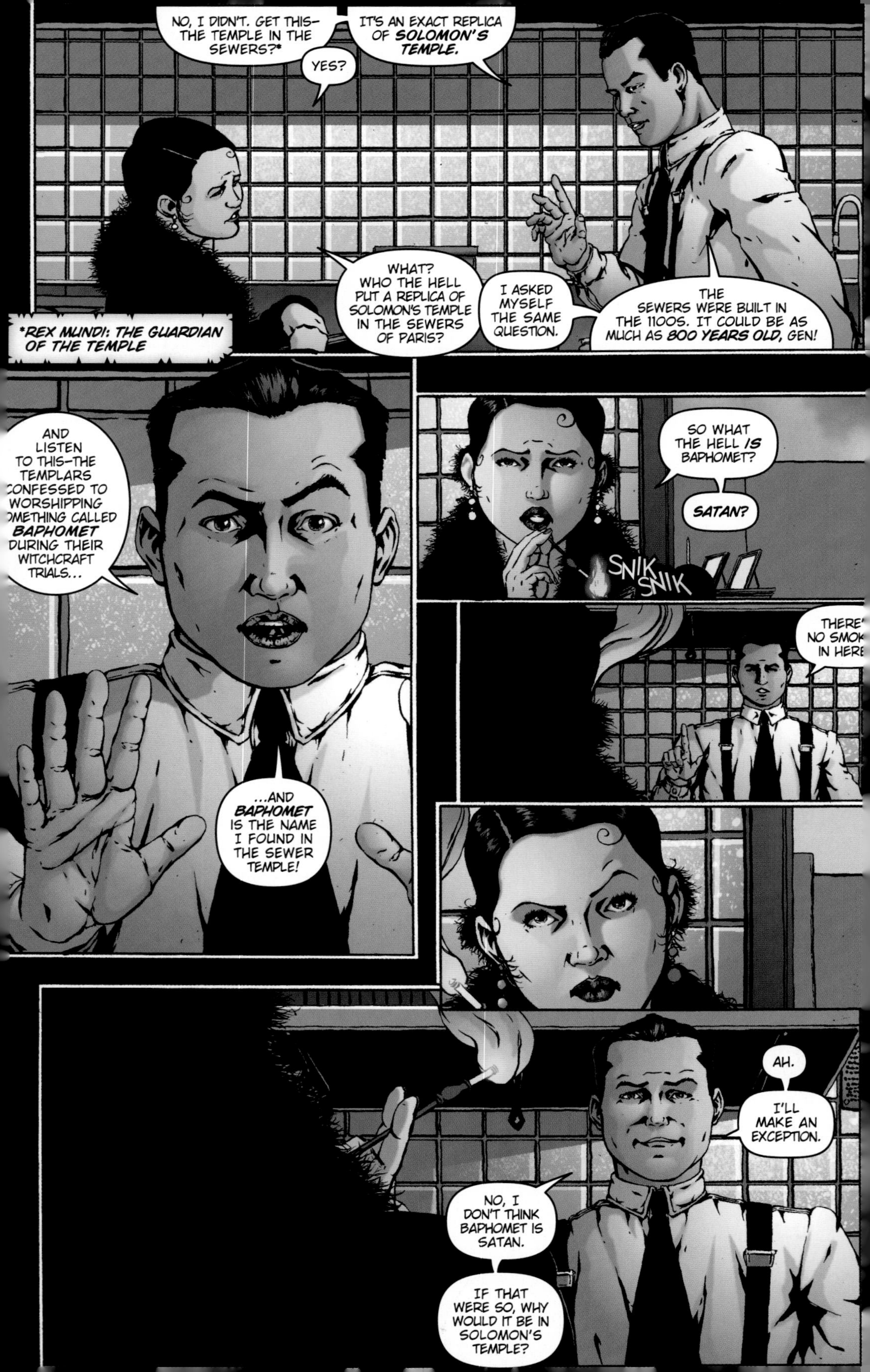

NO, I DIDN'T. GET THIS– THE TEMPLE IN THE SEWERS?*
YES?
IT'S AN EXACT REPLICA OF **SOLOMON'S TEMPLE.**
WHAT? WHO THE HELL PUT A REPLICA OF SOLOMON'S TEMPLE IN THE SEWERS OF PARIS?
I ASKED MYSELF THE SAME QUESTION.
THE SEWERS WERE BUILT IN THE 1100S. IT COULD BE AS MUCH AS **800 YEARS OLD**, GEN!
*REX MUNDI: THE GUARDIAN OF THE TEMPLE
AND LISTEN TO THIS–THE TEMPLARS CONFESSED TO WORSHIPPING OMETHING CALLED **BAPHOMET** DURING THEIR WITCHCRAFT TRIALS...
...AND **BAPHOMET** IS THE NAME I FOUND IN THE SEWER TEMPLE!
SO WHAT THE HELL *IS* BAPHOMET?
SATAN?
SNIK SNIK
THERE' NO SMOK IN HERE
AH.
I'LL MAKE AN EXCEPTION.
NO, I DON'T THINK BAPHOMET IS SATAN.
IF THAT WERE SO, WHY WOULD IT BE IN SOLOMON'S TEMPLE?

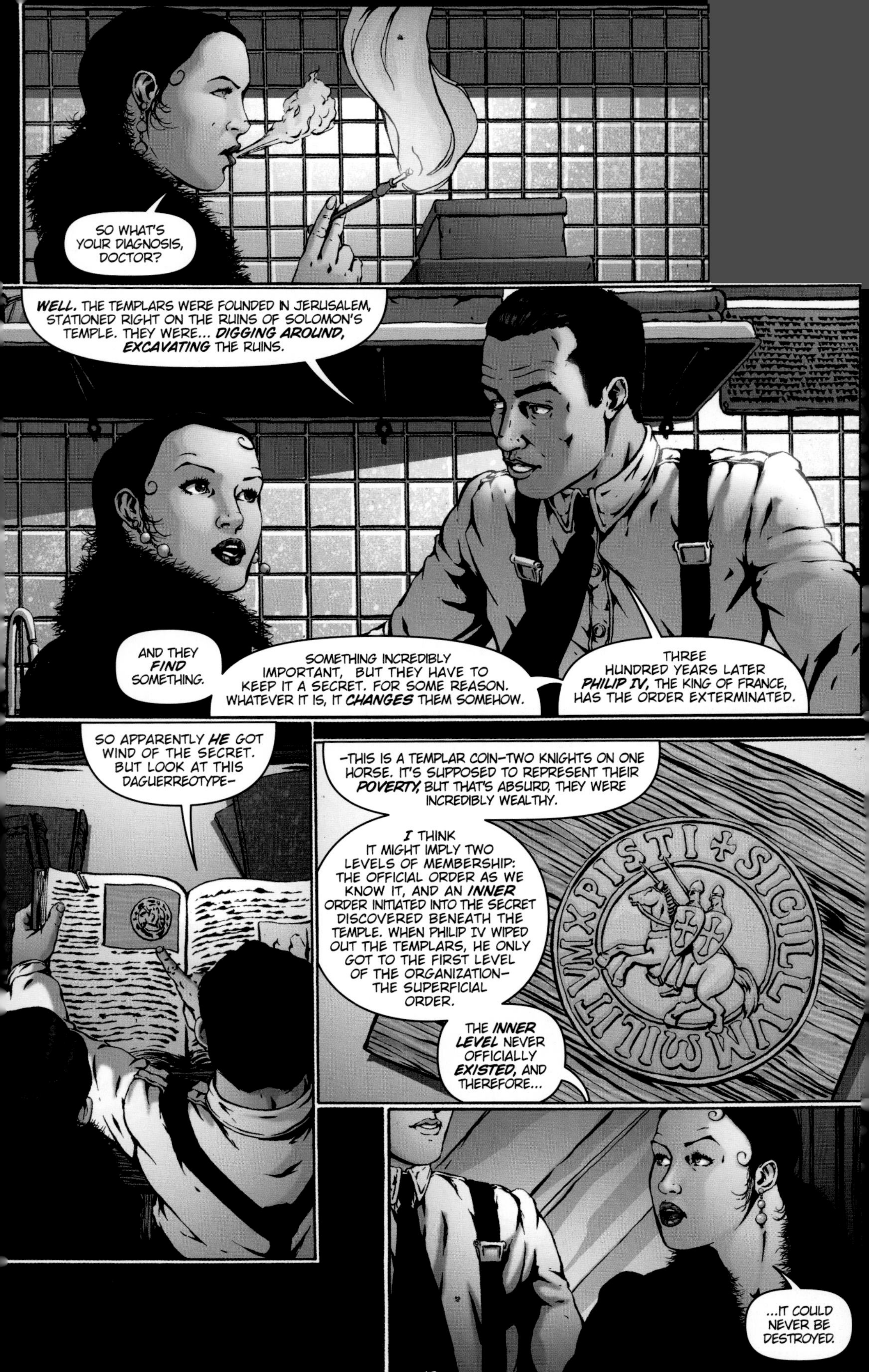
SO WHAT'S YOUR DIAGNOSIS, DOCTOR?
WELL. THE TEMPLARS WERE FOUNDED IN JERUSALEM, STATIONED RIGHT ON THE RUINS OF SOLOMON'S TEMPLE. THEY WERE... **DIGGING AROUND, EXCAVATING** THE RUINS.
AND THEY **FIND** SOMETHING.
SOMETHING INCREDIBLY IMPORTANT, BUT THEY HAVE TO KEEP IT A SECRET. FOR SOME REASON. WHATEVER IT IS, IT **CHANGES** THEM SOMEHOW.
THREE HUNDRED YEARS LATER **PHILIP IV,** THE KING OF FRANCE, HAS THE ORDER EXTERMINATED.
SO APPARENTLY **HE** GOT WIND OF THE SECRET. BUT LOOK AT THIS DAGUERREOTYPE–
–THIS IS A TEMPLAR COIN–TWO KNIGHTS ON ONE HORSE. IT'S SUPPOSED TO REPRESENT THEIR **POVERTY,** BUT THAT'S ABSURD, THEY WERE INCREDIBLY WEALTHY.
I THINK IT MIGHT IMPLY TWO LEVELS OF MEMBERSHIP: THE OFFICIAL ORDER AS WE KNOW IT, AND AN **INNER** ORDER INITIATED INTO THE SECRET DISCOVERED BENEATH THE TEMPLE. WHEN PHILIP IV WIPED OUT THE TEMPLARS, HE ONLY GOT TO THE FIRST LEVEL OF THE ORGANIZATION– THE SUPERFICIAL ORDER.
SIGILLVM MILITVM XPISTI
THE **INNER LEVEL** NEVER OFFICIALLY **EXISTED,** AND THEREFORE...
...IT COULD NEVER BE DESTROYED.

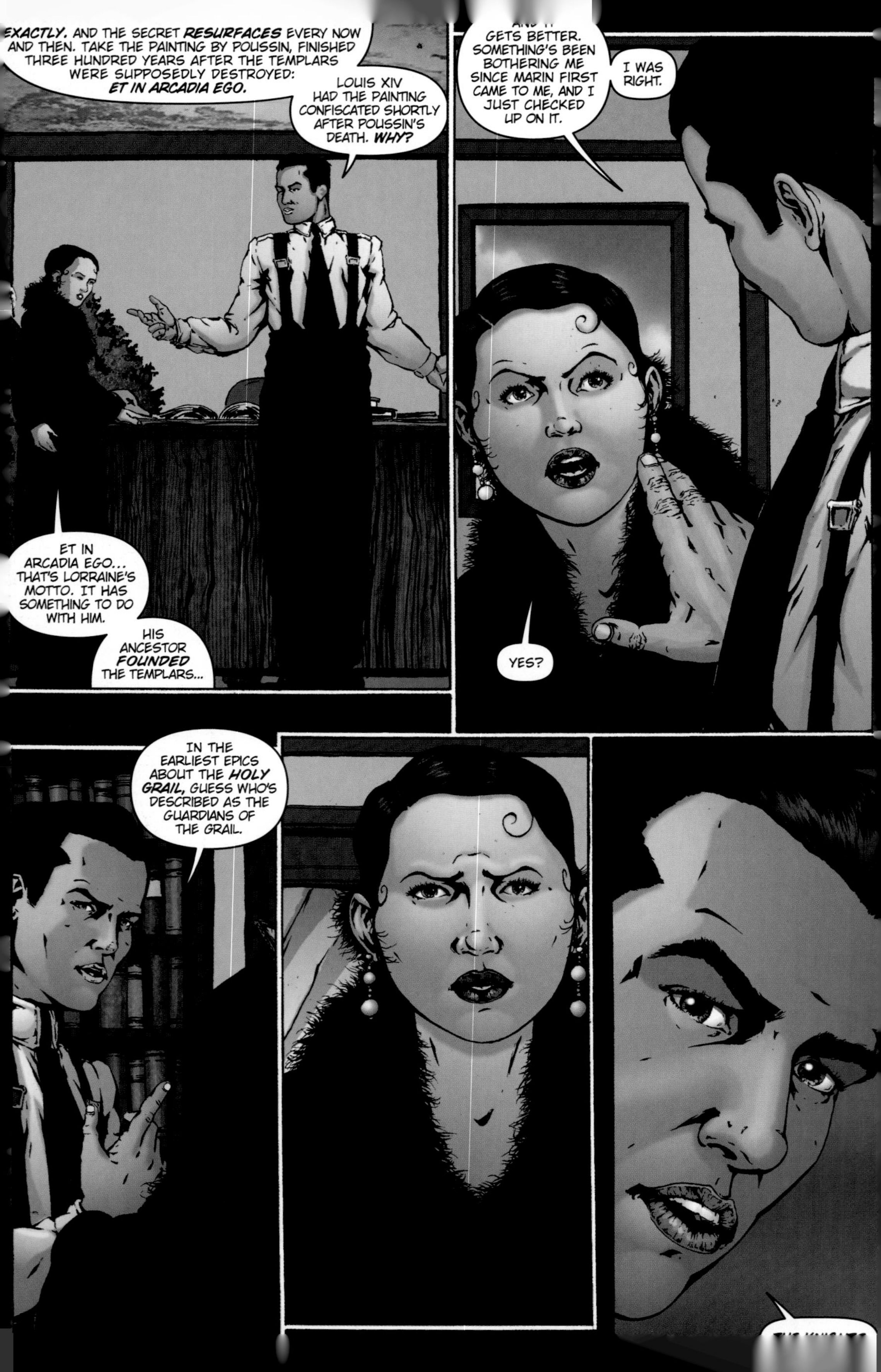
EXACTLY. AND THE SECRET RESURFACES EVERY NOW AND THEN. TAKE THE PAINTING BY POUSSIN, FINISHED THREE HUNDRED YEARS AFTER THE TEMPLARS WERE SUPPOSEDLY DESTROYED: ET IN ARCADIA EGO.
LOUIS XIV HAD THE PAINTING CONFISCATED SHORTLY AFTER POUSSIN'S DEATH. WHY?
ET IN ARCADIA EGO... THAT'S LORRAINE'S MOTTO. IT HAS SOMETHING TO DO WITH HIM.
HIS ANCESTOR FOUNDED THE TEMPLARS...
GETS BETTER. SOMETHING'S BEEN BOTHERING ME SINCE MARIN FIRST CAME TO ME, AND I JUST CHECKED UP ON IT.
I WAS RIGHT.
YES?
IN THE EARLIEST EPICS ABOUT THE HOLY GRAIL, GUESS WHO'S DESCRIBED AS THE GUARDIANS OF THE GRAIL.

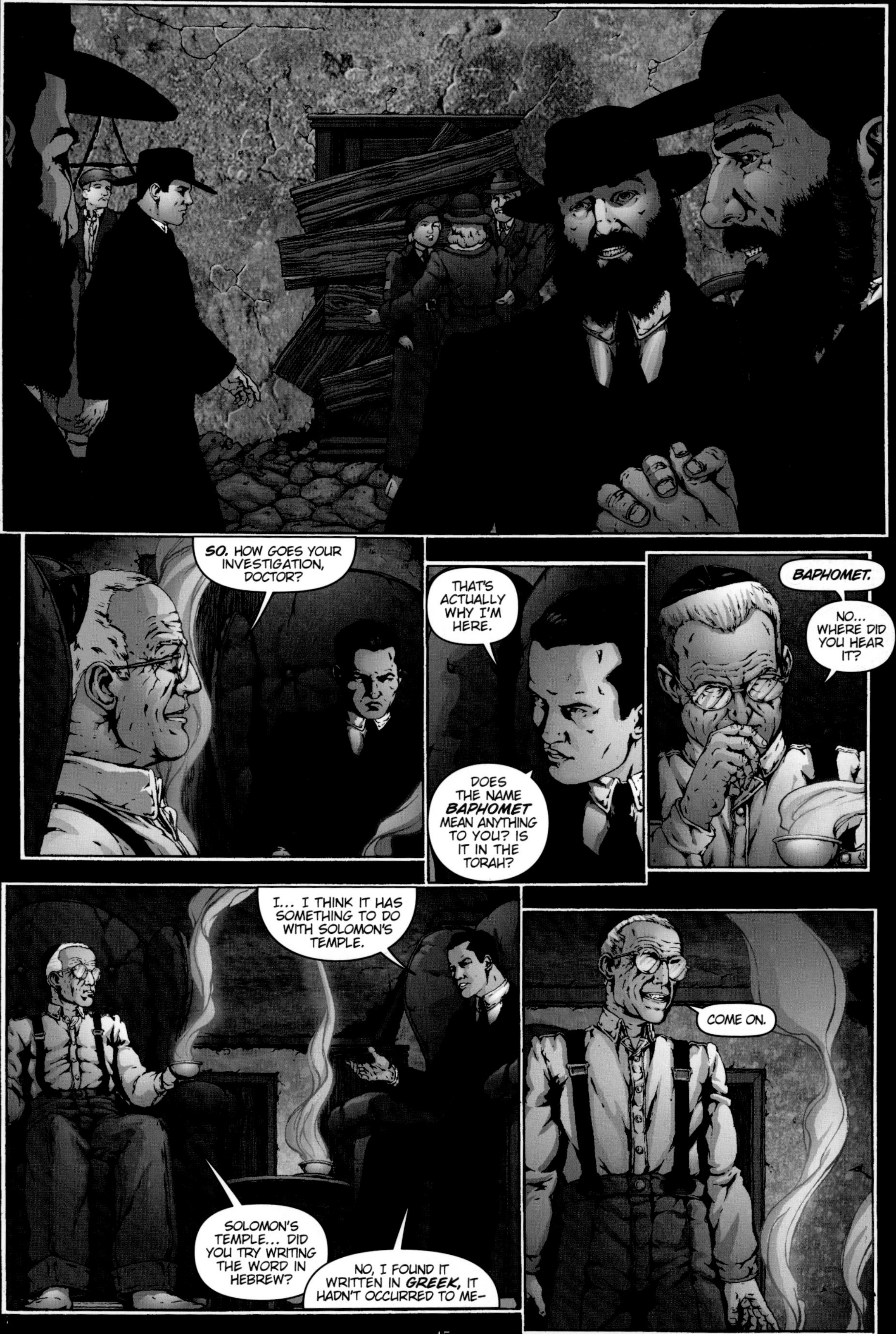
SO. HOW GOES YOUR INVESTIGATION, DOCTOR?
THAT'S ACTUALLY WHY I'M HERE.
DOES THE NAME BAPHOMET MEAN ANYTHING TO YOU? IS IT IN THE TORAH?
BAPHOMET.
NO... WHERE DID YOU HEAR IT?
I... I THINK IT HAS SOMETHING TO DO WITH SOLOMON'S TEMPLE.
SOLOMON'S TEMPLE... DID YOU TRY WRITING THE WORD IN HEBREW?
NO, I FOUND IT WRITTEN IN GREEK, IT HADN'T OCCURRED TO ME-
COME ON.

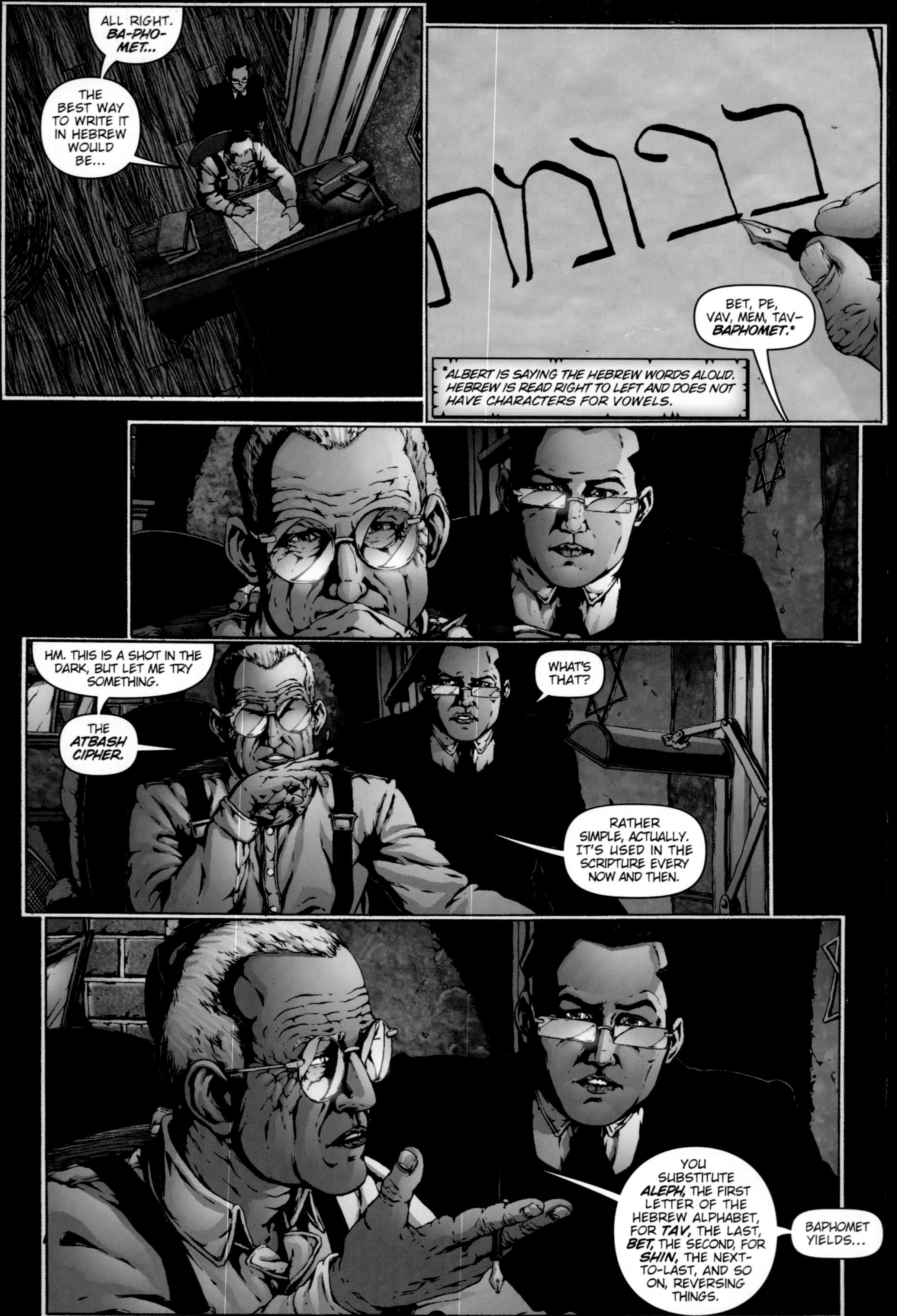
ALL RIGHT. BA-PHO-MET...
THE BEST WAY TO WRITE IT IN HEBREW WOULD BE...
בפומת
BET, PE, VAV, MEM, TAV– BAPHOMET.*
*ALBERT IS SAYING THE HEBREW WORDS ALOUD. HEBREW IS READ RIGHT TO LEFT AND DOES NOT HAVE CHARACTERS FOR VOWELS.
HM. THIS IS A SHOT IN THE DARK, BUT LET ME TRY SOMETHING.
THE ATBASH CIPHER.
WHAT'S THAT?
RATHER SIMPLE, ACTUALLY. IT'S USED IN THE SCRIPTURE EVERY NOW AND THEN.
YOU SUBSTITUTE ALEPH, THE FIRST LETTER OF THE HEBREW ALPHABET, FOR TAV, THE LAST, BET, THE SECOND, FOR SHIN, THE NEXT-TO-LAST, AND SO ON, REVERSING THINGS.
BAPHOMET YIELDS...

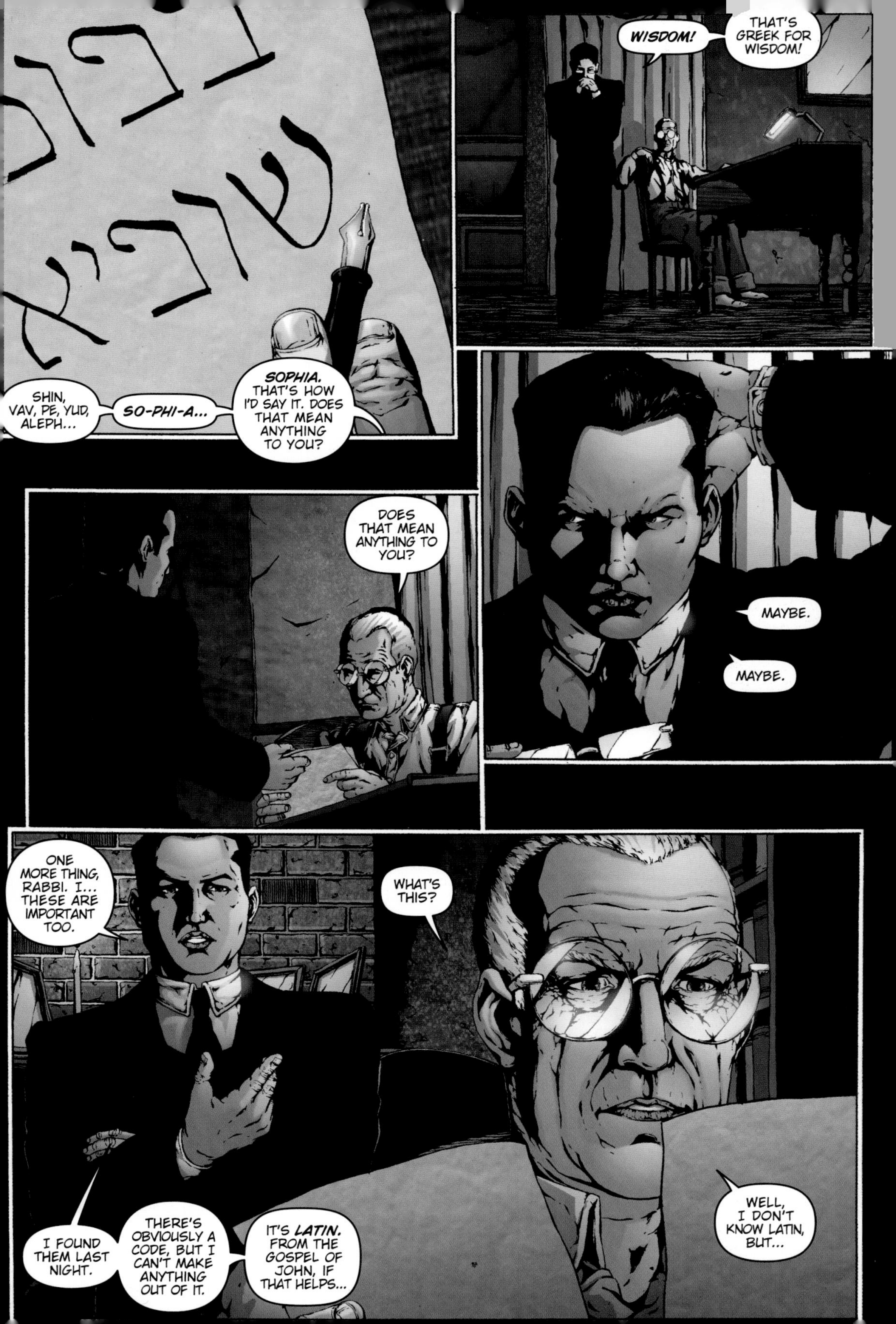
SHIN, VAV, PE, YUD, ALEPH...
SO-PHI-A...
SOPHIA. THAT'S HOW I'D SAY IT. DOES THAT MEAN ANYTHING TO YOU?
WISDOM!
THAT'S GREEK FOR WISDOM!
DOES THAT MEAN ANYTHING TO YOU?
MAYBE.
MAYBE.
ONE MORE THING, RABBI. I... THESE ARE IMPORTANT TOO.
WHAT'S THIS?
I FOUND THEM LAST NIGHT.
THERE'S OBVIOUSLY A CODE, BUT I CAN'T MAKE ANYTHING OUT OF IT.
IT'S LATIN. FROM THE GOSPEL OF JOHN, IF THAT HELPS...
WELL, I DON'T KNOW LATIN, BUT...

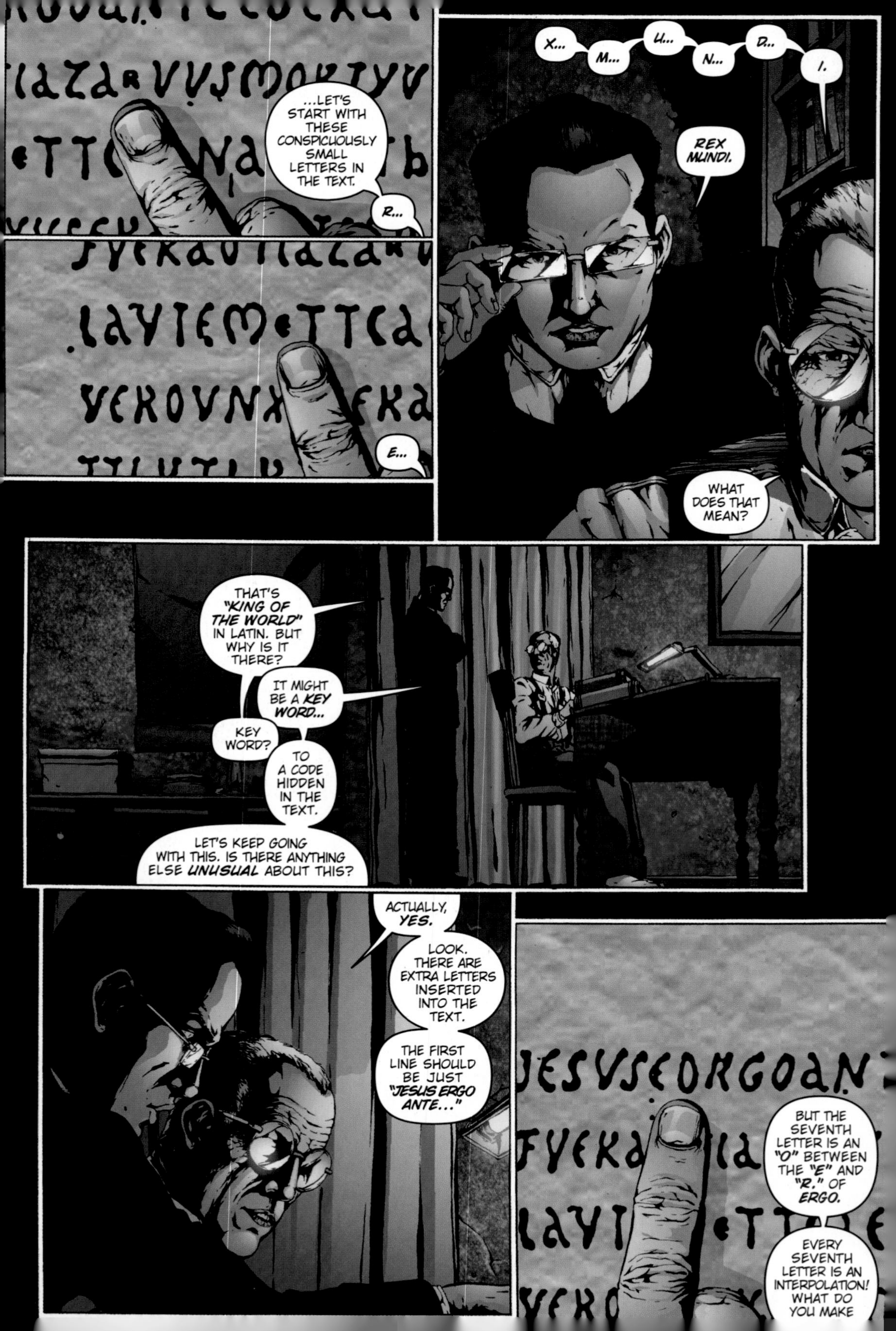
...LET'S START WITH THESE CONSPICUOUSLY SMALL LETTERS IN THE TEXT.
R...
E...
X...
M...
U...
N...
D...
I.
REX MUNDI.
WHAT DOES THAT MEAN?
THAT'S "KING OF THE WORLD" IN LATIN. BUT WHY IS IT THERE?
IT MIGHT BE A KEY WORD...
KEY WORD?
TO A CODE HIDDEN IN THE TEXT.
LET'S KEEP GOING WITH THIS. IS THERE ANYTHING ELSE UNUSUAL ABOUT THIS?
ACTUALLY, YES.
LOOK. THERE ARE EXTRA LETTERS INSERTED INTO THE TEXT.
THE FIRST LINE SHOULD BE JUST "JESUS ERGO ANTE..."
BUT THE SEVENTH LETTER IS AN "O" BETWEEN THE "E" AND "R." OF ERGO.
EVERY SEVENTH LETTER IS AN INTERPOLATION! WHAT DO YOU MAKE

HOLD ON. WHAT'S THIS? THIS ISN'T A *ROMAN* LETTER...

YOU'RE RIGHT. THAT'S AN *OMEGA*. LAST LETTER IN THE GREEK ALPHABET.

STRANGE...

AND HERE'S AN UPPER-CASE *"A"* NEAR THE BEGINNING. IT'S THE ONLY ONE. ALL THE REST ARE LOWER CASE...

WAIT, IT'S NOT AN "A," IT'S AN *ALPHA*, THE FIRST LETTER OF THE GREEK ALPHABET!

THIS REMINDS ME OF SOMETHING...

YES?

SOMETHING JESUS SAYS... "I AM THE ALPHA AND THE OMEGA." THE BEGINNING AND THE END.

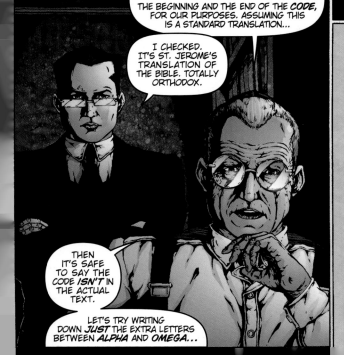

THE BEGINNING AND THE END OF THE *CODE*, FOR OUR PURPOSES. ASSUMING THIS IS A STANDARD TRANSLATION...

I CHECKED. IT'S ST. JEROME'S TRANSLATION OF THE BIBLE. TOTALLY ORTHODOX.

THEN IT'S SAFE TO SAY THE CODE *ISN'T* IN THE ACTUAL TEXT.

LET'S TRY WRITING DOWN *JUST* THE EXTRA LETTERS BETWEEN *ALPHA* AND *OMEGA*...

OOPJIBKQAAEHPQ
XALBLNJLGHDHFPPK
XGYOPHCXUUDVXXTQ
ARGLJJFXURZJXQYT
BOTBSYDOHGOHZXU
EXFEDPLBIIUAGCE
BLHNVJNIFLQATA
CMUANGTSARNJHFH
LGO___NERO

THERE.

JUST A JUMBLE...

NOW HOLD ON. THIS IS WHERE REX MUNDI COMES IN.

I HAVE A HUNCH THIS IS A *VIGENÈRE SUBSTITUTION.**

WHAT'S THAT?

A METHOD OF ENCRYPTION BASED ON A TABLE OF SHIFTING ALPHABETS AND A KEY WORD. VERY HARD TO CRACK WITHOUT THE KEY WORD.

I'M GUESSING OUR KEY IS *REX MUNDI.*

FOR MORE INFORMATION ON VIGENÈRE SUBSTITUTION SEE WWW.REXMUNDI.NET.

WELL THAT'S GREAT...

...IT'S JUST ANOTHER MEANINGLESS JUMBLE.

GSMVDONZREBTKEAIDFI
AEZJPULCCKYAOPSMTXKY
DUATJOEDAYPGVAKYAQN
TDSHEXLFPKYCKOGLVJPRA
NVHMYWLDRGBOZOOPFA
CADSOZRYXTKPPDRRDGN
TKZJXZGMGLAHAG

I'M SORRY, DOCTOR, I REALLY THOUGHT WE WERE ONTO SOMETHING. I GUESS IT WAS TOO MUCH TO HOPE WHOEVER WENT THROUGH THE TROUBLE OF CODING THE SCROLL WOULD INCLUDE THE KEY RIGHT IN THE TEXT.

WHAT IS REX MUNDI FOR THEN?

A RED HERRING PERHAPS? SOMETHING THE CODE MAKER INSERTED TO THROW US OFF.

IT'S JUST TOO OBVIOUS TO BE MEANINGFUL.

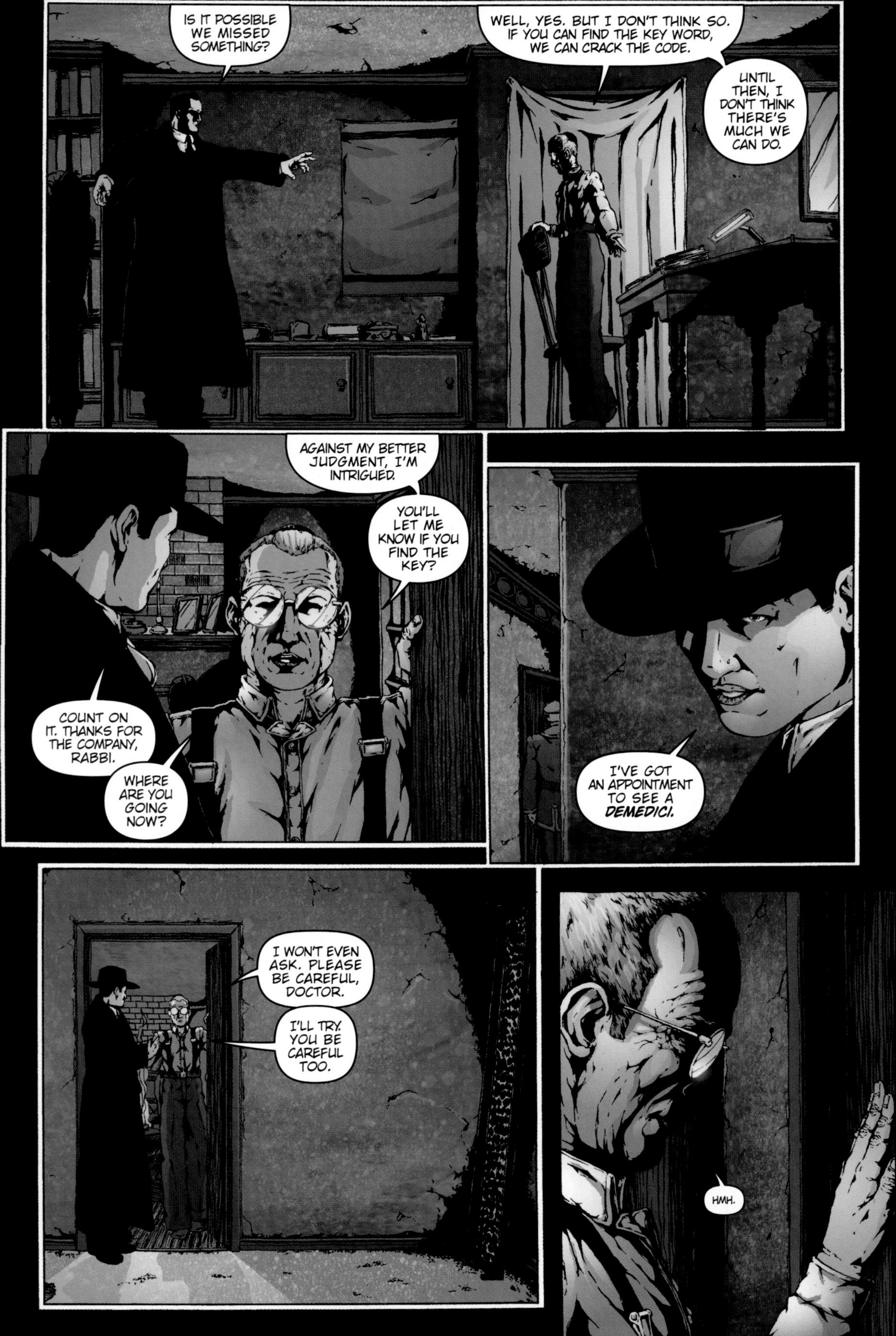
IS IT POSSIBLE WE MISSED SOMETHING?
WELL, YES. BUT I DON'T THINK SO. IF YOU CAN FIND THE KEY WORD, WE CAN CRACK THE CODE.
UNTIL THEN, I DON'T THINK THERE'S MUCH WE CAN DO.
AGAINST MY BETTER JUDGMENT, I'M INTRIGUED.
YOU'LL LET ME KNOW IF YOU FIND THE KEY?
COUNT ON IT. THANKS FOR THE COMPANY, RABBI.
WHERE ARE YOU GOING NOW?
I'VE GOT AN APPOINTMENT TO SEE A DEMEDICI.
I WON'T EVEN ASK. PLEASE BE CAREFUL, DOCTOR.
I'LL TRY. YOU BE CAREFUL TOO.
HMH.

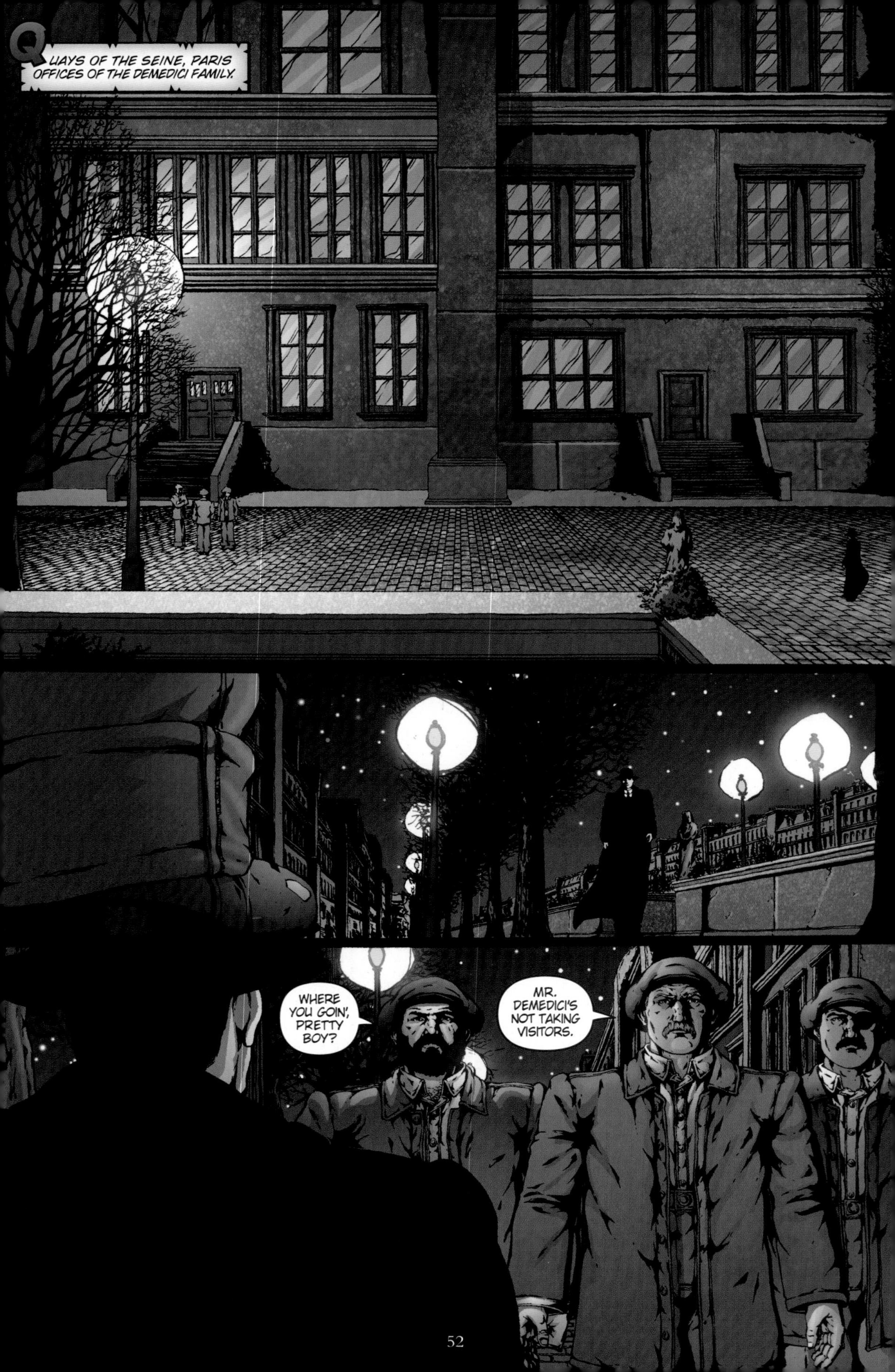
QUAYS OF THE SEINE, PARIS
OFFICES OF THE DEMEDICI FAMILY.
WHERE YOU GOIN', PRETTY BOY?
MR. DEMEDICI'S NOT TAKING VISITORS.

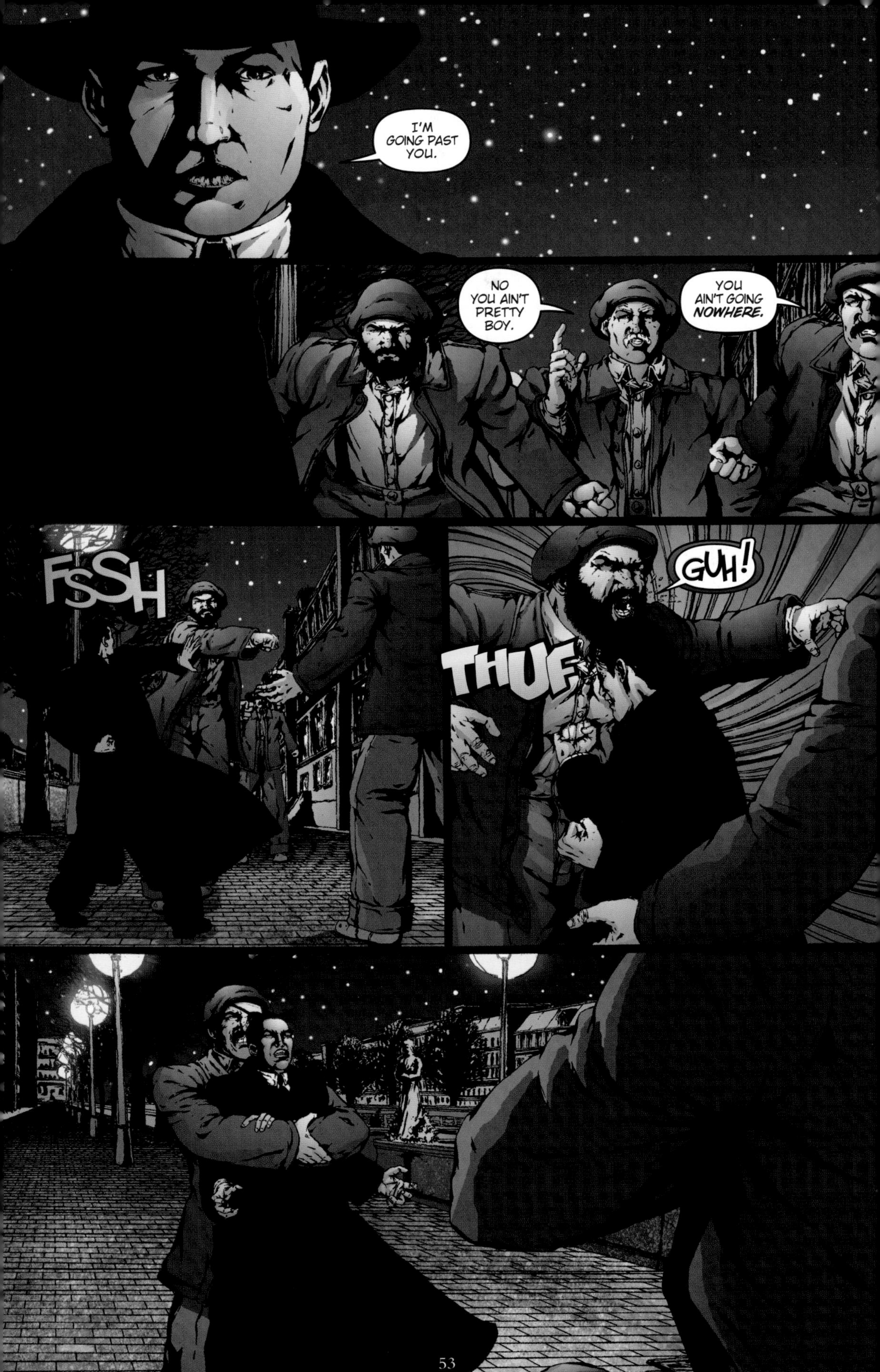
I'M GOING PAST YOU.
NO YOU AIN'T PRETTY BOY.
YOU AIN'T GOING **NOWHERE.**
FSSH
GUH!
THUF

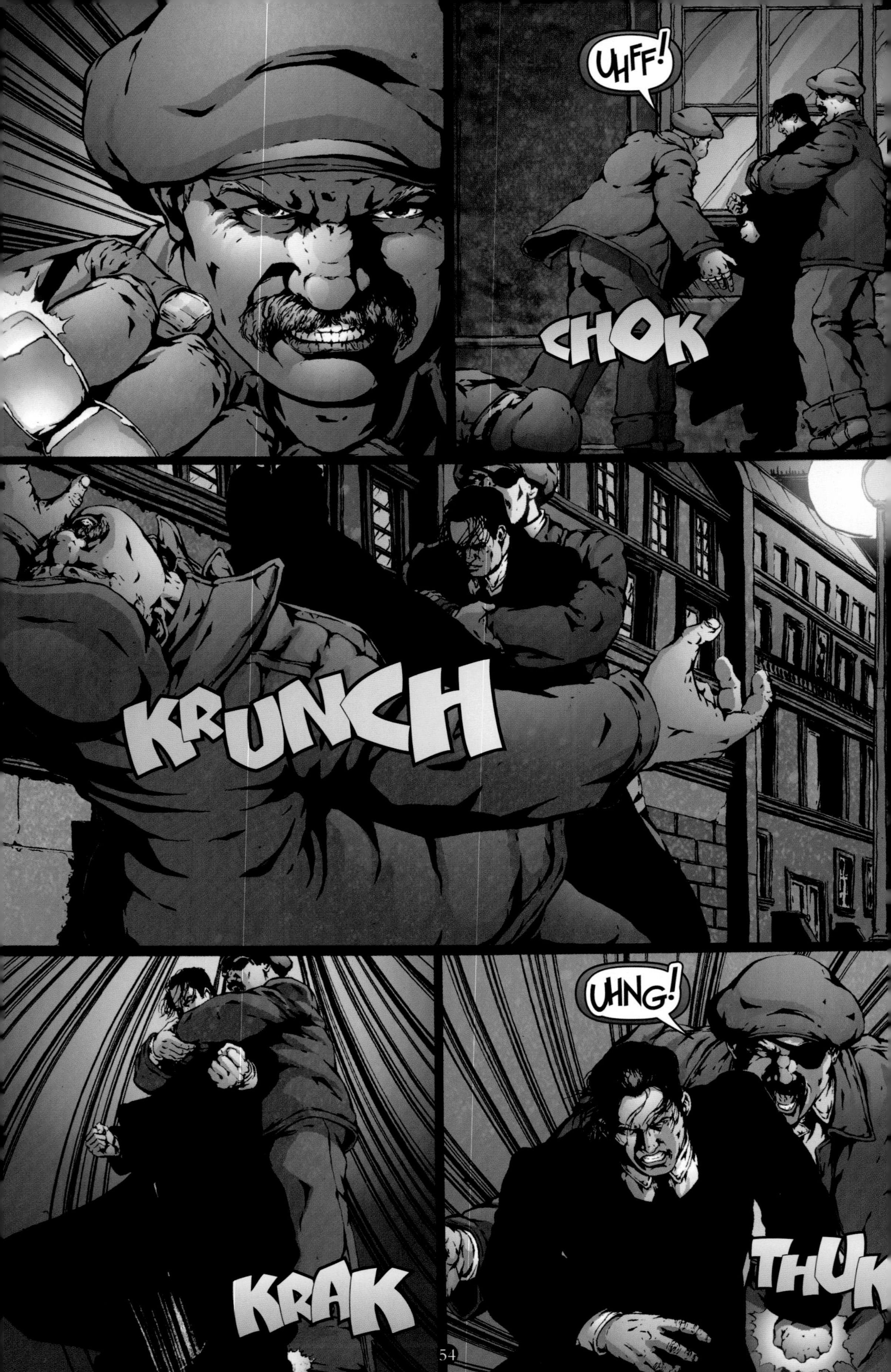
UHFF!
CHOK
KRUNCH
KRAK
UHNG!
THUK

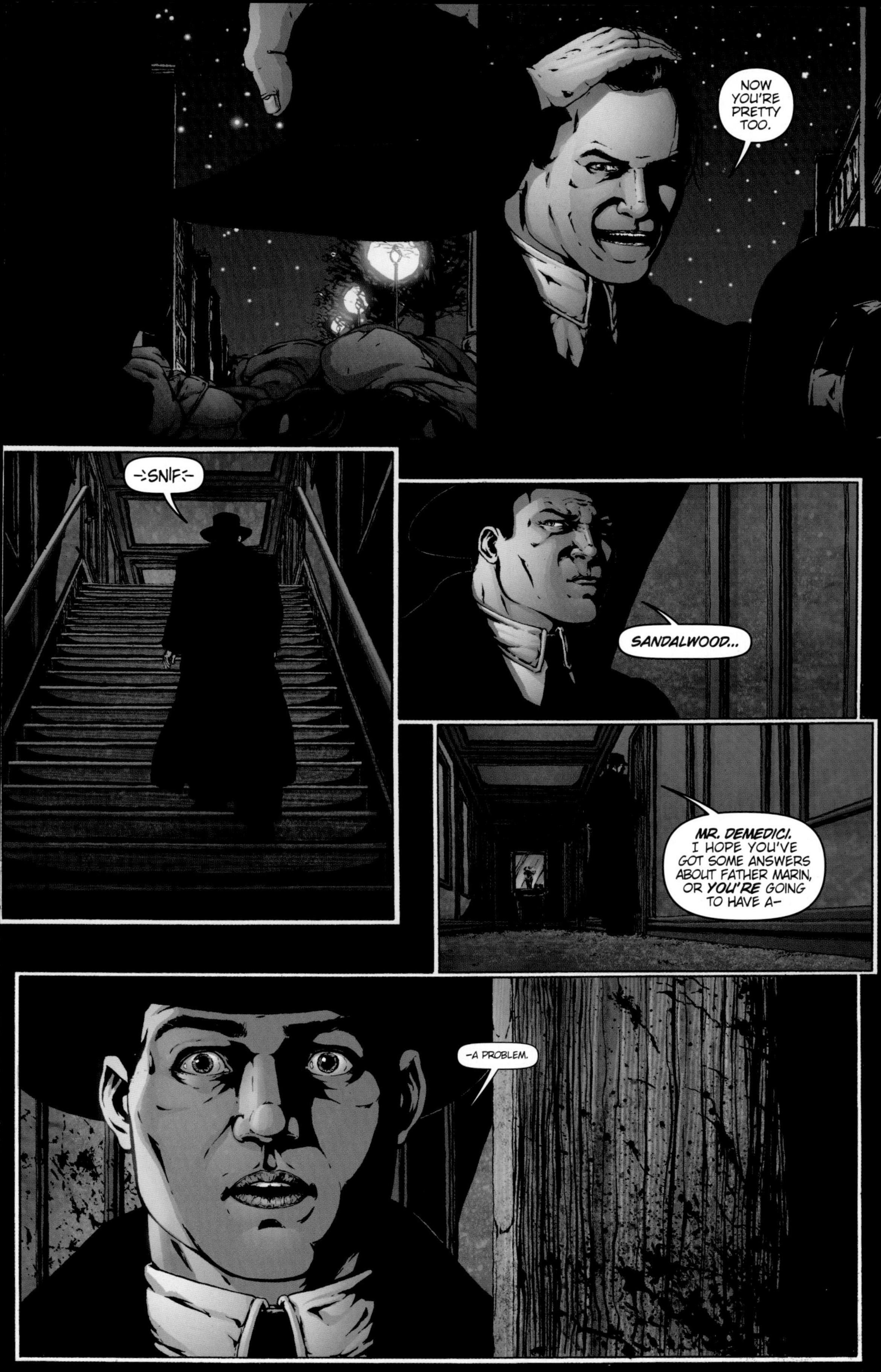
NOW YOU'RE PRETTY TOO.
-SNIF-
SANDALWOOD...
MR. DEMEDICI. I HOPE YOU'VE GOT SOME ANSWERS ABOUT FATHER MARIN, OR YOU'RE GOING TO HAVE A-
-A PROBLEM.

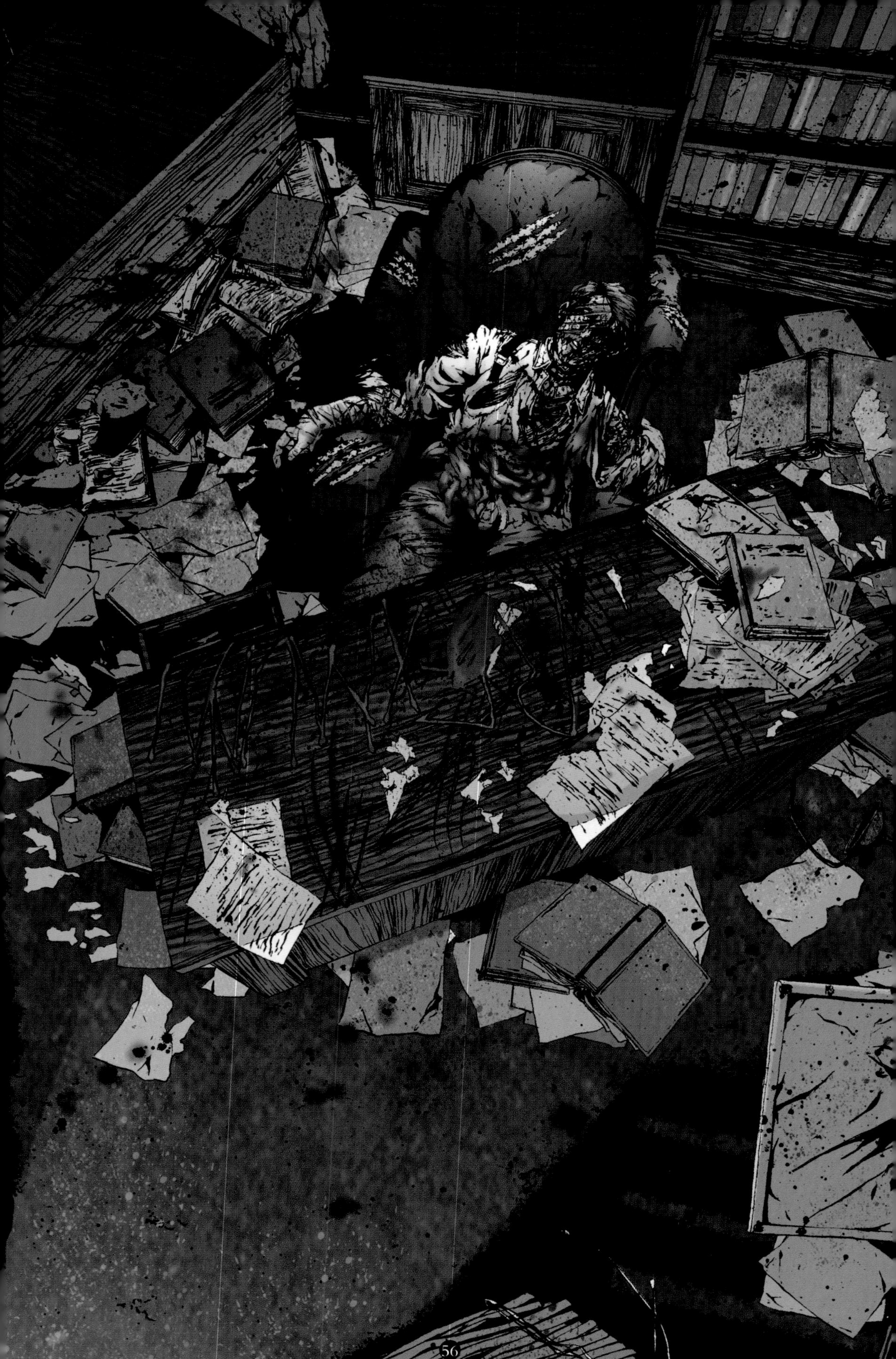

Le Journal de la Liberté

Paris' leading anglophone newspaper • vol. 205, no. 102 • Oct. 25, MCMXXXIII

Papal Seal

Editors in Chief: M. Tait Bergstrom, M. Matthew Pasteris. **Story Editor:** M. Arvid Nelson. **Art Editors:** M. EricJ, M. Jeromy Cox. **Photography Editor:** M. Alexander Waldman. **Layout Supervisor:** M. William Kartalopoulos. **Editors Emeritus:** M. Clark A. Smith, M. Howard P. Lovecraft, M. Robert E. Howard. Redacted by the Holy Parisian Inquisition under the direction of His Excellency Archbishop Emile-Jean Ireneaux. Le Journal de Liberté is printed under the benign auspices of his most puissant majesty KING LOUIS XXII of FRANCE. GOD SAVE THE KING.

of Approval

HOLY FATHER CALLS ECUMENICAL COUNCIL

first in nearly 400 years; topics to be discussed include Holy Church's relation to the state

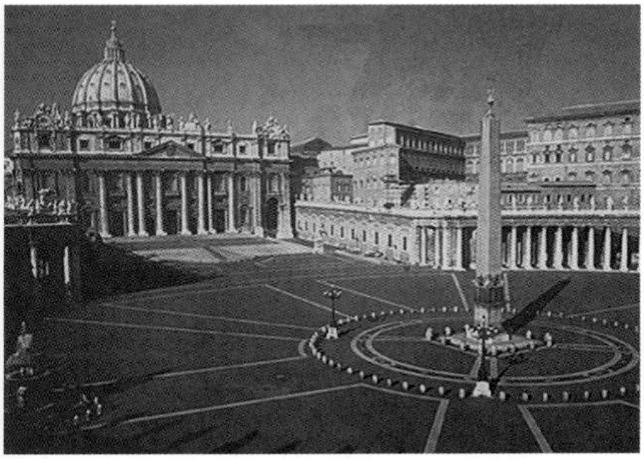

St. Peter's Basilica, where Pope John XIV has convened the first Ecumenical Council since Trent concluded in 1563.

Vatican Hill, Rome – Citing "rising spiritual and religious tension among the nations of Christ," Pope John XIV has declared the convention of an Ecumenical Council to settle theological disputes and formalize Church rulings on matters of faith.

It is the first since the Council of Trent, which began in 1545 and took place in discontinuous sessions until 1563. Trent formalized the anathematization of Martin Luther and officially declared the so-called "Protestant" movement a heresy subject to the persecution of the Holy Inquisition.

"The Holy Father believes the nations of Europe are once again in a very precarious spiritual position," Papal Nuncio Honore Guéant said.

The Council will convene at the Vatican over a period spanning anywhere from a month to a few years.

"It all depends on how much debate there is," Guéant said.

It is expected to cover topics ranging from the surge of nationalism amongst the peoples of Europe to the nature of salvation.

"Nationalism poses a great danger to the human soul because it places the State before God," Guéant said. "It is a form of idolatry, make no mistake."

"There is also a strong sentiment amongst the ecclesiastical community that despite Trent, the doctrine of salvation has not been explained with enough force," Guéant said. "A soul can only attain the Kingdom of Heaven through the Church."

Although this has been a part of Christian teaching for a very long time, Guéant said lingering Lutheran sentiments were still leading people astray.

"We need to show people that the power of the Church is absolute. Faith in Christ is faith in the Church, and vice-versa. this is what Christ meant when he said 'I am the Alpha and the Omega'."

Equally important, he said, was the sanctity of the institution of kingship.

"Christian Kings receive a mandate to rule from God and swear loyalty to the Church. This is a vital component of the Christian social order, and there is much evidence for it in scripture," Guéant said.

According to Guéant, it is even possible that this sentiment may become canonized.

"This is one of the areas about which there is debate, so it is difficult to say. The most important thing, to my mind, is the recognition of the fact that Kings receive their mandate to rule from God through the Church and the Church alone."

Guéant said the Holy Father was not convening the council out of fear the world was abandoning God.

"The Pope is the vicar of Christ," he said. "As long as people need Christ, they will need the Church."

BRITISH TROOPS OPEN FIRE ON ANGRY CROWD IN SHANGHAI

Shanghai, Cathay – British Royal Marines opened fire on a crowd in Shanghai yesterday when, according to colonial officials, a demonstration against English rule turned "ugly."

A Chinese casualty report was not available, per British policy. No British troops were harmed.

"It was a demonstration of dockworkers. They're always a rowdy crowd," said Viceroy Jonathan Mowbry, in charge of British concession in Shanghai. "This time it simply boiled over. The louts made a break for the British consulate, and our troops had no choice."

The demonstration began over what Shanghai natives consider the British viceroyalty's inability–or unwillingness–to put an end to opium smuggling.

"Opium is destroying our country. The British turn a blind eye to the rampant smuggling," a chinaman who spoke on the condition of anonymity said.

"Rubbish," Mowbry said. "If the Chinese would open up their ports we wouldn't have this smuggling problem, which far exceeds anyone's ability to control."

Asked whether he feared a revisitation of the Opium Riots of 1928, Mowbry was dismissive.

"We showed the superiority of British military technology during the riots. I daresay the rabble-rousers aren't anxious to go at it

continued on page A9

Prussians Re-Affirm Support for Habsburg Presence in Serbia; Tzar Expresses "Displeasure"

Belgrade, Serbia – Prussian Chancellor Karl von Haugwitz issued a statement yesterday reaffirming Prussian support for Emperor Rudolph's continued presence in the troubled Balkan province in a move that will strengthen Austrian claims to the land – and further strain Russo-Prussian relations.

"The German people recognize the right of Emperor Rudolph to bring peace and prosperity to the troubled Serbian nation," von Haugwitz wrote in the statement, "and we recognize the legitimacy of their continued presence in that country."

Russian officials expressed the Tzar's misgivings about the Prussian statement.

"Russia has long-standing economic and cultural ties to Serbia. We dispute the claim that the Austrians have a 'sole right' to occupy Serbia, especially against the will of the Serbian people," Yevgeny Morischenko, Russian ambassador to France, said.

However, in the same statement, von Haugwitz declared Prussian support for the freedom of the northern Italian republics from Austrian influence.

"It is the Kaiser's belief that the Italian people are in a position to determine their own political destiny," von Haugwitz wrote.

"In political terms, the Prussians are trying to have it both ways," French Foreign Ministry official Artaud Farrand said. "They see a threat in the Russians, so they want to court the Habsburgs. But they also see a threat in France and England, so they want to court the Italians. They are walking a precarious line, because they are caught between two powers. It is the classic problem of

continued on page A2

INSIDE

Plus sanctimonious editorials by eds. A. Nelson and EricJ

LE JOURNAL SPECIAL: A NATION DIVIDED

FORMER UNITED STATES OF AMERICA

"NEBRASKA CORRIDOR"

CITY-STATE of NEW YORK

- FEDERAL REPUBLIC OF AMERICA
- CONFEDERATE STATES OF AMERICA
- DISPUTED TERRITORIES

The lands of the former continental United States of America. The failed United States Constitution is regarded as "incontrovertible proof of the impossibility of popular government." The Federal Republic of America (FRA) and the Confederate states of America (CSA) are drained by chronic border skirmishes and a vast, lawless western frontier.

"No one dared as highly or failed as catastrophically, as the founding fathers of the United States of America." So says Winston Churchill, first lord of the British admiralty. His sentiment perfectly sums up the prevailing wisdom regarding the ill-fated "American experiment."

The United States of America was coming into eminence as a regional power when it was torn asunder by a brutal four-year civil war from 1861-1864. It never recovered.

"There is a tragic quality to the American experiment," Sir Emile Desrossiers of the Royal Academy of Historians, said. "Tragic because it began with such noble goals and such high aspirations. But there was always a tension in the country between North and South. It proved too much for a government based on popular elections to bear."

In this Le Journal special, we examine the history of American Civil War.

A Brief History of the War

The political conflict that ripped the United States apart began with a difference of opinion about the right of states versus the power of the federal government. Southern people generally believed state government authority superceded that of the national or "federal" government, while northern people generally believed the opposite.

This debate became explosive because it factored into the question of the legitimacy of slavery. War inevitably erupted.

The English crown was instrumental in the success of the Confederacy over the Union. Still smarting over the loss of its American colonies, England supplied the Confederacy with the supplies it needed to protract the war into a brutal stalemate.

"England had to swallow a lot of bile to aid the Confederacy," Desrossiers said. "At the time, revenge was more important than moral qualms about slavery."

Union resolve wavered in the face of the horrors of Southern general Nathan Bedford-Forrest's campaign of wholesale destruction in Pennsylvania, the so-called "scorched earth policy," and the failure of Northern general Ulysses Grant to take the key Southern town of Vicksburg. Abraham Lincoln lost the presidential election of 1864. On taking office, President George McClellan sued for peace, and the Confederate States of America was born.

To this day an uneasy equilibrium exists between North and the South. Petty, economically draining border wars occur almost every year. Economists generally agree the CSA's dependence on slave labor, facilitated by Dutch and Italian merchant princes, means the Southern economy will always be stunted, while chronic political instability weakens the North.

Neither the CSA or the FRA have the wherewithal to take place in international or even regional politics; they are barely able to muster the resources to squabble with each other.

The West—Still Wild

The collapse of the Union created a very large problem, in the form of the western territories of the former United States. Confederacy policy dictated new territories could decide their own fate, but the federal North saw itself as the sole inheritor of the lands. The debate flared into violence on more than one occasion. Most of the former territories are now a part of the FRA, but the South was able to consolidate its hold on the lands north and west of Texas (see map above).

A large swath of the western lands remain disputed. Called the "Nebraska Corridor," it is a wide-open, lawless domain. The law of the gun prevails, and powerful cattle ranchers have all the sway of feudal lords. The cattle barons serve a dual purpose, according to Desrossiers.

"They provide beef for the cities of the North and the South, and they are a sort of proxy law-enforcement agency given the vacuum of government control."

"It's not a place for the faint of heart," says James McCreedy, a Wyoming rancher. "It is a constant battle against bandits and cattle thieves. "But there are G-d-fearing men out here too."

Desrossiers believes it is not that simple.

"The distinction between a cattle baron and a well-organized gang of bandits is exceedingly hazy," he said. "In the final summa-tion, no one suffers more than the native population, the Indians."

The City-State of New York

One must specify "state" or "country" when one refers to New York. The war against the South was never popular in the Union's greatest city; draft riots broke out more than once, and the city had close economic ties to the slaveholding South.

When a city legislature declared secession from the Union in 1864, a combination of corruption at the highest levels of the McClellan administration and war-weariness led to the FRA's unexpected recognition of the independence of the City-State of New York.

The arrangement is profitable for both the North and the South; New York City acts as a kind of economic broker between the two nations.

"Not since the demise of ancient Athens has there been a system of government like that of New York City," New York mayor Fiorello LaGuardia said. "I think democracy can only really succeed on a municipal level. I believe New York City boasts the purest form of democracy the world has ever seen."

The Persistence of Slavery

To many, the most troubling aspect of the CSA is the persistence of slavery within its borders.

Southerners defend the institution vigorously.

"This is our way of life. No one has a right to come in and tell someone to change his way of life just because he doesn't like it," Arthur McClune, a Georgia peanut farmer, said. "My forefathers fought and died for this principle."

"Slavery is, as Dr. Livingston said, the sore of the world," Desrossiers said. "There's no getting around the revulsion most people feel for the institution. It has made the CSA an international pariah."

The CSA has certainly not made any concessions to the international community, but their status might be changing fast. In the past few years, oil has been discovered in the fields of Texas and Oklahoma.

"Oil is the future. It will become the life-blood of nations within our lifetime." David-Louis Plantard, the Duke of Lorraine, said. "It's hard to argue with that sort of power."

⚜

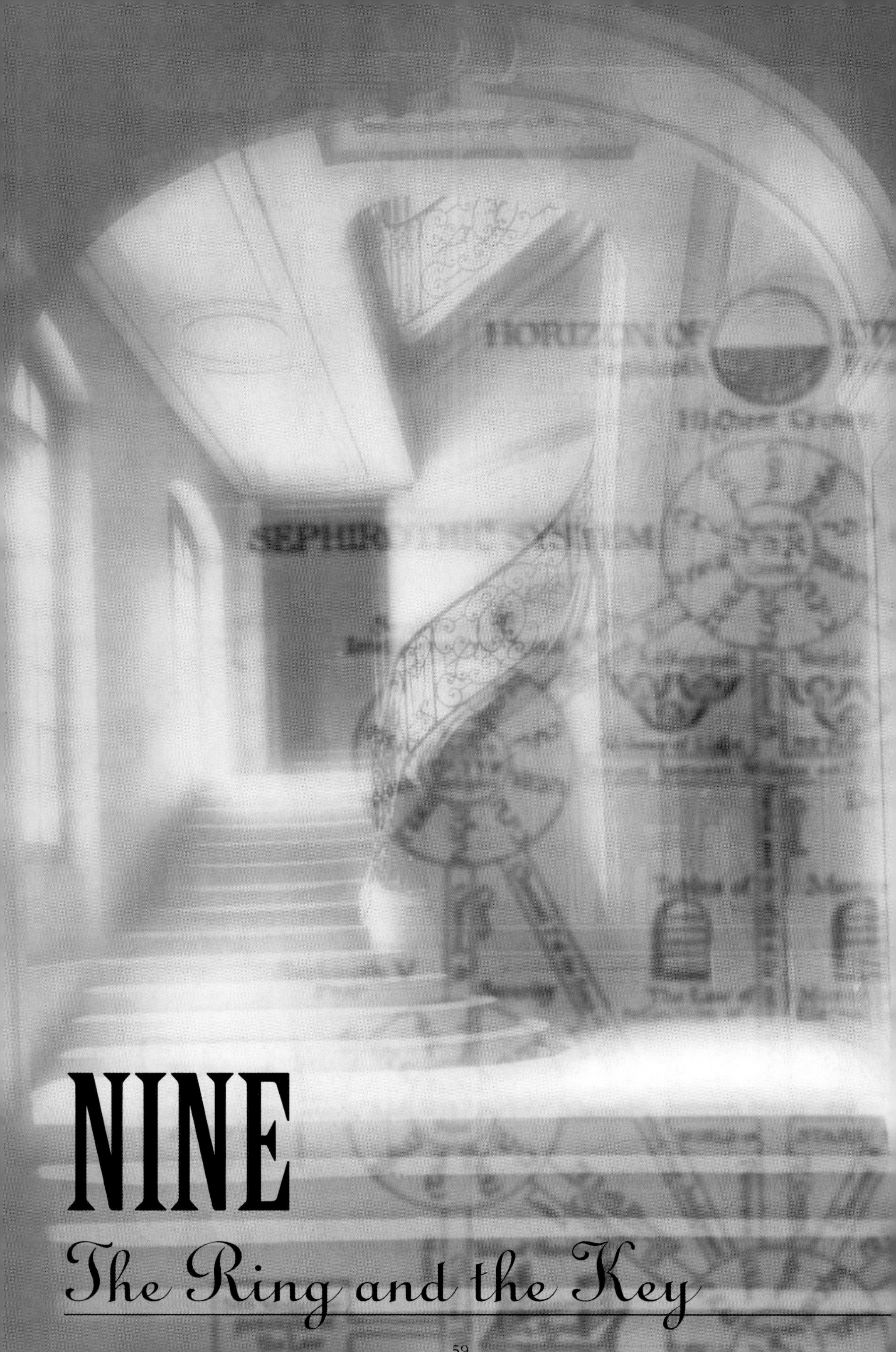

NINE
The Ring and the Key

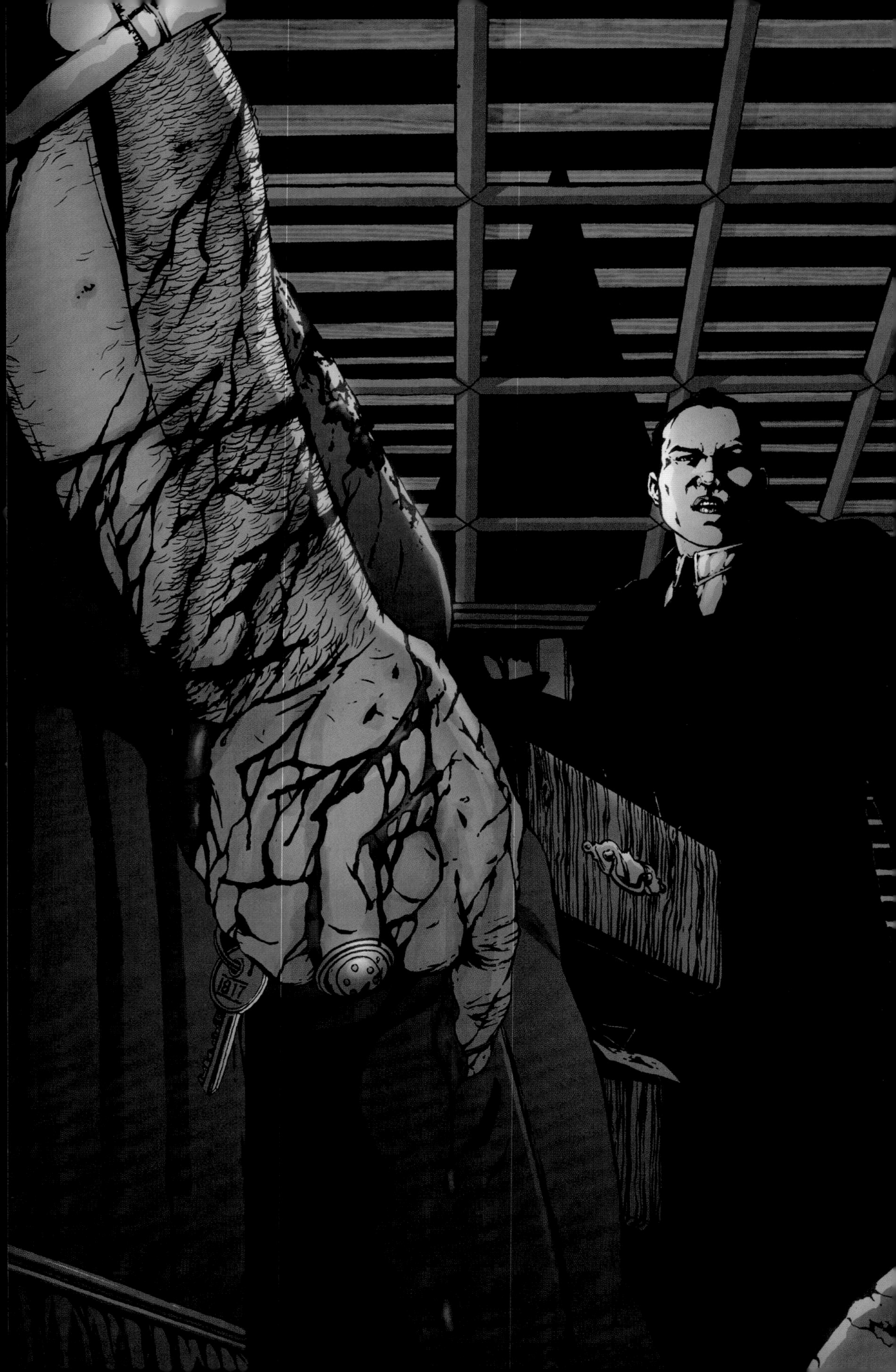
1817

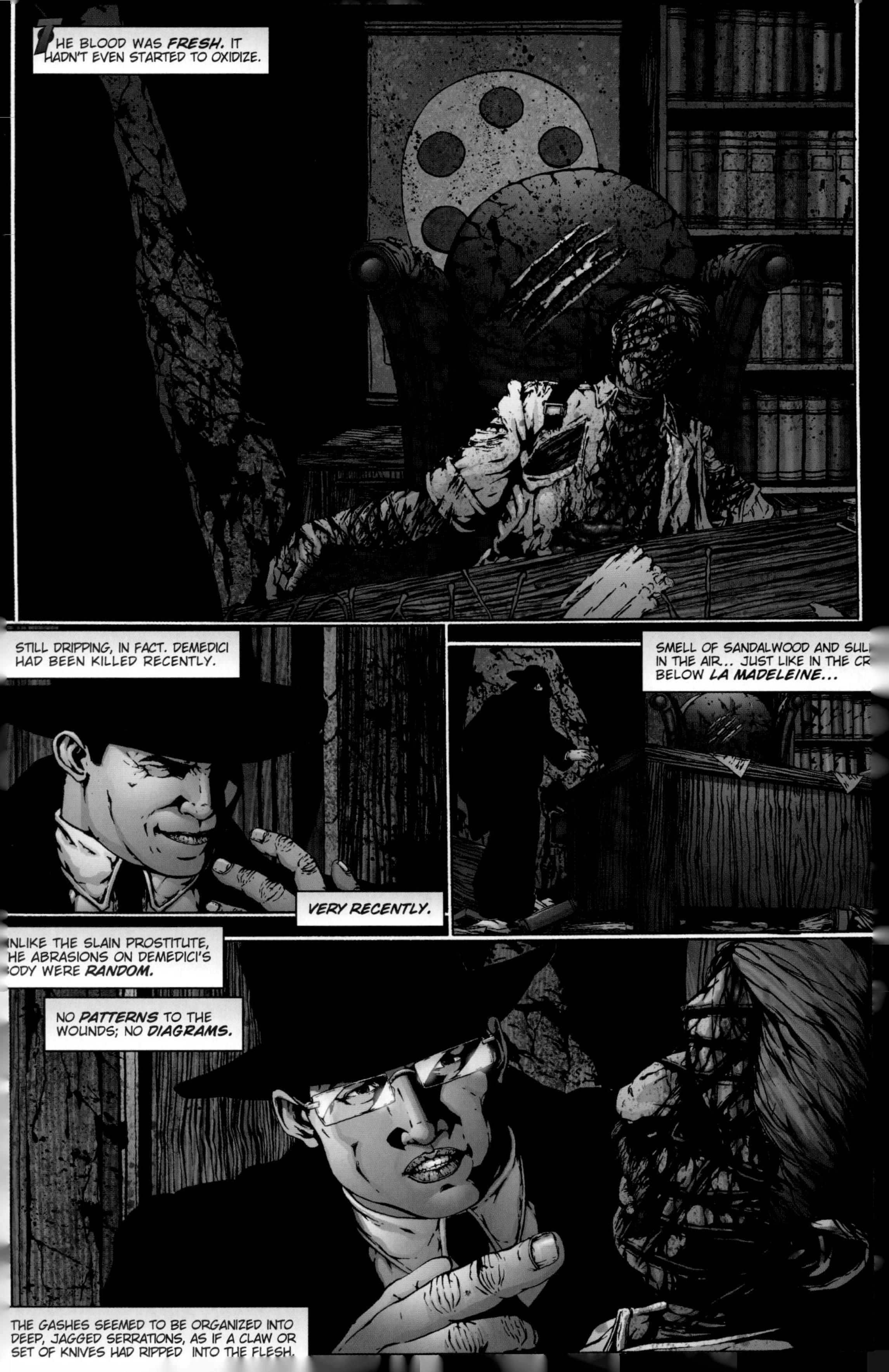
THE BLOOD WAS FRESH. IT HADN'T EVEN STARTED TO OXIDIZE.
STILL DRIPPING, IN FACT. DEMEDICI HAD BEEN KILLED RECENTLY.
VERY RECENTLY.
SMELL OF SANDALWOOD AND SUL IN THE AIR... JUST LIKE IN THE CR BELOW LA MADELEINE...
NLIKE THE SLAIN PROSTITUTE, HE ABRASIONS ON DEMEDICI'S ODY WERE RANDOM.
NO PATTERNS TO THE WOUNDS; NO DIAGRAMS.
THE GASHES SEEMED TO BE ORGANIZED INTO DEEP, JAGGED SERRATIONS, AS IF A CLAW OR SET OF KNIVES HAD RIPPED INTO THE FLESH.

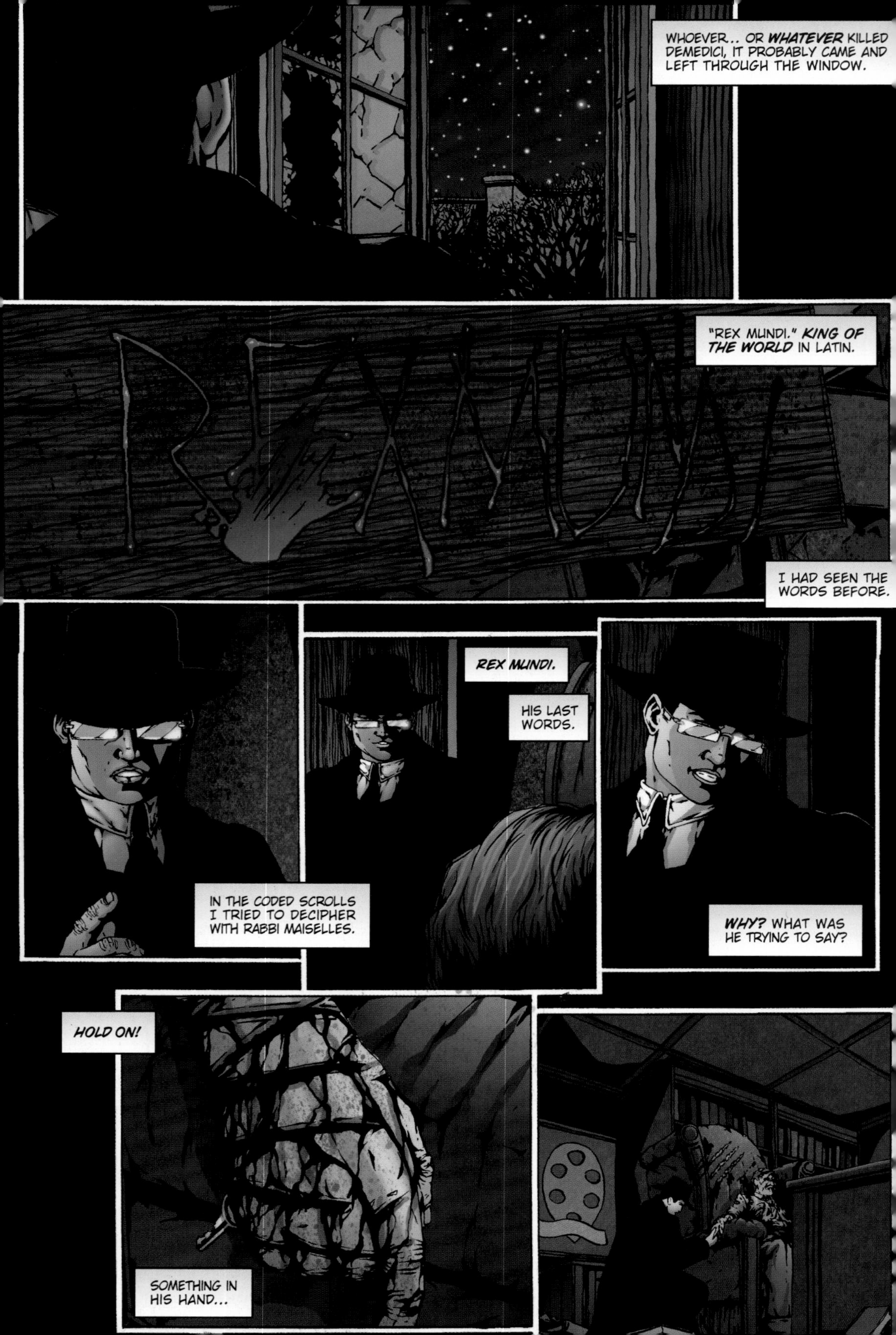
WHOEVER... OR WHATEVER KILLED DEMEDICI, IT PROBABLY CAME AND LEFT THROUGH THE WINDOW.
"REX MUNDI." KING OF THE WORLD IN LATIN.
I HAD SEEN THE WORDS BEFORE.
IN THE CODED SCROLLS I TRIED TO DECIPHER WITH RABBI MAISELLES.
REX MUNDI.
HIS LAST WORDS.
WHY? WHAT WAS HE TRYING TO SAY?
HOLD ON!
SOMETHING IN HIS HAND...

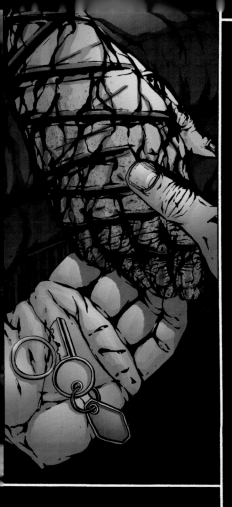

IT LOOKED LIKE A KEY TO A SAFE DEPOSIT BOX.

WHERE?

AND THE RING.

JUST A PLAIN BAND OF GOLD.

WHY DID HE PUT IT IN HIS PALM WITH THE KEY BEFORE HE DIED? WHAT WAS HE TRYING TO COMMUNICATE?

HUGE STACKS OF BILLS.

THOUSANDS OF FRANCS.

UNTOUCHED.

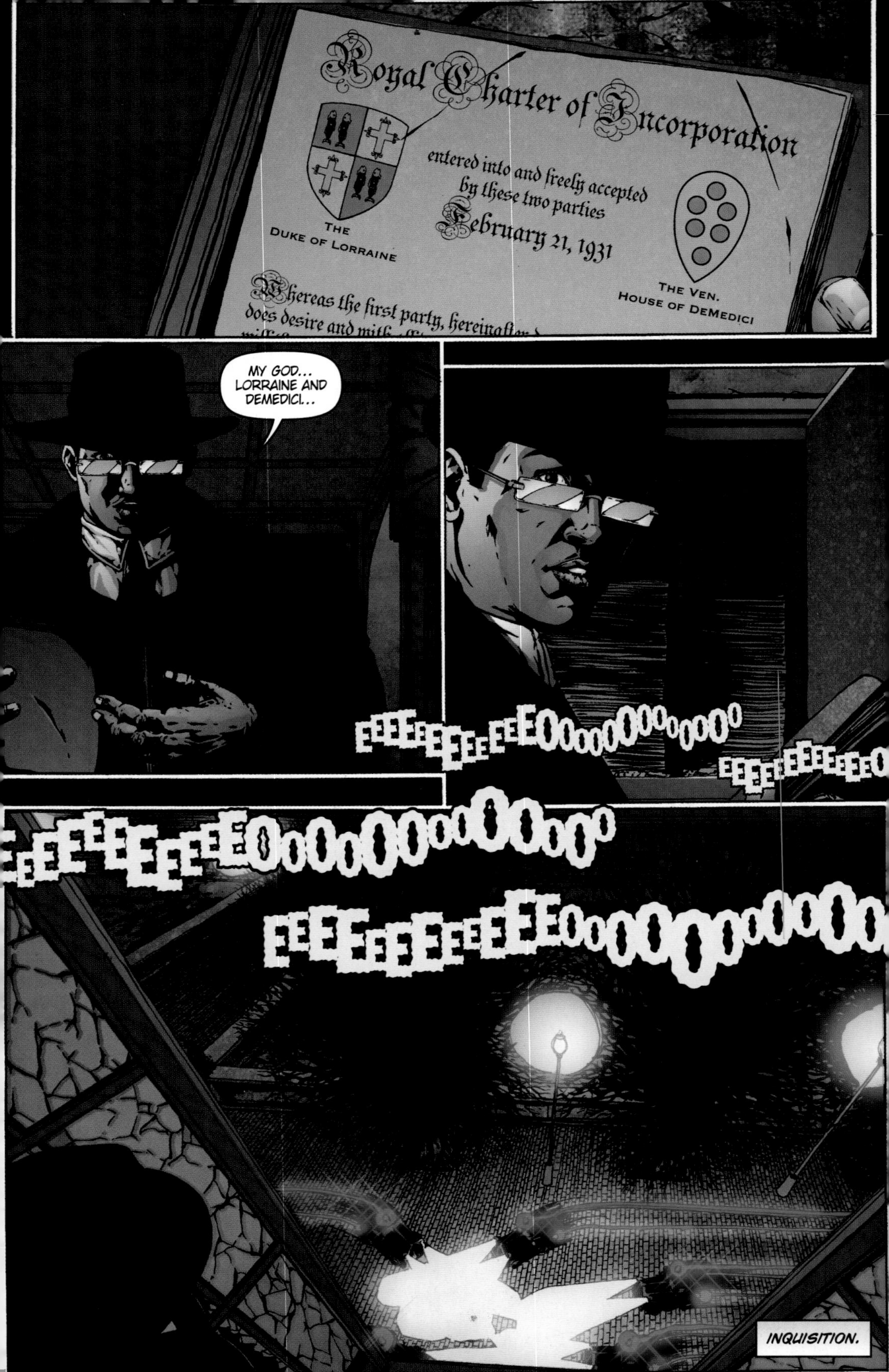
Royal Charter of Incorporation
entered into and freely accepted by these two parties
February 21, 1931
The Duke of Lorraine
The Ven. House of DeMedici
Whereas the first party,
does desire and
MY GOD... LORRAINE AND DEMEDICI...
EEEEEEEEEEEEOOOOOOOOOOO
EEEEEEEEEEO
EEEEEEEEEEEOOOOOOOOOOOOO
EEEEEEEEEEEEEOOOOOOOOOOOO
INQUISITION.

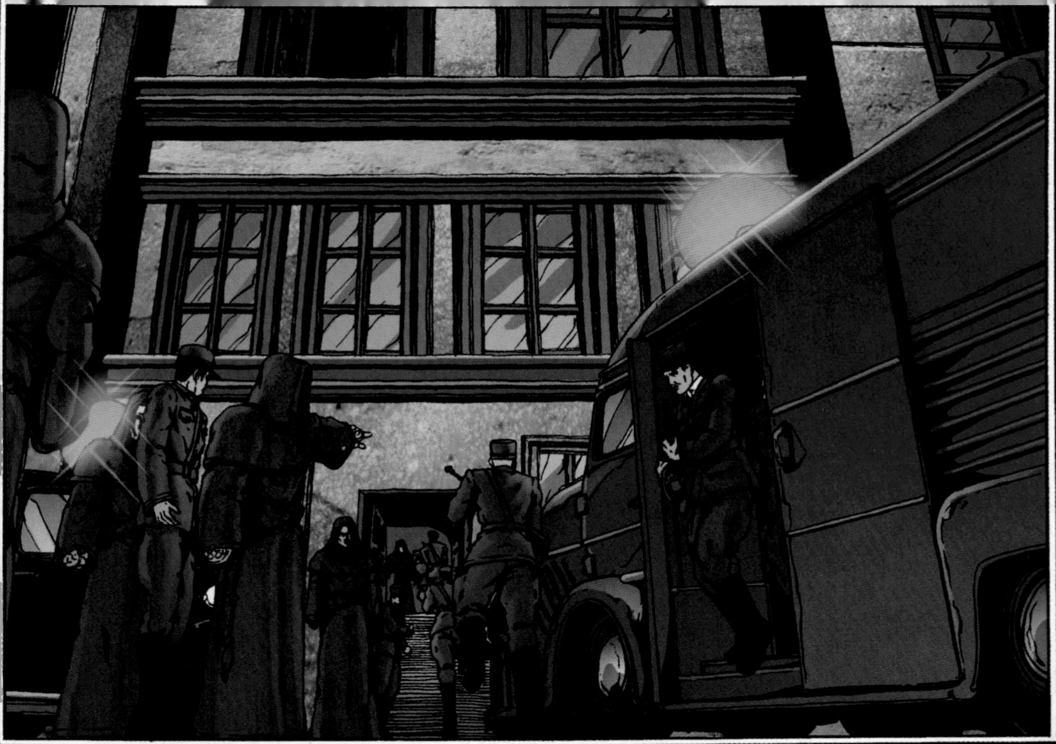

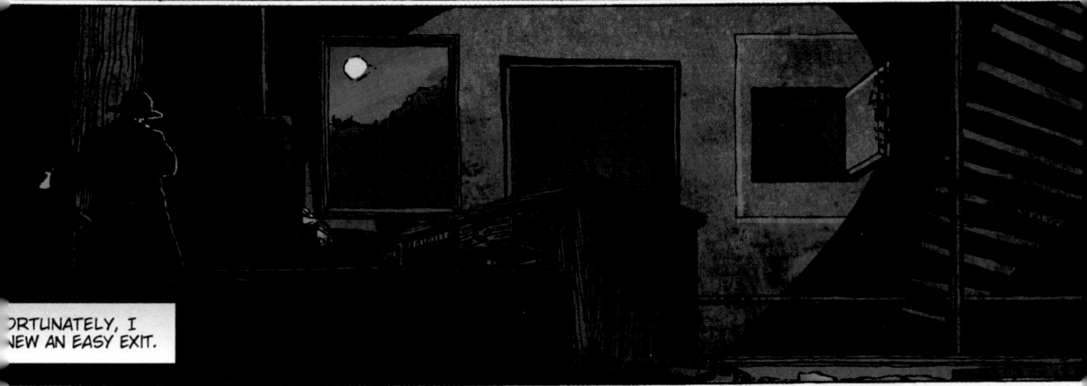
ORTUNATELY, I
NEW AN EASY EXIT.

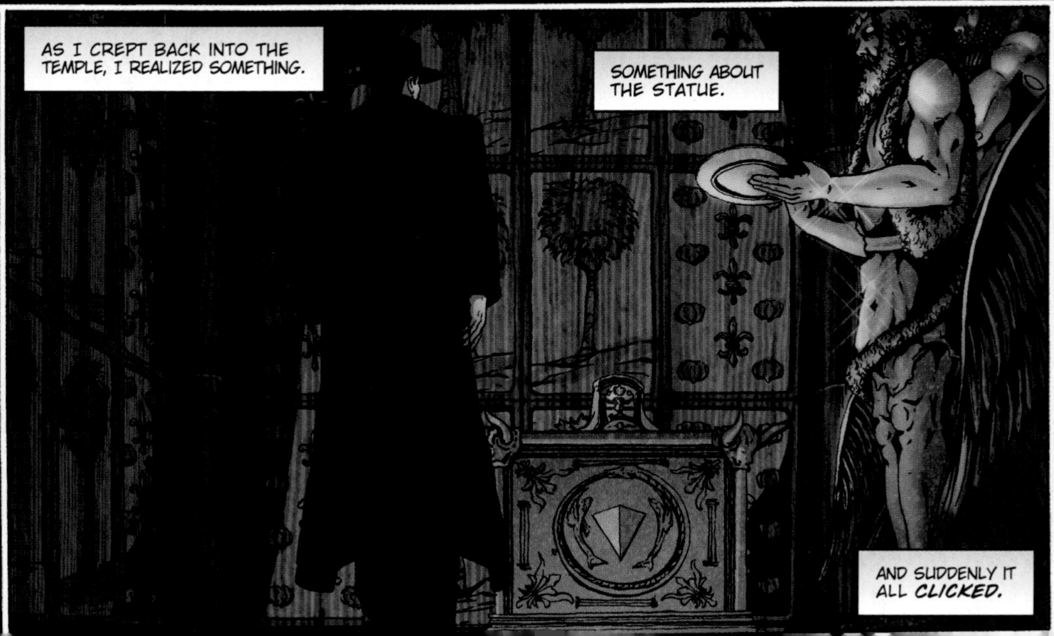
AS I CREPT BACK INTO THE TEMPLE, I REALIZED SOMETHING.
SOMETHING ABOUT THE STATUE.
AND SUDDENLY IT ALL *CLICKED.*

JOHN.

THE STATUE WAS OF *JOHN THE BAPTIST.**

*MORE INFORMATION ON JOHN THE BAPTIST AT WWW.REXMUNDI.NET

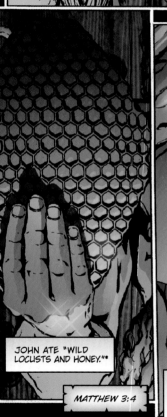

JOHN ATE "WILD LOCUSTS AND HONEY."*

MATTHEW 3:4

HE WAS MURDERED BY KING HEROD, *BEHEADED,* HIS HEAD DELIVERED TO HERODIAS' DAUGHTER ON A *CHARGER.*

BUT JOHN WAS A PERFECTLY LEGITIMATE SAINT...

...WHY BUILD A *SECRET TEMPLE* TO HIM?

BAPHOMET.

A CODE FOR *SOPHIA,* GREEK FOR *WISDOM.*

WAS *JOHN* THE IDENTITY OF *BAPHOMET?*

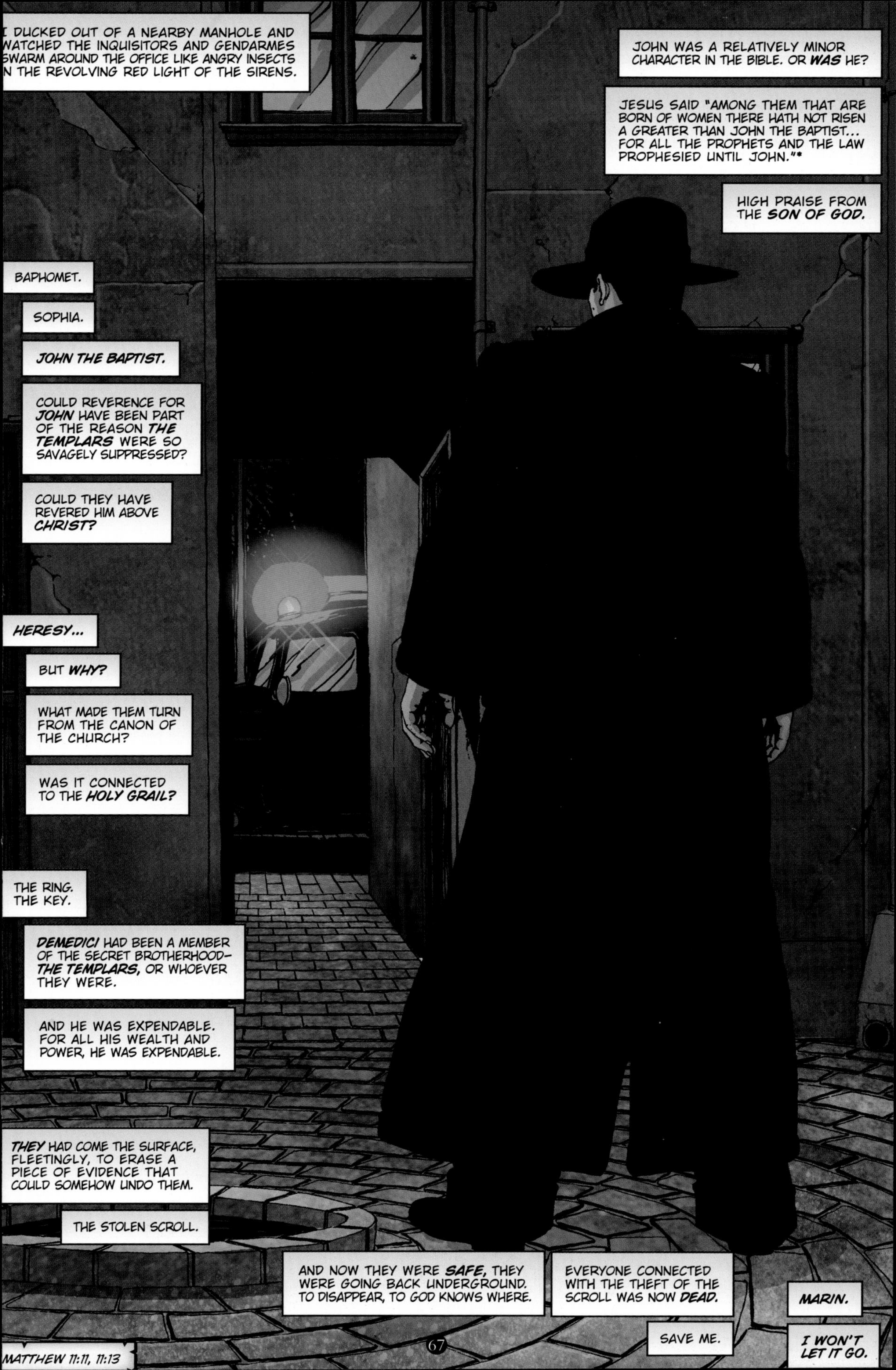
I DUCKED OUT OF A NEARBY MANHOLE AND WATCHED THE INQUISITORS AND GENDARMES SWARM AROUND THE OFFICE LIKE ANGRY INSECTS IN THE REVOLVING RED LIGHT OF THE SIRENS.
JOHN WAS A RELATIVELY MINOR CHARACTER IN THE BIBLE. OR ***WAS*** HE?
JESUS SAID "AMONG THEM THAT ARE BORN OF WOMEN THERE HATH NOT RISEN A GREATER THAN JOHN THE BAPTIST... FOR ALL THE PROPHETS AND THE LAW PROPHESIED UNTIL JOHN."*
HIGH PRAISE FROM THE ***SON OF GOD.***
BAPHOMET.
SOPHIA.
JOHN THE BAPTIST.
COULD REVERENCE FOR ***JOHN*** HAVE BEEN PART OF THE REASON ***THE TEMPLARS*** WERE SO SAVAGELY SUPPRESSED?
COULD THEY HAVE REVERED HIM ABOVE ***CHRIST?***
HERESY...
BUT ***WHY?***
WHAT MADE THEM TURN FROM THE CANON OF THE CHURCH?
WAS IT CONNECTED TO THE ***HOLY GRAIL?***
THE RING. THE KEY.
DEMEDICI HAD BEEN A MEMBER OF THE SECRET BROTHERHOOD- ***THE TEMPLARS,*** OR WHOEVER THEY WERE.
AND HE WAS EXPENDABLE. FOR ALL HIS WEALTH AND POWER, HE WAS EXPENDABLE.
THEY HAD COME THE SURFACE, FLEETINGLY, TO ERASE A PIECE OF EVIDENCE THAT COULD SOMEHOW UNDO THEM.
THE STOLEN SCROLL.
AND NOW THEY WERE ***SAFE,*** THEY WERE GOING BACK UNDERGROUND. TO DISAPPEAR, TO GOD KNOWS WHERE.
EVERYONE CONNECTED WITH THE THEFT OF THE SCROLL WAS NOW ***DEAD.***
MARIN.
SAVE ME.
I WON'T LET IT GO.
MATTHEW 11:11, 11:13

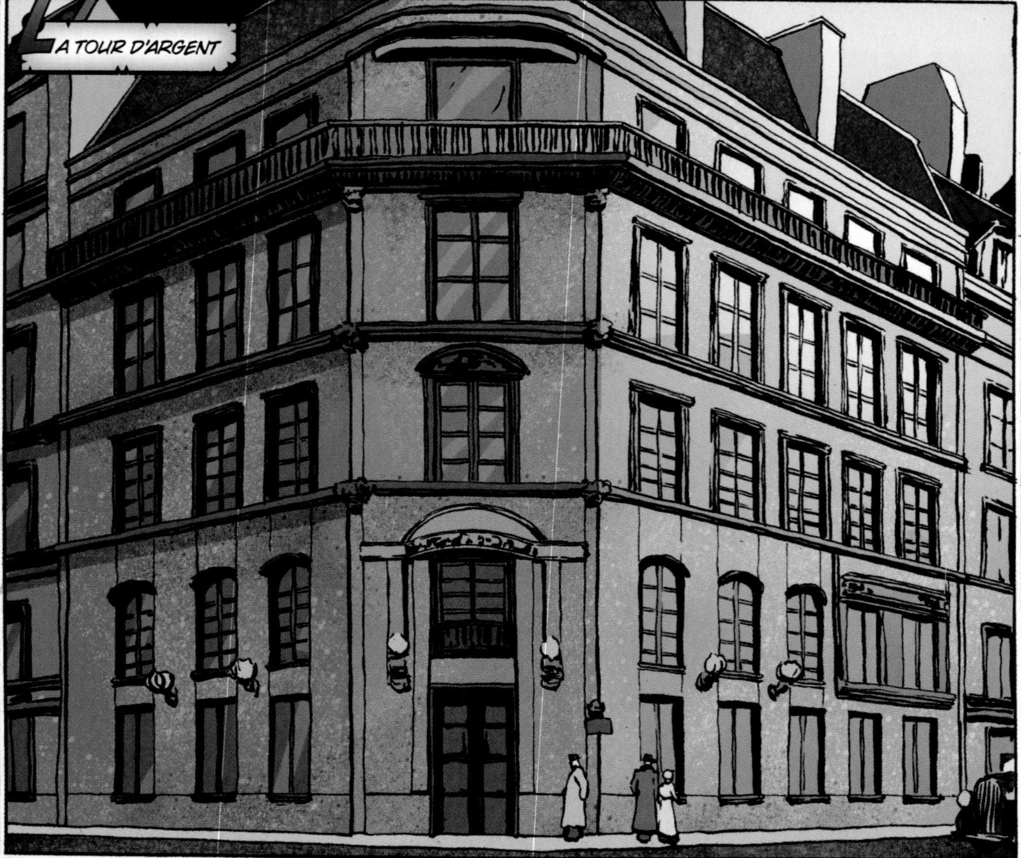
LA TOUR D'ARGENT
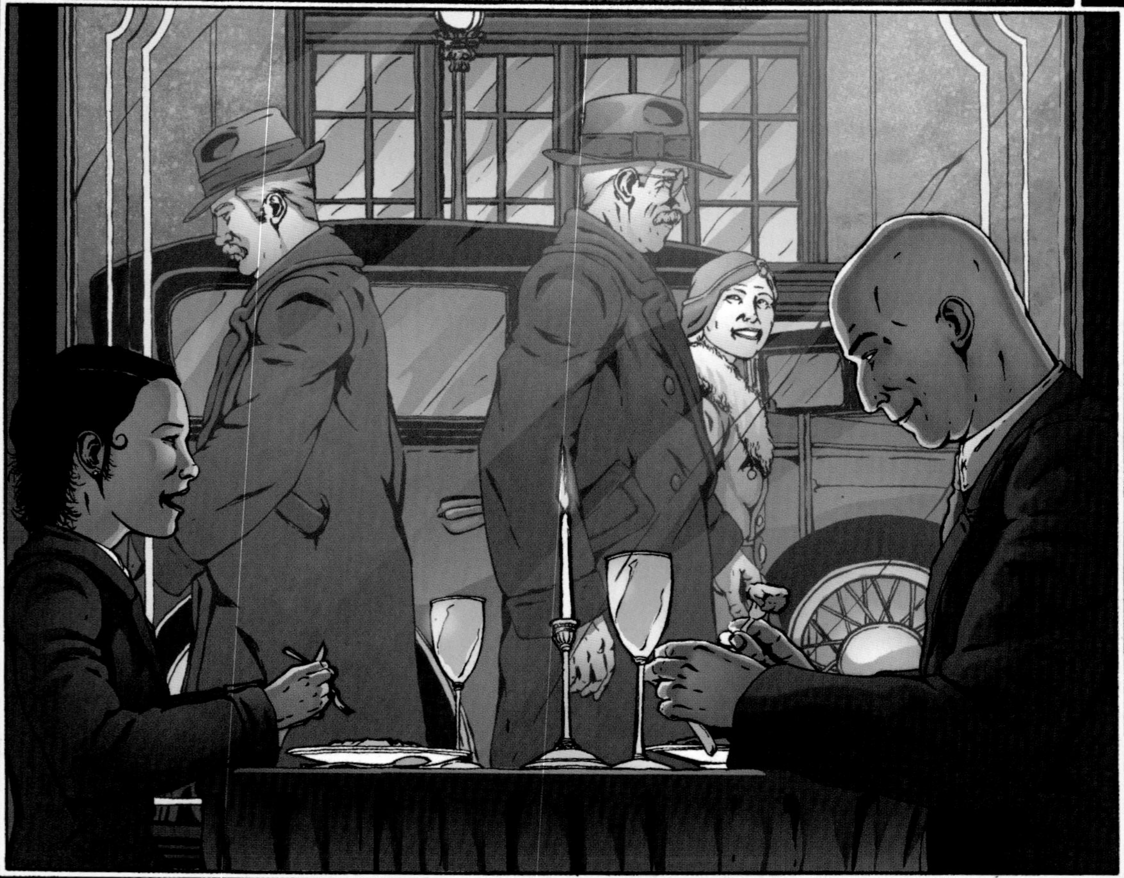

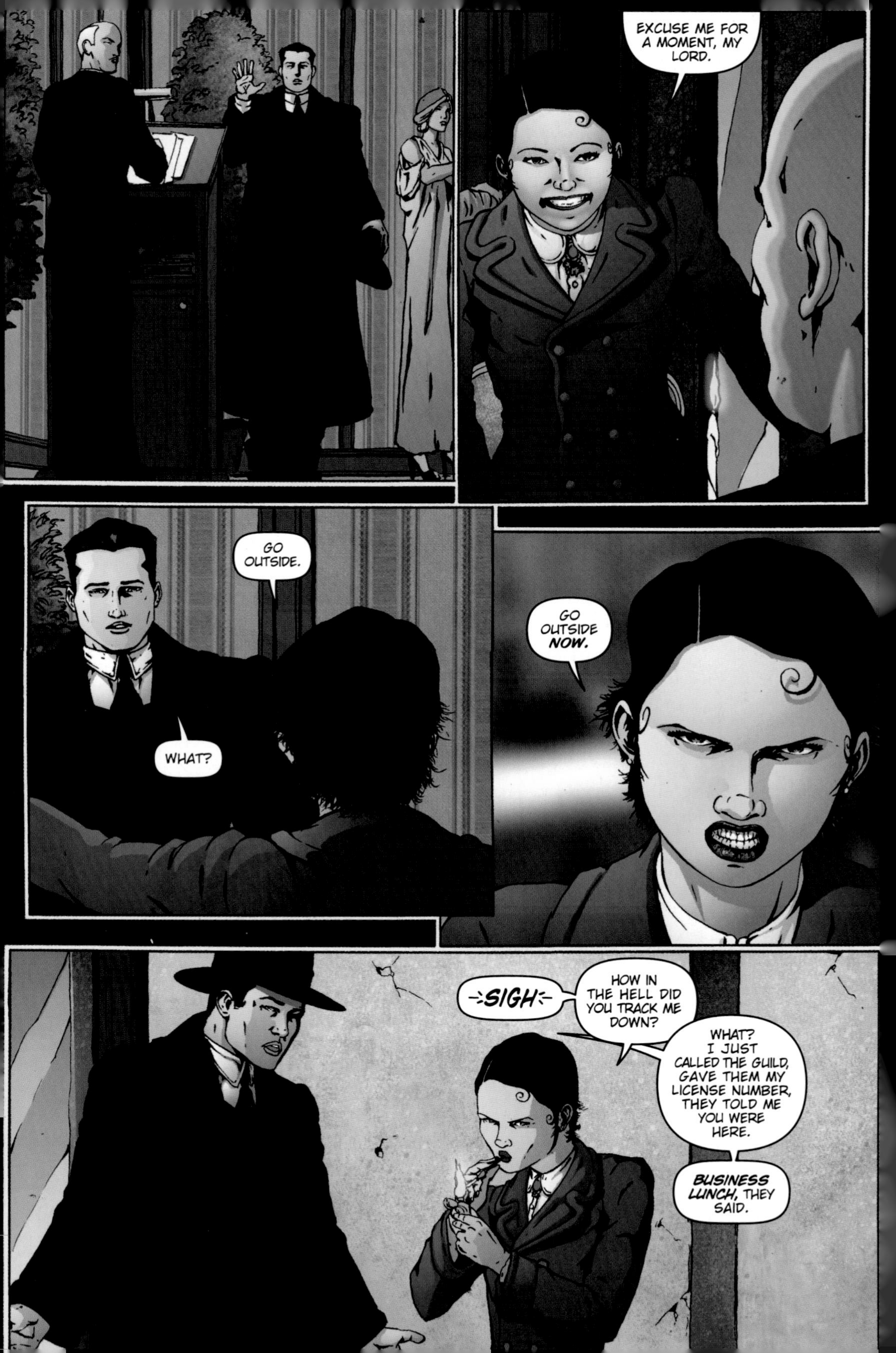
EXCUSE ME FOR A MOMENT, MY LORD.
GO OUTSIDE.
WHAT?
GO OUTSIDE NOW.
-SIGH-
HOW IN THE HELL DID YOU TRACK ME DOWN?
WHAT? I JUST CALLED THE GUILD, GAVE THEM MY LICENSE NUMBER, THEY TOLD ME YOU WERE HERE.
BUSINESS LUNCH, THEY SAID.

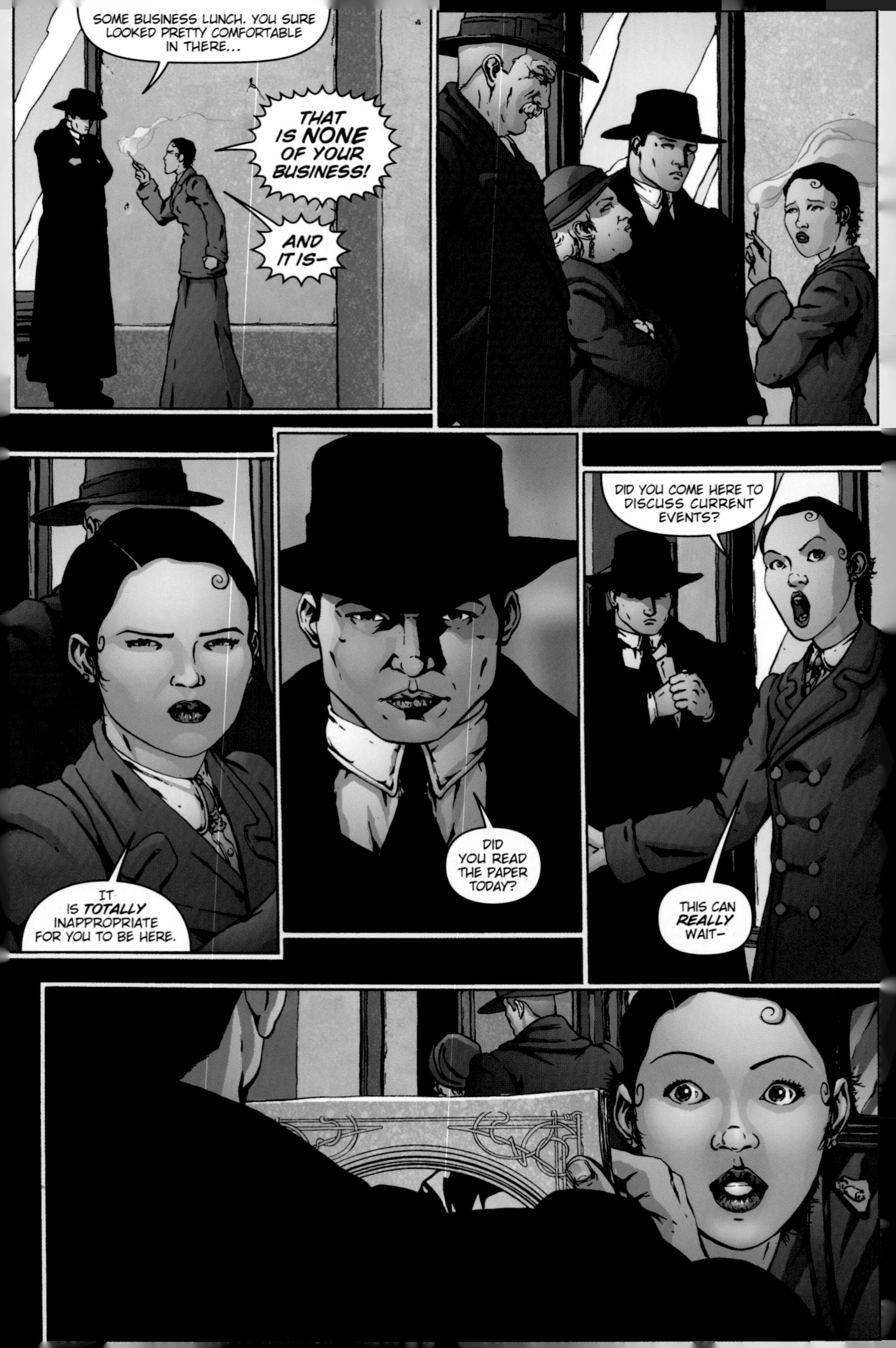
SOME BUSINESS LUNCH. YOU SURE LOOKED PRETTY COMFORTABLE IN THERE...
THAT IS NONE OF YOUR BUSINESS!
AND IT IS-
IT IS TOTALLY INAPPROPRIATE FOR YOU TO BE HERE.
DID YOU READ THE PAPER TODAY?
DID YOU COME HERE TO DISCUSS CURRENT EVENTS?
THIS CAN REALLY WAIT-

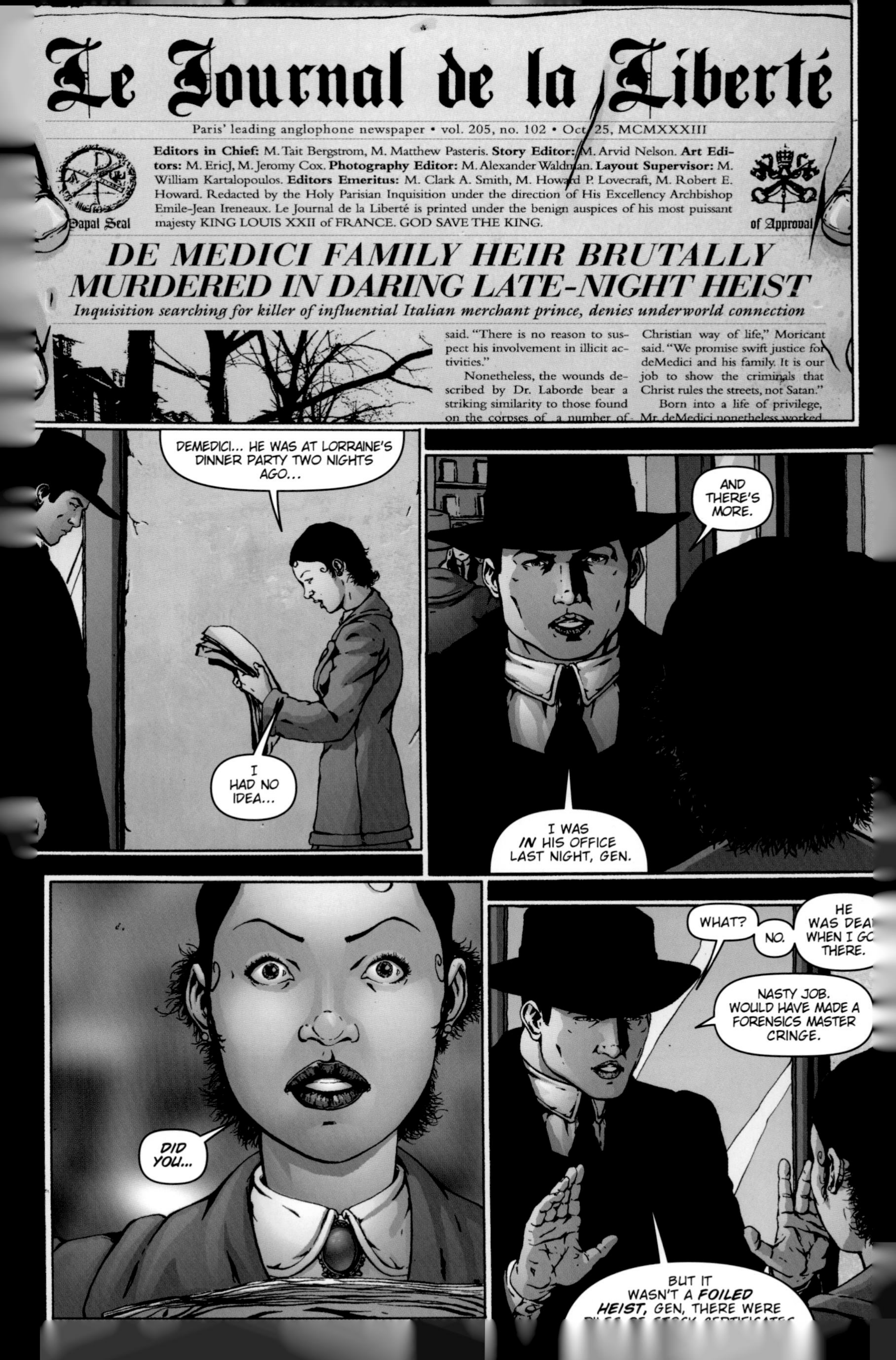
Le Journal de la Liberté
Paris' leading anglophone newspaper • vol. 205, no. 102 • Oct 25, MCMXXXIII
Papal Seal
of Approval
Editors in Chief: M. Tait Bergstrom, M. Matthew Pasteris. Story Editor: M. Arvid Nelson. Art Editors: M. EricJ, M. Jeromy Cox. Photography Editor: M. Alexander Waldman. Layout Supervisor: M. William Kartalopoulos. Editors Emeritus: M. Clark A. Smith, M. Howard P. Lovecraft, M. Robert E. Howard. Redacted by the Holy Parisian Inquisition under the direction of His Excellency Archbishop Emile-Jean Ireneaux. Le Journal de la Liberté is printed under the benign auspices of his most puissant majesty KING LOUIS XXII of FRANCE. GOD SAVE THE KING.
DE MEDICI FAMILY HEIR BRUTALLY MURDERED IN DARING LATE-NIGHT HEIST
Inquisition searching for killer of influential Italian merchant prince, denies underworld connection
said. "There is no reason to suspect his involvement in illicit activities."
Nonetheless, the wounds described by Dr. Laborde bear a striking similarity to those found
Christian way of life," Moricant said. "We promise swift justice for deMedici and his family. It is our job to show the criminals that Christ rules the streets, not Satan."
Born into a life of privilege,
DEMEDICI... HE WAS AT LORRAINE'S DINNER PARTY TWO NIGHTS AGO...
I HAD NO IDEA...
AND THERE'S MORE.
I WAS IN HIS OFFICE LAST NIGHT, GEN.
DID YOU...
WHAT?
NO.
NASTY JOB. WOULD HAVE MADE A FORENSICS MASTER CRINGE.
BUT IT WASN'T A FOILED HEIST, GEN, THERE WERE

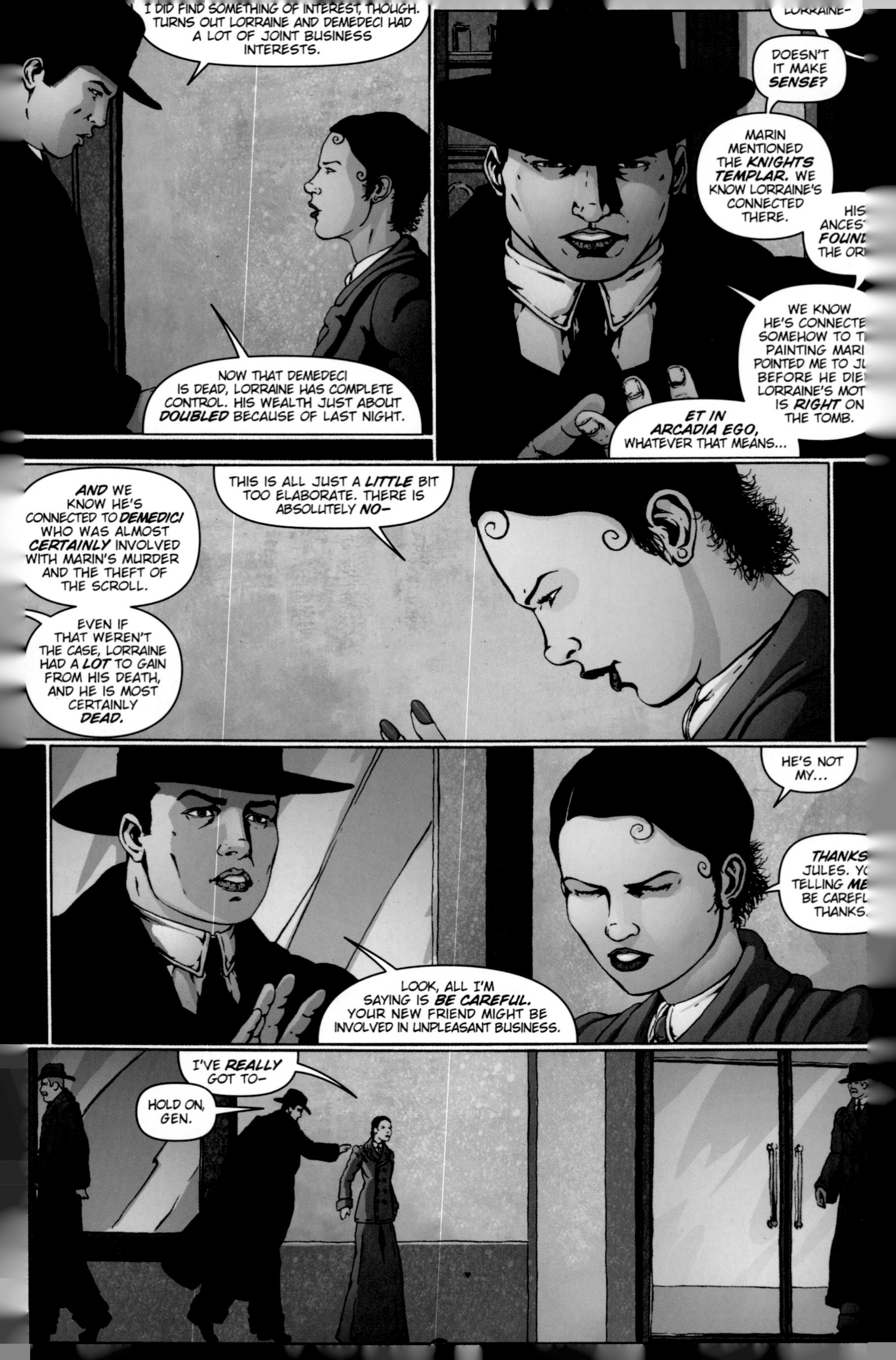
I DID FIND SOMETHING OF INTEREST, THOUGH. TURNS OUT LORRAINE AND DEMEDECI HAD A LOT OF JOINT BUSINESS INTERESTS.
NOW THAT DEMEDECI IS DEAD, LORRAINE HAS COMPLETE CONTROL. HIS WEALTH JUST ABOUT DOUBLED BECAUSE OF LAST NIGHT.
LORRAINE-
DOESN'T IT MAKE SENSE?
MARIN MENTIONED THE KNIGHTS TEMPLAR. WE KNOW LORRAINE'S CONNECTED THERE.
HIS ANCES FOUN THE OR
WE KNOW HE'S CONNECTE SOMEHOW TO T PAINTING MAR POINTED ME TO J BEFORE HE DIE LORRAINE'S MOT IS RIGHT ON THE TOMB.
ET IN ARCADIA EGO, WHATEVER THAT MEANS...
AND WE KNOW HE'S CONNECTED TO DEMEDICI WHO WAS ALMOST CERTAINLY INVOLVED WITH MARIN'S MURDER AND THE THEFT OF THE SCROLL.
EVEN IF THAT WEREN'T THE CASE, LORRAINE HAD A LOT TO GAIN FROM HIS DEATH, AND HE IS MOST CERTAINLY DEAD.
THIS IS ALL JUST A LITTLE BIT TOO ELABORATE. THERE IS ABSOLUTELY NO-
LOOK, ALL I'M SAYING IS BE CAREFUL. YOUR NEW FRIEND MIGHT BE INVOLVED IN UNPLEASANT BUSINESS.
HE'S NOT MY...
THANKS JULES. Y TELLING ME BE CAREF THANKS.
I'VE REALLY GOT TO-
HOLD ON, GEN.

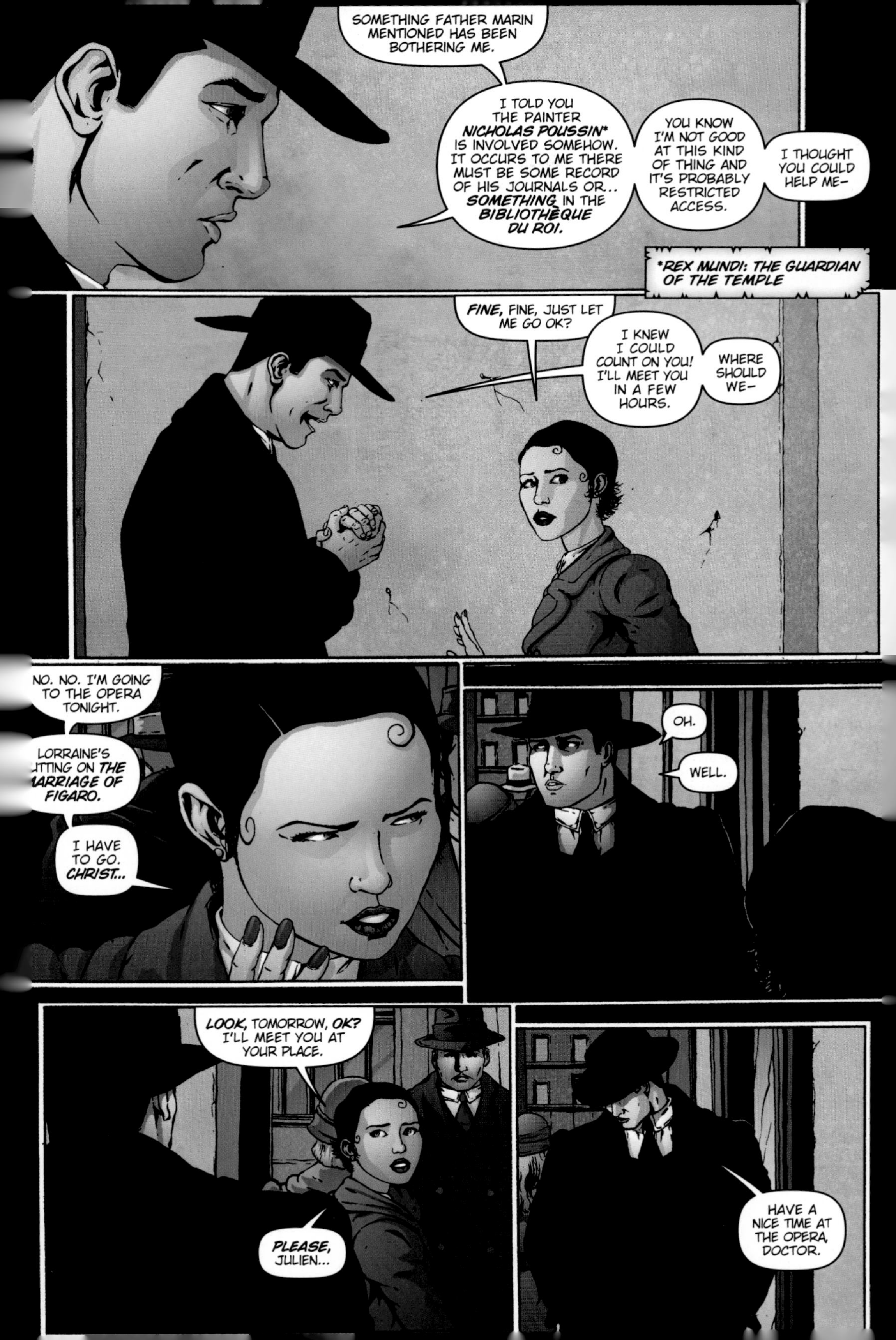
SOMETHING FATHER MARIN MENTIONED HAS BEEN BOTHERING ME.
I TOLD YOU THE PAINTER NICHOLAS POUSSIN* IS INVOLVED SOMEHOW. IT OCCURS TO ME THERE MUST BE SOME RECORD OF HIS JOURNALS OR... SOMETHING IN THE BIBLIOTHÈQUE DU ROI.
YOU KNOW I'M NOT GOOD AT THIS KIND OF THING AND IT'S PROBABLY RESTRICTED ACCESS.
I THOUGHT YOU COULD HELP ME-
*REX MUNDI: THE GUARDIAN OF THE TEMPLE
FINE, FINE, JUST LET ME GO OK?
I KNEW I COULD COUNT ON YOU! I'LL MEET YOU IN A FEW HOURS.
WHERE SHOULD WE-
NO. NO. I'M GOING TO THE OPERA TONIGHT.
LORRAINE'S
THE
FIGARO.
I HAVE TO GO. CHRIST...
OH.
WELL.
LOOK, TOMORROW, OK? I'LL MEET YOU AT YOUR PLACE.
PLEASE, JULIEN...
HAVE A NICE TIME AT THE OPERA, DOCTOR.

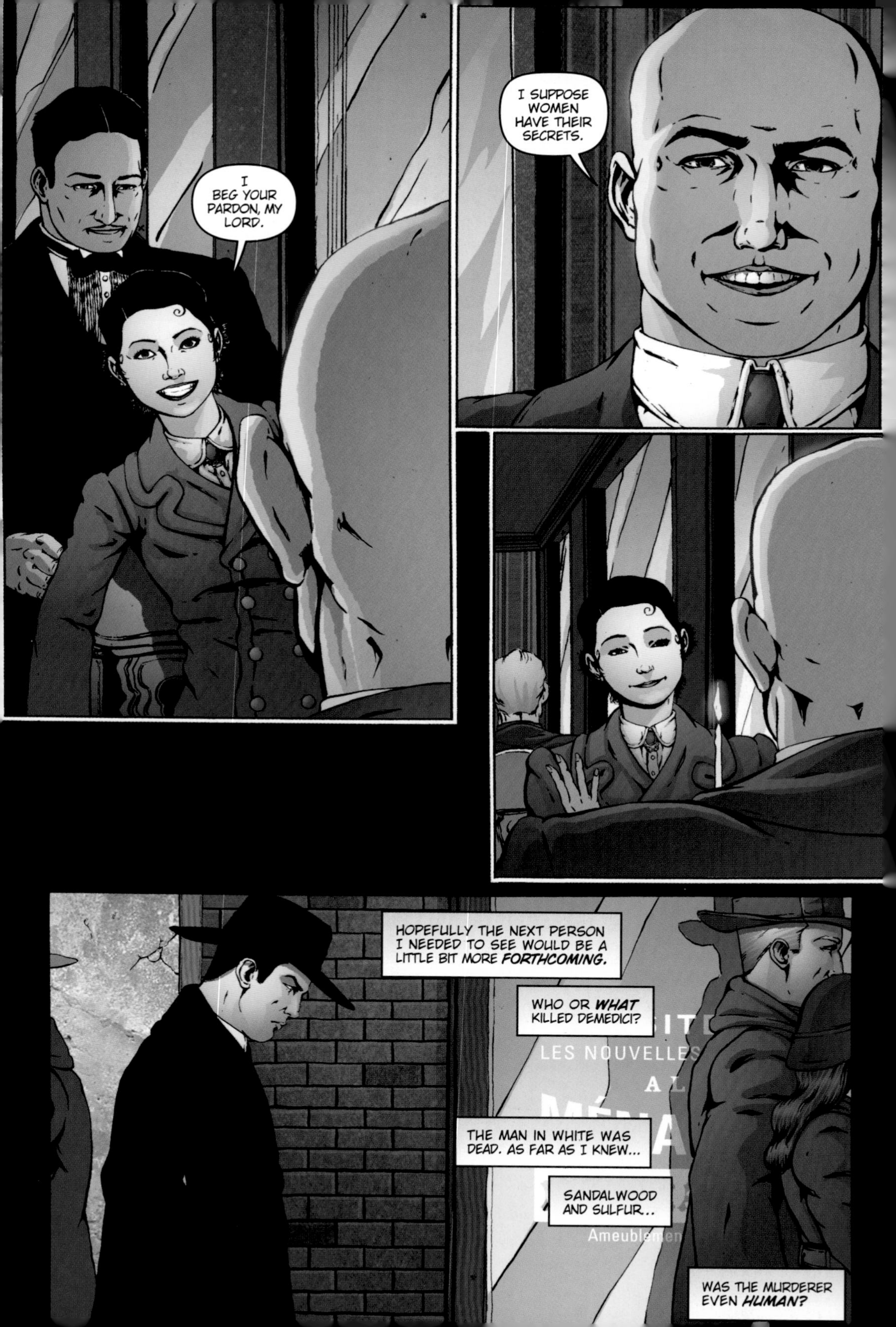
I BEG YOUR PARDON, MY LORD.
I SUPPOSE WOMEN HAVE THEIR SECRETS.
HOPEFULLY THE NEXT PERSON I NEEDED TO SEE WOULD BE A LITTLE BIT MORE *FORTHCOMING.*
WHO OR *WHAT* KILLED DEMEDICI?
LES NOUVELLES
THE MAN IN WHITE WAS DEAD. AS FAR AS I KNEW...
SANDALWOOD AND SULFUR..
WAS THE MURDERER EVEN *HUMAN?*

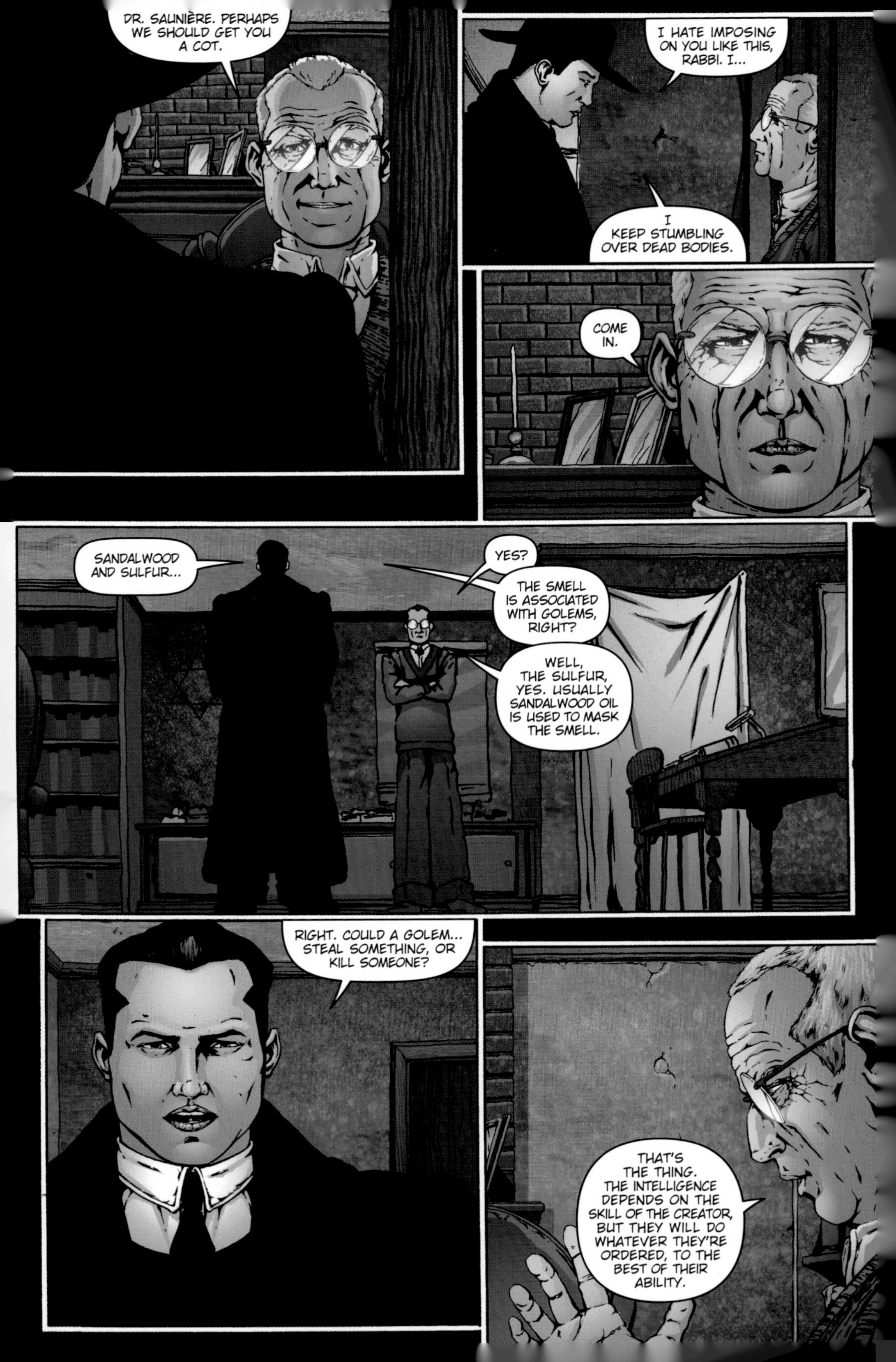
DR. SAUNIÈRE. PERHAPS WE SHOULD GET YOU A COT.
I HATE IMPOSING ON YOU LIKE THIS, RABBI. I...
I KEEP STUMBLING OVER DEAD BODIES.
COME IN.
SANDALWOOD AND SULFUR...
YES?
THE SMELL IS ASSOCIATED WITH GOLEMS, RIGHT?
WELL, THE SULFUR, YES. USUALLY SANDALWOOD OIL IS USED TO MASK THE SMELL.
RIGHT. COULD A GOLEM... STEAL SOMETHING, OR KILL SOMEONE?
THAT'S THE THING. THE INTELLIGENCE DEPENDS ON THE SKILL OF THE CREATOR, BUT THEY WILL DO WHATEVER THEY'RE ORDERED, TO THE BEST OF THEIR ABILITY.

SUCH A THING?

FOREHEAD OR EVEN IN THE MOUTH—WILL BE THE WORD *LIFE* WRITTEN IN HEBREW.

COME, I'LL SHOW YOU.

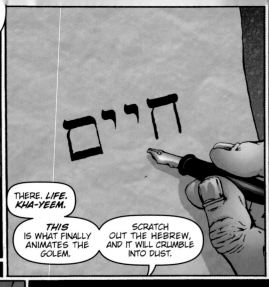

חיים

THERE. *LIFE.* KHA-YEEM.

THIS IS WHAT FINALLY ANIMATES THE GOLEM.

SCRATCH OUT THE HEBREW, AND IT WILL CRUMBLE INTO DUST.

ONE WORD CAN DO *THAT?*

IT'S THE FINAL STEP IN A LONG RITUAL PROCESS.

HEBREW IS A MYSTICAL LANGUAGE, DOCTOR.

THE LANGUAGE IN WHICH MOSES RECEIVED THE TEN COMMANDMENTS. THE LANGUAGE IN WHICH ABRAHAM SPOKE TO *GOD.*

IT HAS TREMENDOUS POWER IF YOU KNOW HOW TO TAP ITS SECRETS.

HOLD ON. I'VE HEARD SORCERERS MAKING INCANTATIONS. IT'S DEFINITELY *NOT* HEBREW.

THAT'S RIGHT. IT'S *AMHARIC,* AN ETHIOPIAN LANGUAGE.

ETHIOPIAN?

IT HAS TO DO WITH THE *ARK OF THE COVENANT.*

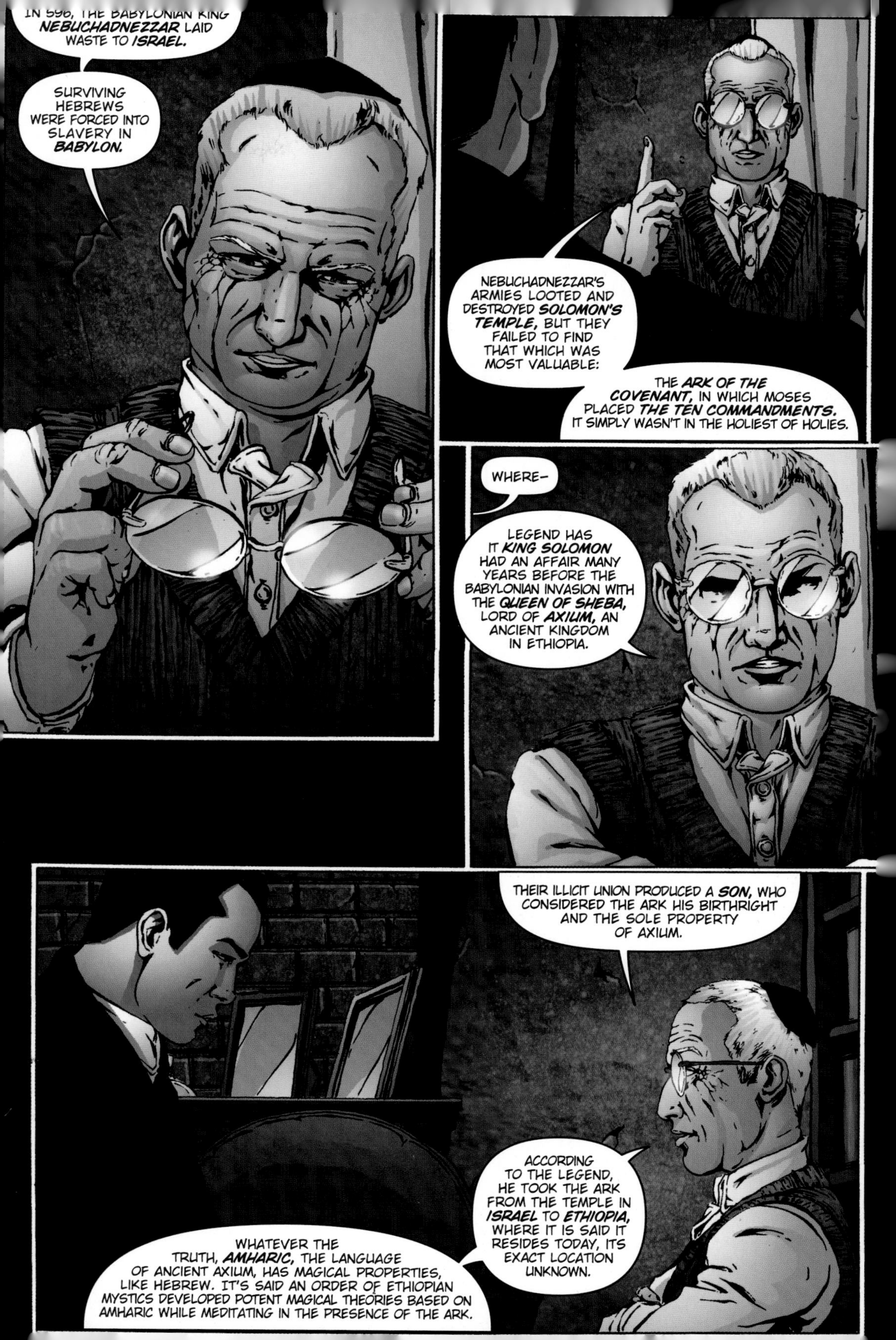
IN 596, THE BABYLONIAN KING NEBUCHADNEZZAR LAID WASTE TO ISRAEL.
SURVIVING HEBREWS WERE FORCED INTO SLAVERY IN BABYLON.
NEBUCHADNEZZAR'S ARMIES LOOTED AND DESTROYED SOLOMON'S TEMPLE, BUT THEY FAILED TO FIND THAT WHICH WAS MOST VALUABLE:
THE ARK OF THE COVENANT, IN WHICH MOSES PLACED THE TEN COMMANDMENTS. IT SIMPLY WASN'T IN THE HOLIEST OF HOLIES.
WHERE–
LEGEND HAS IT KING SOLOMON HAD AN AFFAIR MANY YEARS BEFORE THE BABYLONIAN INVASION WITH THE QUEEN OF SHEBA, LORD OF AXIUM, AN ANCIENT KINGDOM IN ETHIOPIA.
THEIR ILLICIT UNION PRODUCED A SON, WHO CONSIDERED THE ARK HIS BIRTHRIGHT AND THE SOLE PROPERTY OF AXIUM.
ACCORDING TO THE LEGEND, HE TOOK THE ARK FROM THE TEMPLE IN ISRAEL TO ETHIOPIA, WHERE IT IS SAID IT RESIDES TODAY, ITS EXACT LOCATION UNKNOWN.
WHATEVER THE TRUTH, AMHARIC, THE LANGUAGE OF ANCIENT AXIUM, HAS MAGICAL PROPERTIES, LIKE HEBREW. IT'S SAID AN ORDER OF ETHIOPIAN MYSTICS DEVELOPED POTENT MAGICAL THEORIES BASED ON AMHARIC WHILE MEDITATING IN THE PRESENCE OF THE ARK.

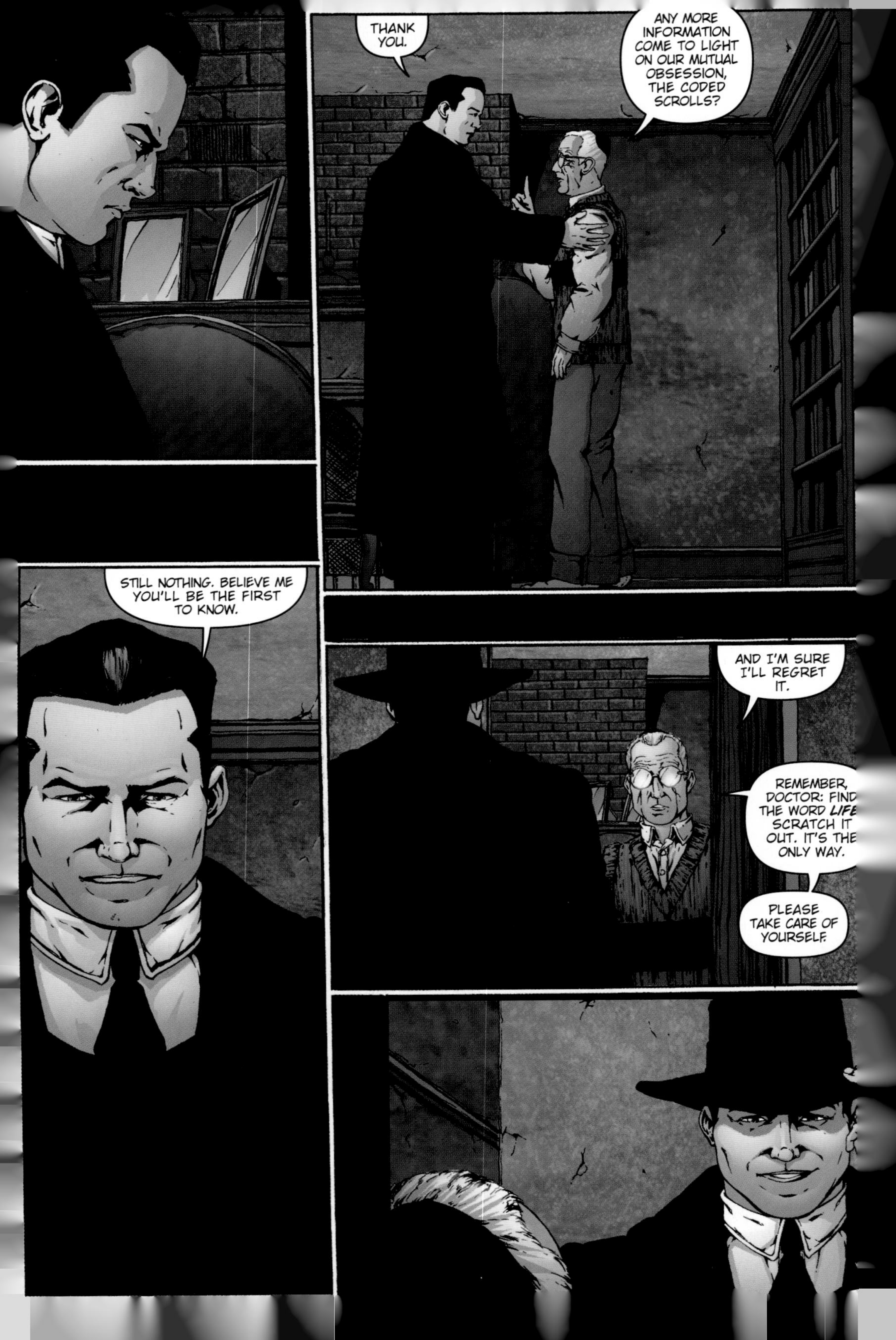
THANK YOU.
ANY MORE INFORMATION COME TO LIGHT ON OUR MUTUAL OBSESSION, THE CODED SCROLLS?
STILL NOTHING. BELIEVE ME YOU'LL BE THE FIRST TO KNOW.
AND I'M SURE I'LL REGRET IT.
REMEMBER, DOCTOR: FIND THE WORD *LIFE* SCRATCH IT OUT. IT'S THE ONLY WAY.
PLEASE TAKE CARE OF YOURSELF.

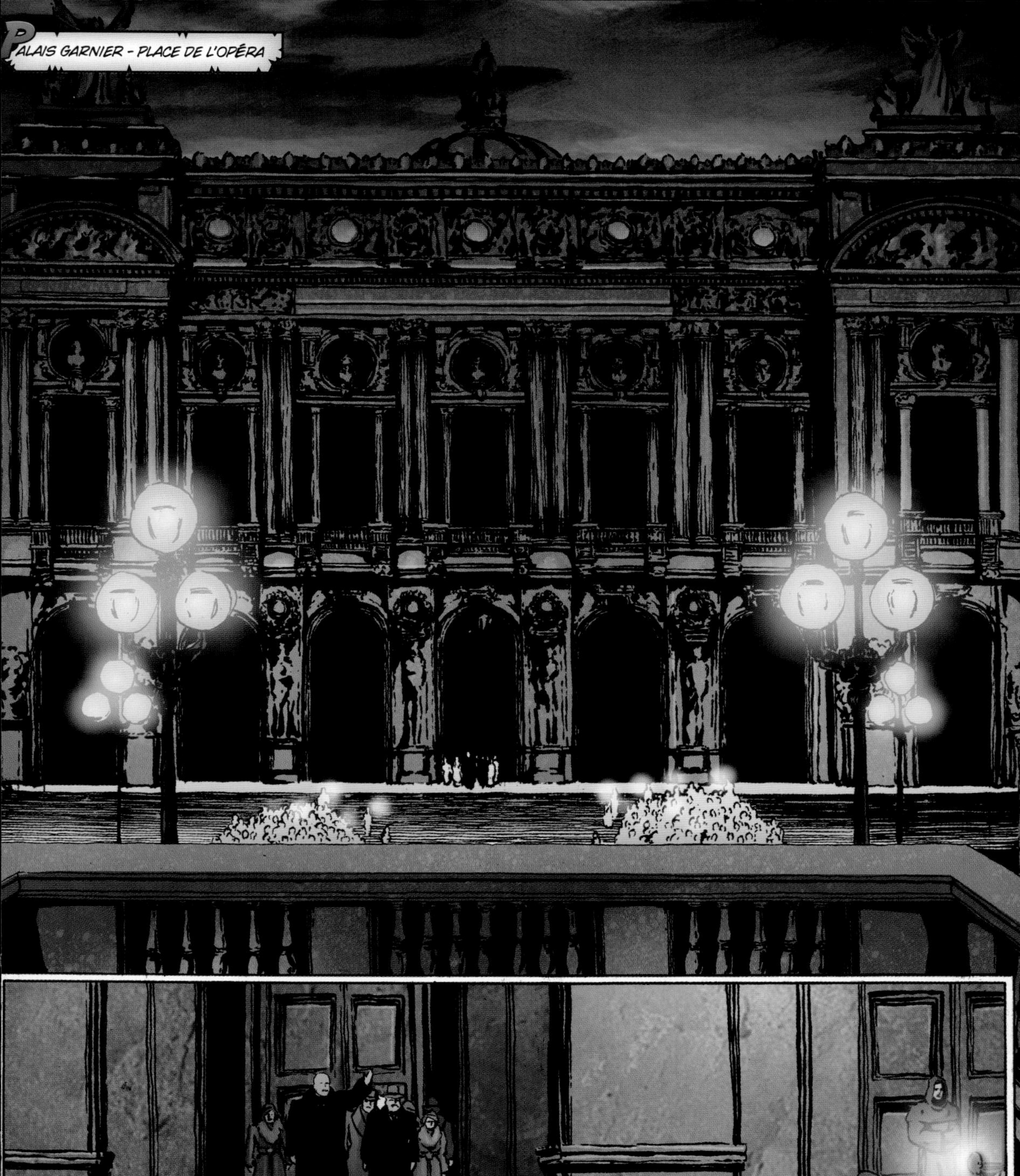
PALAIS GARNIER - PLACE DE L'OPÉRA
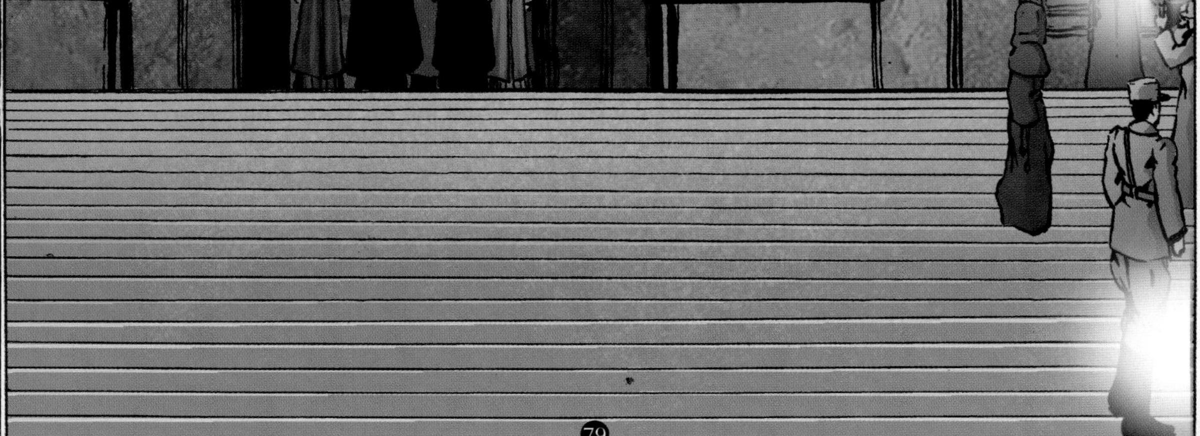

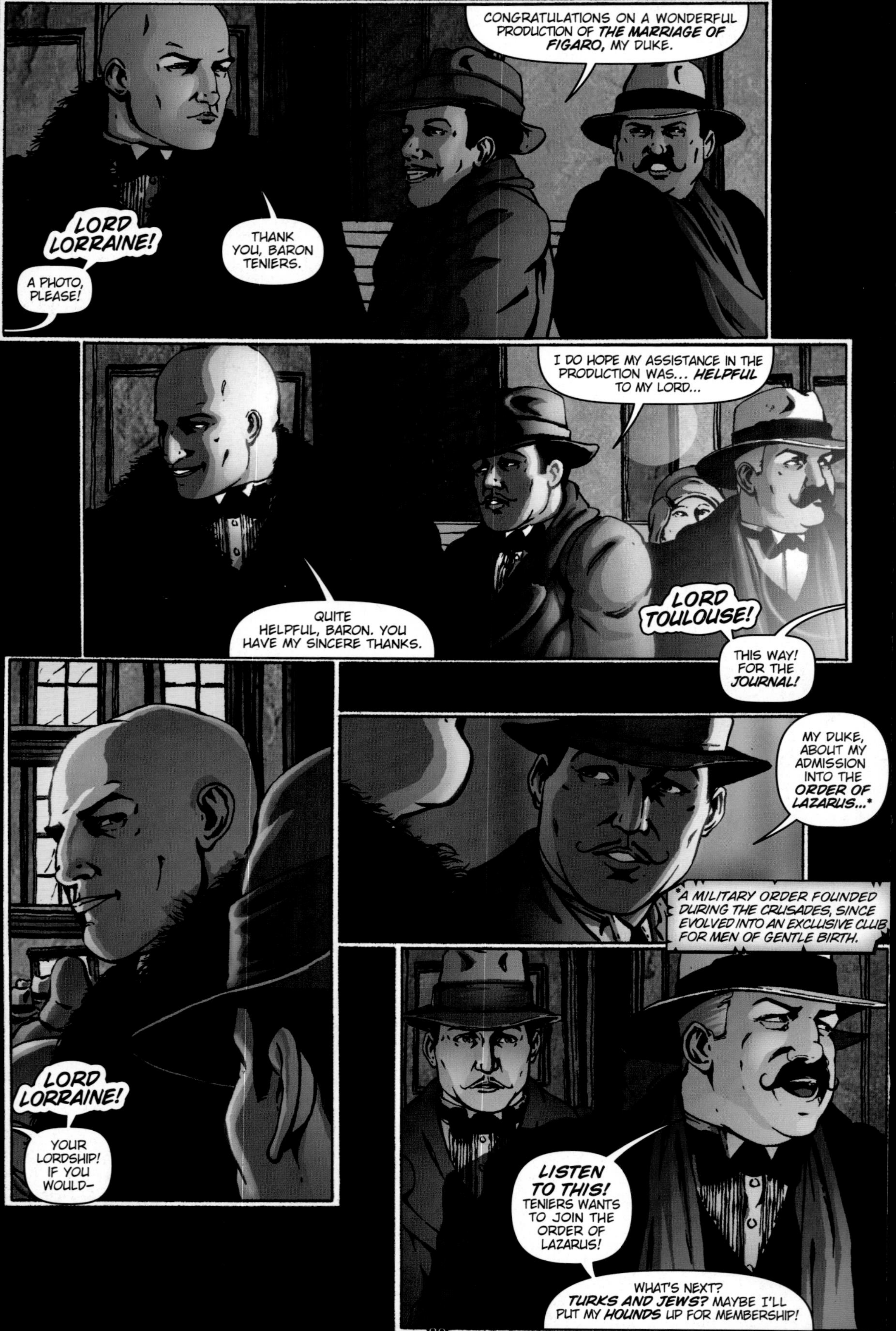

CONGRATULATIONS ON A WONDERFUL PRODUCTION OF THE MARRIAGE OF FIGARO, MY DUKE.
LORD LORRAINE!
A PHOTO, PLEASE!
THANK YOU, BARON TENIERS.
I DO HOPE MY ASSISTANCE IN THE PRODUCTION WAS... HELPFUL TO MY LORD...
QUITE HELPFUL, BARON. YOU HAVE MY SINCERE THANKS.
LORD TOULOUSE!
THIS WAY! FOR THE JOURNAL!
LORD LORRAINE!
YOUR LORDSHIP! IF YOU WOULD-
MY DUKE, ABOUT MY ADMISSION INTO THE ORDER OF LAZARUS...*
*A MILITARY ORDER FOUNDED DURING THE CRUSADES, SINCE EVOLVED INTO AN EXCLUSIVE CLUB FOR MEN OF GENTLE BIRTH.
LISTEN TO THIS! TENIERS WANTS TO JOIN THE ORDER OF LAZARUS!
WHAT'S NEXT? TURKS AND JEWS? MAYBE I'LL PUT MY HOUNDS UP FOR MEMBERSHIP!

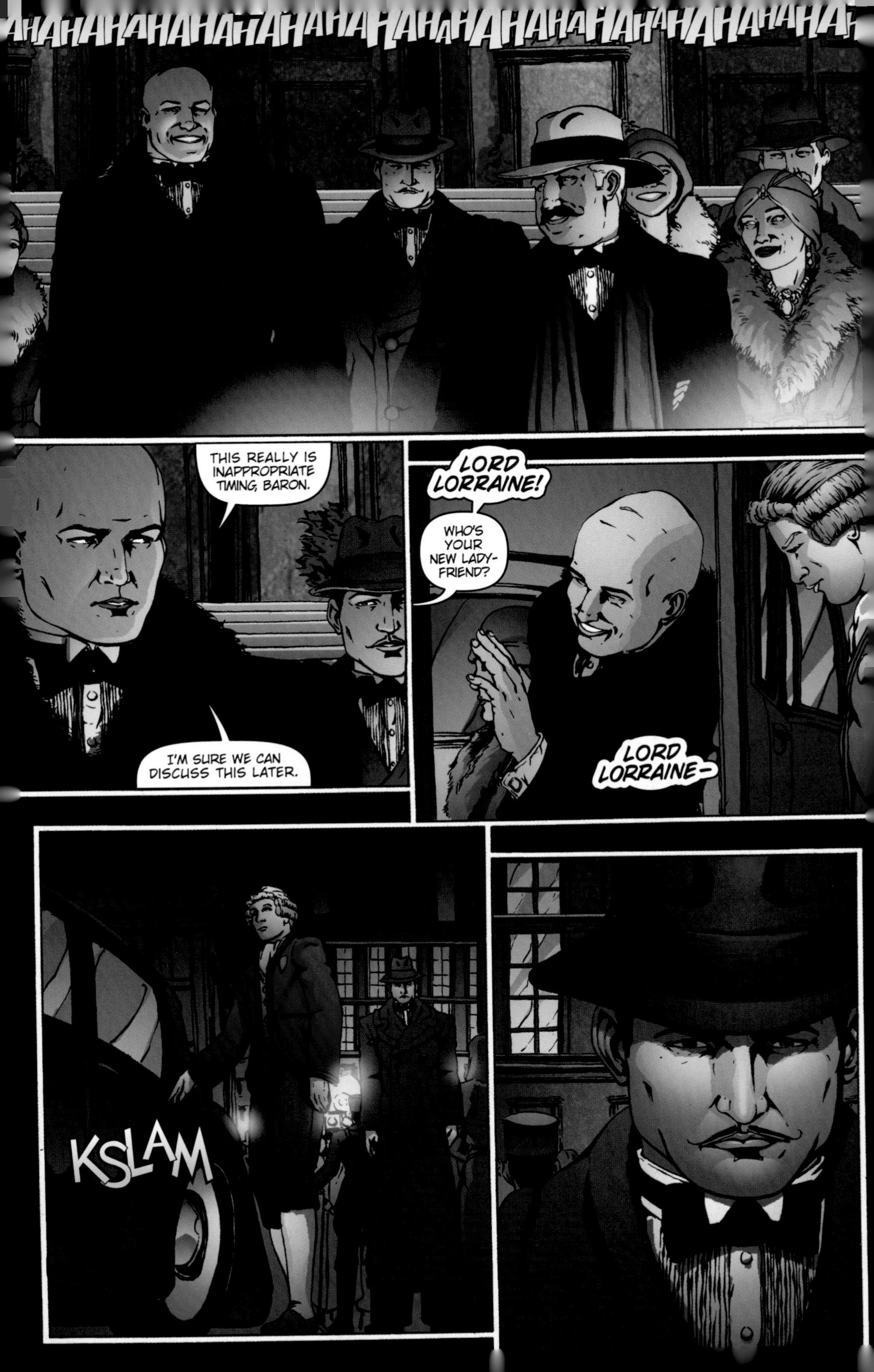

AHAHAHAHAHAHAHAHAHAHAHAHAHAHAHAHAHAHAHAHAHA
THIS REALLY IS INAPPROPRIATE TIMING, BARON.
I'M SURE WE CAN DISCUSS THIS LATER.
LORD LORRAINE!
WHO'S YOUR NEW LADY-FRIEND?
LORD LORRAINE-
KSLAM

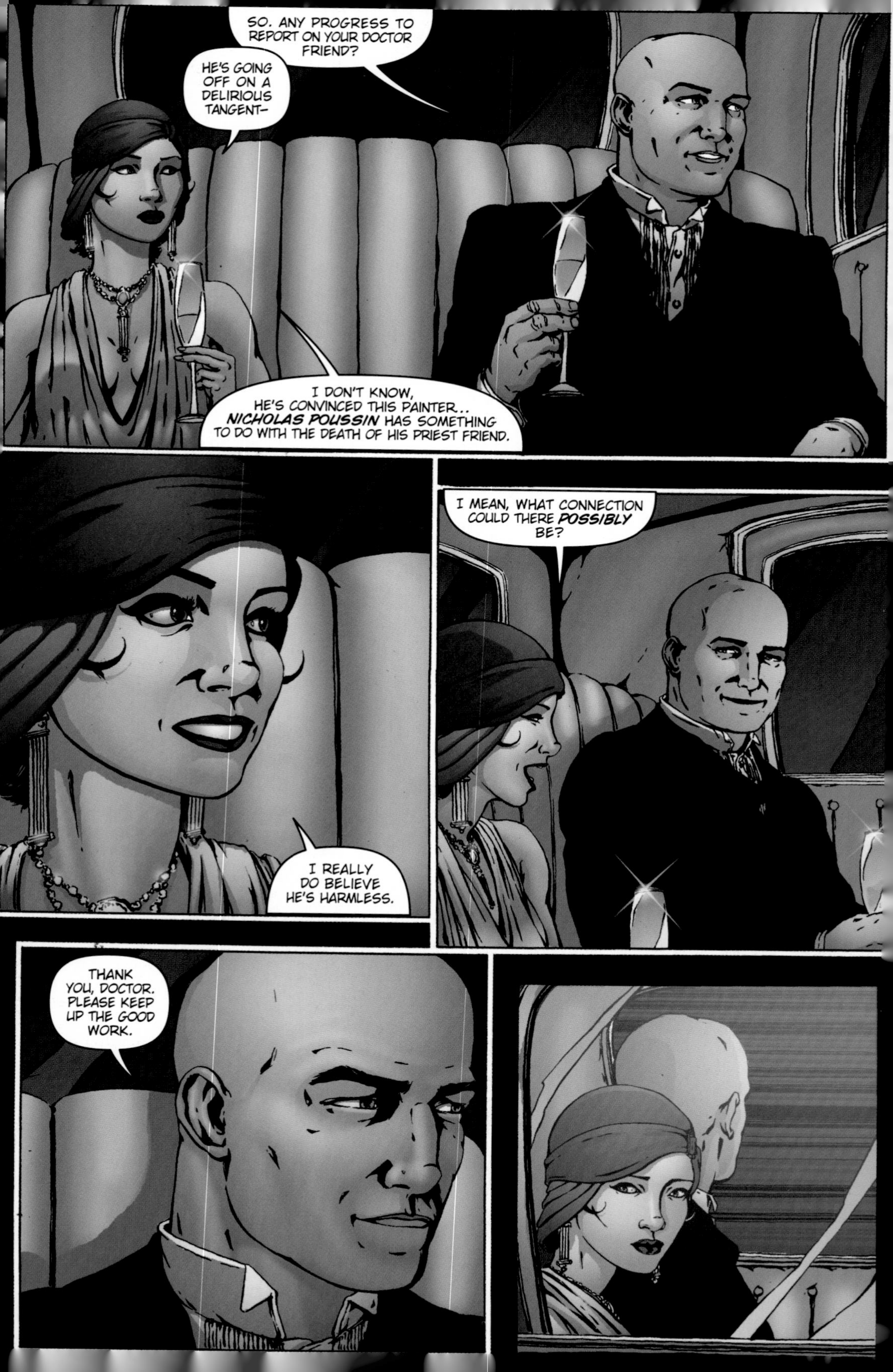
SO. ANY PROGRESS TO REPORT ON YOUR DOCTOR FRIEND?
HE'S GOING OFF ON A DELIRIOUS TANGENT–
I DON'T KNOW, HE'S CONVINCED THIS PAINTER... NICHOLAS POUSSIN HAS SOMETHING TO DO WITH THE DEATH OF HIS PRIEST FRIEND.
I REALLY DO BELIEVE HE'S HARMLESS.
I MEAN, WHAT CONNECTION COULD THERE POSSIBLY BE?
THANK YOU, DOCTOR. PLEASE KEEP UP THE GOOD WORK.

Le Journal de la Liberté

Paris' leading anglophone newspaper • vol. 205, no. 102 • Oct. 25, MCMXXXIII

Papal Seal

Editors in Chief: M. Tait Bergstrom, M. Matthew Pasteris. **Story Editor:** M. Arvid Nelson. **Art Editors:** M. EricJ, M. Jeromy Cox. **Photography Editor:** M. Alexander Waldman. **Layout Supervisor:** M. William Kartalopoulos. **Editors Emeritus:** M. Clark A. Smith, M. Howard P. Lovecraft, M. Robert E. Howard. Redacted by the Holy Parisian Inquisition under the direction of His Excellency Archbishop Emile-Jean Ireneaux. Le Journal de la Liberté is printed under the benign auspices of his most puissant majesty KING LOUIS XXII of FRANCE. GOD SAVE THE KING.

of Approval

DE MEDICI FAMILY HEIR BRUTALLY MURDERED IN DARING LATE-NIGHT HEIST

Inquisition searching for killer of influential Italian merchant prince, denies underworld connection

Quays of the Seine, where Hugo deMedici's much-abused corpse was found. Inquisition officials have not named a suspect but promise "swift justice."

Paris – Hugo deMedici, a powerful figure in the deMedici family financial empire, was found slain in a riverside office building early this morning.

Inquisitors and gendarmerie officers rushed to the scene on a tipoff from an anonymous informant.

DeMedici was pronounced dead on the scene by Antione Laborde, a forensic attaché from the Guild of Physicians.

"He sustained deep lacerations to his limbs, face and torso. The cause of death was shock and blood-loss," Laborde said.

Members of the Inquisition refused to comment on the motivation for the crime beyond simple greed.

"DeMedici was a wealthy man," Grand Inquisitor Moricant, chief representative of the Church on the scene, said. "We are treating this as a robbery-homicide, the work of opportunistic thugs."

Inquisition officials said "significant" amounts of currency and stock certificates had been looted from the office.

Moricant denied a connection to the wave of underworld killings over the past few weeks.

"DeMedici was a regular churchgoer and an outstanding member of the community," he said. "There is no reason to suspect his involvement in illicit activities."

Nonetheless, the wounds described by Dr. Laborde bear a striking similarity to those recently found on the corpses of a number of hoodlums.

Moricant dismissed the connection. "If the circumstances seem similar to murders committed over the past few weeks, it is only because all degenerate and criminals types have a disposition towards excessive violence and rage."

"Right now, our theory is that killer or killers forcibly entered deMedici's office sometime early in the morning. DeMedici resisted, and the intruders became overzealous," a gendarmerie officer said. "The crime scene is in a terrible state. Like a swarm of locusts came through."

Dr. Laborde confirmed that the wounds on deMedici's body were largely defensive in nature.

"He put up a fight, right to the very end, it seems," he said.

Inquisitors said they had no suspects, but that an apprehension was "only a matter of time."

"Crimes such as this, directed at pillars of the community, are nothing less than assaults on our Christian way of life," Moricant said. "We promise swift justice for deMedici and his family. It is our job to show the criminals that Christ rules the streets, not Satan."

Born into a life of privilege, Mr. deMedici nonetheless worked hard to attain the status he enjoyed in the deMedici empire.

"He never took anything in life for granted," his father, Cosimo deMedici, said. "He was a loving son and a vital asset to our organization. His mother, his siblings, myself, we're all in a state of disbelief."

DeMedici began as a humble clerk in a capital investment firm run by his father in Florence, but in a short while he climbed his way to to the top of his family's empire. He attributed his success to his "bottom-up" experience in an interview earlier this year.

But deMedici wasn't content simply making money. He became interested in politics at an early age, and was one of the most vocal supporters of the Duke of Lorraine in business circles.

"Lord Lorraine expresses his deep regret and sadness at this sudden an unexplainable loss of life," Baron Robert Teniers, a spokesman for the Duke of Lorraine, said.

Lorraine and deMedici forged *continued on page B1*

LORDS OF THE SPANISH MARCHES PROCLAIM SUPPORT FOR DUKE OF LORRAINE

Navarre, Aragon and Castile pledge support for Duke in upset for French Crown

The Spanish Marches – The Marquises of Aragon, Castile and Navarre yesterday proclaimed endorsement of the policy of French territorial expansion in the Iberian peninsula.

"We believe the time has come to turn the tide of Islam back from Europe," Alonzo deGonzaga, a spokesman for the three Lords of the Marches, said. "And we believe Lord Lorraine is the man to do it."

The "Lords of the Marches," as they are known, are feudal landholders on the border between France and the Emirate of Cordova. They enjoy ancient privileges of autonomy from the King of France in return for their steadfast defense against moorish incursions.

Over the centuries the Lords have been the first line of defense against Islam in Western Europe, and as such have enjoyed the gratitude and good will of the French Crown.

Now, that might all be about to change.

"His Majesty King Louis thinks this is a dangerous road to take, and it could jeopardize our mutual interests," Mayor of the Court Charles Martel said.

The Marquises insist they are strengthening the position of the King, not weakening it.

Not so, said Hall of the Robe member Eustache Lambert, a close ally of the King.

"The best person to determine what's best for France is the king, not a group of scruffy Spanish robber-lords."

Lorraine dismissed allegations he was deliberately antagonizing *continued on page A9*

LE JOURNAL SPECIAL: THE HOLY HIERARCHY

The lands of St. Peter & environs

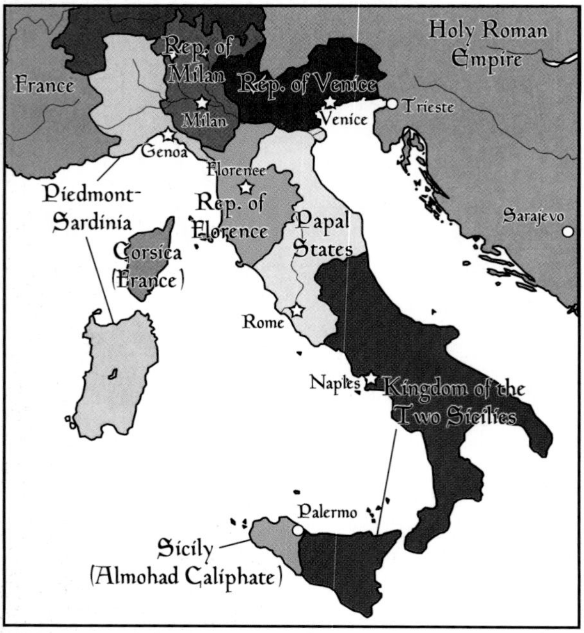

Holy Roman Empire
Rep. of Milan
France
Rep. of Venice
Milan
Venice
Trieste
Genoa
Florence
Piedmont-Sardinia
Rep. of Florence
Papal States
Sarajevo
Corsica (France)
Rome
Naples
Kingdom of the Two Sicilies
Palermo
Sicily (Almohad Caliphate)

The Church's holdings are most concentrated in the Italian peninsula, but it also possesses large amounts of land throughout Europe, the result of centuries of charitable donations.

His Holiness Pope John XIV announced yesterday a general convocation of bishops to discuss matters of theology and the future course of the church. Such a meeting, an "ecumenical council," has not occurred in over 350 years.

The term "catholic" means "universal," and no word could better describe the Church. It is the most powerful organization in the world, overseeing the coronations of emperors and providing spiritual guidance to all Christians, like a big brother.

In this special edition of *Le Journal de la Liberté,* we examine the organization of the Church and the civilizing, stabilizing effect it has on humanity as a whole.

"Ego Sum Caesar": The Papacy

"Ego Sum Caesar" – *I am Caesar* in Latin. Thus spoke Pope Boniface VIII in 1302, and in doing so he perfectly summed up the role of the Pope.

"The Holy Father wields an enormous amount of power," said Brother Eugène Lourié, a Carmelite monk and Church historian, said.

"If the Church is Christ's mystical body, then the Pope is the head. Christ ordained St. Peter to be His heir, and this divine right to rule has been passed down unbroken over the centuries to each successive pope."

"In a more mundane sense, the Church is, quite literally, the transubstantiation of the Roman Empire," Brother Eugène said.

As the social and political apparatus of the Roman Empire began to collapse, the Church assumed the mantle of leadership.

"There wasn't anyone else to do the job," Brother Eugène said. "The Church was the only institution with the organizational infrastructure to fill the vacuum of power."

Just as Caesar ruled Rome, so does the Pope rule the Church.

The Pope governs through the institution of the *Curia*, the assembly of ministries that assist him in governing the Holy See.

"Everything flows from the Holy Father," Brother Eugène said. "Every member of the Ecclesiastical hierarchy above a priest is appointed by the Pope."

The Body of the Church

Below pope is the rank of *cardinal.* Cardinals participate directly in the Curia government and advise the Pope on matters spiritual and temporal. When a pope dies, the cardinals conduct a closed door election, called the *Conclave,* to determine the new Pope. Most often, but not always, the successor pope is a member of the College of Cardinals.

"Cardinals seem to make the best Popes because they are attuned to both the spiritual and political needs of the Church," Brother Eugène said. "There have been a few instances in which men of great faith but little experience have been elected to the Throne of St. Peter. These occasions have mostly proved disasters."

The administration of the Church outside the Vatican falls to the next ranks in descending order: *Archbishops* and *Bishops*.

Archbishops rule over a *province*, a large swath of land composed of several *dioceses*. A diocese is the territory under the control of a Bishop. Bishops, in turn, ordain priests who preside over a *parish*, the smallest subdivision of land in the Church hierarchy. Priests perform mass for lay Christians and ensure their souls travel to heaven after death.

"Of course, it's not as simple as all that," Brother Eugène said. "There are many officials within the Church who do not preside over a diocese or a parish. Instead they provide special services. For example, there is the office of a *Papal Nuncio*, an ambassador of the Church, or an appointment as the director of the regional activities of the Holy Inquisition."

Religious Orders - A Body Apart

"Scholars think that when Christianity became the state religion of Rome, people who previously would have sought martyrdom instead became hermits and monks, the most famous of which is St. Anthony," Brother Eugène said. "Who knows? Fifteen hundred years ago instead of wearing these robes I might have been turning on a spit in a Roman dungeon."

Most religious orders were founded in the Middle Ages by men of renown faith and intellect. The founder of an order creates a *rule*, a set of guidelines by which a person who decides to enter must abide.

Monastic orders, such as the Carmelites, generally require a life of "poverty, chastity and obedience," Brother Eugène said. "Obedience to the head of our order and to Christ."

Other orders, such as the Jesuits, founded in part in response the heresy of Lutheranism, enforce a less strict code of conduct and do not require communal life.

The Inquisition: The Sword of Christ

One order in particular, the Dominicans, serves a very special function: members of their order constitute the majority of the Holy Inquisition.

Christ said "I am come not to bring peace but a sword. He was referring to the Inquisition," Inquisitor and Dominican friar Augusto Santiago said.

The Inquisition was founded in the Middle Ages to combat rampant heresy. While this mandate still obtains, it has also evolved into a secular police force.

"The problems facing the Church and Christian society at large are legion," Brother Santiago said. "Witchcraft, heresy, devil worship and organized crime threaten to destroy our cherished values. The Inquisition is at war with the forces of darkness."

Secular law enforcement, according to Brother Santiago, is ill-equipped to deal with the myriad problems.

"We are as hard on ourself as we are on the enemies of Christ," he said. "Secular law enforcement provides the Inquisition with valuable auxiliary support, but the task of tending Christ's flock must be left to the shepherds, not the wolves."

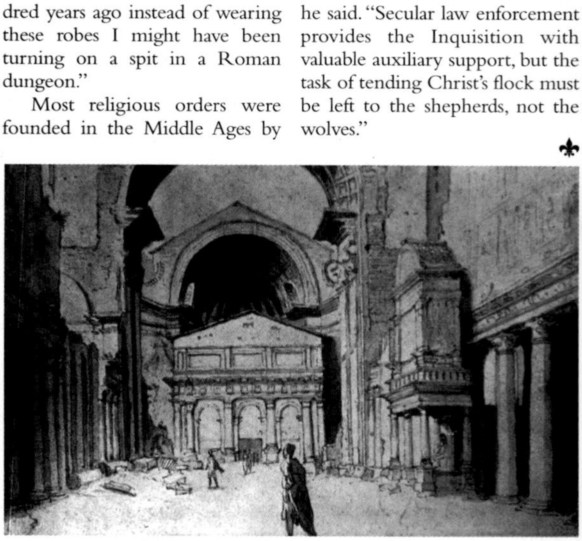

St. Peter's Basilica, the center of the Holy Church, in the early 1500s

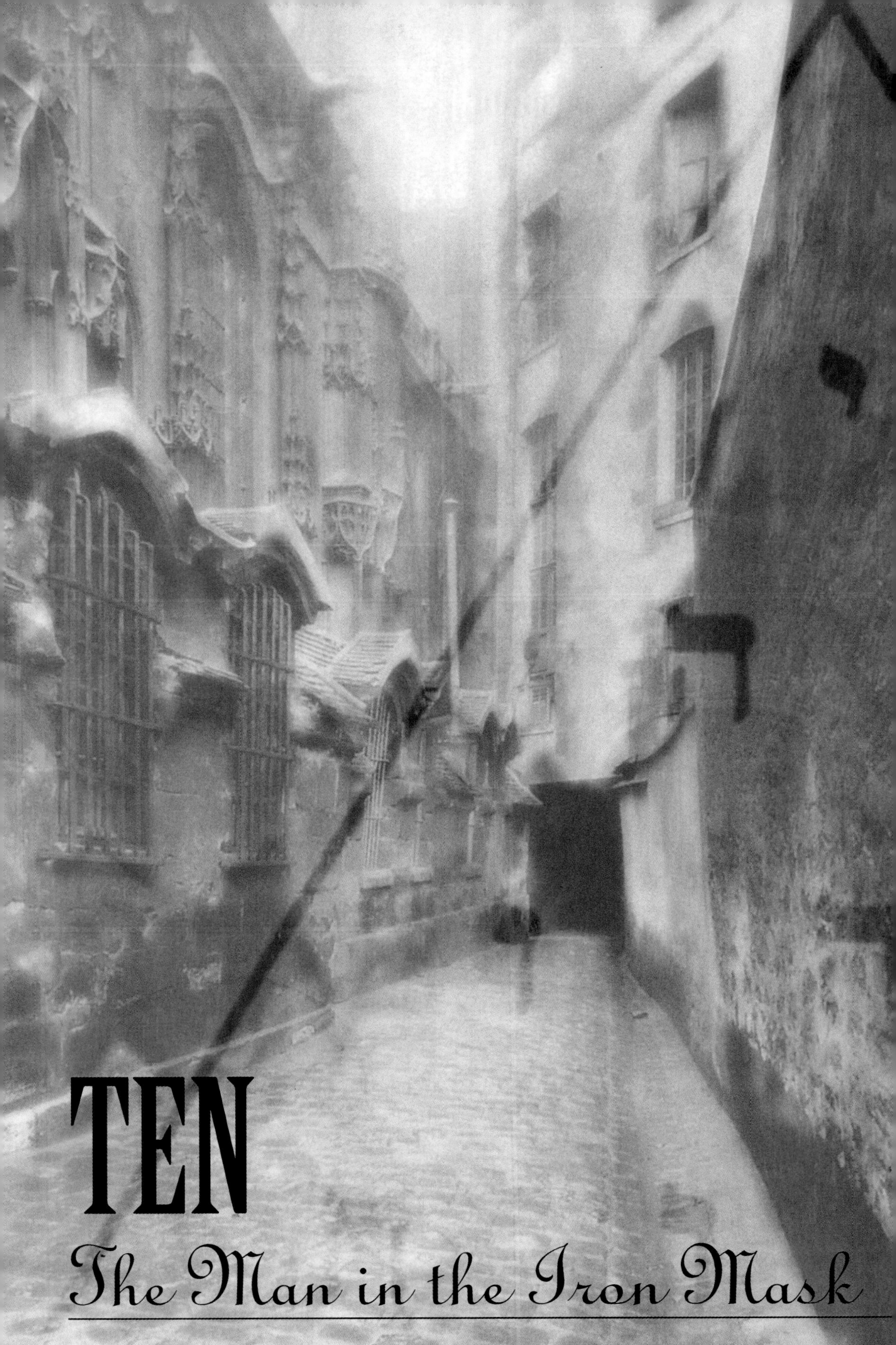

TEN
The Man in the Iron Mask

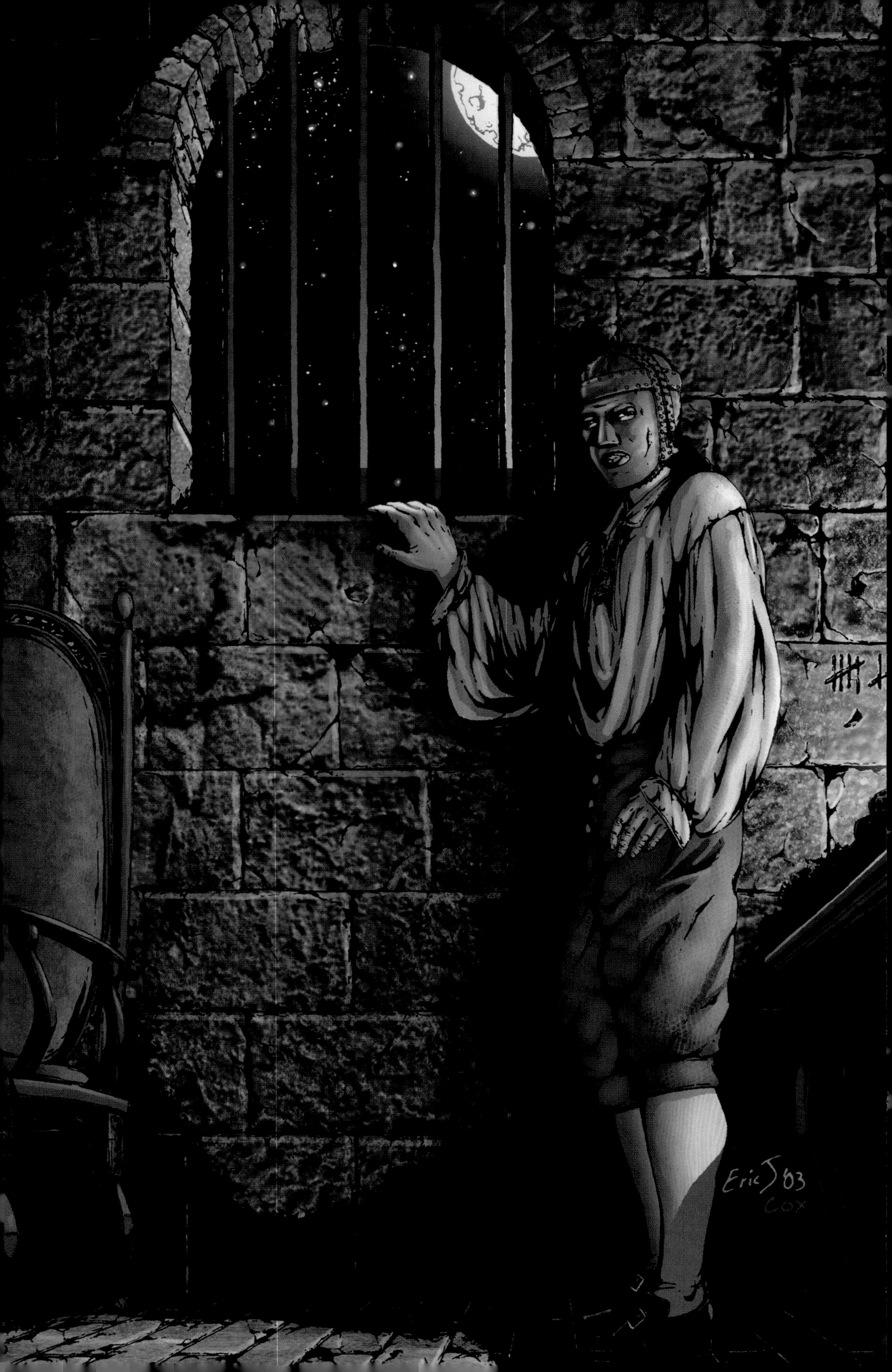
Eric J '03
COX

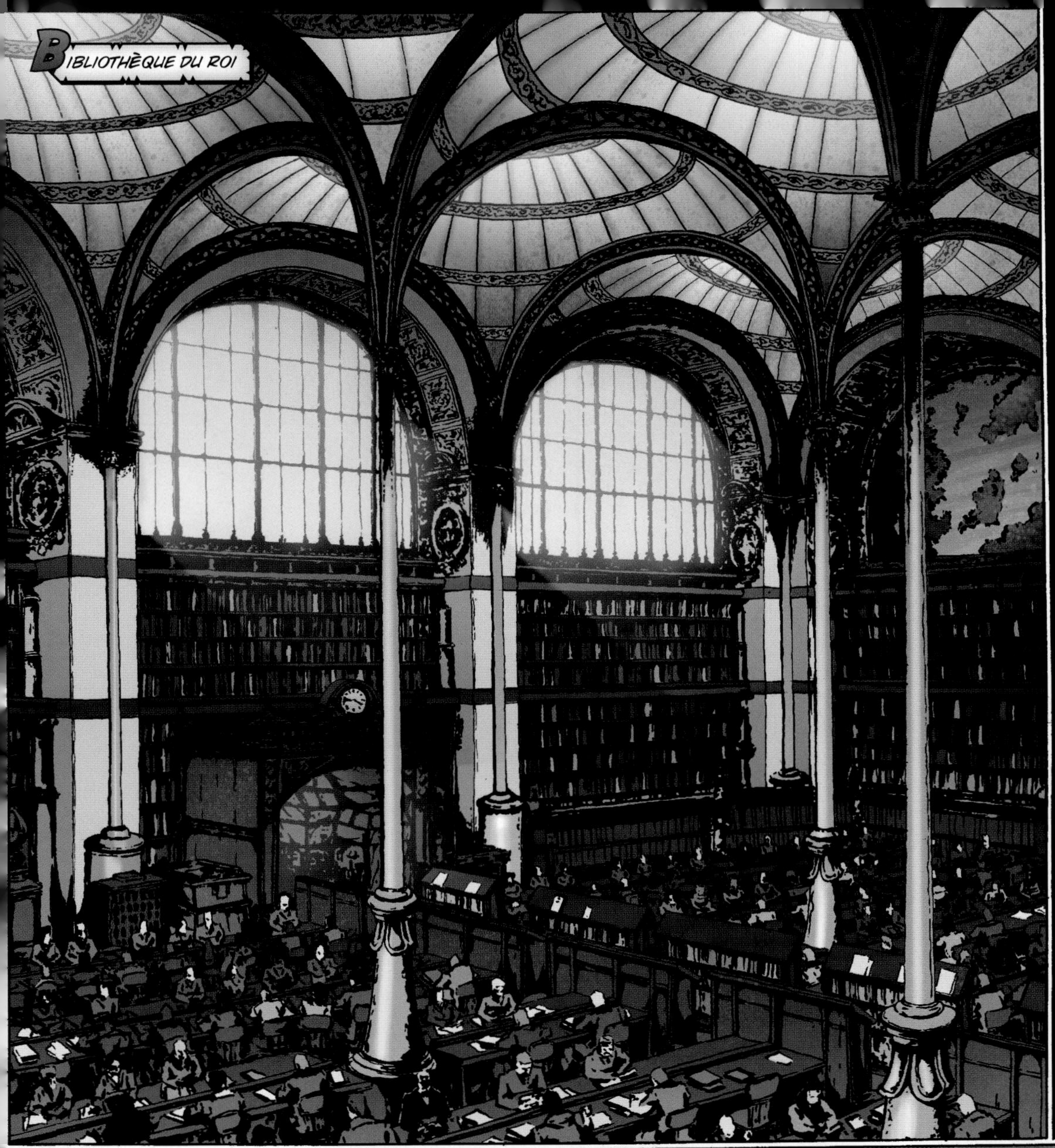
BIBLIOTHÈQUE DU ROI

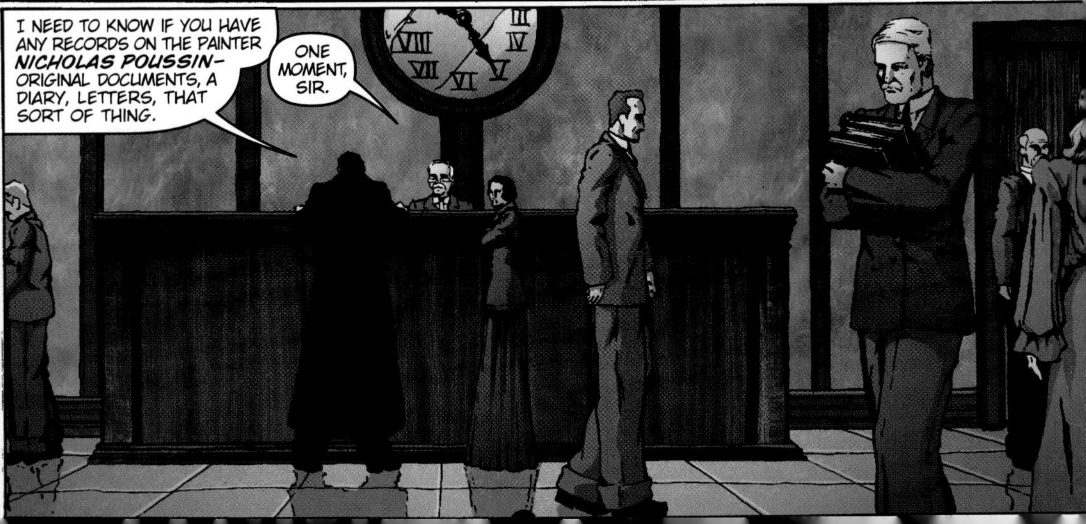
I NEED TO KNOW IF YOU HAVE ANY RECORDS ON THE PAINTER NICHOLAS POUSSIN- ORIGINAL DOCUMENTS, A DIARY, LETTERS, THAT SORT OF THING.
ONE MOMENT, SIR.

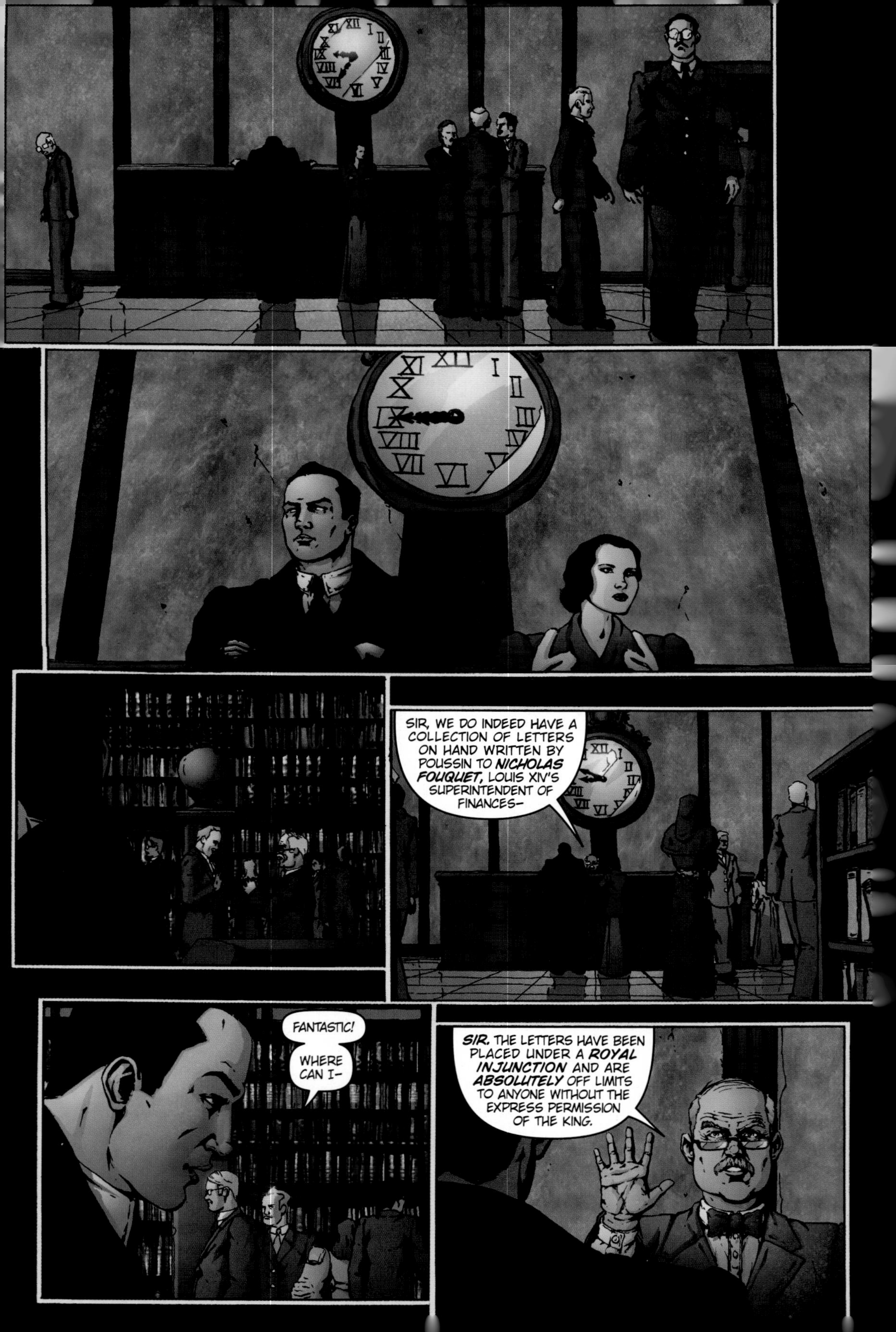
SIR, WE DO INDEED HAVE A COLLECTION OF LETTERS ON HAND WRITTEN BY POUSSIN TO ***NICHOLAS FOUQUET,*** LOUIS XIV'S SUPERINTENDENT OF FINANCES-
FANTASTIC!
WHERE CAN I-
SIR, THE LETTERS HAVE BEEN PLACED UNDER A ***ROYAL INJUNCTION*** AND ARE ***ABSOLUTELY*** OFF LIMITS TO ANYONE WITHOUT THE EXPRESS PERMISSION OF THE KING.

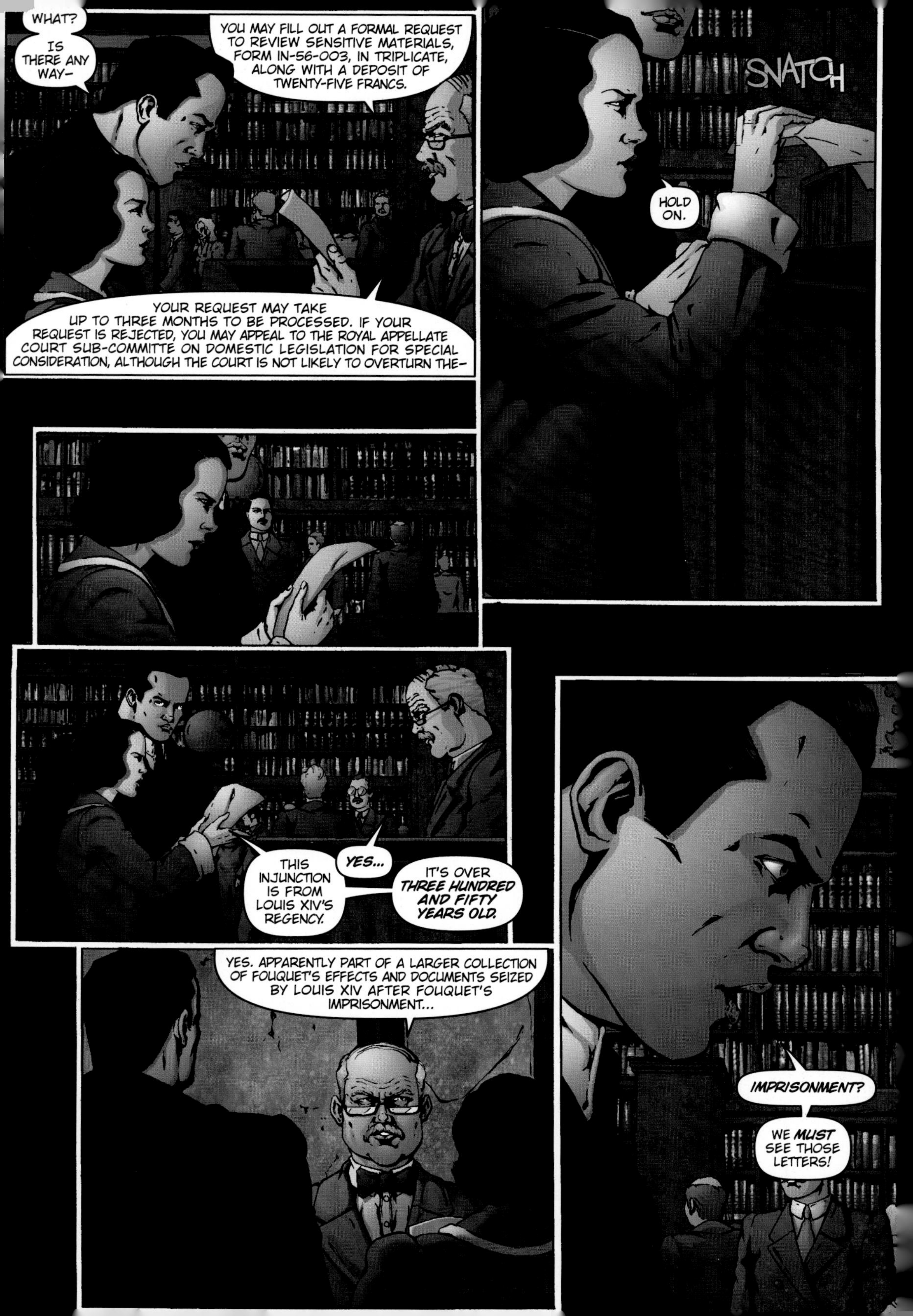
WHAT? IS THERE ANY WAY-
YOU MAY FILL OUT A FORMAL REQUEST TO REVIEW SENSITIVE MATERIALS, FORM IN-56-003, IN TRIPLICATE, ALONG WITH A DEPOSIT OF TWENTY-FIVE FRANCS.
YOUR REQUEST MAY TAKE UP TO THREE MONTHS TO BE PROCESSED. IF YOUR REQUEST IS REJECTED, YOU MAY APPEAL TO THE ROYAL APPELLATE COURT SUB-COMMITTE ON DOMESTIC LEGISLATION FOR SPECIAL CONSIDERATION, ALTHOUGH THE COURT IS NOT LIKELY TO OVERTURN THE-
SNATCH
HOLD ON.
THIS INJUNCTION IS FROM LOUIS XIV'S REGENCY.
YES...
IT'S OVER THREE HUNDRED AND FIFTY YEARS OLD.
YES. APPARENTLY PART OF A LARGER COLLECTION OF FOUQUET'S EFFECTS AND DOCUMENTS SEIZED BY LOUIS XIV AFTER FOUQUET'S IMPRISONMENT...
IMPRISONMENT?
WE MUST SEE THOSE LETTERS!

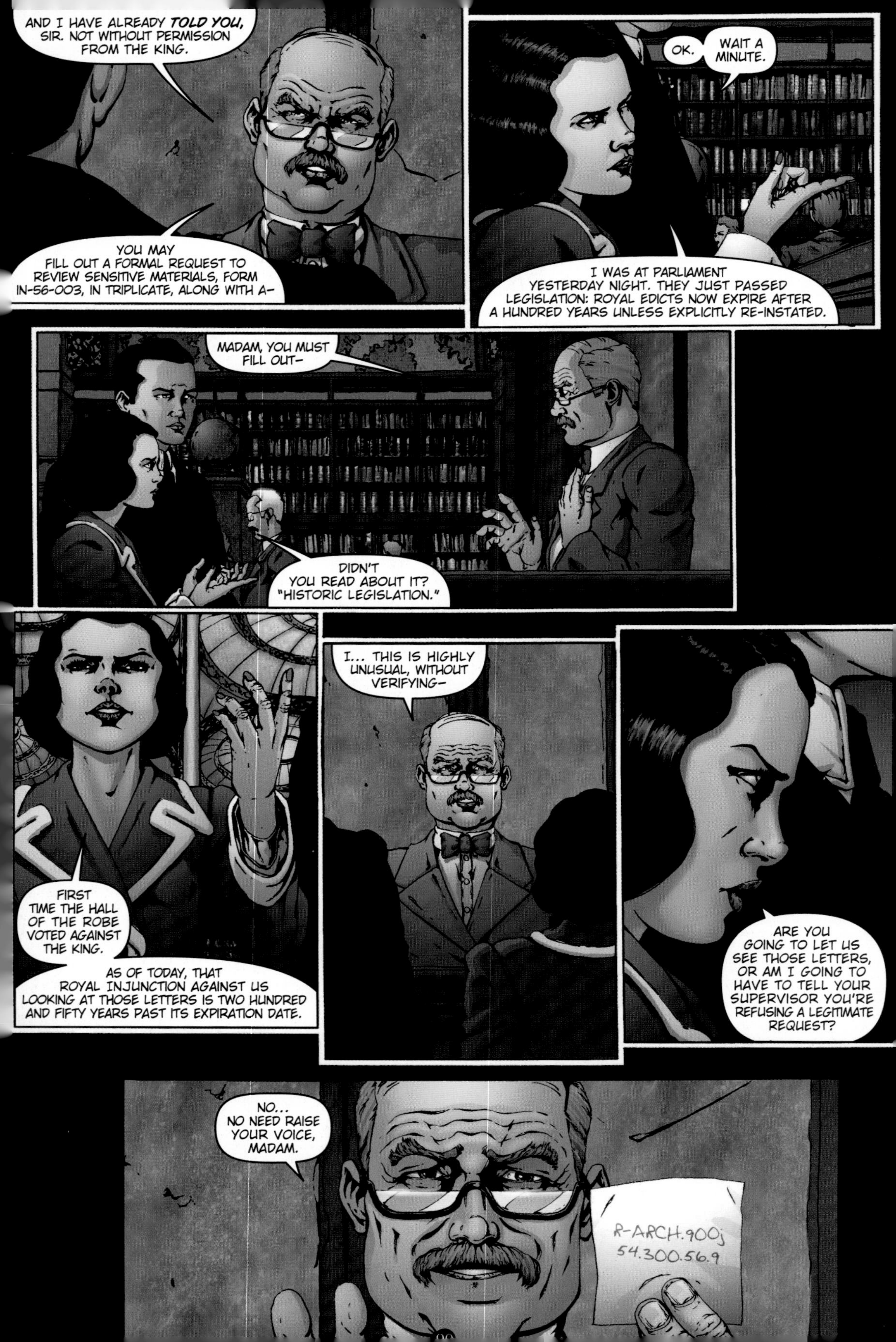
AND I HAVE ALREADY *TOLD YOU,* SIR. NOT WITHOUT PERMISSION FROM THE KING.
YOU MAY FILL OUT A FORMAL REQUEST TO REVIEW SENSITIVE MATERIALS, FORM IN-56-003, IN TRIPLICATE, ALONG WITH A-
OK.
WAIT A MINUTE.
I WAS AT PARLIAMENT YESTERDAY NIGHT. THEY JUST PASSED LEGISLATION: ROYAL EDICTS NOW EXPIRE AFTER A HUNDRED YEARS UNLESS EXPLICITLY RE-INSTATED.
MADAM, YOU MUST FILL OUT-
DIDN'T YOU READ ABOUT IT? "HISTORIC LEGISLATION."
FIRST TIME THE HALL OF THE ROBE VOTED AGAINST THE KING.
AS OF TODAY, THAT ROYAL INJUNCTION AGAINST US LOOKING AT THOSE LETTERS IS TWO HUNDRED AND FIFTY YEARS PAST ITS EXPIRATION DATE.
I... THIS IS HIGHLY UNUSUAL, WITHOUT VERIFYING-
ARE YOU GOING TO LET US SEE THOSE LETTERS, OR AM I GOING TO HAVE TO TELL YOUR SUPERVISOR YOU'RE REFUSING A LEGITIMATE REQUEST?
NO... NO NEED RAISE YOUR VOICE, MADAM.
R-ARCH.900j
54.300.56.9

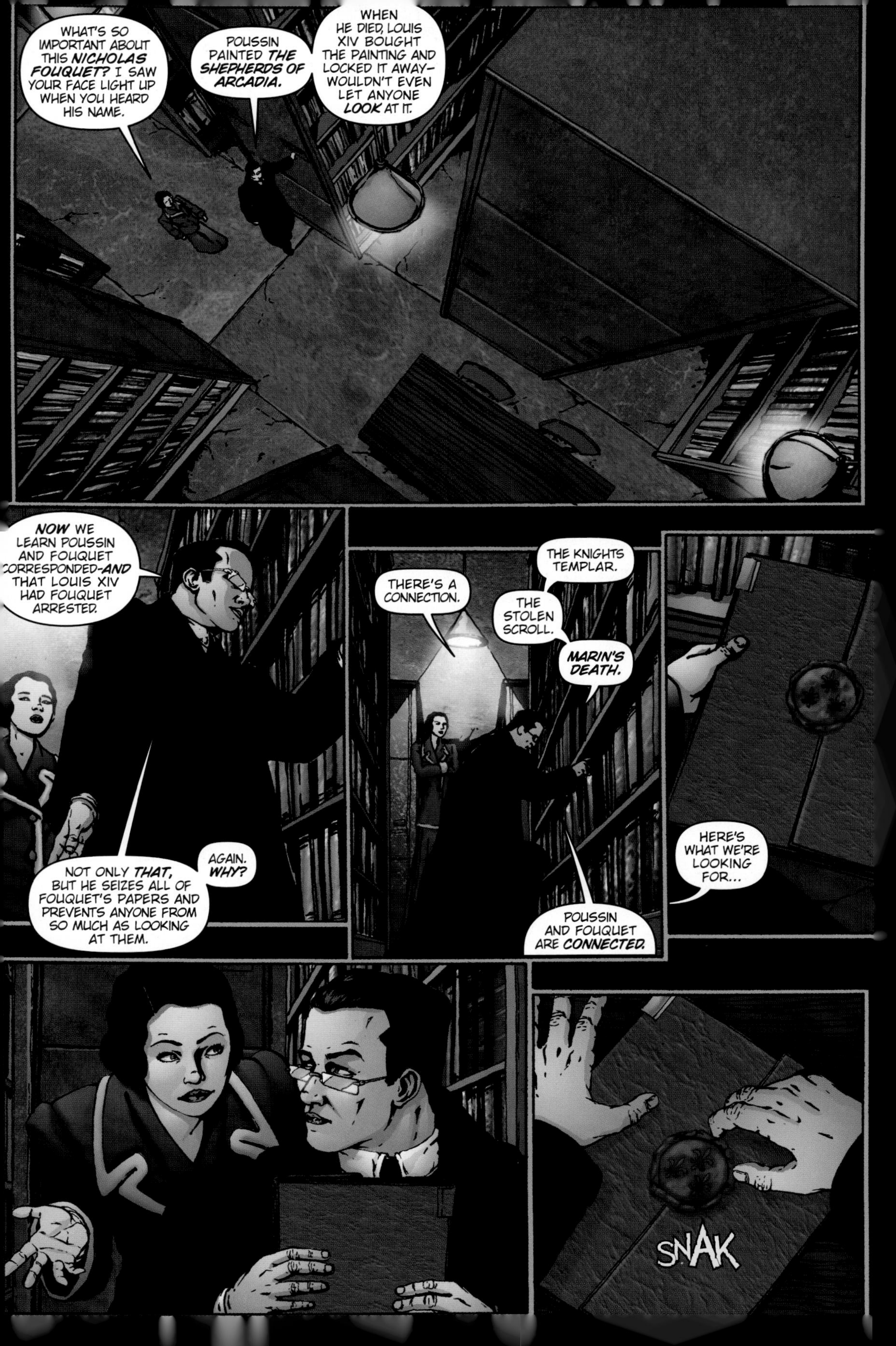
WHAT'S SO IMPORTANT ABOUT THIS NICHOLAS FOUQUET? I SAW YOUR FACE LIGHT UP WHEN YOU HEARD HIS NAME.
POUSSIN PAINTED THE SHEPHERDS OF ARCADIA.
WHEN HE DIED, LOUIS XIV BOUGHT THE PAINTING AND LOCKED IT AWAY--WOULDN'T EVEN LET ANYONE LOOK AT IT.
NOW WE LEARN POUSSIN AND FOUQUET CORRESPONDED--AND THAT LOUIS XIV HAD FOUQUET ARRESTED.
NOT ONLY THAT, BUT HE SEIZES ALL OF FOUQUET'S PAPERS AND PREVENTS ANYONE FROM SO MUCH AS LOOKING AT THEM.
AGAIN. WHY?
THERE'S A CONNECTION.
THE KNIGHTS TEMPLAR.
THE STOLEN SCROLL.
MARIN'S DEATH.
POUSSIN AND FOUQUET ARE CONNECTED.
HERE'S WHAT WE'RE LOOKING FOR...
SNAK

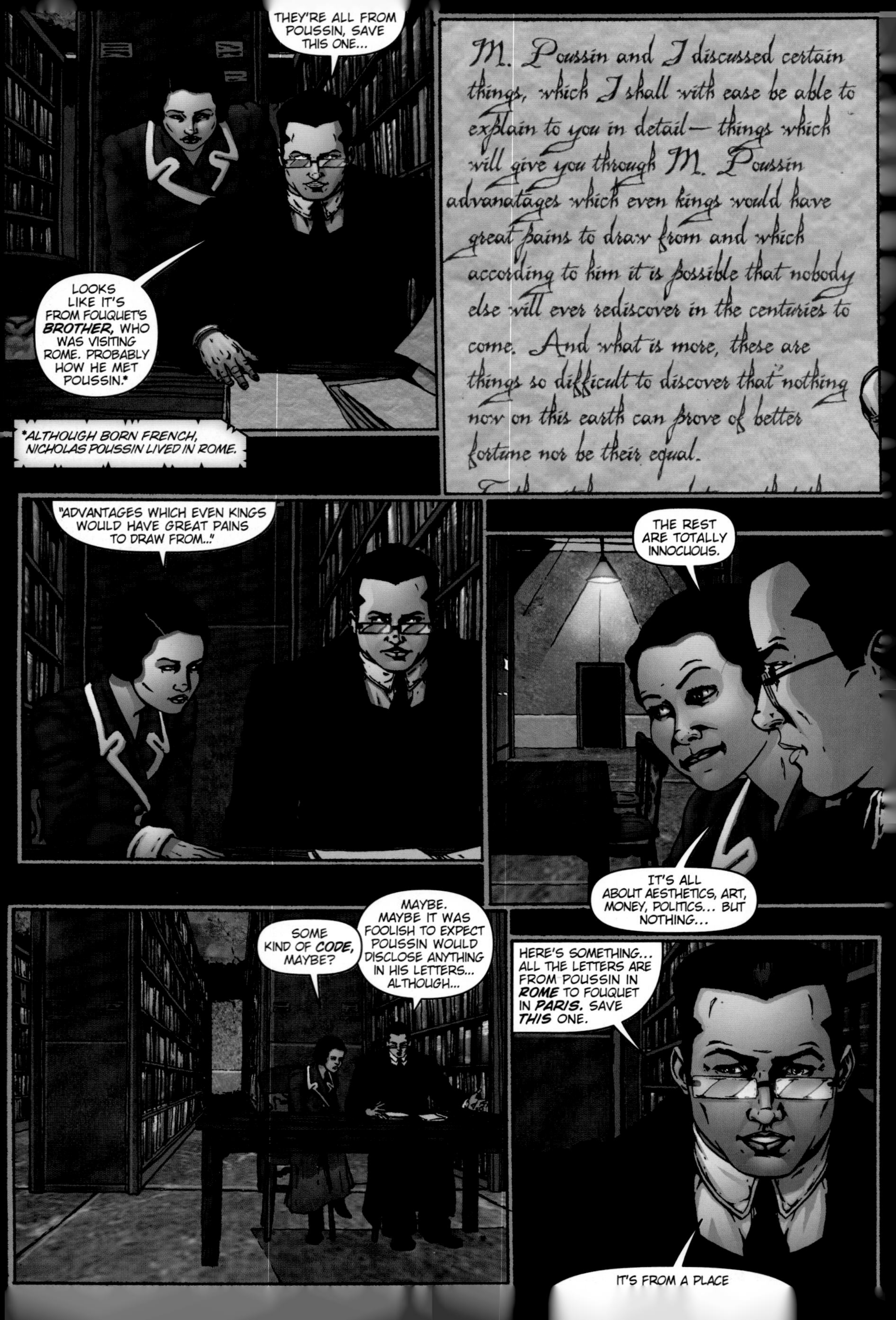
THEY'RE ALL FROM POUSSIN, SAVE THIS ONE...
LOOKS LIKE IT'S FROM FOUQUET'S BROTHER, WHO WAS VISITING ROME. PROBABLY HOW HE MET POUSSIN.*
*ALTHOUGH BORN FRENCH, NICHOLAS POUSSIN LIVED IN ROME.
M. Poussin and I discussed certain things, which I shall with ease be able to explain to you in detail— things which will give you through M. Poussin advanatages which even kings would have great pains to draw from and which according to him it is possible that nobody else will ever rediscover in the centuries to come. And what is more, these are things so difficult to discover that nothing now on this earth can prove of better fortune nor be their equal.
"ADVANTAGES WHICH EVEN KINGS WOULD HAVE GREAT PAINS TO DRAW FROM..."
THE REST ARE TOTALLY INNOCUOUS.
IT'S ALL ABOUT AESTHETICS, ART, MONEY, POLITICS... BUT NOTHING...
SOME KIND OF CODE, MAYBE?
MAYBE. MAYBE IT WAS FOOLISH TO EXPECT POUSSIN WOULD DISCLOSE ANYTHING IN HIS LETTERS... ALTHOUGH...
HERE'S SOMETHING... ALL THE LETTERS ARE FROM POUSSIN IN ROME TO FOUQUET IN PARIS. SAVE THIS ONE.
IT'S FROM A PLACE

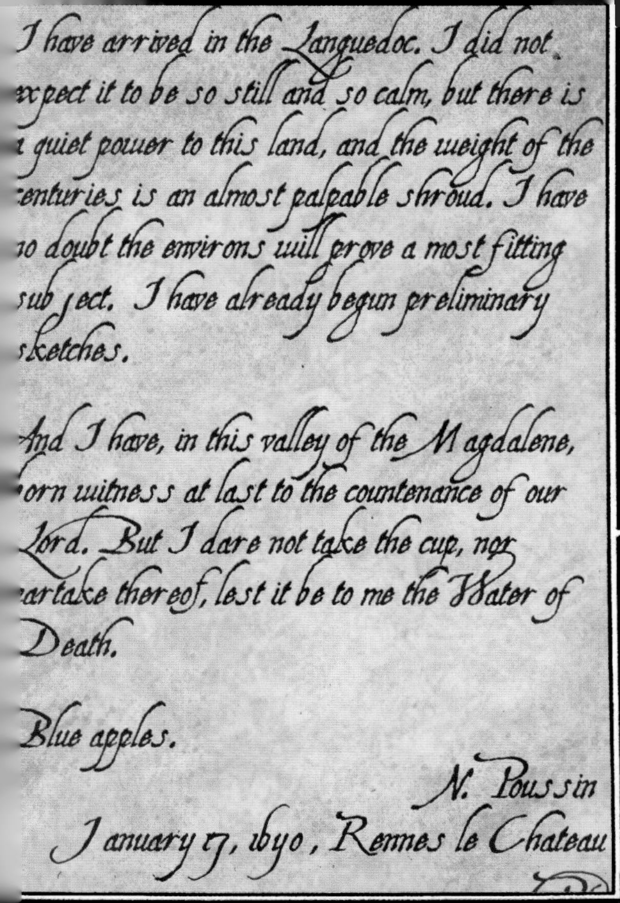

I have arrived in the Languedoc. I did not expect it to be so still and so calm, but there is a quiet power to this land, and the weight of the centuries is an almost palpable shroud. I have no doubt the environs will prove a most fitting subject. I have already begun preliminary sketches.

And I have, in this valley of the Magdalene, born witness at last to the countenance of our Lord. But I dare not take the cup, nor partake thereof, lest it be to me the Water of Death.

Blue apples.

N. Poussin

January 17, 1670, Rennes le Chateau

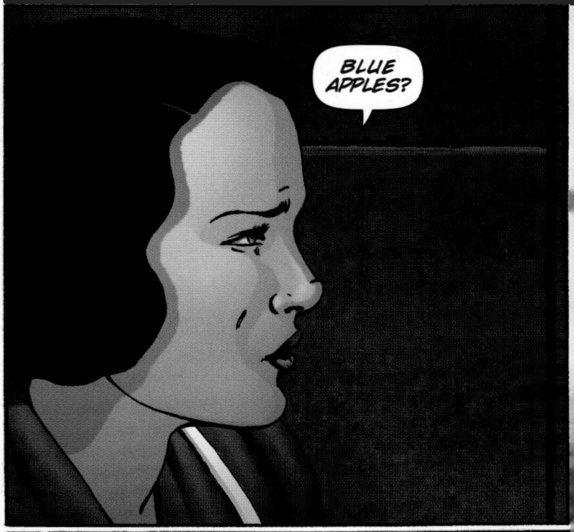
BLUE APPLES?

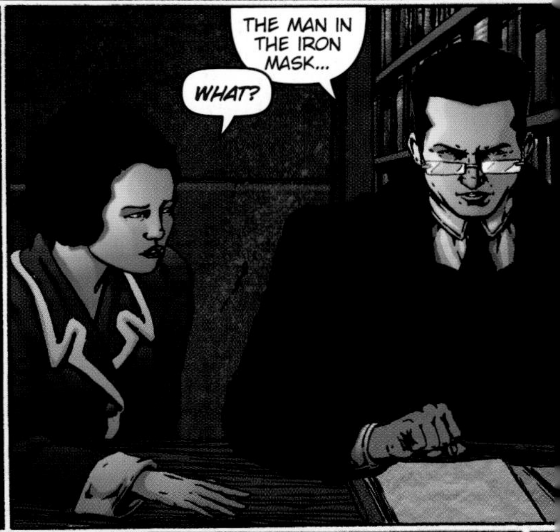
THE MAN IN THE IRON MASK...
WHAT?

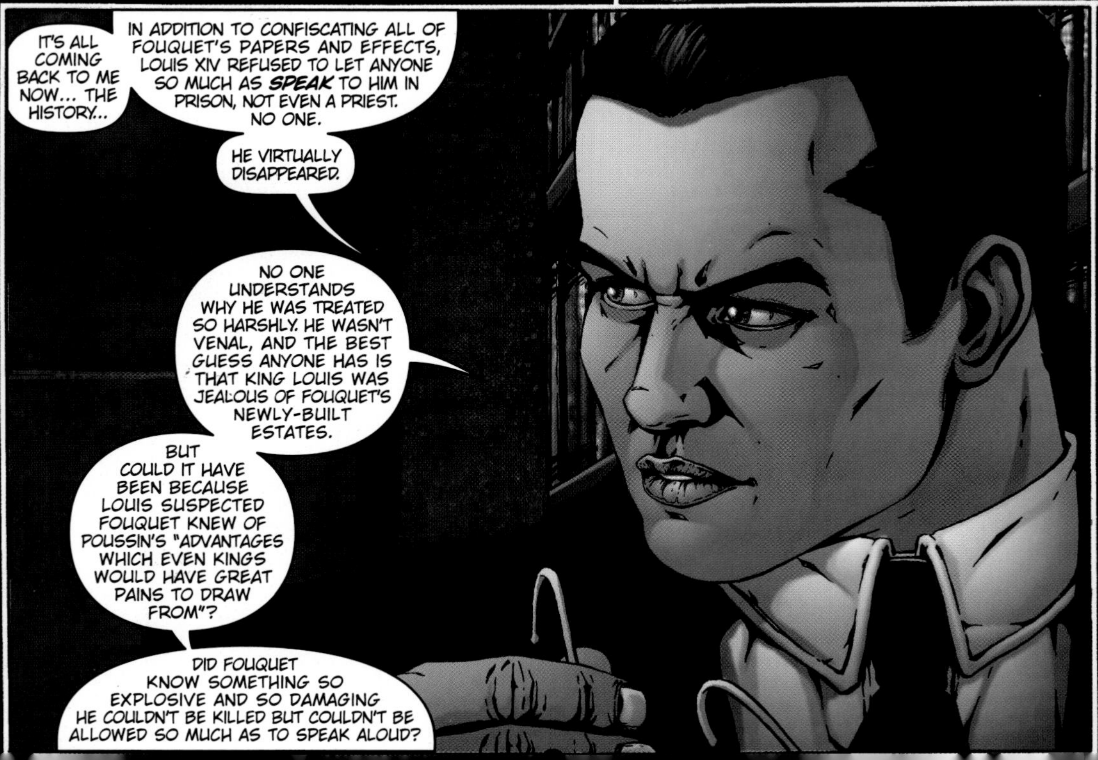
IT'S ALL COMING BACK TO ME NOW... THE HISTORY...
IN ADDITION TO CONFISCATING ALL OF FOUQUET'S PAPERS AND EFFECTS, LOUIS XIV REFUSED TO LET ANYONE SO MUCH AS SPEAK TO HIM IN PRISON, NOT EVEN A PRIEST. NO ONE.
HE VIRTUALLY DISAPPEARED.
NO ONE UNDERSTANDS WHY HE WAS TREATED SO HARSHLY. HE WASN'T VENAL, AND THE BEST GUESS ANYONE HAS IS THAT KING LOUIS WAS JEALOUS OF FOUQUET'S NEWLY-BUILT ESTATES.
BUT COULD IT HAVE BEEN BECAUSE LOUIS SUSPECTED FOUQUET KNEW OF POUSSIN'S "ADVANTAGES WHICH EVEN KINGS WOULD HAVE GREAT PAINS TO DRAW FROM"?
DID FOUQUET KNOW SOMETHING SO EXPLOSIVE AND SO DAMAGING HE COULDN'T BE KILLED BUT COULDN'T BE ALLOWED SO MUCH AS TO SPEAK ALOUD?

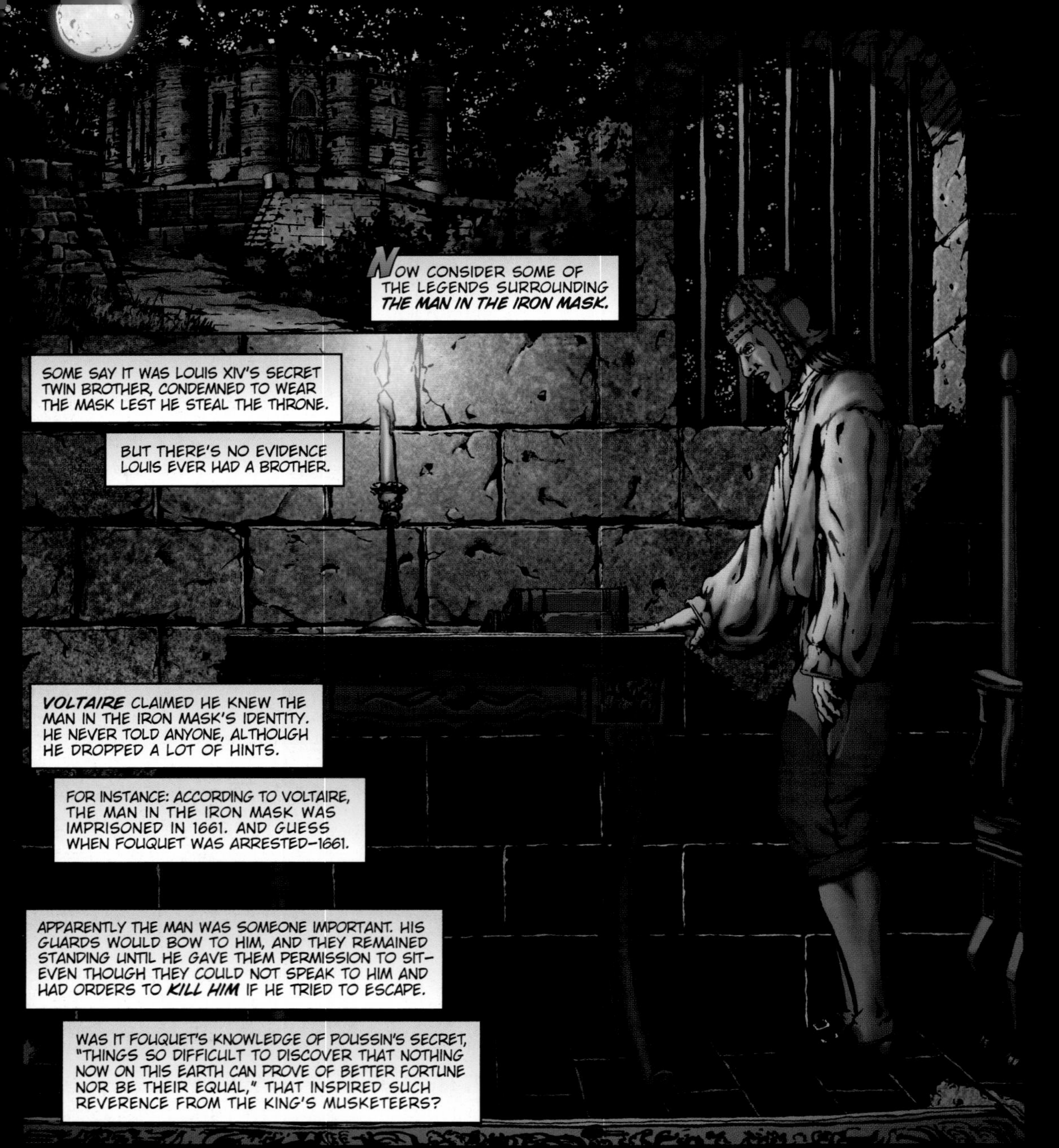
NOW CONSIDER SOME OF THE LEGENDS SURROUNDING ***THE MAN IN THE IRON MASK.***
SOME SAY IT WAS LOUIS XIV'S SECRET TWIN BROTHER, CONDEMNED TO WEAR THE MASK LEST HE STEAL THE THRONE.
BUT THERE'S NO EVIDENCE LOUIS EVER HAD A BROTHER.
VOLTAIRE CLAIMED HE KNEW THE MAN IN THE IRON MASK'S IDENTITY. HE NEVER TOLD ANYONE, ALTHOUGH HE DROPPED A LOT OF HINTS.
FOR INSTANCE: ACCORDING TO VOLTAIRE, THE MAN IN THE IRON MASK WAS IMPRISONED IN 1661. AND GUESS WHEN FOUQUET WAS ARRESTED—1661.
APPARENTLY THE MAN WAS SOMEONE IMPORTANT. HIS GUARDS WOULD BOW TO HIM, AND THEY REMAINED STANDING UNTIL HE GAVE THEM PERMISSION TO SIT—EVEN THOUGH THEY COULD NOT SPEAK TO HIM AND HAD ORDERS TO ***KILL HIM*** IF HE TRIED TO ESCAPE.
WAS IT FOUQUET'S KNOWLEDGE OF POUSSIN'S SECRET, "THINGS SO DIFFICULT TO DISCOVER THAT NOTHING NOW ON THIS EARTH CAN PROVE OF BETTER FORTUNE NOR BE THEIR EQUAL," THAT INSPIRED SUCH REVERENCE FROM THE KING'S MUSKETEERS?

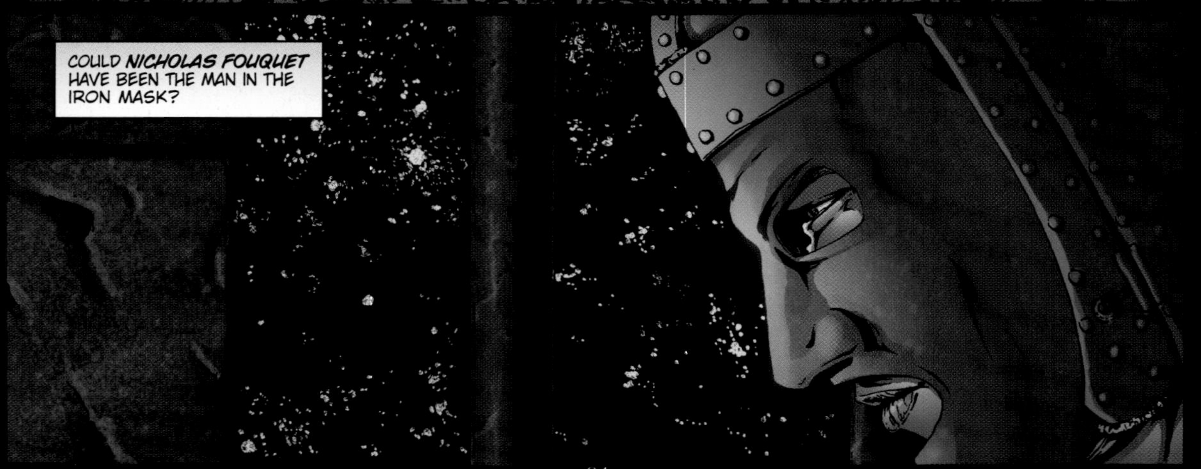
COULD ***NICHOLAS FOUQUET*** HAVE BEEN THE MAN IN THE IRON MASK?

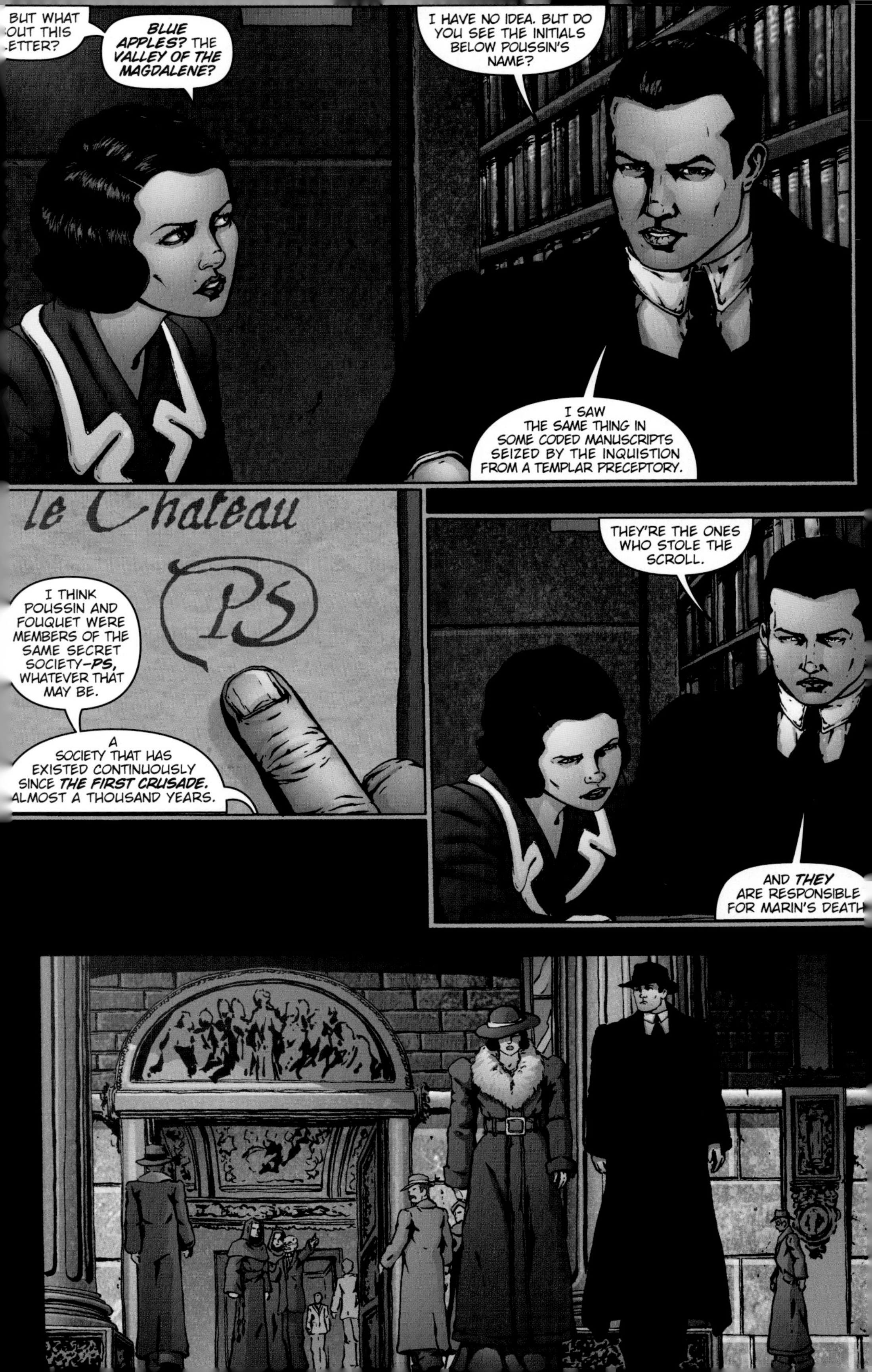
BUT WHAT OUT THIS ETTER?
BLUE APPLES? THE VALLEY OF THE MAGDALENE?
I HAVE NO IDEA. BUT DO YOU SEE THE INITIALS BELOW POUSSIN'S NAME?
I SAW THE SAME THING IN SOME CODED MANUSCRIPTS SEIZED BY THE INQUISTION FROM A TEMPLAR PRECEPTORY.
le Chateau
PS
I THINK POUSSIN AND FOUQUET WERE MEMBERS OF THE SAME SECRET SOCIETY–PS, WHATEVER THAT MAY BE.
A SOCIETY THAT HAS EXISTED CONTINUOUSLY SINCE THE FIRST CRUSADE. ALMOST A THOUSAND YEARS.
THEY'RE THE ONES WHO STOLE THE SCROLL.
AND THEY ARE RESPONSIBLE FOR MARIN'S DEATH

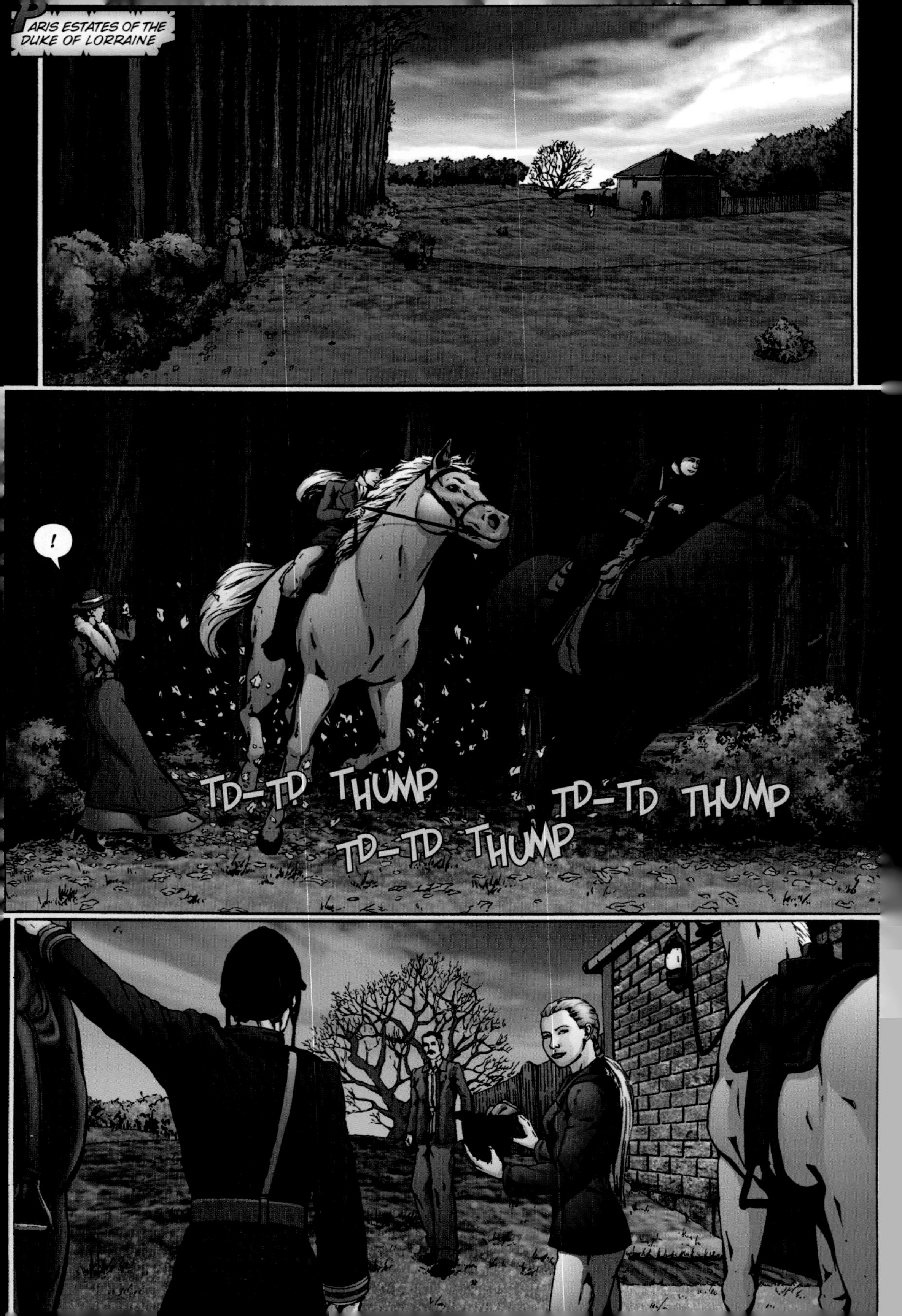
PARIS ESTATES OF THE DUKE OF LORRAINE
!
TD-TD THUMP
TD-TD THUMP
TD-TD THUMP

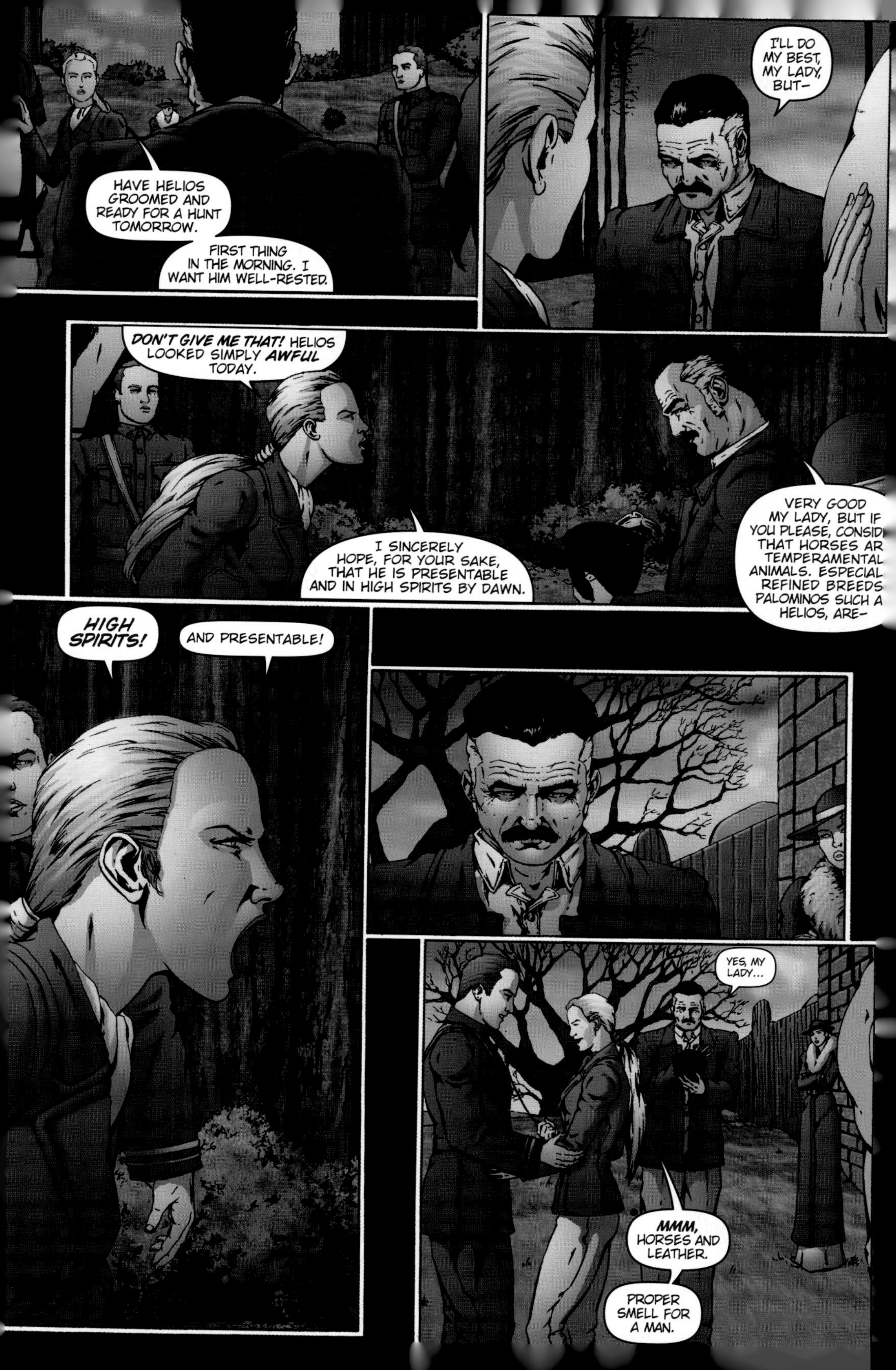
HAVE HELIOS GROOMED AND READY FOR A HUNT TOMORROW.
FIRST THING IN THE MORNING. I WANT HIM WELL-RESTED.
I'LL DO MY BEST, MY LADY, BUT-
DON'T GIVE ME THAT! HELIOS LOOKED SIMPLY AWFUL TODAY.
I SINCERELY HOPE, FOR YOUR SAKE, THAT HE IS PRESENTABLE AND IN HIGH SPIRITS BY DAWN.
VERY GOOD MY LADY, BUT IF YOU PLEASE, CONSID THAT HORSES AR TEMPERAMENTAL ANIMALS. ESPECIAL REFINED BREEDS PALOMINOS SUCH A HELIOS, ARE-
HIGH SPIRITS!
AND PRESENTABLE!
YES, MY LADY...
MMM, HORSES AND LEATHER.
PROPER SMELL FOR A MAN.

CARE TO GIVE ME ANOTHER RIDING LESSON?

WHY, YES MY LADY. AND I DARESAY THE CURRICULUM WILL BE TO YOUR LIKING.

PRAY, DON'T SPARE THE CROP.

SHE TREATS ANIMALS BETTER THAN PEOPLE.

ALL IN A DAY'S WORK, DOCTOR TOURNON.

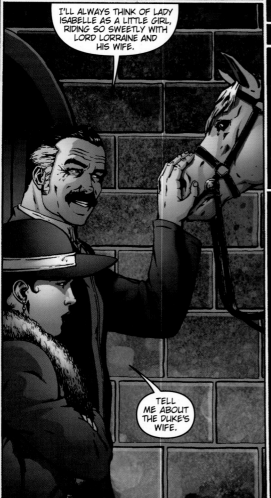

I'LL ALWAYS THINK OF LADY ISABELLE AS A LITTLE GIRL, RIDING SO SWEETLY WITH LORD LORRAINE AND HIS WIFE.

TELL ME ABOUT THE DUKE'S WIFE.

SHE WAS FROM AN OLD FAMILY WITH MORE PRESTIGE THAN MONEY, BUT LORD LORRAINE LOVED HER VERY MUCH. WHEN THEY WERE NEWLYWED HIS FAMILY FORTUNE WAS ALL BUT GONE— HE HAD TO SELL MOST OF HIS LAND.

MYSELF AND A FEW OTHER SERVANTS WERE ALL THEY COULD AFFORD TO KEEP ON. BUT THEY NEVER SEEMED TO PAY IT ANY MIND, THEY WERE JUST HAPPY TO BE TOGETHER.

WHEN THEIR DAUGHTER CAME ALONG, IT SEEMED LIKE EVERYTHING WAS... JUST... RIGHT WITH THE WORLD. NOT ONLY FOR THEM, BUT FOR US TOO, THE SERVANTS. LIKE THE YEARS WERE SPUN OUT OF GOLD.

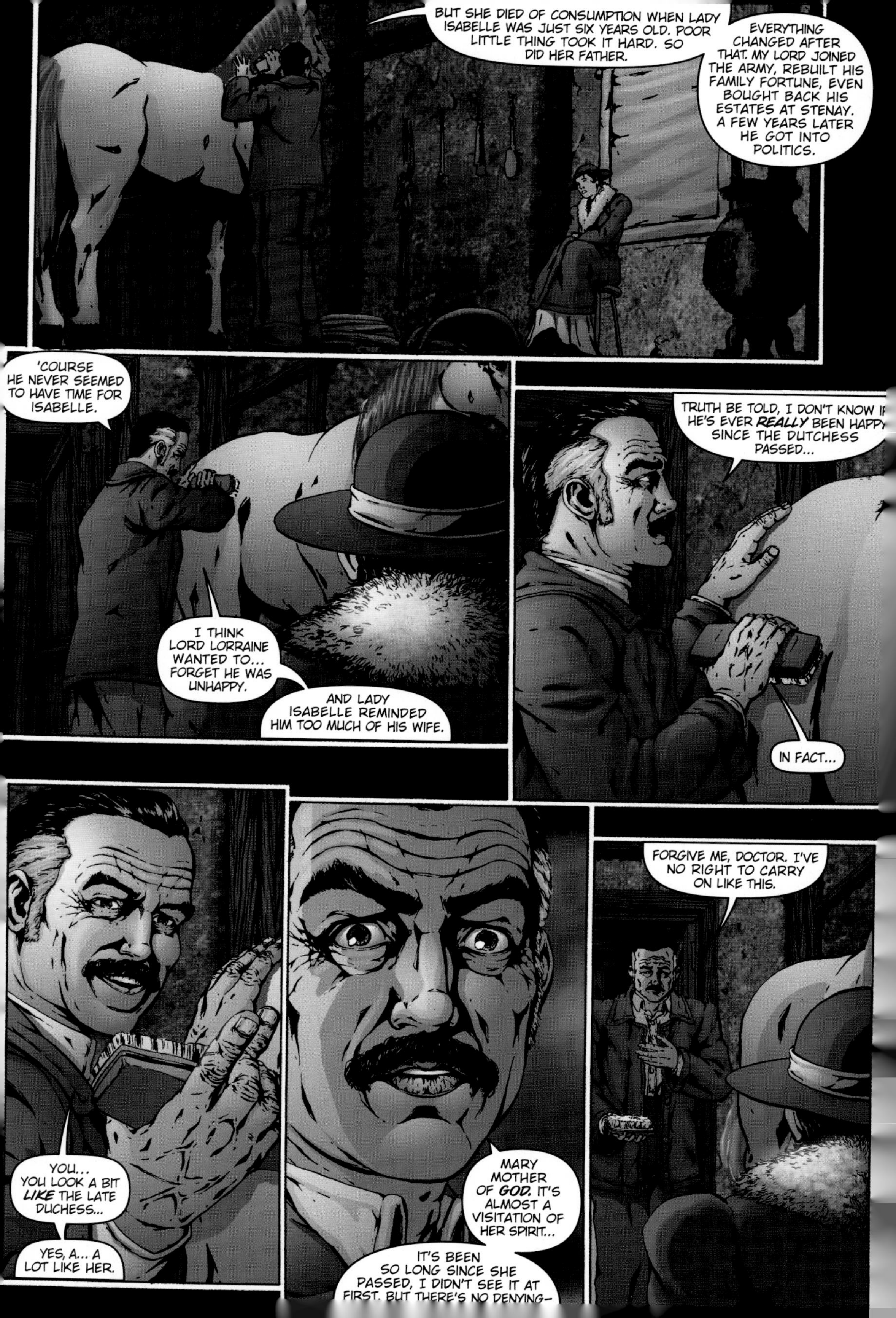
BUT SHE DIED OF CONSUMPTION WHEN LADY ISABELLE WAS JUST SIX YEARS OLD. POOR LITTLE THING TOOK IT HARD. SO DID HER FATHER.
EVERYTHING CHANGED AFTER THAT. MY LORD JOINED THE ARMY, REBUILT HIS FAMILY FORTUNE, EVEN BOUGHT BACK HIS ESTATES AT STENAY. A FEW YEARS LATER HE GOT INTO POLITICS.
'COURSE HE NEVER SEEMED TO HAVE TIME FOR ISABELLE.
I THINK LORD LORRAINE WANTED TO... FORGET HE WAS UNHAPPY.
AND LADY ISABELLE REMINDED HIM TOO MUCH OF HIS WIFE.
TRUTH BE TOLD, I DON'T KNOW IF HE'S EVER ***REALLY*** BEEN HAPPY SINCE THE DUTCHESS PASSED...
IN FACT...
YOU... YOU LOOK A BIT ***LIKE*** THE LATE DUCHESS...
YES, A... A LOT LIKE HER.
MARY MOTHER OF ***GOD.*** IT'S ALMOST A VISITATION OF HER SPIRIT...
IT'S BEEN SO LONG SINCE SHE PASSED, I DIDN'T SEE IT AT FIRST. BUT THERE'S NO DENYING–
FORGIVE ME, DOCTOR. I'VE NO RIGHT TO CARRY ON LIKE THIS.

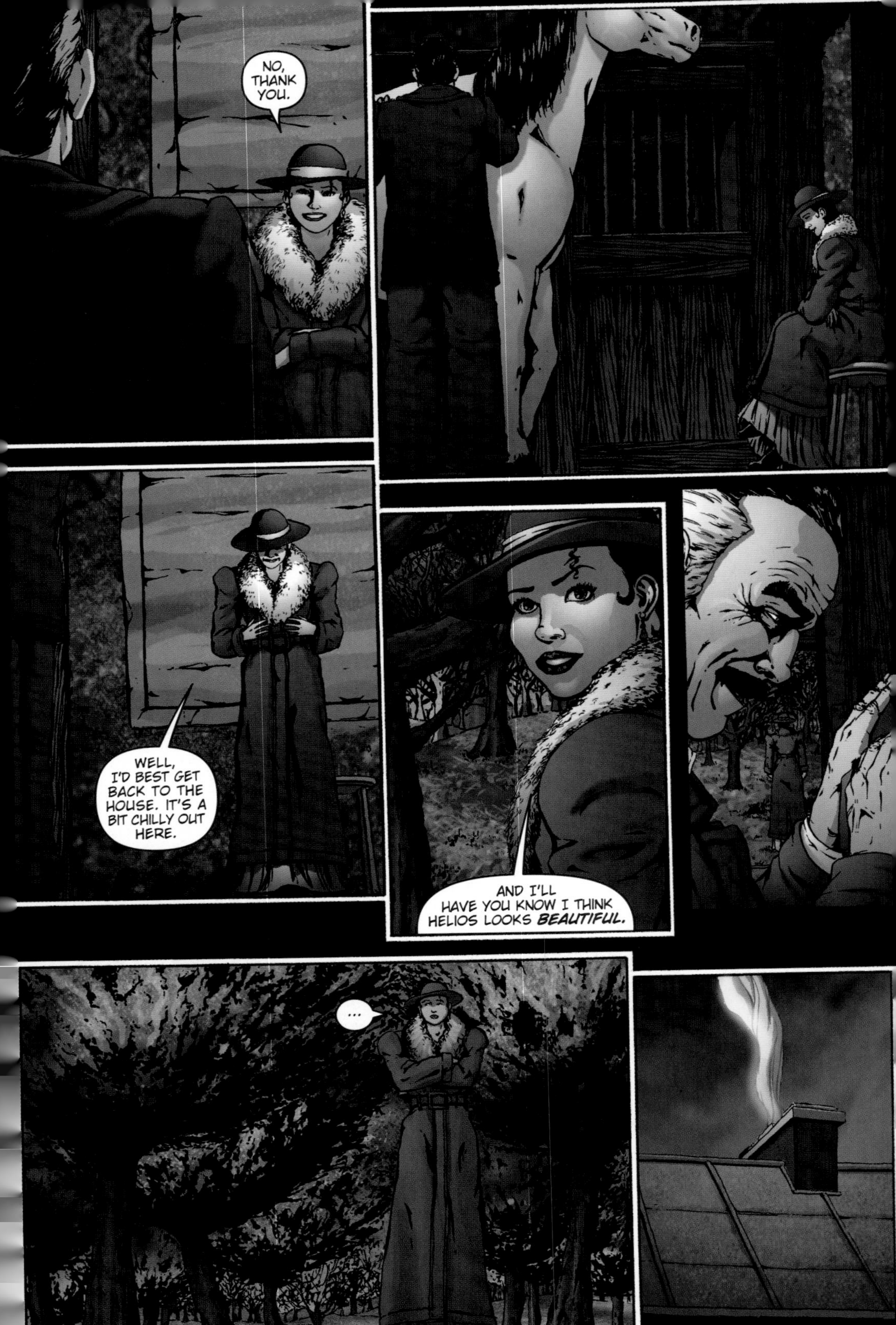
NO, THANK YOU.
WELL, I'D BEST GET BACK TO THE HOUSE. IT'S A BIT CHILLY OUT HERE.
AND I'LL HAVE YOU KNOW I THINK HELIOS LOOKS **BEAUTIFUL.**
...

AMANDE PLANTARD DE ST. CLA
XXXIV DUCHESS OF LORRAI

Beloved Wife
1895–1921

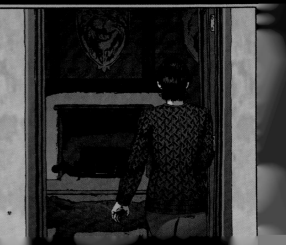

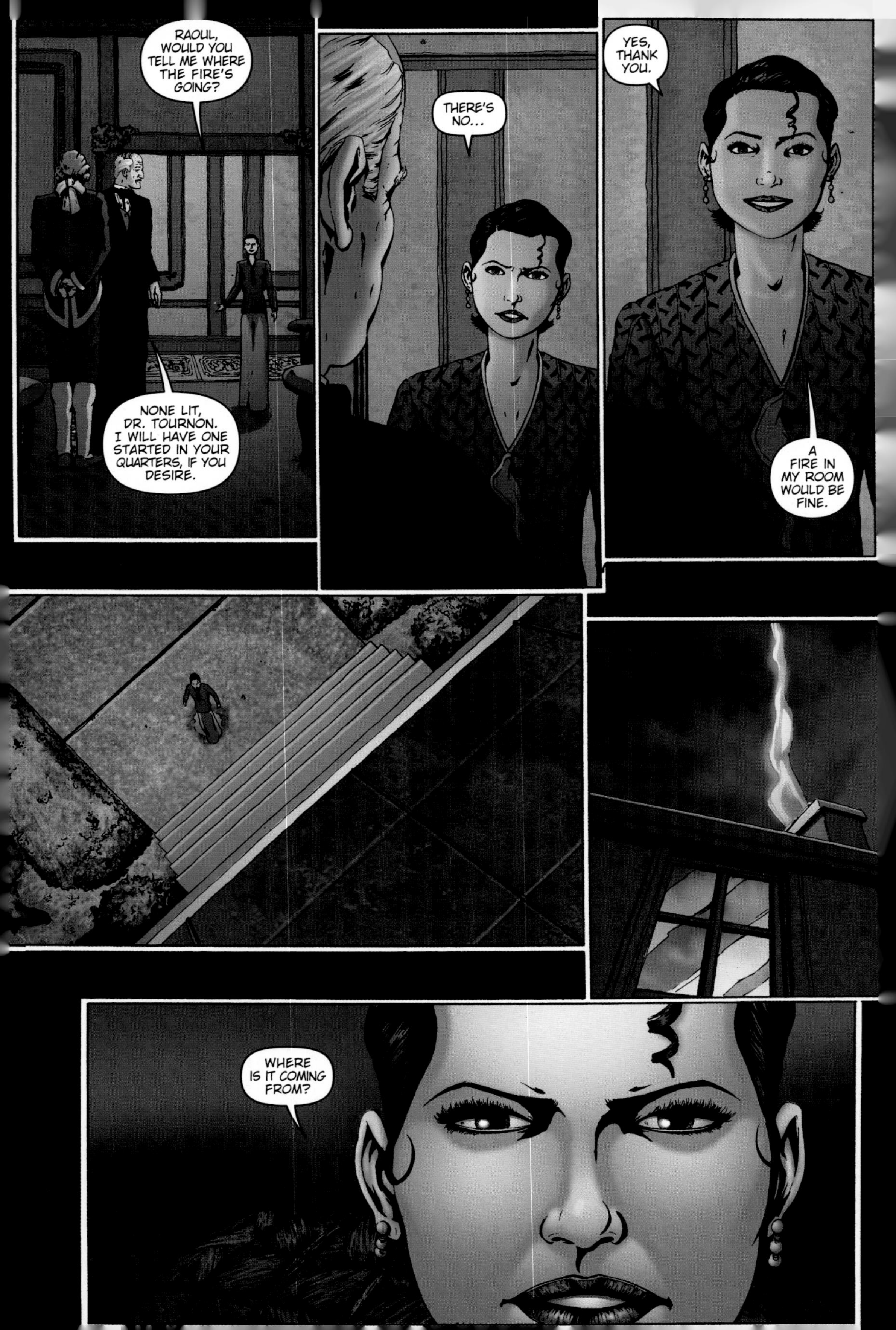
RAOUL, WOULD YOU TELL ME WHERE THE FIRE'S GOING?
NONE LIT, DR. TOURNON. I WILL HAVE ONE STARTED IN YOUR QUARTERS, IF YOU DESIRE.
THERE'S NO...
YES, THANK YOU.
A FIRE IN MY ROOM WOULD BE FINE.
WHERE IS IT COMING FROM?

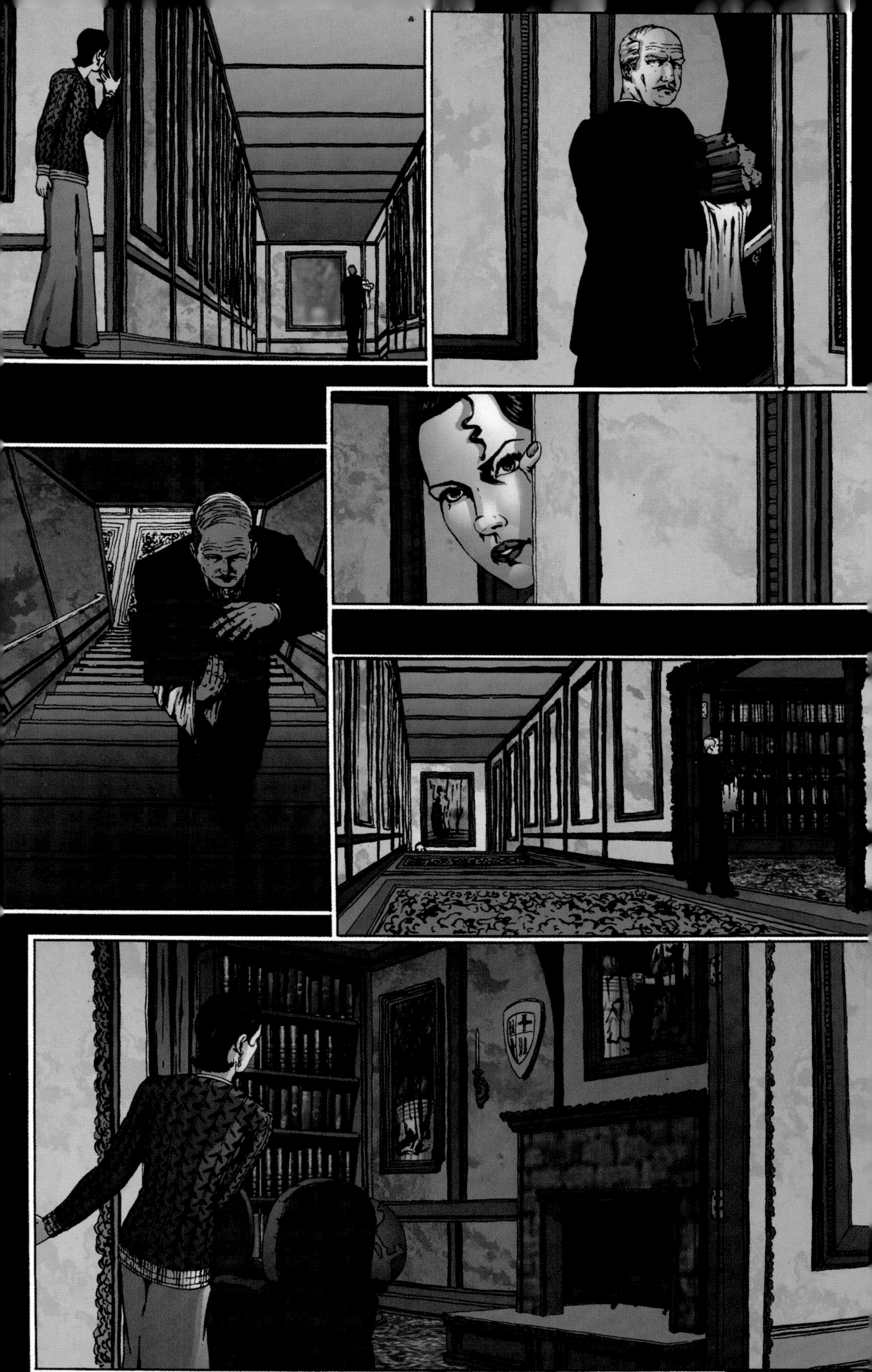

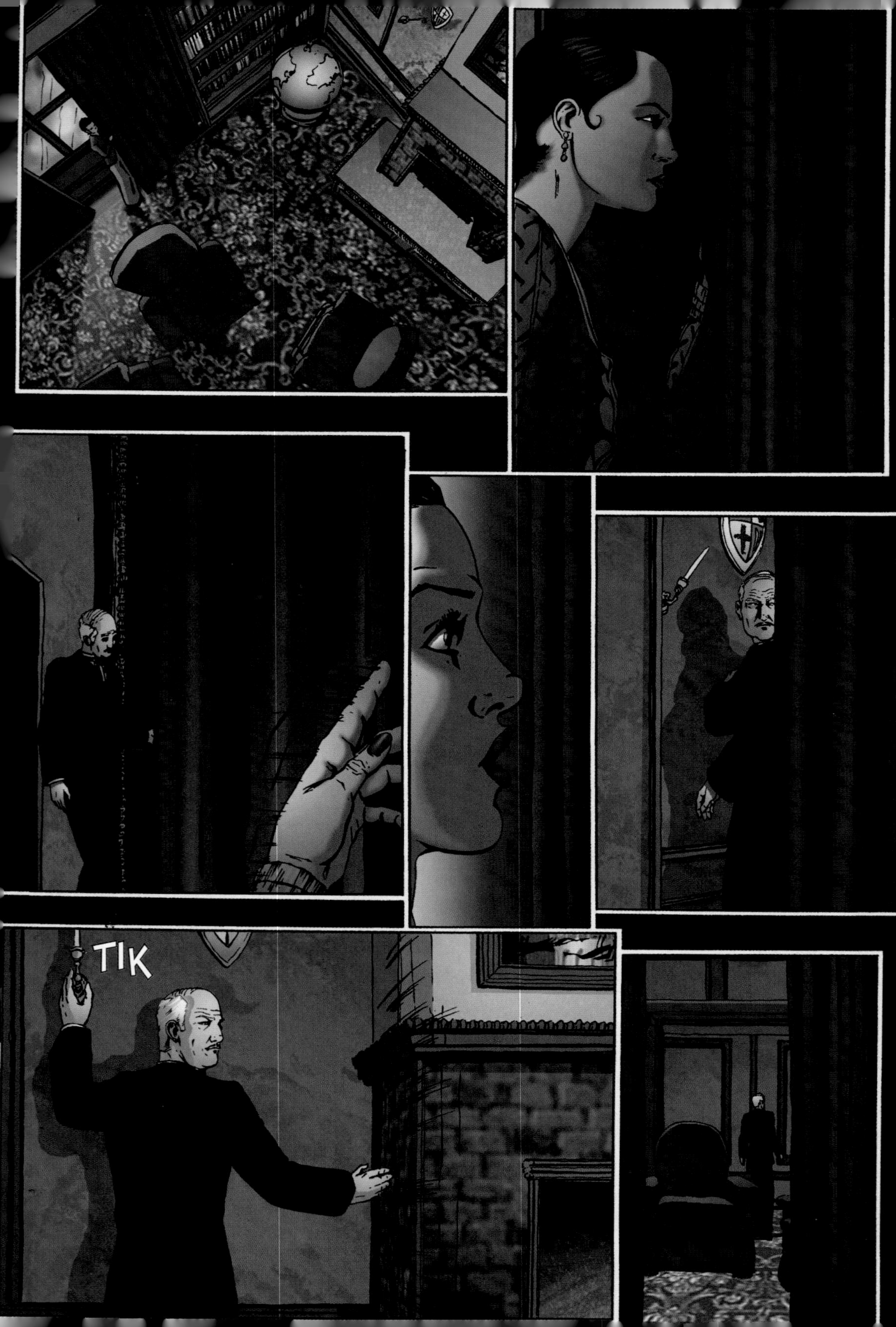
TIK

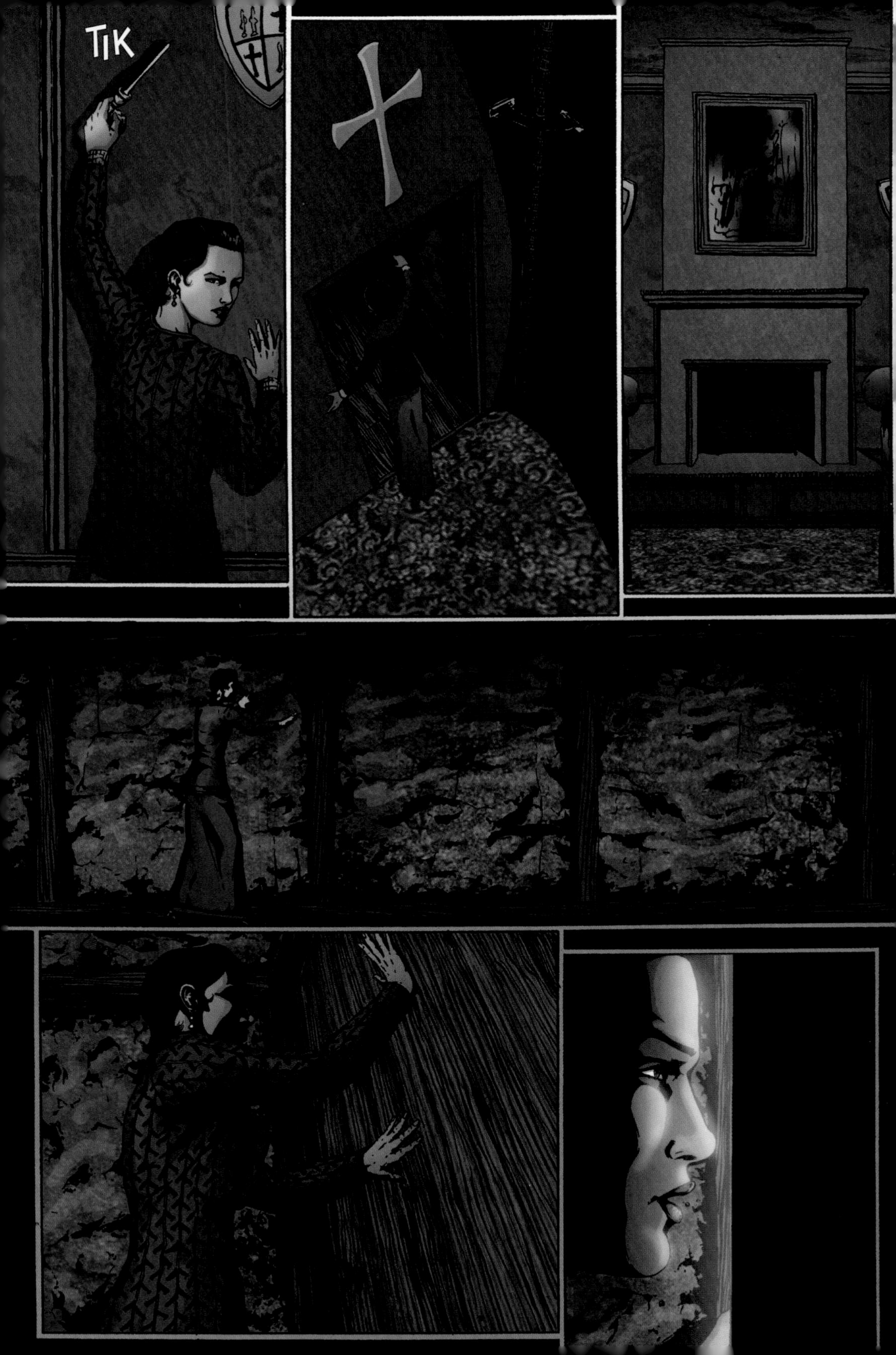
TIK

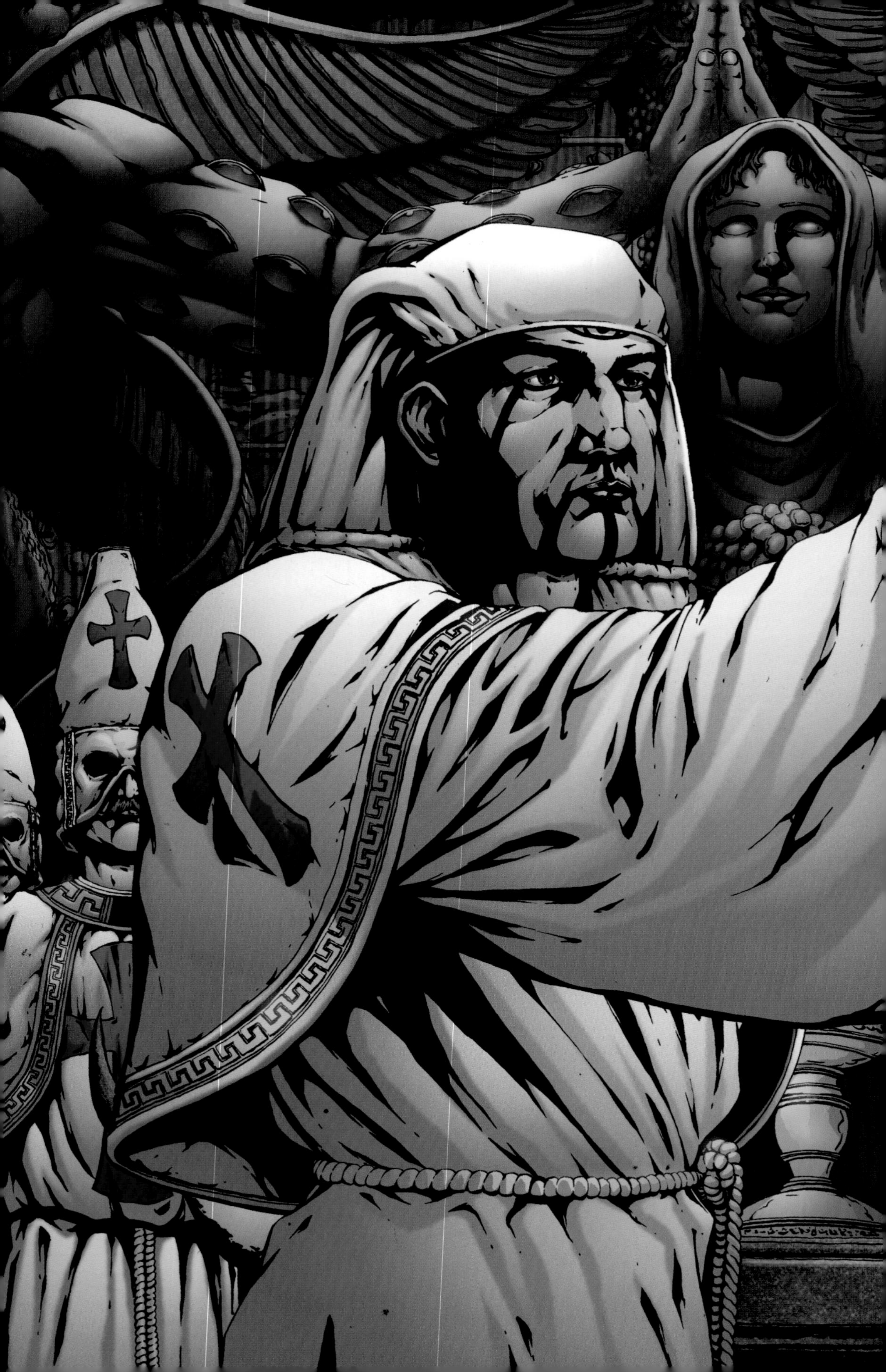

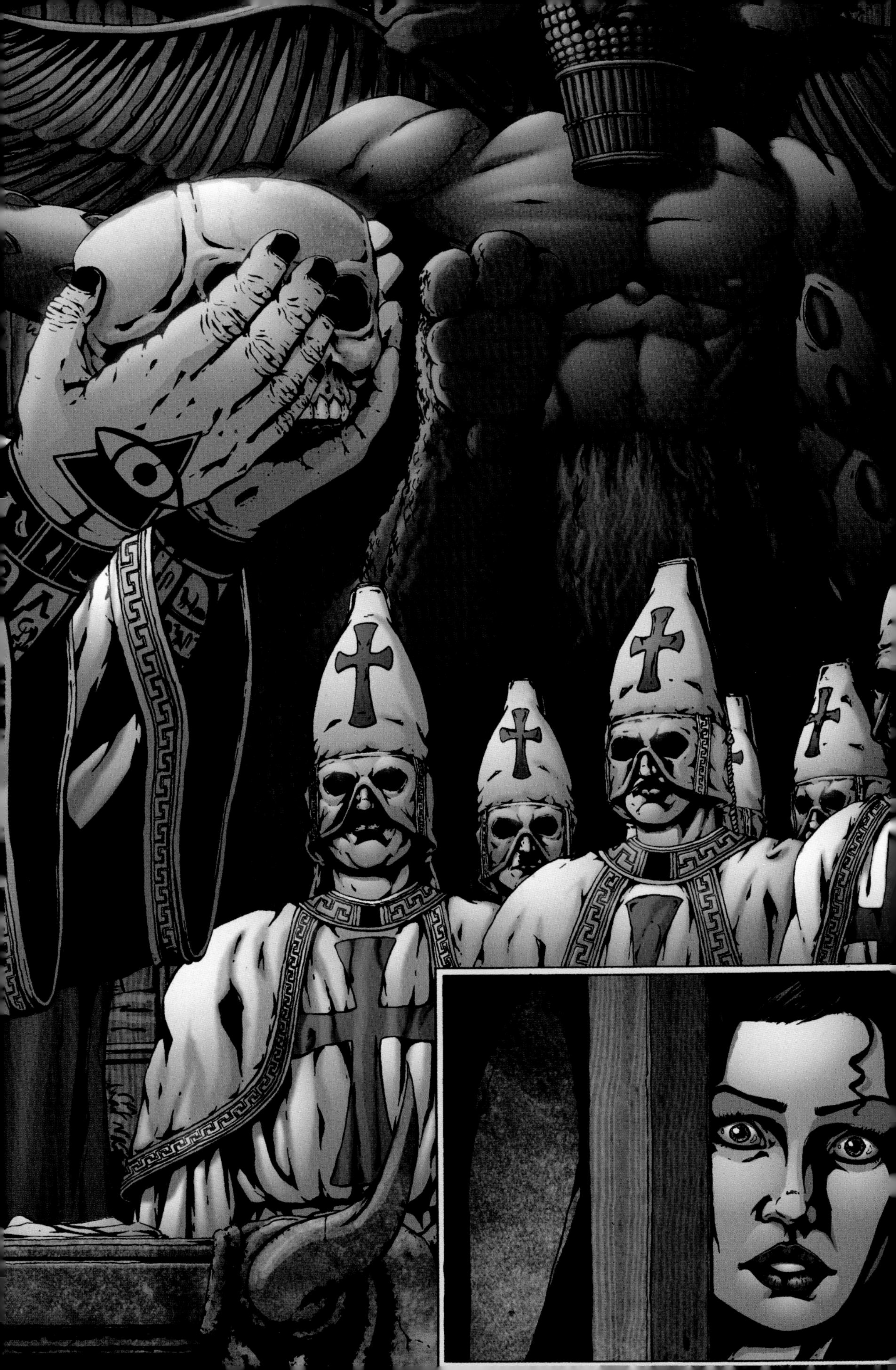

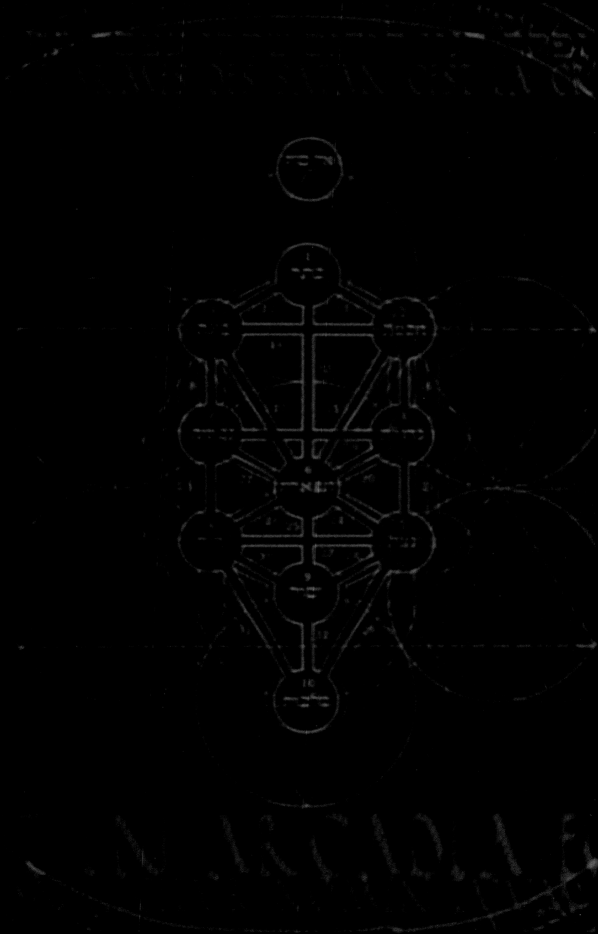

Le Journal de la Liberté

Paris' leading anglophone newspaper • vol. 205, no. 103 • Oct. 26, MCMXXXIII

Papal Seal

Editors in Chief: M. Tait Bergstrom, M. Matthew Pasteris. **Story Editor:** M. Arvid Nelson. **Art Editors:** M. EricJ, M. Jeromy Cox. **Photography Editor:** M. Alexander Waldman. **Layout Supervisor:** M. William Kartalopoulos. **Editors Emeritus:** M. Clark A. Smith, M. Howard P. Lovecraft, M. Robert E. Howard. Redacted by the Holy Parisian Inquisition under the direction of His Excellency Archbishop Emile-Jean Ireneaux. Le Journal de la Liberté is printed under the benign auspices of his most puissant majesty KING LOUIS XXII of FRANCE. GOD SAVE THE KING.

of Approval

HALL OF THE ROBE VOTES AGAINST KING ON DOMESTIC LEGISLATION

New law is "innocuous," but political implications might foreshadow a rebellion in Parliament

The Assemblé Nationale, sight of the "betrayal" of the Crown.

The bill passed into law yesterday night is hardly worth mentioning. But the way in which it was passed could signal historic changes in France's political landscape.

For the first time ever, both houses of Parliament – the Hall of the Sword and the Hall of the Robe – acted in unison against the will of the King.

King Louis XXII's advisors and spokesmen made it clear they were disappointed by passage of the law, which was introduced by the Count of Toulouse in Hall of the Sword several weeks earlier.

The bill called for an expiration of royal injunctions after 100 years. It passed by a wide margin in the Sword, as was expected.

The broad support for the bill in the Hall of the Robe was not.

According to Jean-Alexis Moncorge, a political advisor to the Hall of the Sword, the Crown has never once lost a fight with Parliament.

"Every time legislation has passed into law under our current system of government, it has either been a three 'yeas', or the Hall of the Robe and the Crown have overpowered the Sword," Moncorge said. "Until now, the Robe has always voted with the King."

This is because the King has the exclusive right to appoint members to the lower house of French parliament, the Hall of the Robe. The King has always stocked the Robe with his most devoted supporters.

But the presumed fealty of the Robe to the King was called into question yesterday.

"This is the first time the Robe has voted against the King," Moncorge said. "What this does is dim the halo of invincibility surrounding the Crown."

Members of the Hall of the Robe played down the significance of the event.

"This is a very small piece of legislation, intended to make our increasingly unmanageable bureaucracy more efficient," said Baronet Aristide deMandeville, Speaker of the Robe. "It should in no way be regarded as an attack on Robe's time-honored tradition of loyalty to the King."

Members of King Louis XXII's court saw a broader context of defiance.

"This is betrayal, pure and simple," said a source close to the king. "The actions of the Hall of the Robe border on treason. His Majesty has been stabbed in the back, plain and simple."

But Lord DeMandeville doesn't think there's any need for concern on the Crown's part.

"We ensured the bill was modified in a number of ways before it was brought to a vote," Lord deMandeville said.

"For instance, the king may renew injunctions as he sees fit once the 100 year time limit is up."

Members of the Hall of the Sword seemed cautiously optimistic about the prospect of more power for their historically marginalized Hall.

"France's great houses have been disorganized and apathetic for many years, but the Duke of Lorraine turned that all around," a member of the Hall of the Sword said.

"And now we've shown that the Robe has the courage to stand up to the King, too. It's the precedent that's important here, not the passage of the bill itself."

Moncorge was inclined to agree.

"It's too early to say for sure, but this could very well signal a new era of political significance for the Hall of the Robe," he said.

This idea was troublesome to advisors close to the king.

"Certain members of the Hall of the Sword have been batting around entirely too much militaristic rhetoric," Charles Martel, Louis XXII's Mayor of the Court, said.

"If the Sword is poised to gain influence, I hope it will be to extend a hand of friendship to our neighbors, but I have my doubts. France and all Christendom could be heading off a precipice."

Royal injunctions are issued at the sole discretion of the king. Only the king may view a royally enjoined document.

Leads in deMedici Murder Scarce; Markets Plunge at News of Financier's Death

Inquisitors are still baffled as to the identity of Hugo deMedici's killer twenty-four hours after his death.

Mr. deMedici was the heir-apparent to the vast deMedici family financial empire.

"The individual responsible for this horrific act was particularly clever," Inquisitor Moricant, lead investigator on the case, said. "While our leads are few, they are promising, and we are following

them diligently."

In particular, Inquisitors are questioning three members of the Guild of Stevedores near the scene of the murder around the time it occurred.

Officials did not list the three men as suspects but potential witnesses of suspicious activity.

Inquisitor Moricant declined to give the names of the three men or comment further on the case.

An elderly woman who lives

in the neighborhood told *Le Journal* she saw a "man dressed in black" walking around the premises of the deMedici offices late that night.

"I was up late at night knitting stockings when I saw him. He went right into the deMedici building," she said.

Inquisitors declined to comment on the woman's testimony.

Meanwhile, markets reacted to

continued on page B4

❈ Society Pages ❈

Who Is the Mysterious Woman on the Arm of the Duke of Lorraine?

She's beautiful, she's stylish, she's a doctor. She's the hottest thing in Paris. Who wouldn't fall for the lovely Dr. Tournon?

Please, ladies, no weeping: France's most eligible – and most elusive – bachelor may be off limits. Lots of women have been seen hanging off Lord Lorraine's arm over the years, but never for more than a few nights in a row. Seems like Lorraine, the man who proves beyond a doubt that bald can be sexy, likes to play it fast and easy.

Until now. For the past two months, Lorraine has attended every party with the same female companion.

Two months? Practically a lifetime for the nubile lord! Lorraine's new flame is a working girl, a member of the Guild of Physicians. The young doctor, Genevieve Tournon, has risen quickly through the ranks of the Guild. In recent months she has become something of a sensation in Paris society with her boyish good looks, wit and impeccable couture.

Discretion, too, may be one of her charms: according to her, she and the Duke are "just good friends." Our diagnosis: this relationship is a lot hotter than she's letting on!

Sweetness, I Was Only Joking

Whoops! Just three hours after a hasty wedding ceremony, young Baroness Brittany Feuillère has petitioned the Papacy for an annulment of her marriage.

The Baroness, who scandalized her family by choosing the life of a professional singer, wed an untitled young man whom she has known "since childhood." Rumor has it the young man was a servant of her family.

A new record for shortest marriage? A publicity stunt for the baroness' upcoming recital? Our dedicated reporters are on the beat!

Paris is Burning

Months after the scandal and there's still no let-up for poor Paris. No, we don't mean our fair city, we mean the now-infamous Paris Huguet-Renoir, heir to her father's sprawling hotel-and-casino empire.

In case you've been living in a Siberian convent, we'll fill you in on the gory details. Paris and a Roumanian count (whose name escapes us) had a secret tryst four months ago – or so they had hoped! Paris and the dashing count, who is twice her age, decided to memorialize the event with a Lumière motion-camera.

Apparently, foresight and intelligence are not among the many gifts God bestowed upon the wealthy socialites.

It seems a member of the Count's entourage, a camera enthusiast, overheard the lovebirds' plan and secretly made a print from the negatives of the two in the act.

Although Pope John XIV has threatened excommunication for anyone caught showing or distributing the film, underground salons all over Europe have been playing copies of the reel incessantly.

The event has scandalized the Huguet-Renoir family. At a dinner party last night, Henrietta Dobson, the wife of a wealthy American banker known for her social slip-ups, confessed her "deepest sympathy" to Paris' mother Beatriz. Appalled by the gaffe, Paris' mother expressed her "deepest sympathy" that Mme Dobson lacked the "etiquette and social grace of a reptile".

Most recently, beautiful-if-not-overtly-interesting-aside-from-the-scandal Paris has been consoling herself modeling the clothes of haute-couture designers with her beloved chihuahua Fifi.

"She's a real professional, considering what she's been through," a photographer said of her. Frankly, we couldn't agree more.

Barely Worth Mentioning

Visiting dignitaries from the Confederate States of America received a terrible shock at yesterday's Rugby World Championships.

During a "half-time" performance, famed performer Janet Témerson bared one of her breasts, causing an uproar amongst the Southerners. The wife of one of the diplomats shrieked and threatened to faint.

A French count nearby reportedly told the shocked Americans "It's only a breast. We have lots of those around here."

A Night at the Opera

David-Louis Plantard de St. Clair, better known to us mortals as the Duke of Lorraine, has done the unthinkable: he's made the Le Journal Society pages twice on the same day!

Lorraine is flying high with his new "good friend" Dr. Genevieve Tournon. And he made a prodigious splash last night at the Palais Garnier opera house, where his production of *The Marriage of Figaro* debuted to wide acclaim from critics and opera-goers.

But surely his majesty King Louis XXII's feathers were ruffled by the Duke's choice of *The Marriage of Figaro*. Written by Mozart, the opera was banned in France until ten years ago because of its "seditious and perfidious content."

It is also said that Mozart, a Freemason, hid references to Masonic institutions and rituals in his works. Church and crown have branded the secretive Freemason movement as "a grave threat to Christian civilization."

Clearly this did not deter the Duke. He was in attendance last night with his usual entourage of political supporters: Dominique Lourié-Modot, Count of Toulouse, and Baron Robert Teniers.

Lord Toulouse was overheard ridiculing Baron Teniers outside the Palais Garnier, but the young Baron took the slight coolly.

Men about town: Lords Lorraine and Toulouse exit the Palais Garnier yesterday evening after the premiere of The Marriage of Figaro. Between them is Lord Lorraine's close confidant, Baron Robert Teniers. Why so glum, Baron? Too many secrets to hide?

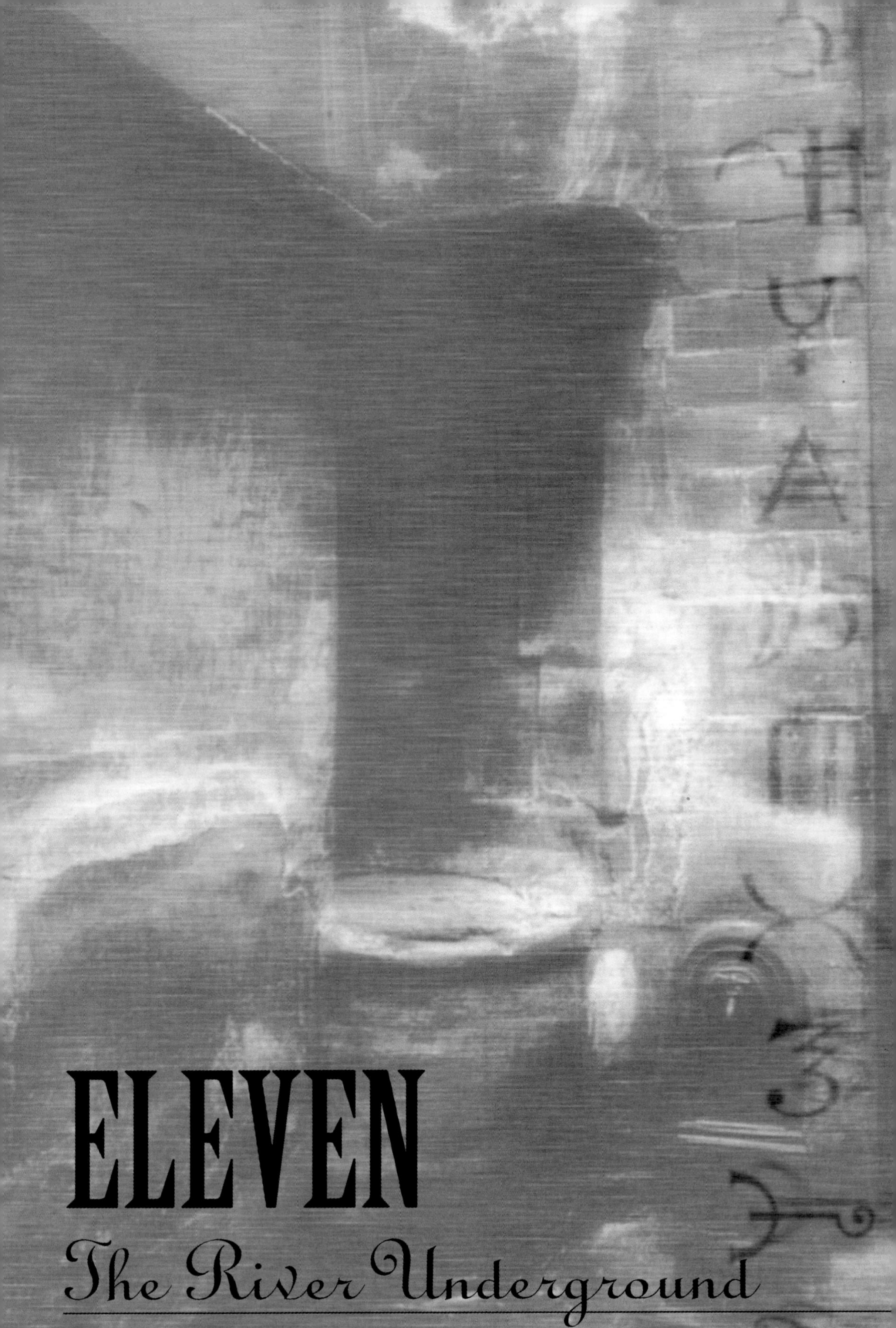

ELEVEN
The River Underground

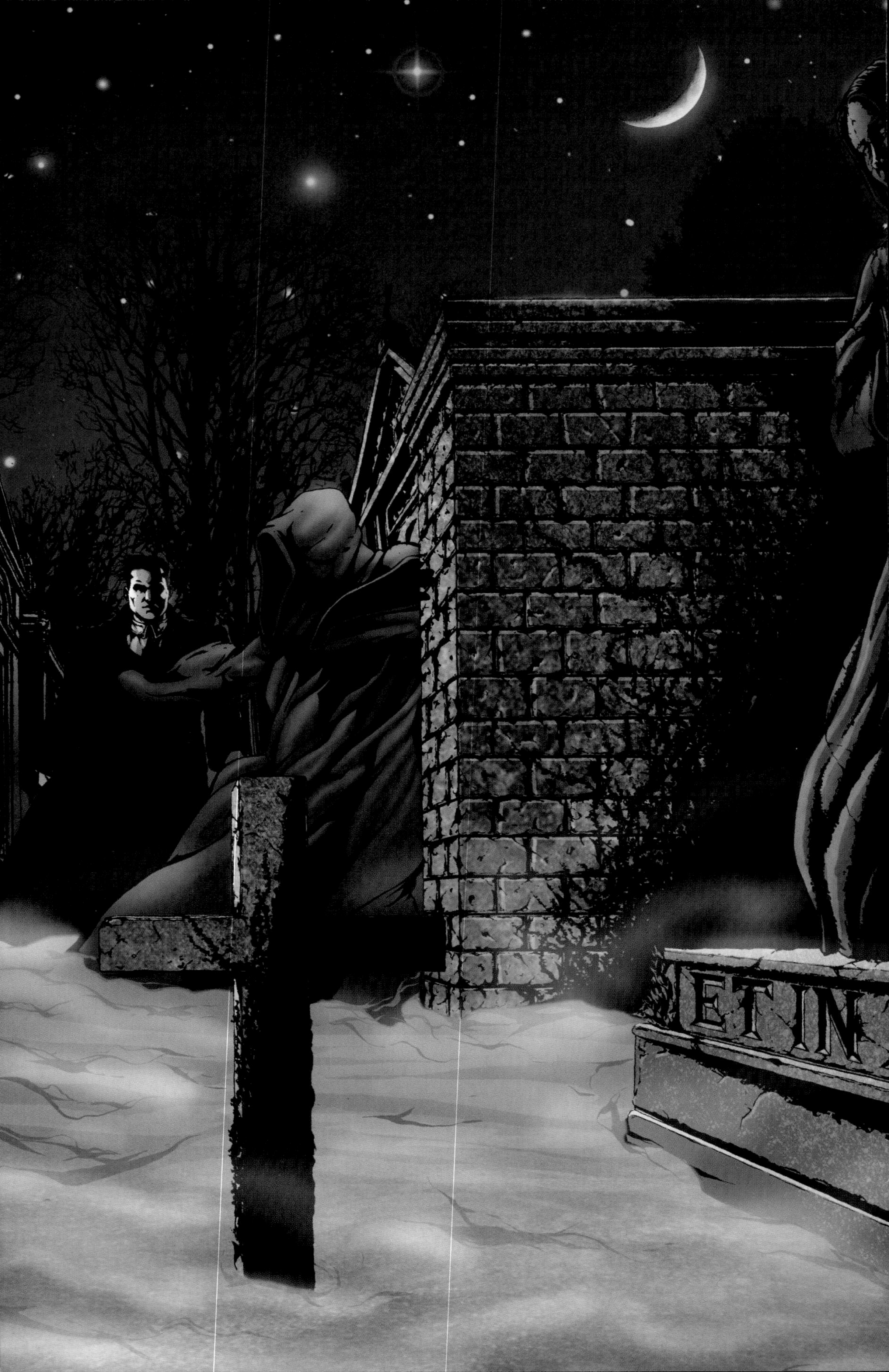
ET IN

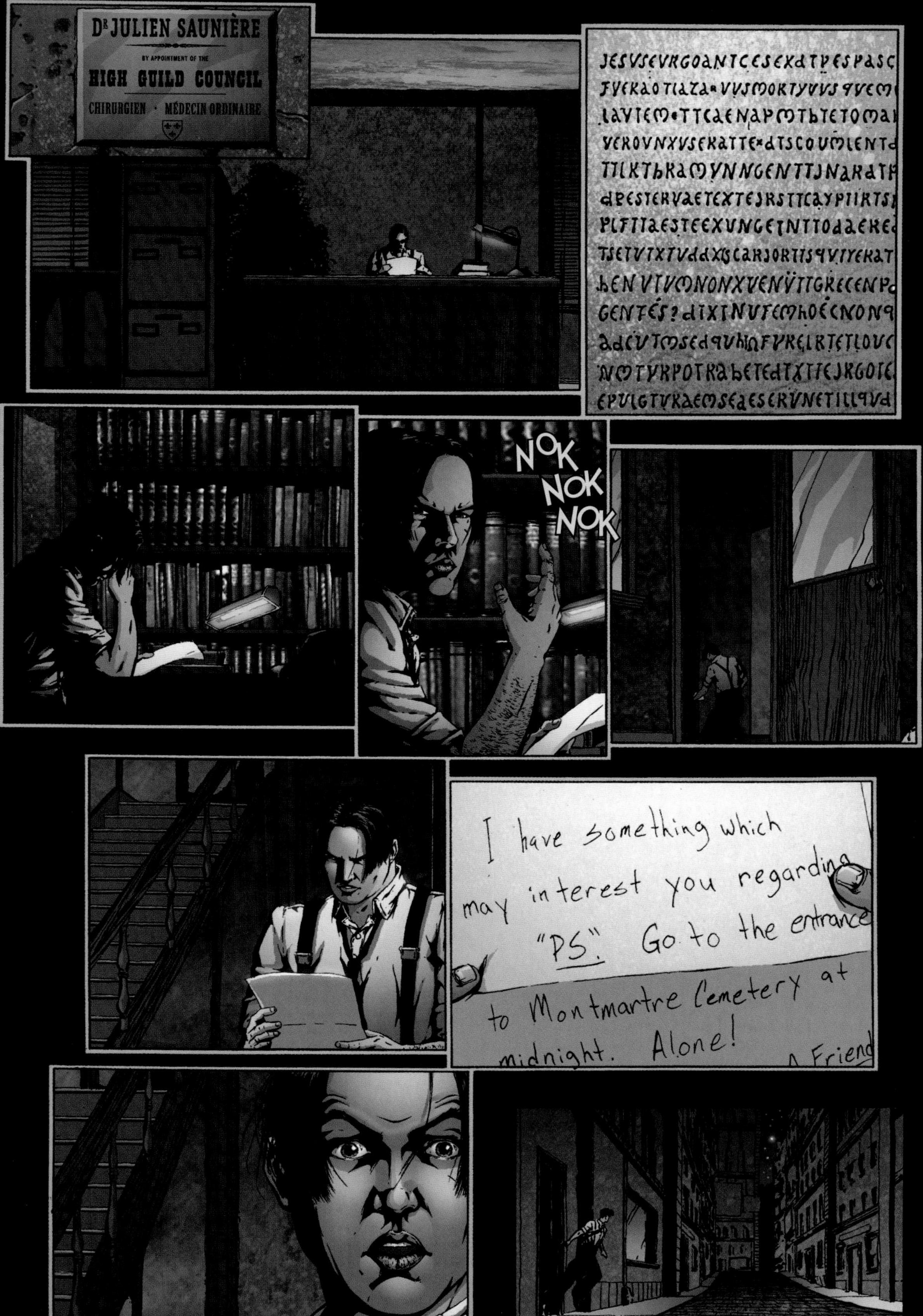
Dr JULIEN SAUNIÈRE
BY APPOINTMENT OF THE
HIGH GUILD COUNCIL
CHIRURGIEN · MÉDECIN ORDINAIRE
NOK NOK NOK
I have something which may interest you regarding "PS". Go to the entrance to Montmartre Cemetery at midnight. Alone!
A Friend

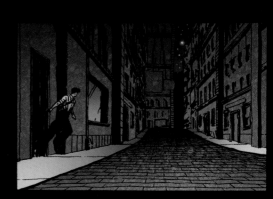

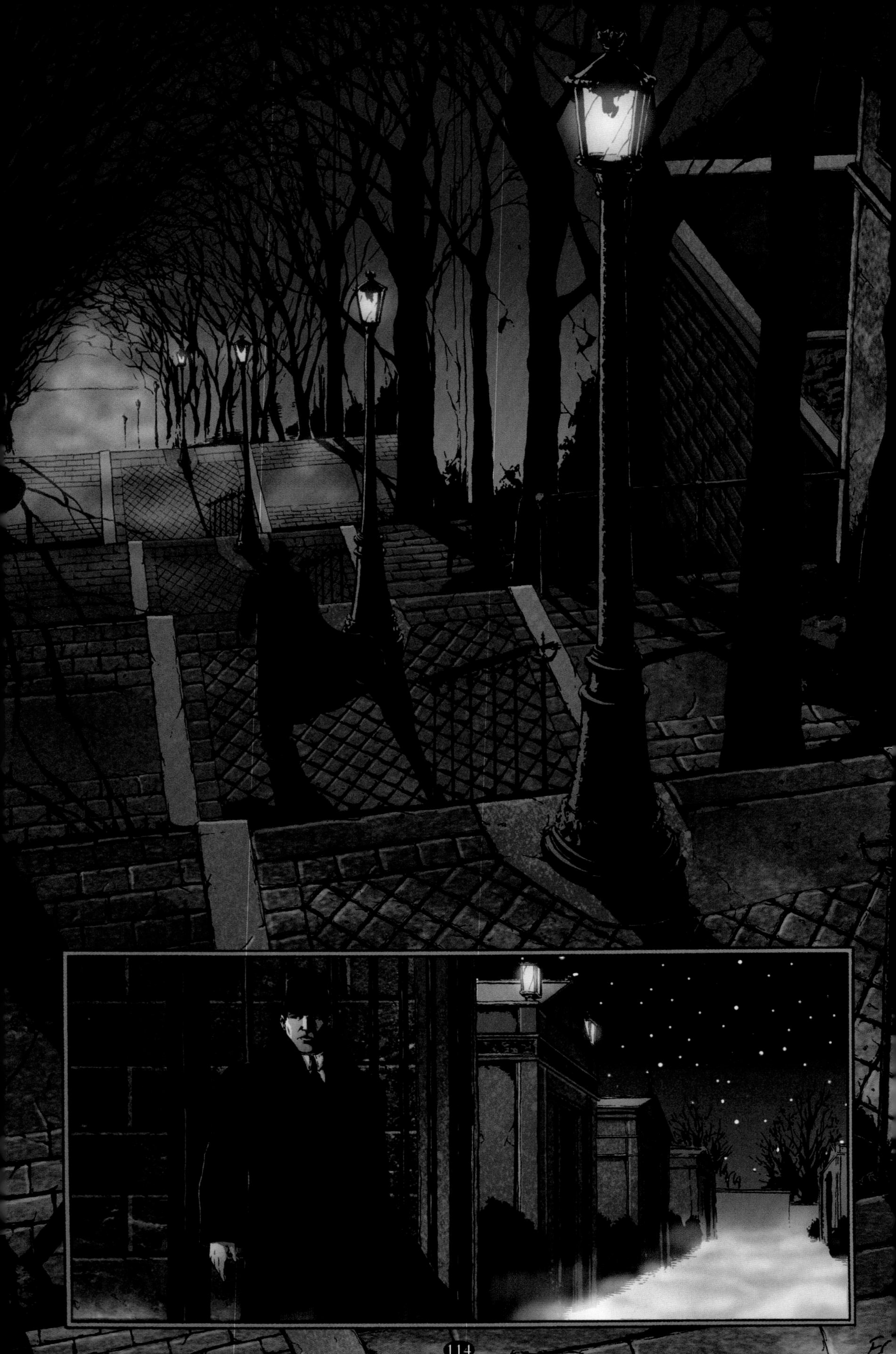

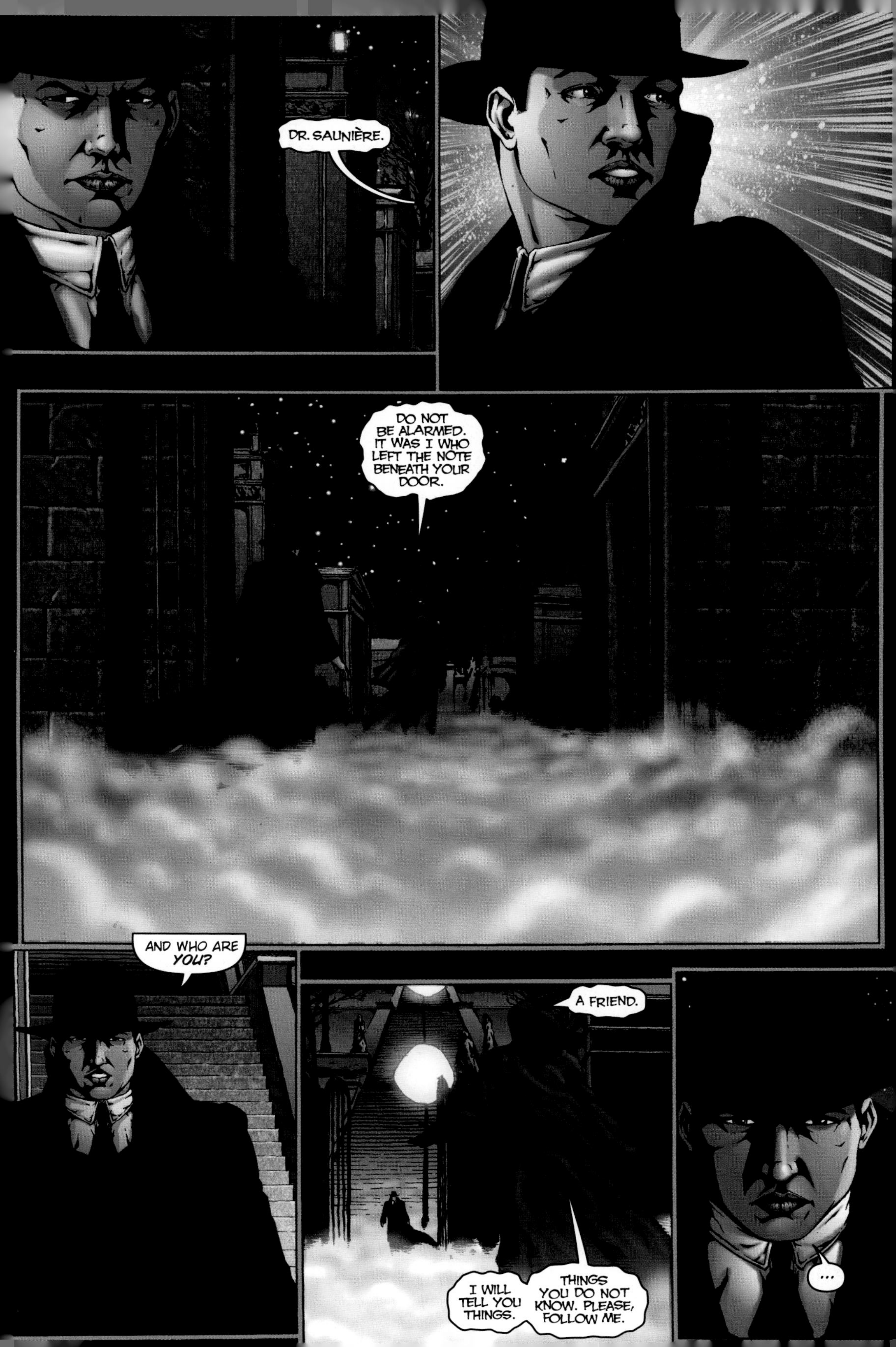
DR. SAUNIÈRE.
DO NOT BE ALARMED. IT WAS I WHO LEFT THE NOTE BENEATH YOUR DOOR.
AND WHO ARE *YOU*?
A FRIEND.
I WILL TELL YOU THINGS.
THINGS YOU DO NOT KNOW. PLEASE, FOLLOW ME.
...

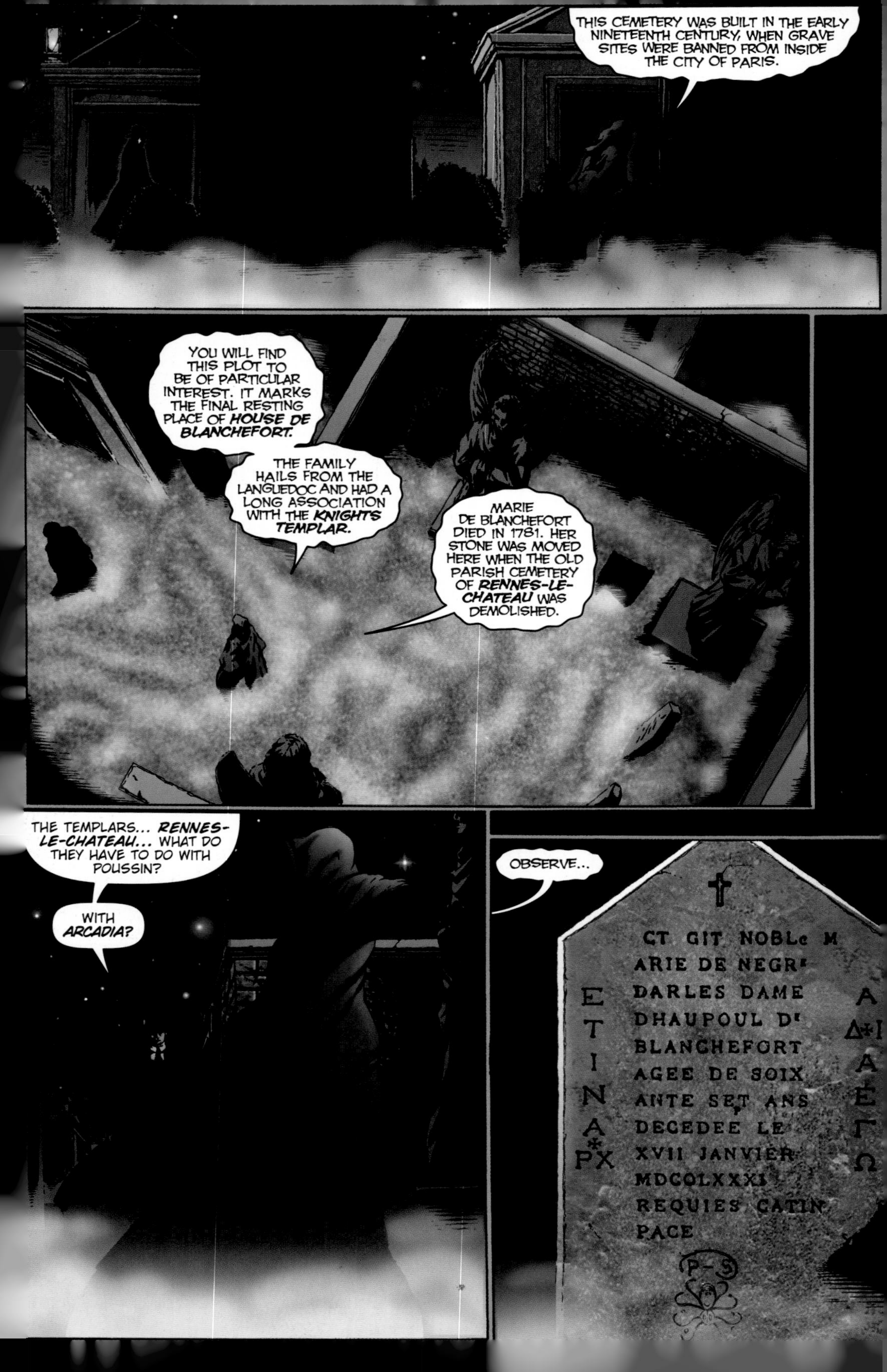
THIS CEMETERY WAS BUILT IN THE EARLY NINETEENTH CENTURY, WHEN GRAVE SITES WERE BANNED FROM INSIDE THE CITY OF PARIS.
YOU WILL FIND THIS PLOT TO BE OF PARTICULAR INTEREST. IT MARKS THE FINAL RESTING PLACE OF HOUSE DE BLANCHEFORT.
THE FAMILY HAILS FROM THE LANGUEDOC AND HAD A LONG ASSOCIATION WITH THE KNIGHTS TEMPLAR.
MARIE DE BLANCHEFORT DIED IN 1781. HER STONE WAS MOVED HERE WHEN THE OLD PARISH CEMETERY OF RENNES-LE-CHATEAU WAS DEMOLISHED.
THE TEMPLARS... RENNES-LE-CHATEAU... WHAT DO THEY HAVE TO DO WITH POUSSIN?
WITH ARCADIA?
OBSERVE...
CT GIT NOBLe M
ARIE DE NEGRe
DARLES DAME
DHAUPOUL De
BLANCHEFORT
AGEE DE SOIX
ANTE SET ANS
DECEDEE LE
XVII JANVIER
MDCOLXXXI
REQUIES CATIN
PACE
ETINAP*X
AΔ*IAEΓΩ
P-S

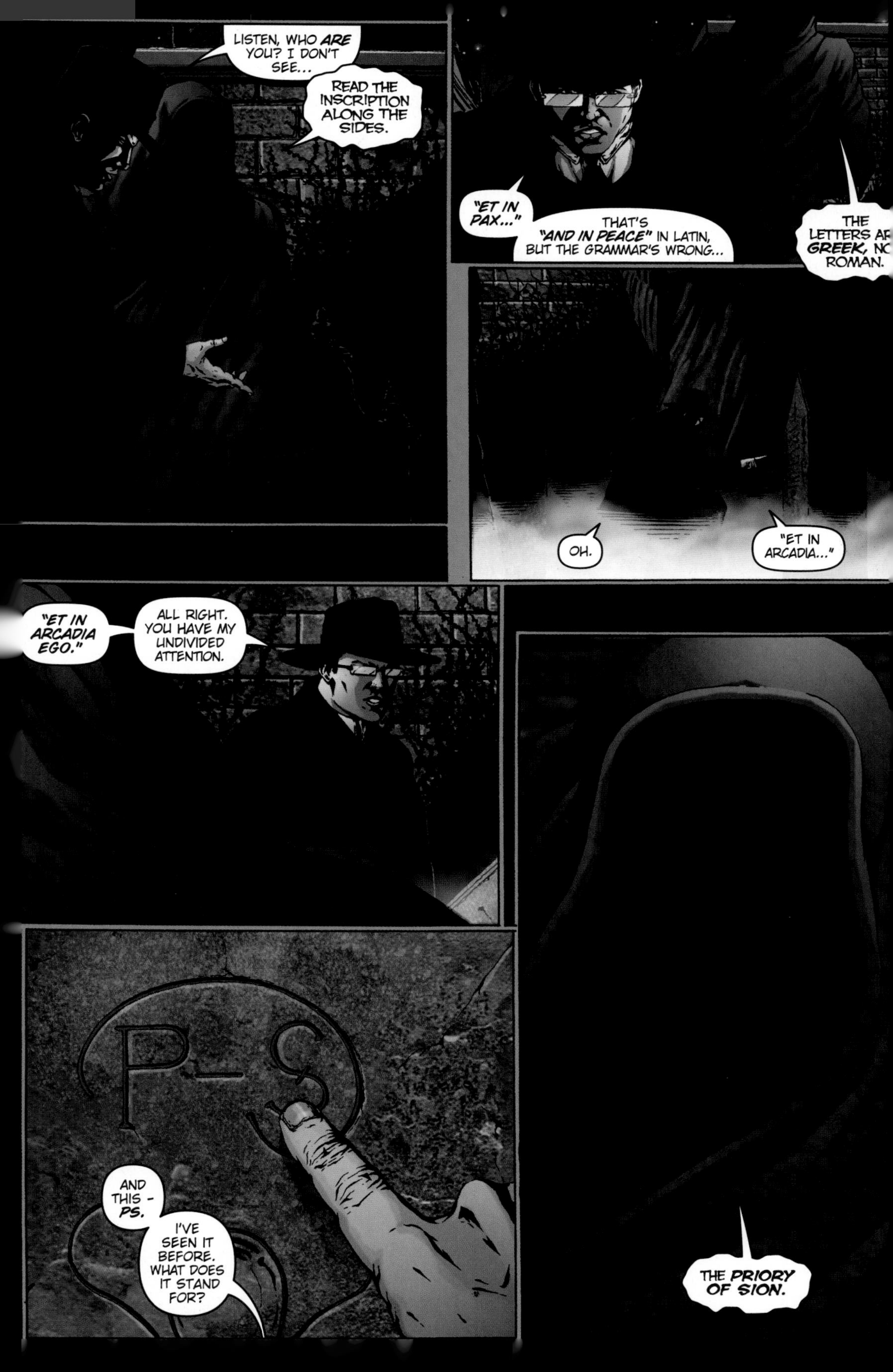

LISTEN, WHO ARE YOU? I DON'T SEE...
READ THE INSCRIPTION ALONG THE SIDES.
"ET IN PAX..."
THAT'S "AND IN PEACE" IN LATIN, BUT THE GRAMMAR'S WRONG...
THE LETTERS AR GREEK, NC ROMAN.
OH.
"ET IN ARCADIA..."
"ET IN ARCADIA EGO."
ALL RIGHT. YOU HAVE MY UNDIVIDED ATTENTION.
P S
AND THIS - PS.
I'VE SEEN IT BEFORE. WHAT DOES IT STAND FOR?
THE PRIORY OF SION.

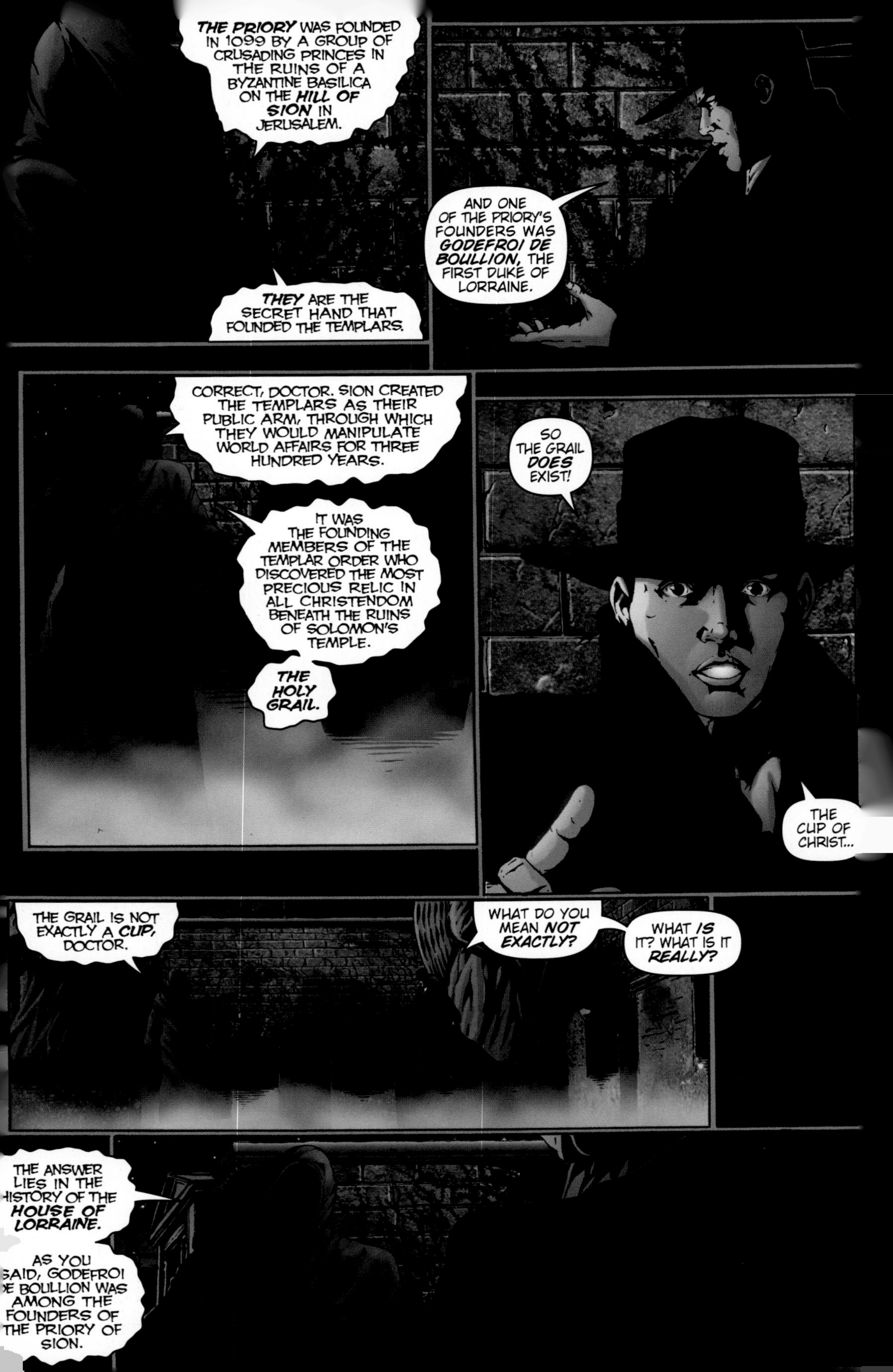
THE PRIORY WAS FOUNDED IN 1099 BY A GROUP OF CRUSADING PRINCES IN THE RUINS OF A BYZANTINE BASILICA ON THE HILL OF SION IN JERUSALEM.
THEY ARE THE SECRET HAND THAT FOUNDED THE TEMPLARS.
AND ONE OF THE PRIORY'S FOUNDERS WAS GODEFROI DE BOULLION, THE FIRST DUKE OF LORRAINE.
CORRECT, DOCTOR. SION CREATED THE TEMPLARS AS THEIR PUBLIC ARM, THROUGH WHICH THEY WOULD MANIPULATE WORLD AFFAIRS FOR THREE HUNDRED YEARS.
IT WAS THE FOUNDING MEMBERS OF THE TEMPLAR ORDER WHO DISCOVERED THE MOST PRECIOUS RELIC IN ALL CHRISTENDOM BENEATH THE RUINS OF SOLOMON'S TEMPLE.
THE HOLY GRAIL.
SO THE GRAIL DOES EXIST!
THE CUP OF CHRIST...
THE GRAIL IS NOT EXACTLY A CUP, DOCTOR.
WHAT DO YOU MEAN NOT EXACTLY?
WHAT IS IT? WHAT IS IT REALLY?
THE ANSWER LIES IN THE HISTORY OF THE HOUSE OF LORRAINE.
AS YOU SAID, GODEFROI DE BOULLION WAS AMONG THE FOUNDERS OF THE PRIORY OF SION.

HOUSE LORRAINE HAS ATTEMPTED TO SIEZE THE THRONE OF FRANCE MANY TIMES THROUGHOUT HISTORY.

KING PHILIP IV DISCOVERED THE TRUE NATURE OF THE TEMPLARS AND PUT THEM TO THE STAKE IN 1307.

MOST OF THE KNIGHTS WERE IGNORANT OF THE PRIORY'S EXISTENCE, AND OF THE EXISTENCE OF THE GRAIL.

THEY DIED BELIEVING THEIR ORDER WAS TRULY INNOCENT OF WITCHCRAFT OR PLOTTING AGAINST THE CROWN.

REQUIEM AETERNAM, DONA EIS DOMINE...

AND KING PHILIP COULD NOT DESTROY THAT WHICH NEVER OFFICIALLY EXISTED: *THE PRIORY ITSELF.*

IT TOOK THE PRIORY CENTURIES TO REGROUP FROM THE DISASTER. IT WOULD NOT BE READY TO STRIKE AGAIN FOR NEARLY 300 YEARS.

IN THE SIXTEENTH CENTURY THE HOUSES OF *LORRAINE* AND *GUISE*, A CADET BRANCH OF LORRAINE, ATTEMPTED TO TAKE THE THRONE.

THEY WAGED A BRUTAL CAMPAIGN OF ASSASSINATION AND INTRIGUE AGAINST THE *VALOIS* KINGS.

BUT BY THE TIME THE VALOIS WERE EXTINCT, HOUSE LORRAINE HAD BEEN SO DEPLETED BY POLITICAL MURDERS IT COULD NOT PRODUCE AN HEIR FOR THE THRONE.

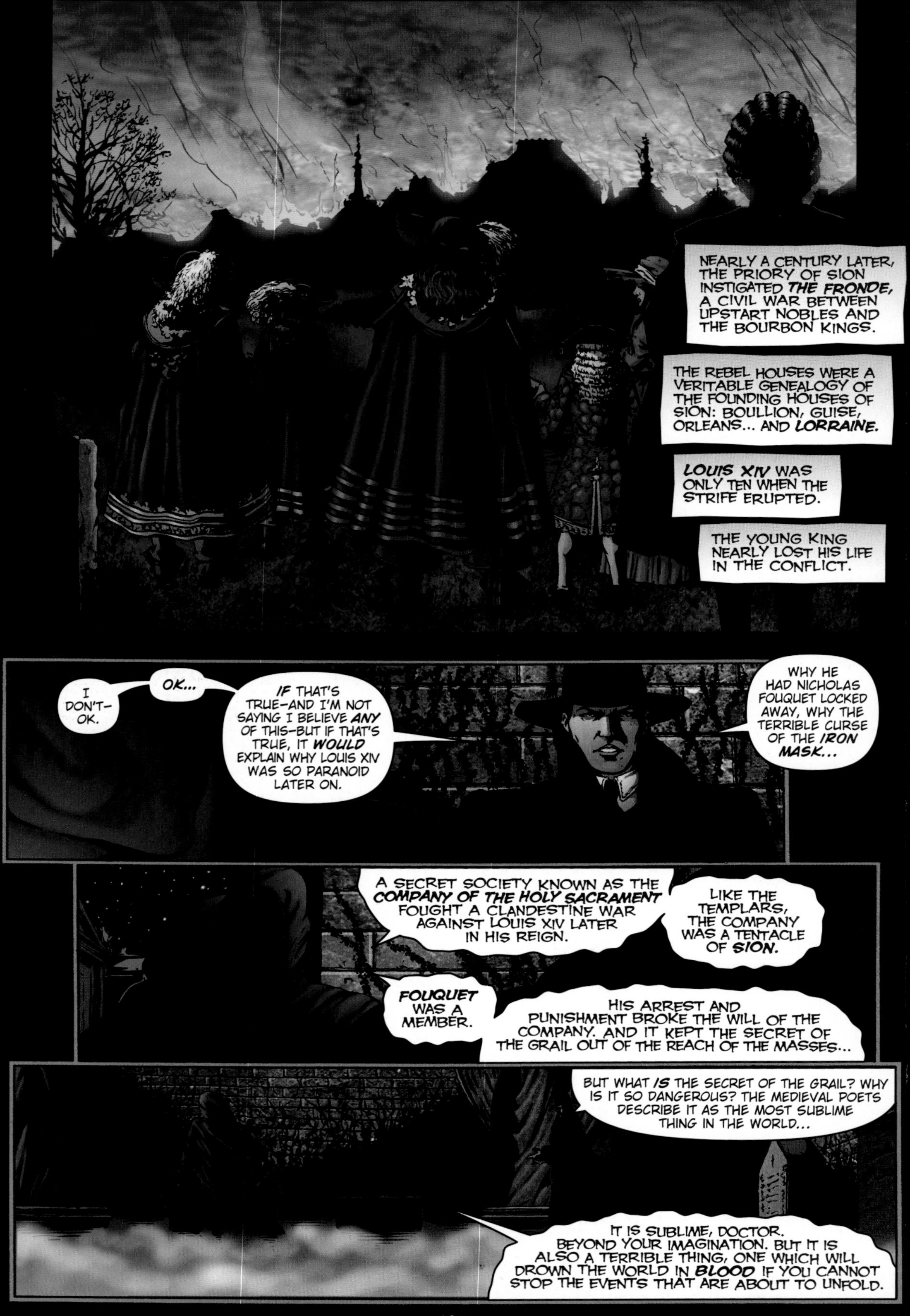
NEARLY A CENTURY LATER, THE PRIORY OF SION INSTIGATED THE FRONDE, A CIVIL WAR BETWEEN UPSTART NOBLES AND THE BOURBON KINGS.
THE REBEL HOUSES WERE A VERITABLE GENEALOGY OF THE FOUNDING HOUSES OF SION: BOULLION, GUISE, ORLEANS... AND LORRAINE.
LOUIS XIV WAS ONLY TEN WHEN THE STRIFE ERUPTED.
THE YOUNG KING NEARLY LOST HIS LIFE IN THE CONFLICT.
I DON'T- OK.
OK...
IF THAT'S TRUE-AND I'M NOT SAYING I BELIEVE ANY OF THIS-BUT IF THAT'S TRUE, IT WOULD EXPLAIN WHY LOUIS XIV WAS SO PARANOID LATER ON.
WHY HE HAD NICHOLAS FOUQUET LOCKED AWAY, WHY THE TERRIBLE CURSE OF THE IRON MASK...
A SECRET SOCIETY KNOWN AS THE COMPANY OF THE HOLY SACRAMENT FOUGHT A CLANDESTINE WAR AGAINST LOUIS XIV LATER IN HIS REIGN.
LIKE THE TEMPLARS, THE COMPANY WAS A TENTACLE OF SION.
FOUQUET WAS A MEMBER.
HIS ARREST AND PUNISHMENT BROKE THE WILL OF THE COMPANY. AND IT KEPT THE SECRET OF THE GRAIL OUT OF THE REACH OF THE MASSES...
BUT WHAT IS THE SECRET OF THE GRAIL? WHY IS IT SO DANGEROUS? THE MEDIEVAL POETS DESCRIBE IT AS THE MOST SUBLIME THING IN THE WORLD...
IT IS SUBLIME, DOCTOR. BEYOND YOUR IMAGINATION. BUT IT IS ALSO A TERRIBLE THING, ONE WHICH WILL DROWN THE WORLD IN BLOOD IF YOU CANNOT STOP THE EVENTS THAT ARE ABOUT TO UNFOLD.

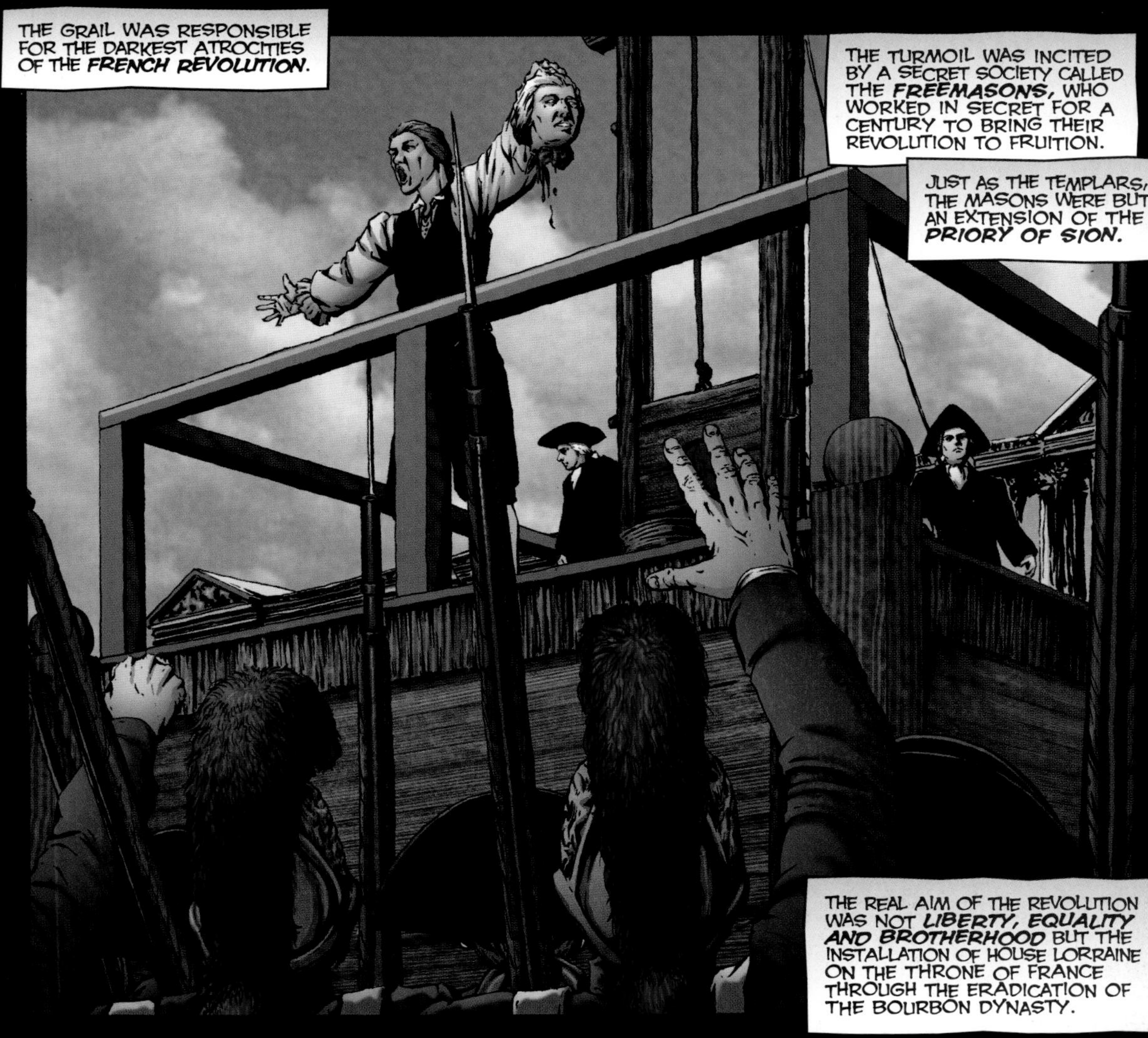
THE GRAIL WAS RESPONSIBLE FOR THE DARKEST ATROCITIES OF THE ***FRENCH REVOLUTION***.
THE TURMOIL WAS INCITED BY A SECRET SOCIETY CALLED THE ***FREEMASONS,*** WHO WORKED IN SECRET FOR A CENTURY TO BRING THEIR REVOLUTION TO FRUITION.
JUST AS THE TEMPLARS, THE MASONS WERE BUT AN EXTENSION OF THE ***PRIORY OF SION.***
THE REAL AIM OF THE REVOLUTION WAS NOT ***LIBERTY, EQUALITY AND BROTHERHOOD*** BUT THE INSTALLATION OF HOUSE LORRAINE ON THE THRONE OF FRANCE THROUGH THE ERADICATION OF THE BOURBON DYNASTY.

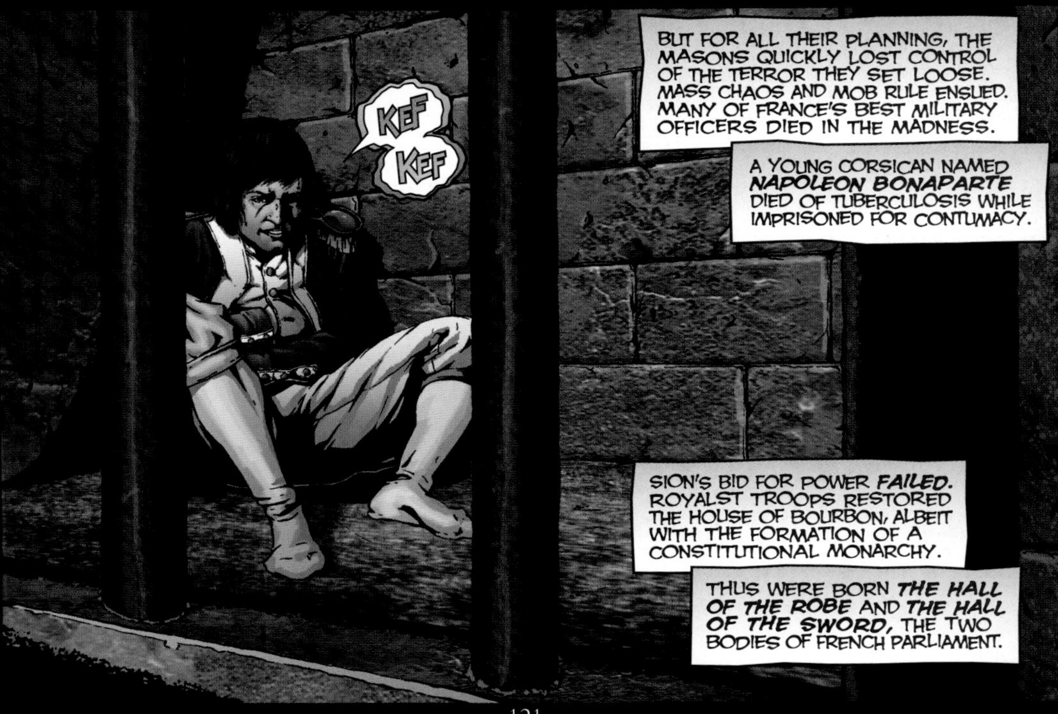
BUT FOR ALL THEIR PLANNING, THE MASONS QUICKLY LOST CONTROL OF THE TERROR THEY SET LOOSE. MASS CHAOS AND MOB RULE ENSUED. MANY OF FRANCE'S BEST MILITARY OFFICERS DIED IN THE MADNESS.
KEF KEF
A YOUNG CORSICAN NAMED ***NAPOLEON BONAPARTE*** DIED OF TUBERCULOSIS WHILE IMPRISONED FOR CONTUMACY.
SION'S BID FOR POWER ***FAILED.*** ROYALST TROOPS RESTORED THE HOUSE OF BOURBON, ALBEIT WITH THE FORMATION OF A CONSTITUTIONAL MONARCHY.
THUS WERE BORN ***THE HALL OF THE ROBE*** AND ***THE HALL OF THE SWORD,*** THE TWO BODIES OF FRENCH PARLIAMENT.

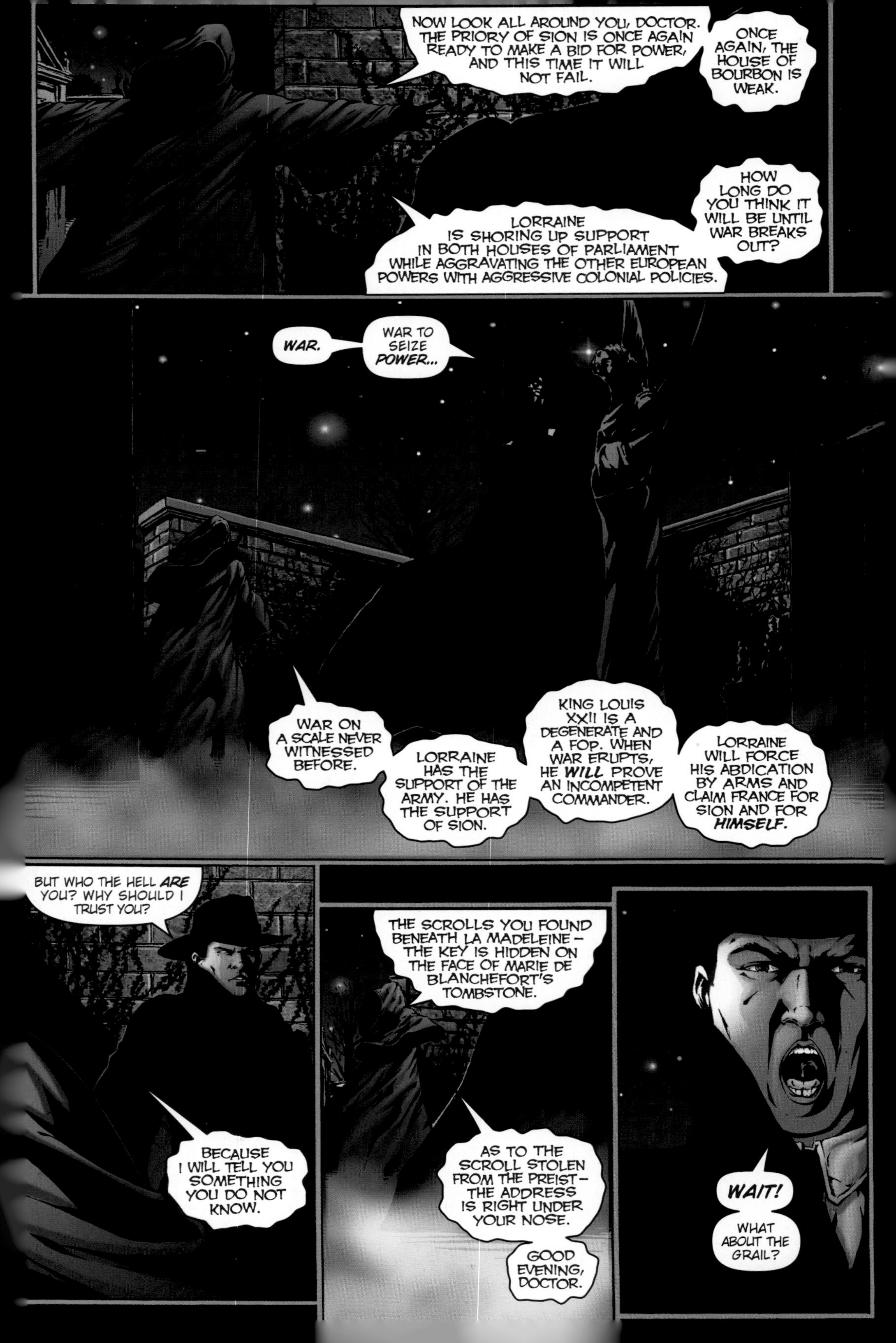
NOW LOOK ALL AROUND YOU, DOCTOR. THE PRIORY OF SION IS ONCE AGAIN READY TO MAKE A BID FOR POWER, AND THIS TIME IT WILL NOT FAIL.
ONCE AGAIN, THE HOUSE OF BOURBON IS WEAK.
LORRAINE IS SHORING UP SUPPORT IN BOTH HOUSES OF PARLIAMENT WHILE AGGRAVATING THE OTHER EUROPEAN POWERS WITH AGGRESSIVE COLONIAL POLICIES.
HOW LONG DO YOU THINK IT WILL BE UNTIL WAR BREAKS OUT?
WAR.
WAR TO SEIZE POWER...
WAR ON A SCALE NEVER WITNESSED BEFORE.
LORRAINE HAS THE SUPPORT OF THE ARMY. HE HAS THE SUPPORT OF SION.
KING LOUIS XXII IS A DEGENERATE AND A FOP. WHEN WAR ERUPTS, HE WILL PROVE AN INCOMPETENT COMMANDER.
LORRAINE WILL FORCE HIS ABDICATION BY ARMS AND CLAIM FRANCE FOR SION AND FOR HIMSELF.
BUT WHO THE HELL ARE YOU? WHY SHOULD I TRUST YOU?
BECAUSE I WILL TELL YOU SOMETHING YOU DO NOT KNOW.
THE SCROLLS YOU FOUND BENEATH LA MADELEINE – THE KEY IS HIDDEN ON THE FACE OF MARIE DE BLANCHEFORT'S TOMBSTONE.
AS TO THE SCROLL STOLEN FROM THE PREIST – THE ADDRESS IS RIGHT UNDER YOUR NOSE.
GOOD EVENING, DOCTOR.
WAIT!
WHAT ABOUT THE GRAIL?

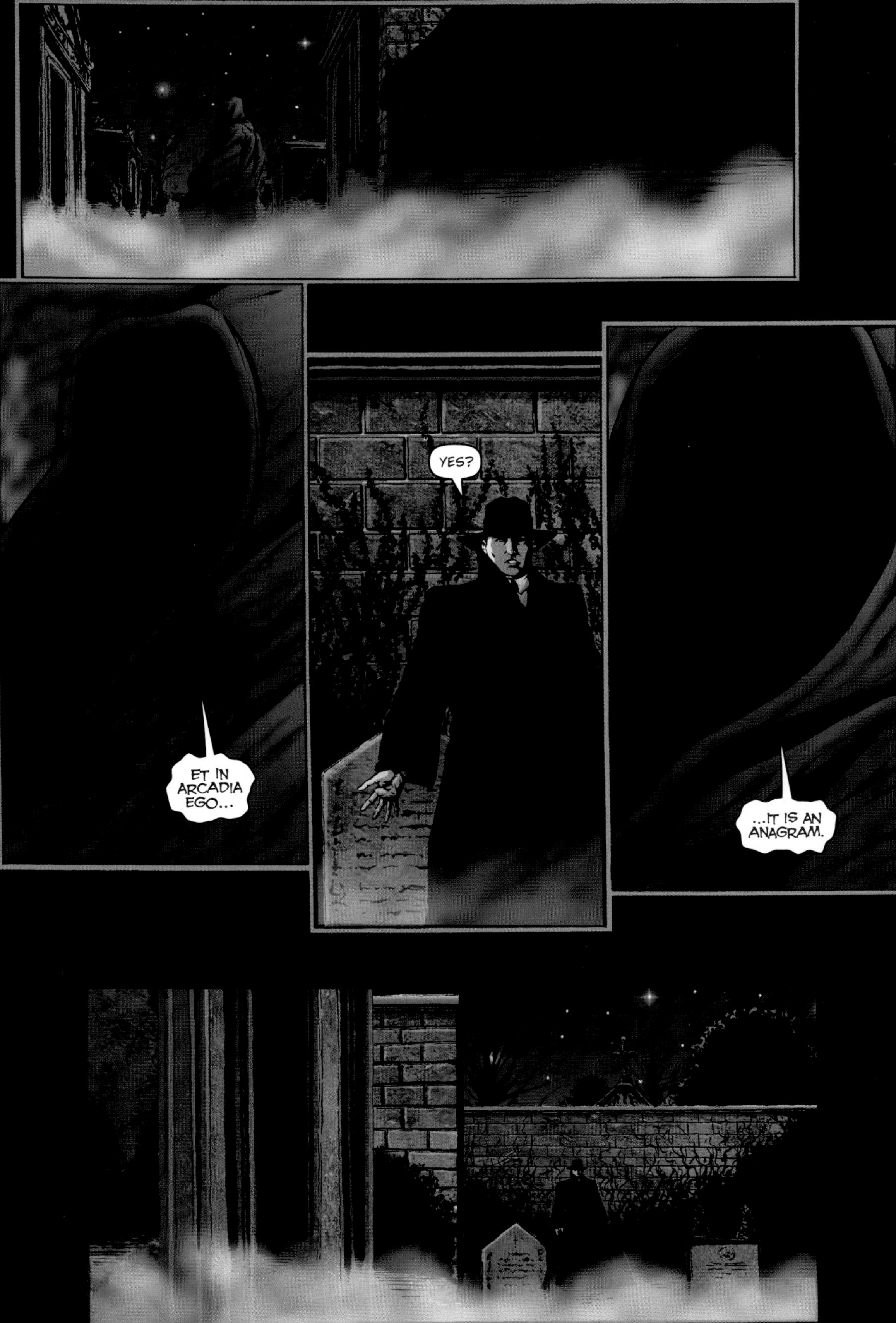
ET IN ARCADIA EGO...
YES?
...IT IS AN ANAGRAM.

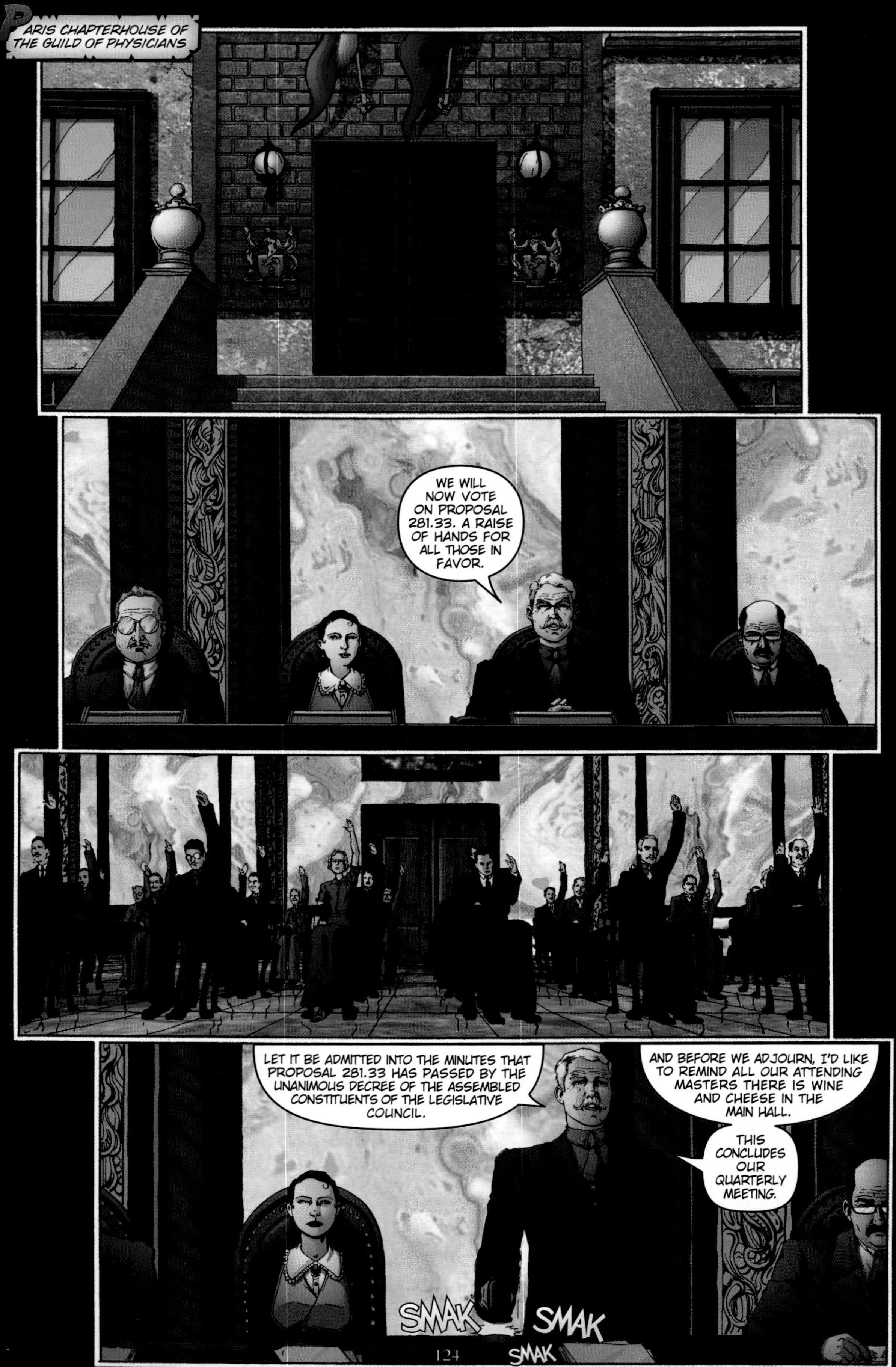
PARIS CHAPTERHOUSE OF THE GUILD OF PHYSICIANS
WE WILL NOW VOTE ON PROPOSAL 281.33. A RAISE OF HANDS FOR ALL THOSE IN FAVOR.
LET IT BE ADMITTED INTO THE MINUTES THAT PROPOSAL 281.33 HAS PASSED BY THE UNANIMOUS DECREE OF THE ASSEMBLED CONSTITUENTS OF THE LEGISLATIVE COUNCIL.
AND BEFORE WE ADJOURN, I'D LIKE TO REMIND ALL OUR ATTENDING MASTERS THERE IS WINE AND CHEESE IN THE MAIN HALL.
THIS CONCLUDES OUR QUARTERLY MEETING.
SMAK
SMAK
SMAK

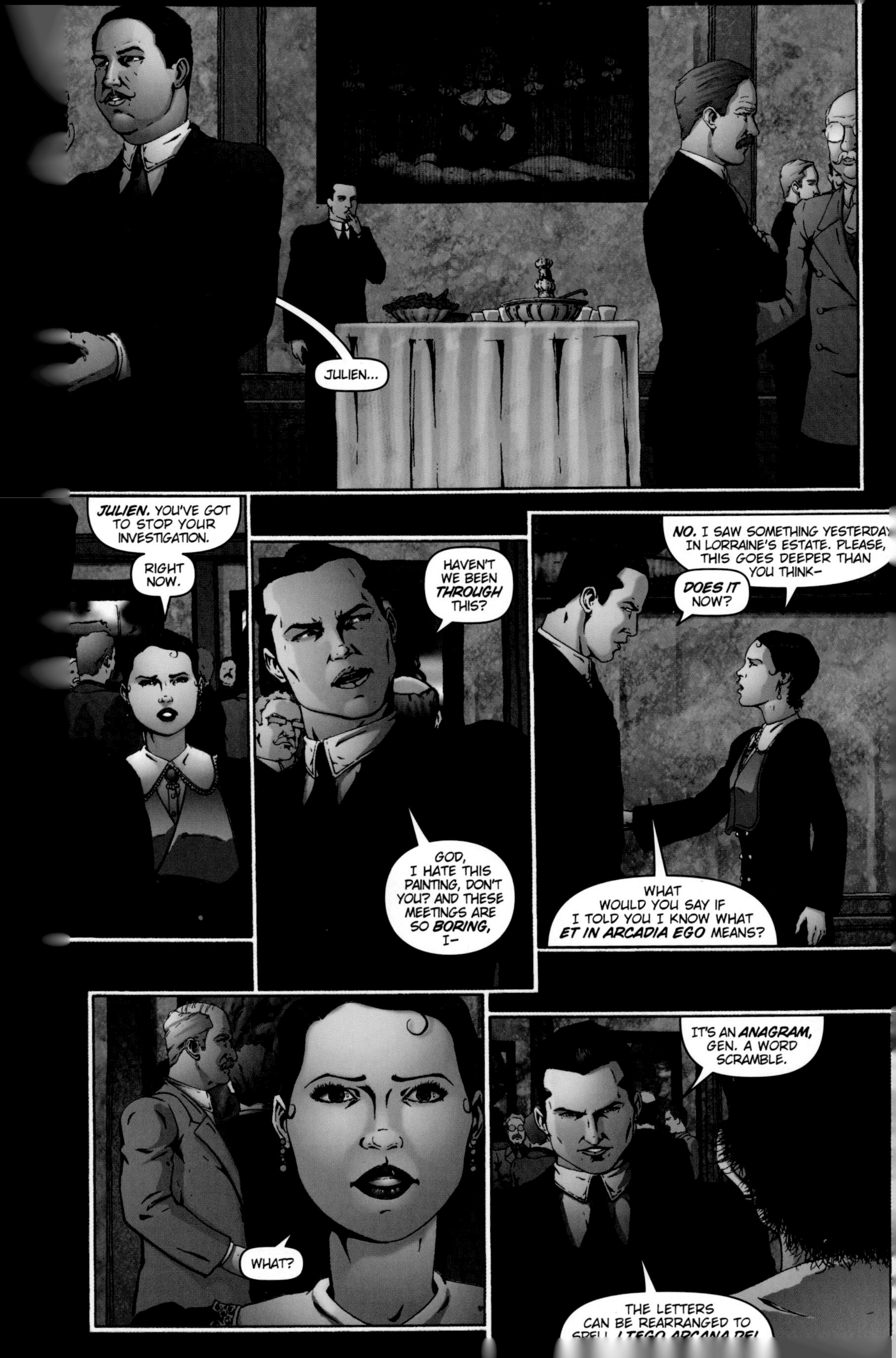
JULIEN...
JULIEN. YOU'VE GOT TO STOP YOUR INVESTIGATION.
RIGHT NOW.
HAVEN'T WE BEEN THROUGH THIS?
GOD, I HATE THIS PAINTING, DON'T YOU? AND THESE MEETINGS ARE SO BORING, I–
NO. I SAW SOMETHING YESTERDAY IN LORRAINE'S ESTATE. PLEASE, THIS GOES DEEPER THAN YOU THINK–
DOES IT NOW?
WHAT WOULD YOU SAY IF I TOLD YOU I KNOW WHAT ET IN ARCADIA EGO MEANS?
WHAT?
IT'S AN ANAGRAM, GEN. A WORD SCRAMBLE.
THE LETTERS CAN BE REARRANGED TO

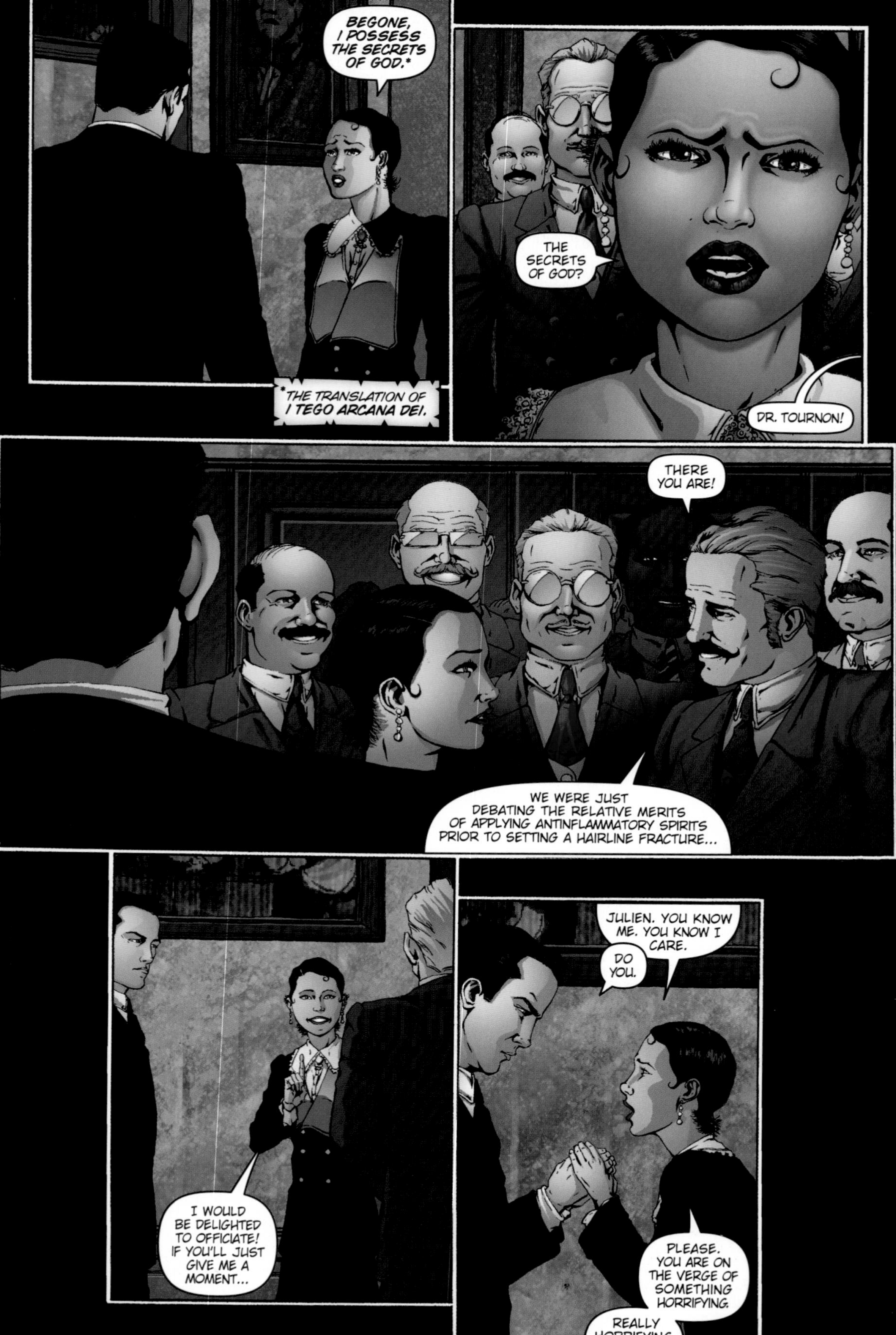
BEGONE, I POSSESS THE SECRETS OF GOD.*
*THE TRANSLATION OF I TEGO ARCANA DEI.
THE SECRETS OF GOD?
DR. TOURNON!
THERE YOU ARE!
WE WERE JUST DEBATING THE RELATIVE MERITS OF APPLYING ANTINFLAMMATORY SPIRITS PRIOR TO SETTING A HAIRLINE FRACTURE...
I WOULD BE DELIGHTED TO OFFICIATE! IF YOU'LL JUST GIVE ME A MOMENT...
JULIEN. YOU KNOW ME. YOU KNOW I CARE.
DO YOU.
PLEASE. YOU ARE ON THE VERGE OF SOMETHING HORRIFYING.
REALLY

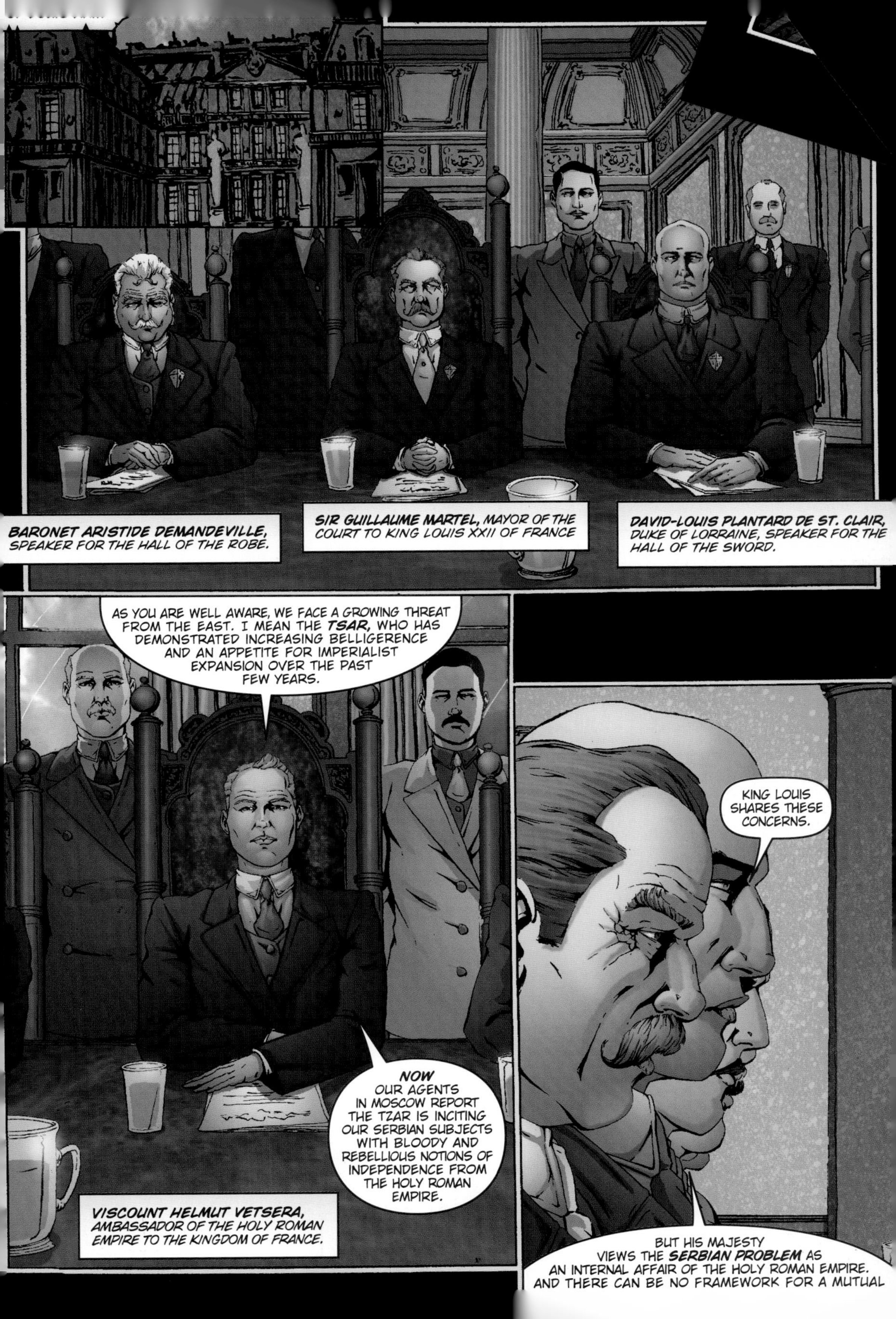

BARONET ARISTIDE DEMANDEVILLE, SPEAKER FOR THE HALL OF THE ROBE.
SIR GUILLAUME MARTEL, MAYOR OF THE COURT TO KING LOUIS XXII OF FRANCE
DAVID-LOUIS PLANTARD DE ST. CLAIR, DUKE OF LORRAINE, SPEAKER FOR THE HALL OF THE SWORD.
AS YOU ARE WELL AWARE, WE FACE A GROWING THREAT FROM THE EAST. I MEAN THE TSAR, WHO HAS DEMONSTRATED INCREASING BELLIGERENCE AND AN APPETITE FOR IMPERIALIST EXPANSION OVER THE PAST FEW YEARS.
NOW OUR AGENTS IN MOSCOW REPORT THE TZAR IS INCITING OUR SERBIAN SUBJECTS WITH BLOODY AND REBELLIOUS NOTIONS OF INDEPENDENCE FROM THE HOLY ROMAN EMPIRE.
VISCOUNT HELMUT VETSERA, AMBASSADOR OF THE HOLY ROMAN EMPIRE TO THE KINGDOM OF FRANCE.
KING LOUIS SHARES THESE CONCERNS.
BUT HIS MAJESTY VIEWS THE SERBIAN PROBLEM AS AN INTERNAL AFFAIR OF THE HOLY ROMAN EMPIRE. AND THERE CAN BE NO FRAMEWORK FOR A MUTUAL

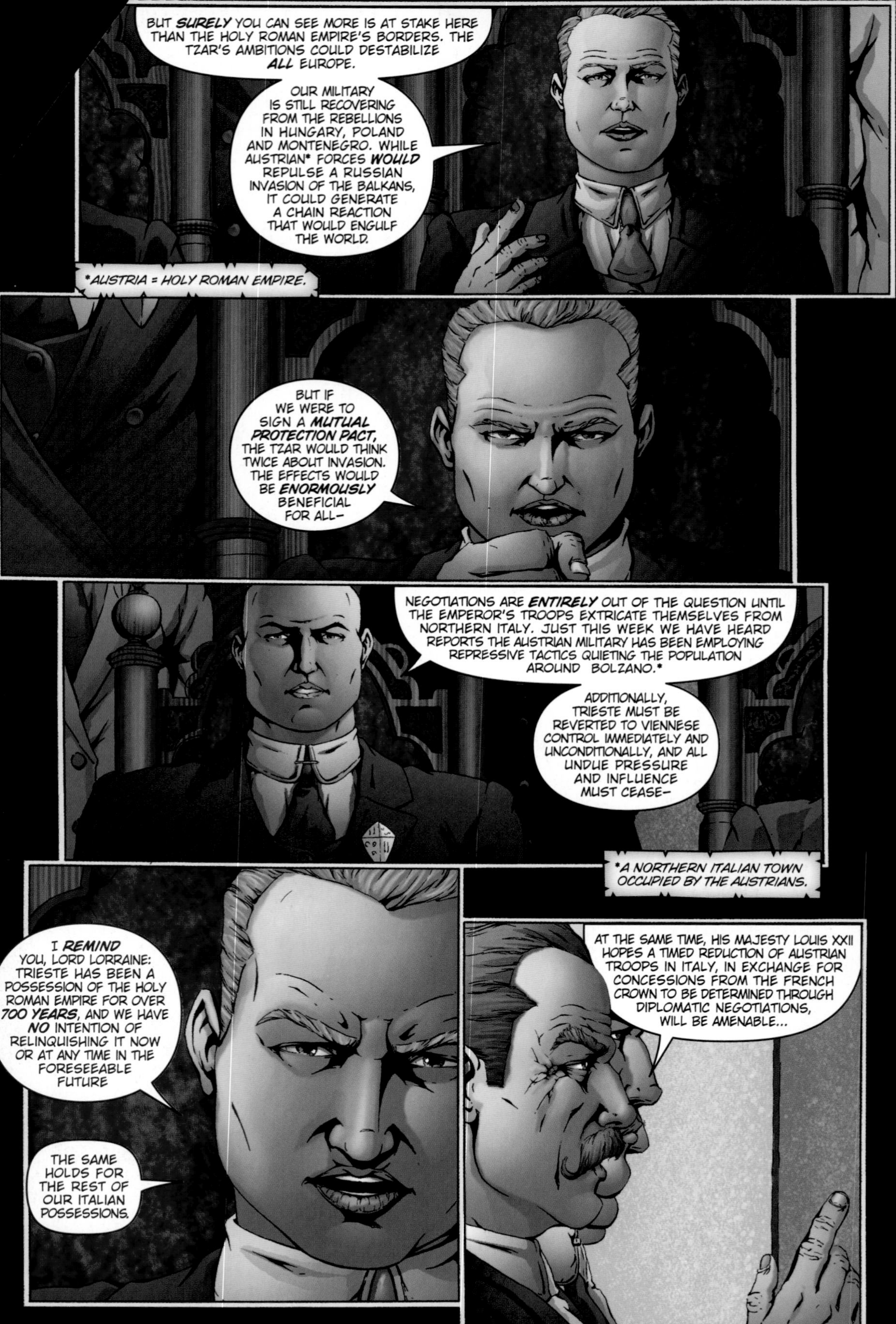
BUT SURELY YOU CAN SEE MORE IS AT STAKE HERE THAN THE HOLY ROMAN EMPIRE'S BORDERS. THE TZAR'S AMBITIONS COULD DESTABILIZE ALL EUROPE.
OUR MILITARY IS STILL RECOVERING FROM THE REBELLIONS IN HUNGARY, POLAND AND MONTENEGRO. WHILE AUSTRIAN* FORCES WOULD REPULSE A RUSSIAN INVASION OF THE BALKANS, IT COULD GENERATE A CHAIN REACTION THAT WOULD ENGULF THE WORLD.
*AUSTRIA = HOLY ROMAN EMPIRE.
BUT IF WE WERE TO SIGN A MUTUAL PROTECTION PACT, THE TZAR WOULD THINK TWICE ABOUT INVASION. THE EFFECTS WOULD BE ENORMOUSLY BENEFICIAL FOR ALL-
NEGOTIATIONS ARE ENTIRELY OUT OF THE QUESTION UNTIL THE EMPEROR'S TROOPS EXTRICATE THEMSELVES FROM NORTHERN ITALY. JUST THIS WEEK WE HAVE HEARD REPORTS THE AUSTRIAN MILITARY HAS BEEN EMPLOYING REPRESSIVE TACTICS QUIETING THE POPULATION AROUND BOLZANO.*
ADDITIONALLY, TRIESTE MUST BE REVERTED TO VIENNESE CONTROL IMMEDIATELY AND UNCONDITIONALLY, AND ALL UNDUE PRESSURE AND INFLUENCE MUST CEASE-
*A NORTHERN ITALIAN TOWN OCCUPIED BY THE AUSTRIANS.
I REMIND YOU, LORD LORRAINE: TRIESTE HAS BEEN A POSSESSION OF THE HOLY ROMAN EMPIRE FOR OVER 700 YEARS, AND WE HAVE NO INTENTION OF RELINQUISHING IT NOW OR AT ANY TIME IN THE FORESEEABLE FUTURE
THE SAME HOLDS FOR THE REST OF OUR ITALIAN POSSESSIONS.
AT THE SAME TIME, HIS MAJESTY LOUIS XXII HOPES A TIMED REDUCTION OF AUSTRIAN TROOPS IN ITALY, IN EXCHANGE FOR CONCESSIONS FROM THE FRENCH CROWN TO BE DETERMINED THROUGH DIPLOMATIC NEGOTIATIONS, WILL BE AMENABLE...

MY EMPEROR HAS MADE HIS POSITION ON THIS SUBJECT **VERY CLEAR.** OUR ITALIAN HOLDINGS ARE NOT NEGOTIABLE.

IS THERE REALLY NO OTHER WAY? WHAT SAYS THE REPRESENTATIVE FROM THE HALL OF THE ROBE?

THE ROBE IS IN COMPLETE CONCURRENCE WITH THE CROWN.

AND WITH **LORD LORRAINE.**

DO YOU REALIZE THE MAGNITUDE OF THE CHAOS THAT COULD ENSUE IF WAR WERE TO BREAK OUT RIGHT NOW? WE ARE HEADED FOR THE EDGE OF A CLIFF.

RULERS MUST BAND **TOGETHER,** IN A SPIRIT OF **COOPERATION,** TO REDUCE TENSION.

IF WE FAIL IN THIS, HOW LONG WILL IT TAKE FOR THE WORLD TO RECOVER? HOW MANY OF OUR SUBJECTS WILL PERISH?

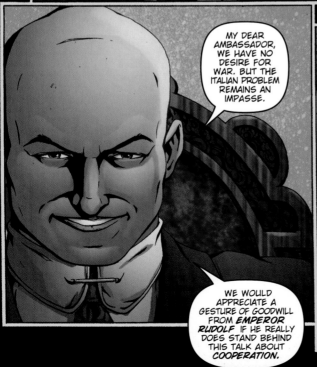

MY DEAR AMBASSADOR, WE HAVE NO DESIRE FOR WAR. BUT THE ITALIAN PROBLEM REMAINS AN IMPASSE.

WE WOULD APPRECIATE A GESTURE OF GOODWILL FROM **EMPEROR RUDOLF** IF HE REALLY DOES STAND BEHIND THIS TALK ABOUT **COOPERATION.**

WE DO INDEED SEEM TO BE AT AN IMPASSE.

AT LEAST FOR THE TIME BEING.

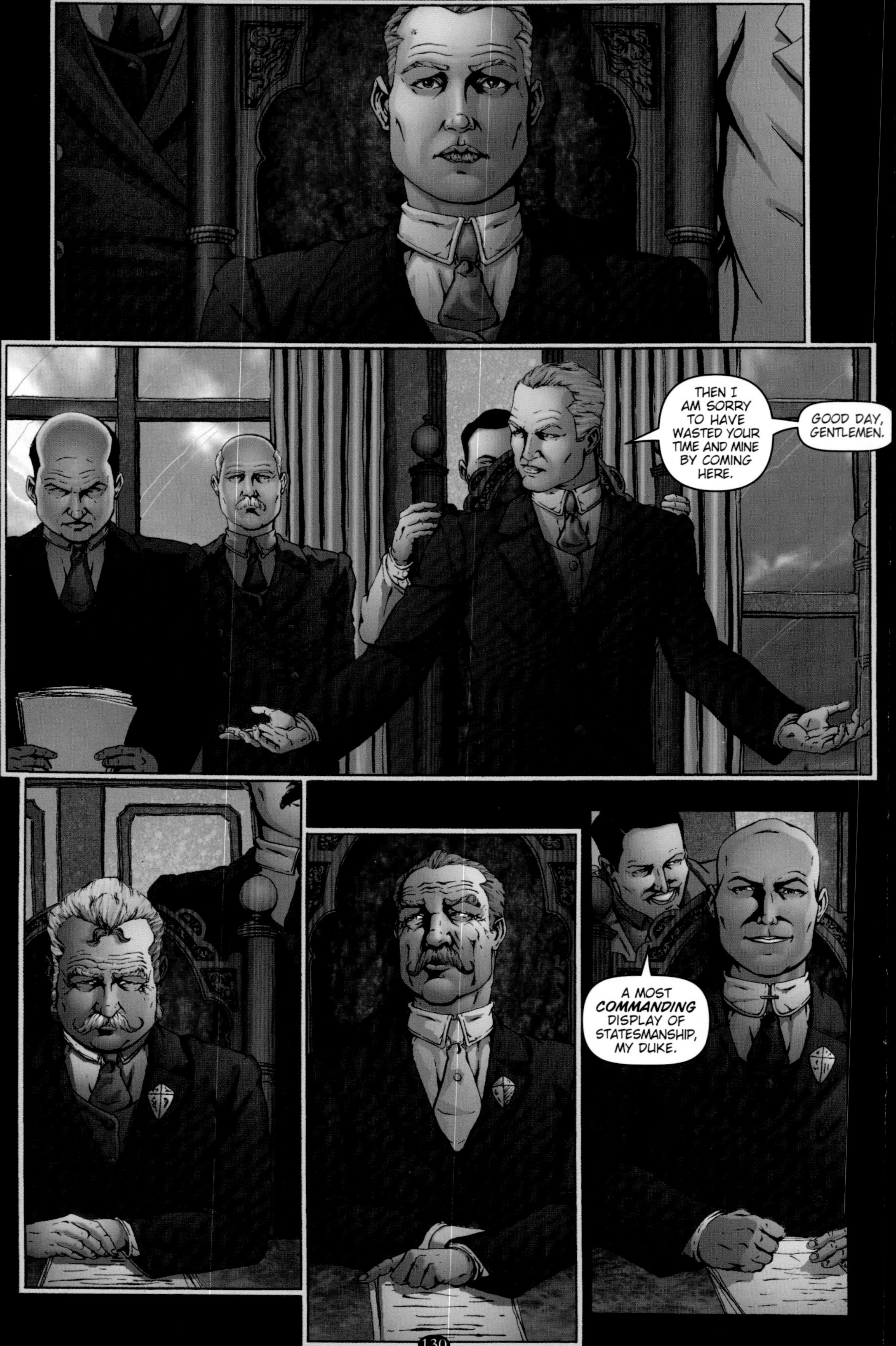
THEN I AM SORRY TO HAVE WASTED YOUR TIME AND MINE BY COMING HERE.
GOOD DAY, GENTLEMEN.
A MOST **COMMANDING** DISPLAY OF STATESMANSHIP, MY DUKE.

DEATH SWORD!

DR. SAUNIÈRE? HAVE YOU GONE COMPLETELY MAD?

NO! DEATH SWORD IS THE KEYWORD TO THE CODE WE DISCOVERED IN THE SCROLLS I BROUGHT YOU.

PRAY, EXPLAIN.

LAST NIGHT, A GRAVE IN MONTMARTRE CEMETERY WAS... BROUGHT TO MY ATTENTION.

IT WAS THE HEADSTONE OF A WOMAN WHOSE FAMILY HAD A LONG HISTORY WITH THE **KNIGHTS TEMPLAR.**

THERE WERE FOUR MISSPELLED OR MISPLACED UPPERCASE LETTERS ON THE TOMBSTONE: **M, O, R,** AND **T.**

CT GIT NOBLe M
ARIE DE NEGRᵉ
DARLES DAME
DHAUPOUL Dᵗ
BLANCHEFORT
AGEE DE SOIX
ANTE SET ANS
DECEDEE LE
XVII JANVIER
MDCOLXXXI
REQUIES CATIN
PACE

E T I N A P X

Δ⚹I A E Ω

MORT. **DEATH.**

AND THERE WERE FOUR CONSPICUOUSLY SUBSCRIPTED LETTERS: **E, P, E, E.**

CT GIT NOBLe M
ARIE DE NEGRᵉ
DARLES DAME
DHAUPOUL Dᵗ
BLANCHEFORT
AGEE DE SOIX
ANTE SET ANS
DECEDEE LE
XVII JANVIER
MDCOLXXXI
REQUIES CATIN
PACE

E T I N A P X

Δ⚹I A E Ω

EPEE. **SWORD.**

TOGETHER IT SPELLS **MORT EPEE.**

I WON'T EVEN ASK HOW YOU GOT THIS. I GUESS THERE'S ONLY ONE WAY TO FIND OUT IF YOU'RE ONTO SOMETHING...

m o r t e p e e m o r t e p e e m
GSMVDONZREBTKEAID

o r t e p e e m o r t e p e e m o r
FIAEZJPULCCKYAOPSM

t e p e e m o r t e p e e m o r t
TXKYDUATJOEDAYPGV

e p e e m o r t e p e e m o r t e p
AKYAQNTDSHEXLFPKYC

e e m o r t e p e e m o r t e p e
KOGLVJPRANVHMYWLD

e m o r t e p e e m o r t e p e
RGBOZOOPFAGADSOZ

e m o r t e p e e m o r t e p e e
RYXTKPPDRRDGNNEVB

m o r t e p e e m o r t e p e e
LCTKZJXZGMGLAHAG

INFORMATION ON THE DECRYPTION:
WWW.REXMUNDI.NET

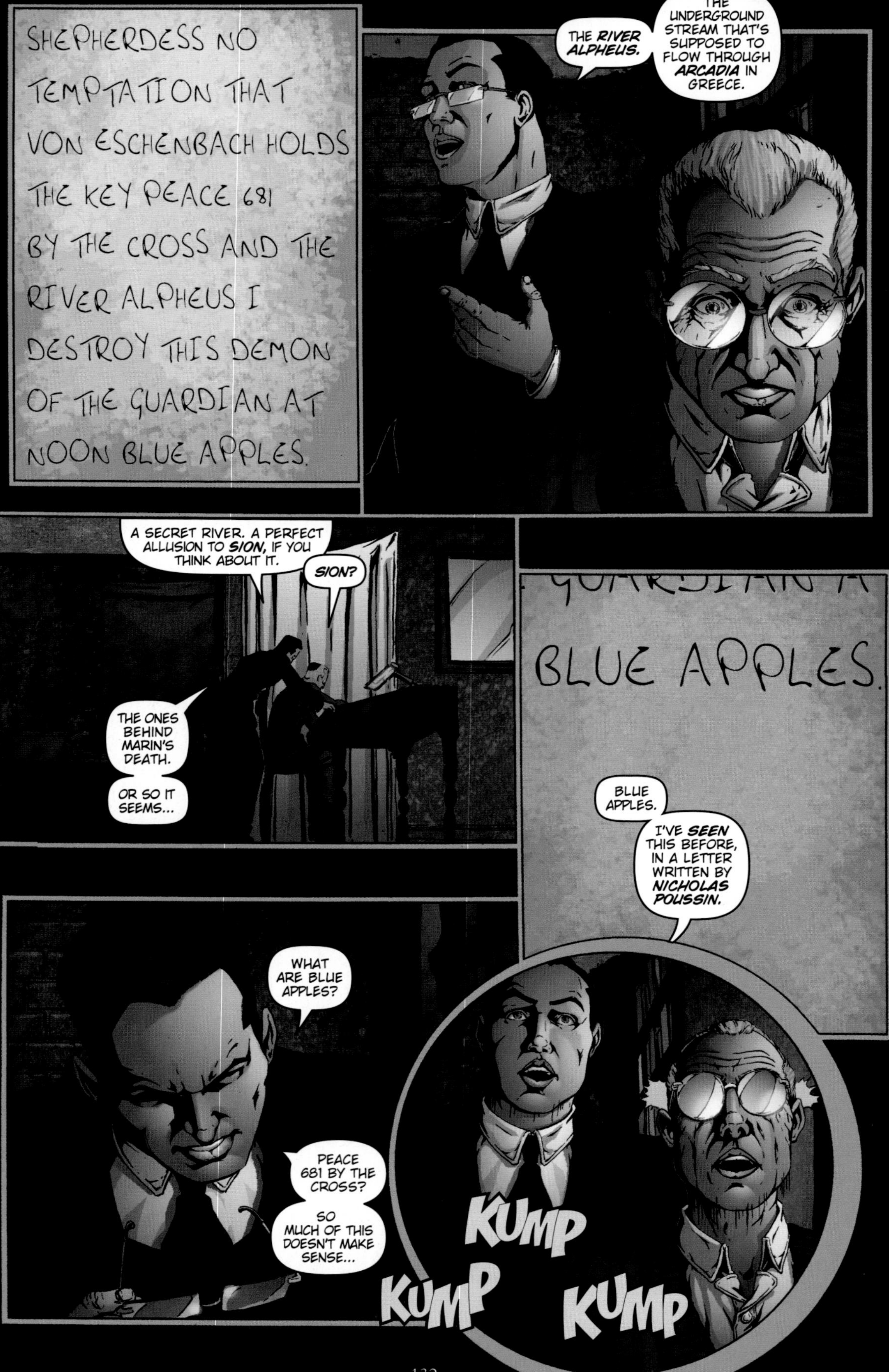
SHEPHERDESS NO TEMPTATION THAT VON ESCHENBACH HOLDS THE KEY PEACE 681 BY THE CROSS AND THE RIVER ALPHEUS I DESTROY THIS DEMON OF THE GUARDIAN AT NOON BLUE APPLES.
THE RIVER ALPHEUS.
THE UNDERGROUND STREAM THAT'S SUPPOSED TO FLOW THROUGH ARCADIA IN GREECE.
A SECRET RIVER. A PERFECT ALLUSION TO SION, IF YOU THINK ABOUT IT.
SION?
THE ONES BEHIND MARIN'S DEATH.
OR SO IT SEEMS...
BLUE APPLES.
BLUE APPLES.
I'VE SEEN THIS BEFORE, IN A LETTER WRITTEN BY NICHOLAS POUSSIN.
WHAT ARE BLUE APPLES?
PEACE 681 BY THE CROSS?
SO MUCH OF THIS DOESN'T MAKE SENSE...
KUMP
KUMP
KUMP

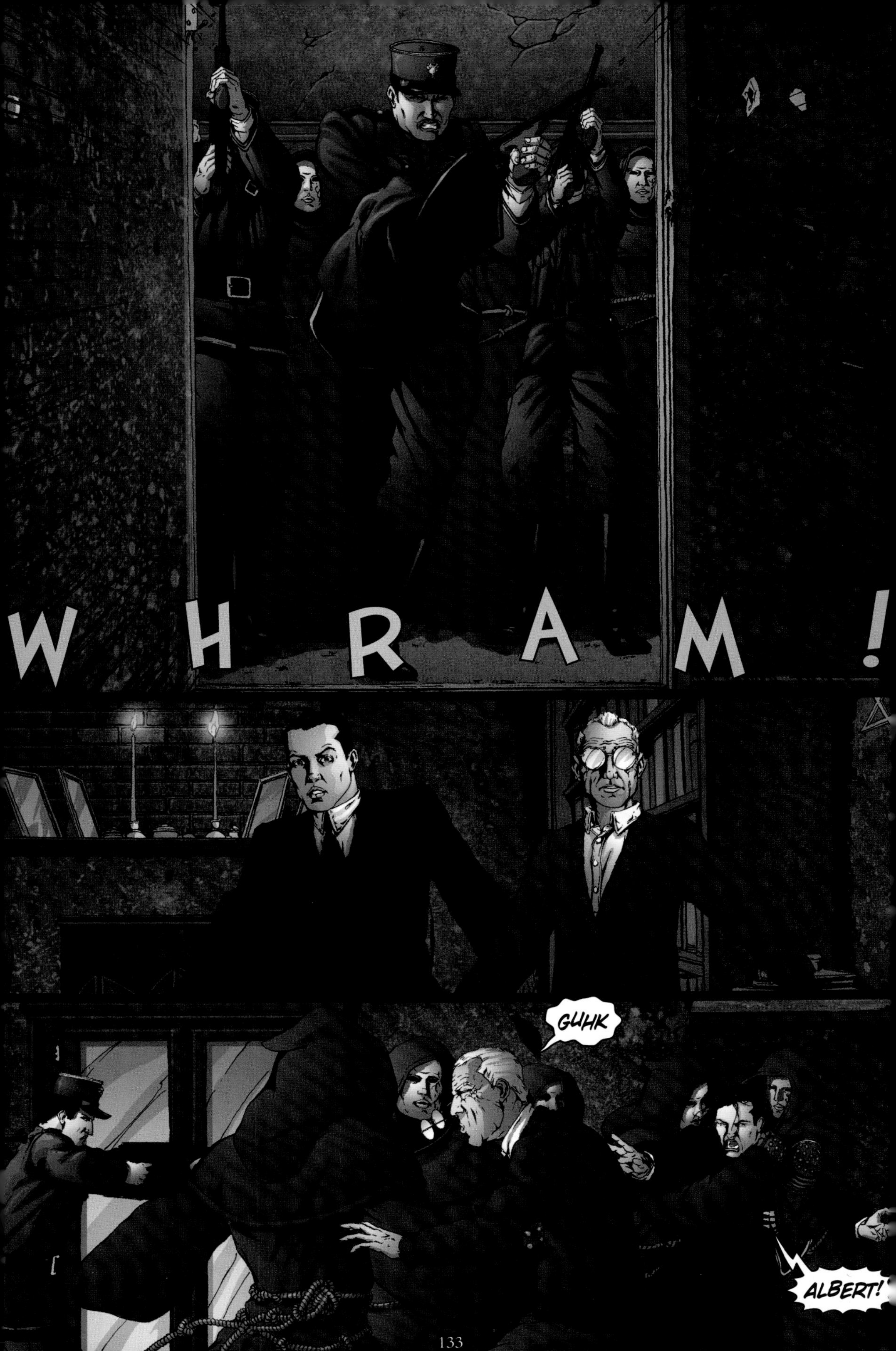
WHRAM!
GUHK
ALBERT!

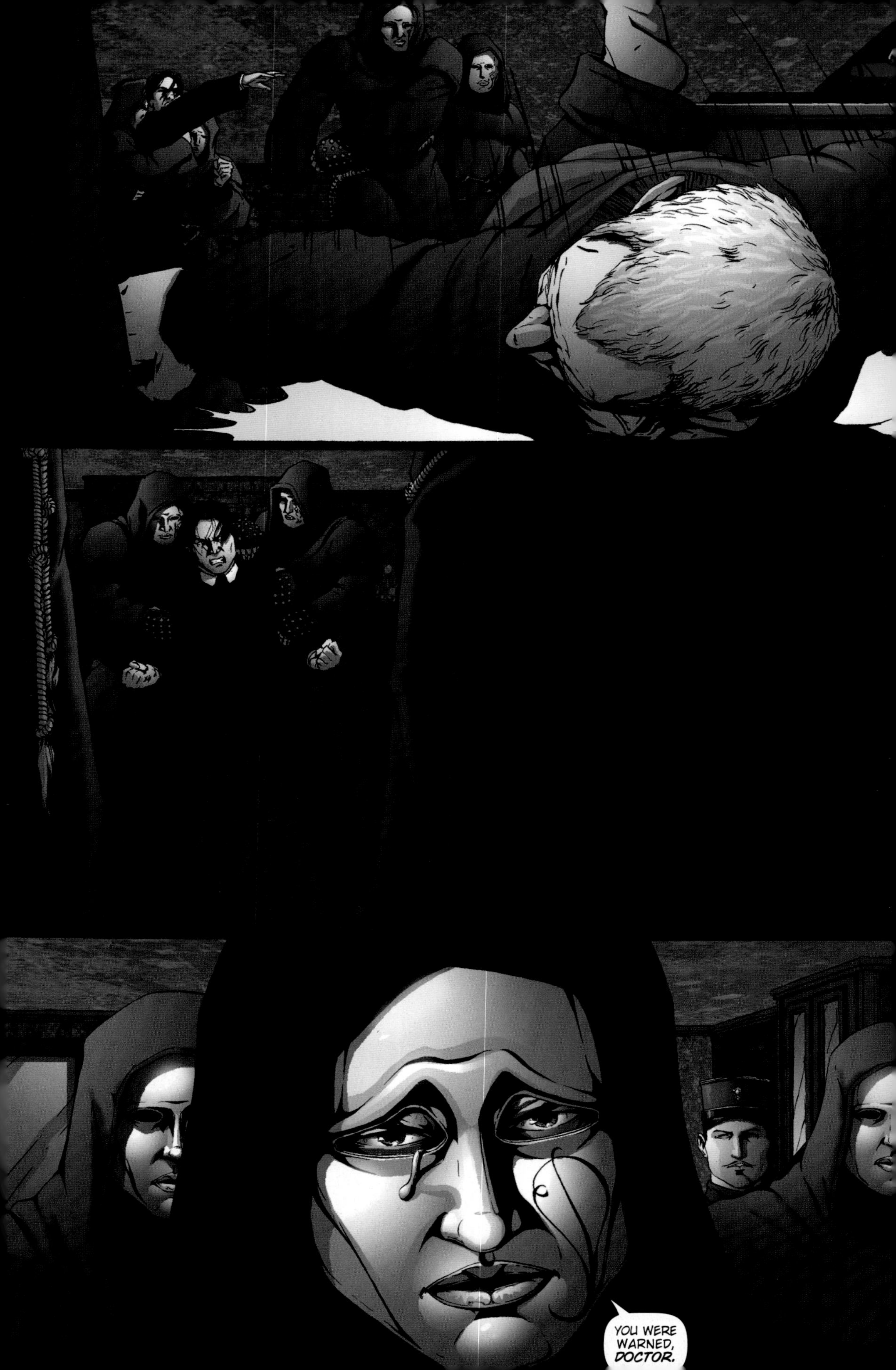
YOU WERE WARNED, DOCTOR.

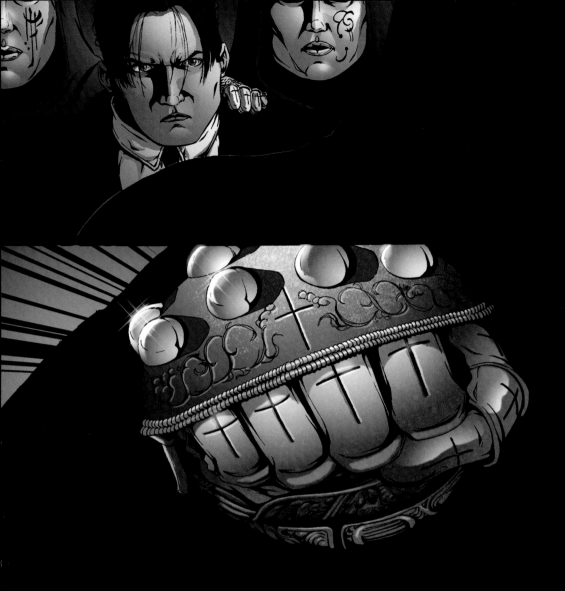

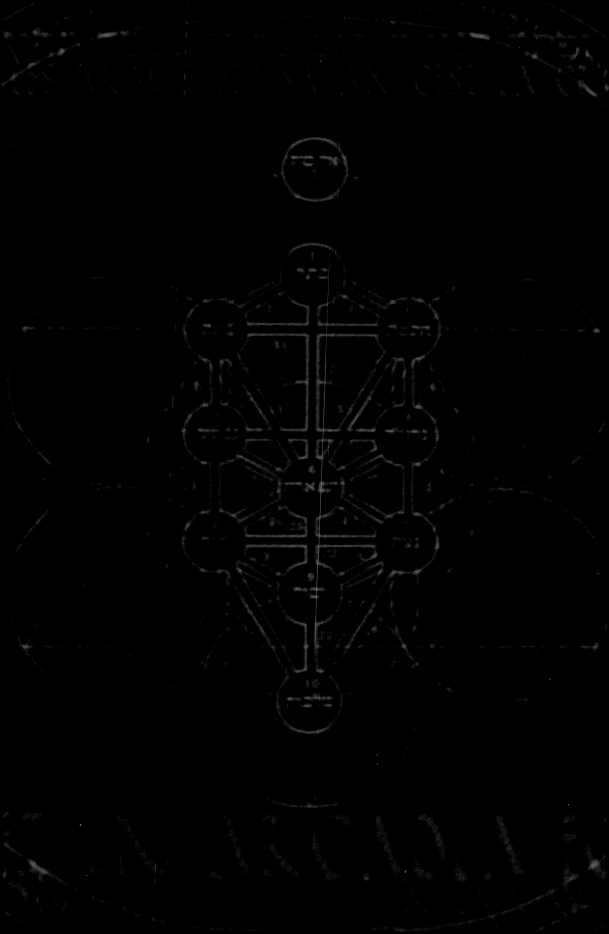

Le Journal de la Liberté

Paris' leading anglophone newspaper • vol. 205, no. 97 • Oct. 27, MCMXXXIII

Papal Seal

Editors in Chief: M. Tait Bergstrom, M. Matthew Pasteris. **Story Editor:** M. Arvid Nelson. **Art Editors:** M. EricJ, M. Jeromy Cox. **Photography Editor:** M. Alexander Waldman. **Layout Supervisor:** M. William Kartalopoulos. **Editors Emeritus:** M. Clark A. Smith, M. Howard P. Lovecraft, M. Robert E. Howard. Redacted by the Holy Parisian Inquisition under the direction of His Excellency Archbishop Emile-Jean Ireneaux. Le Journal de Liberté is printed under the benign auspices of his most puissant majesty KING LOUIS XXII of FRANCE.

GOD SAVE THE KING.

of Approval

SUPPORT FOR KING'S POLICIES ERODING IN PARLIAMENT

King's advisors express concern, dismay over recent defections in Hall of the Robe but remain confident

Versailles, Paris — The rank-and-file members of the Hall of the Robe, Louis XXII's bastion of support, continue to defect to Lord Lorraine, the crown's most vocal opponent.

Publicly, the crown's spokesmen remain dismissive. But private anxieties over the king's evaporating political base are surfacing.

"I think it's safe to say we're looking at a trend now," said a member of Louis' court. "It's impossible to say what the effect will be, but it's a cause of some concern."

The political shake-up started earlier this week, when Baron Aristide deMandeville, leading member of the Hall of the Sword and the King's close ally, announced a dramatic policy reversal.

While he once condemned Lord Lorraine's policies and "warmongering and myopic," deMandeville now calls Lorraine's

aggressive foreign stance "a clarion call for the French Kingdom."

"France had only two options, global supremacy or abject servitude as an Arab or German satrapy," deMandeville said in his floor speech announcing his changed intentions four days ago. DeMandeville has not been available for comment since his abrupt shift.

"Baron deMandeville is entitled to his opinions, but King Louis find his reversal most dishonorable," crown spokesman Sir Jean Dasté said.

"We welcome any addition to our ranks," Baron Robert Teniers, a spokesman for the Duke of Lorraine, said. "It's occurring to more and more people that the path to security for France lies in strength, not weakness."

Whatever his reasons, deMandeville's disavowal of the King has triggered a small but

Versailles, Court of Louis XXII. The tranquility of the gardens belies growing turmoil as King Louis faces an insurrection in Parliament.

growing number of defections in the Hall of the Robe. Such a move would have been unthinkable before. So far, a dozen Robe members have changed allegiances.

"DeMandeville gave courage to those of us in the Robe who were uncomfortable with the King's policies," junior Robe member and recent defector Count Ralph Perou Weigand said.

Yesterday, this newfound independence was felt dramatically when the Robe voted against the King's wishes on a bill — the first time since its inception in 1802.

While the king has the power to appoint members to the Hall of the Robe, under France's constitution only the Robe may expel its own.

"I can't see the Robe voting out a member because of this, at least not for the time being. But if things get much worse, action might be taken," loyalist Robe member Jean-Claude Dhien said. The King will have the last word on the subject according to him.

"Let's not forget the majority of the Robe still supports the King. We will consult him on any issue concerning His kingdom."

FRA President Franklin Delano Roosevelt Announces Detention of Alleged English Spies; Edward VIII Expresses "Outrage"

Washington, DC, FRA — Five British nationals have been detained by Bureau of Investigation (BOI) agents on charges they illegally obtained "top secret information vital to the security of the Federal Republic of America," according to BOI spokesman J. Edgar Hoover.

The men, whose identities have not been released, allegedly worked through the British Embassy in Washington, D.C.

President Roosevelt announced the arrests jointly with Hoover in a press conference on the White House Lawn yesterday

afternoon. Roosevelt praised Hoover for his diligence in tracking down "foreign nationals who seek to compromise the safety of American citizens."

"It is no secret that a vast network of underground English royalists is at work in Washington, trying to undermine the very fabric of our societal values," Hoover said.

He would not comment on the nature of the secrets allegedly stolen, save to say that the arrests concern "fortifications and defenses on the Mason-Dixon line."

The Mason-Dixon line separates the Federal Republic of America and the Confederate States of America. Each side is wary of a surprise invasion by the other.

"We have sent a clear message to the Confederates and their allies: their attempts to undermine our way of life will fail," Roosevelt said.

The English crown was quick to condemn the move.

"These charges are scurrilous *continued on page A13*

High-Level French Officials to Discuss Territorial Disputes, Instability with Austrian Ambassador

Versailles, Paris — Relations between the Holy Roman Empire and France have been frosty for several generations. However, a shift towards friendlier footing may be imminent.

In a potentially historic gesture, Austrian Ambassador Viscount Helmut Von Vetsera has extended an invitation to the French political establishment, hoping, in his words, "to establish a mutual framework of trust and cooperation."

In attendance at the talks scheduled for today will be Vetsera himself, Lord Lorraine, Speaker for the Sword, the King's spokesman Sir Charles Martel, and Baron Aristide deMandeville, Speaker for the Robe.

Lorraine is openly mistrustful of the Austrians, a fact reflected in his voting record, while Martel is a

strong advocate of greater cooperation amongst Christian monarchs.

Attention is therefore focused on Lord deMandeville, who did a theatrical about-face on the floor of the Hall of the Robe four days ago. Once a staunch ally of King Louis, he declared support for Lord Lorraine, his former political arch-rival.

"It mystified a lot of people," a member of the Hall of the Sword said. "So this is a touchstone for his recent change of heart. We'll see if he means it or not."

Security and international stability are expected to be high on Ambassador Vetsera's agenda. In recent years, the Austrian army has been severely strained suppressing rebellions in its outlying provinces. It now faces external threats from *continued on page A*

E JOURNAL SPECIAL:
The Holy Roman Empire

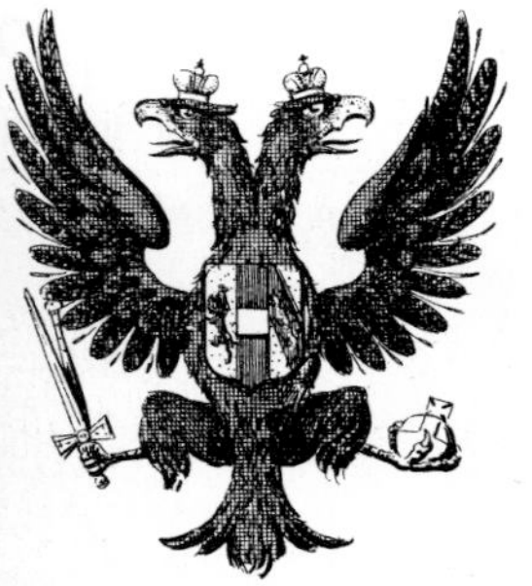

'he two-headed eagle, symbol of the Ioly Roman Empire and the Iabsburg dynasty.

he Holy Roman Empire (HRE) is one of the oldest despotisms in con-nuous existence. Although the Iabsburgs have had a firm grip on this rawling, polyglot empire for over ght hundred years, recent events have ft many wondering about its future. this special section of Le Journal de Liberté, *we take a look at the his-ry of the HRE, at its current state of fairs, and what it all means to the erage Parisian citizen.*

e Origins of the Empire

Voltaire famously said the HRE "neither Holy, nor Roman, nor Empire." A more common name r the Habsburg domains is the *ustro-Hungarian Empire*, since the o most prominent ethnic popu-ions of the empire, the Magyars Hungary and the Germans of ıstria, are its virtual masters.

The name "Holy Roman npire" was coined during the ign of Charlemagne, crowned Novus Constantinus" by Pope o II in the year 800 AD. ıarlemagne was seen as a new ıristian Emperor in the tradition Constantine the Great, and the pellation Holy Roman Empire emed an appropriate description r his lands.

The character and dimensions the HRE have changed since edieval times, but the Habsburg nasty, considered the heirs to ıarlemagne's legacy, have provid- a thread of continuity through- t the empire's turbulent history.

e House of Habsburg-Lothringen

The venerable House of ıbsburg-Lothringen has an illus-ous past. "Their pedigree has oduced more monarchs than any ıer," according to Sir Jean-Marc fayette, Royal Herald of the ench College of Arms.

Over the years, the Habsburgs have ceded some political power to provincial councils and the *Reichsrat*, the national legislative council.

But none should question who really commands the empire.

"Control over military and for-eign affairs is the sole domain of the Emperor," Viscount Helmut Von Vetsera, Ambassador of the Holy Roman Empire to the Kingdom of France, said.

Emperor Rudolf: The Prodigal Son

Rudolf von Habsburg-Lothringen is the current Emperor. He was unusually old before he ascended to the throne; his father Franz-Josef took the title at the age of eighteen. Rudolf was obliged to wait to wait until his father abdicated in 1906. He was 64 years old at the time.

The Emperor had a difficult relationship with his father; Franz Josef was strictly conservative, while young Rudolf was liberally mind-ed. Rumors abounded that the young Rudolph, then an archduke, tried to kill himself in 1889 at an imperial hunting lodge in Mayerling, Austria.

However, Rudolf's anticlerical and anti-social opinions mellowed later on in life, and now he cham-pions the causes closest to his late father's heart.

"...Nor an Empire"

Although the Habsburgs con-sider themselves German Emperors, their subjects include Ukrainians, Poles, Italians, Roumanians, Slavs, Magyars, Ruthenes, and Bohemians, to name a few. This mixture of eth-nicities is "extremely volatile," according to Lord Vetsera.

The many ethnic groups of the empire are prone to unrest and out-right rebellion when they feel the yoke of Habsburg rule is too heavy.

"Our Emperor must carefully balance the concerns of all His sub-jects. Granting too much freedom to one minority may cause resent-ment amongst others," Vestera said. "But at its core, the Holy Roman Empire is a German Empire. This is what provides us with stability."

Some believe this attitude of German superiority actually adds to the chronic unrest within the Empire. Not all the Emperor's sub-jects are happy to be ruled by what they consider a foreign power.

"It's simply not tenable," Hall of the Robe member Sir Jean-Paul Gartier said. "Emperor Rudolf's father nearly caused a civil war by announcing he would be coronated King of Bohemia. Rudolf won't dare make the same mistake. And they have made so many recent concessions to the Hungarians that the other minori-ties are extremely unhappy."

According to some, the divi-sions amongst the myriad ethnic groups can be considered an asset to the Emperor.

"They bicker intensely with one another, so there's no impetus for a collective movement against the Habsburgs," said a source with-in the Imperial Ministry of State.

Indeed, politics in the empire are a noisy, contentious affair. Members of the Reichsrat are even known to bang on drums and blast trumpets during the speeches of opposition party members.

But no one argues the revolu-tionary, nationalist tendencies amongst the HRE's subjects pro-mote the empire's stability.

The Keystone of Europe

"Our internal differences are a natural result of geography. We are at the crossroads of the world," Baron Lajos Ferenczy, a member of the Hungarian Parliament, said. "To our east lie the Ottomans. To the north, Russia, and to the west Italy and Prussia. This is why the two-headed eagle is our symbol: we must be vigilant in all directions."

Tension electrifies every one of the HRE's frontiers. Serbian nationalists in the east are widely believed to have the support of Tzar Nicholas II. To the west, the Austrian occupation of norther Italy engenders ill will amongst th monarchs of France and England particularly in regard to Adriati port of Trieste.

Austro-Hungarian officials se this disharmony as a direct threat t the whole of Europe.

"We are the keystone o Europe," Ambassador Vetsera said "We are the Christian vanguar against the Mohammedan threat o the Turks. If we fall, so does a Europe." Charles Martel, mayor o the court to King Louis XXII, i inclined to agree.

"Austria-Hungary must not b allowed to disintegrate, or all th nations of Europe risk exposin themselves to a conflict beyon anyone's power to contain. Th time has never been more critical.'

But a growing chorus o French politicians disagree wit this point of view.

"The problems faced b Austria-Hungary are of its ow making," Lord Lorraine, Speaker fo the Hall of the Sword said. "W cannot be held accountable fo their bad management."

Whatever the case, most agre the Holy Roman Empire is in a position of unprecedented weakness

"Over the last decade, th Austrian army has been sorel taxed suppressing rebellions i Croatia, Galicia and Hungary. W came close to the precipice, an we're only inching away very slow-ly," a source within the Hofburg palace said. "One sharp tug could send the Holy Roman Empire ove the edge."

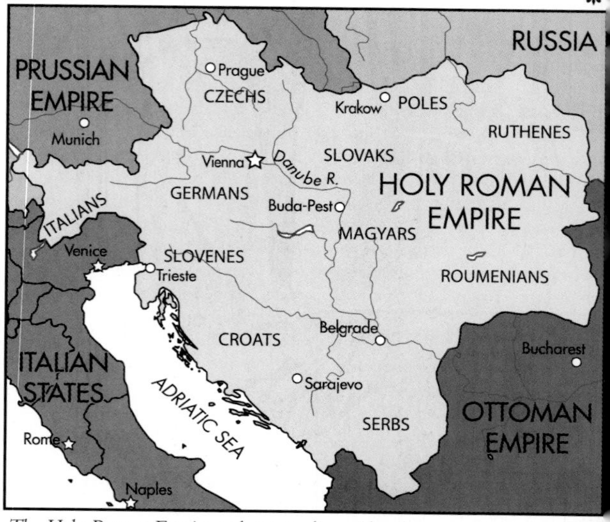
RUSSIA
PRUSSIAN EMPIRE
Prague
CZECHS
Krakow
POLES
RUTHENES
Munich
SLOVAKS
Vienna
Danube R.
GERMANS
HOLY ROMAN EMPIRE
Buda-Pest
ITALIANS
MAGYARS
Venice
SLOVENES
Trieste
ROUMENIANS
Belgrade
CROATS
Bucharest
ITALIAN STATES
Sarajevo
ADRIATIC SEA
SERBS
OTTOMAN EMPIRE
Rome
Naples

The Holy Roman Empire and surroundings. Also shown are the many ethnic groups within the Empire. "A volatile mix," according to Ambassador Vetsera.

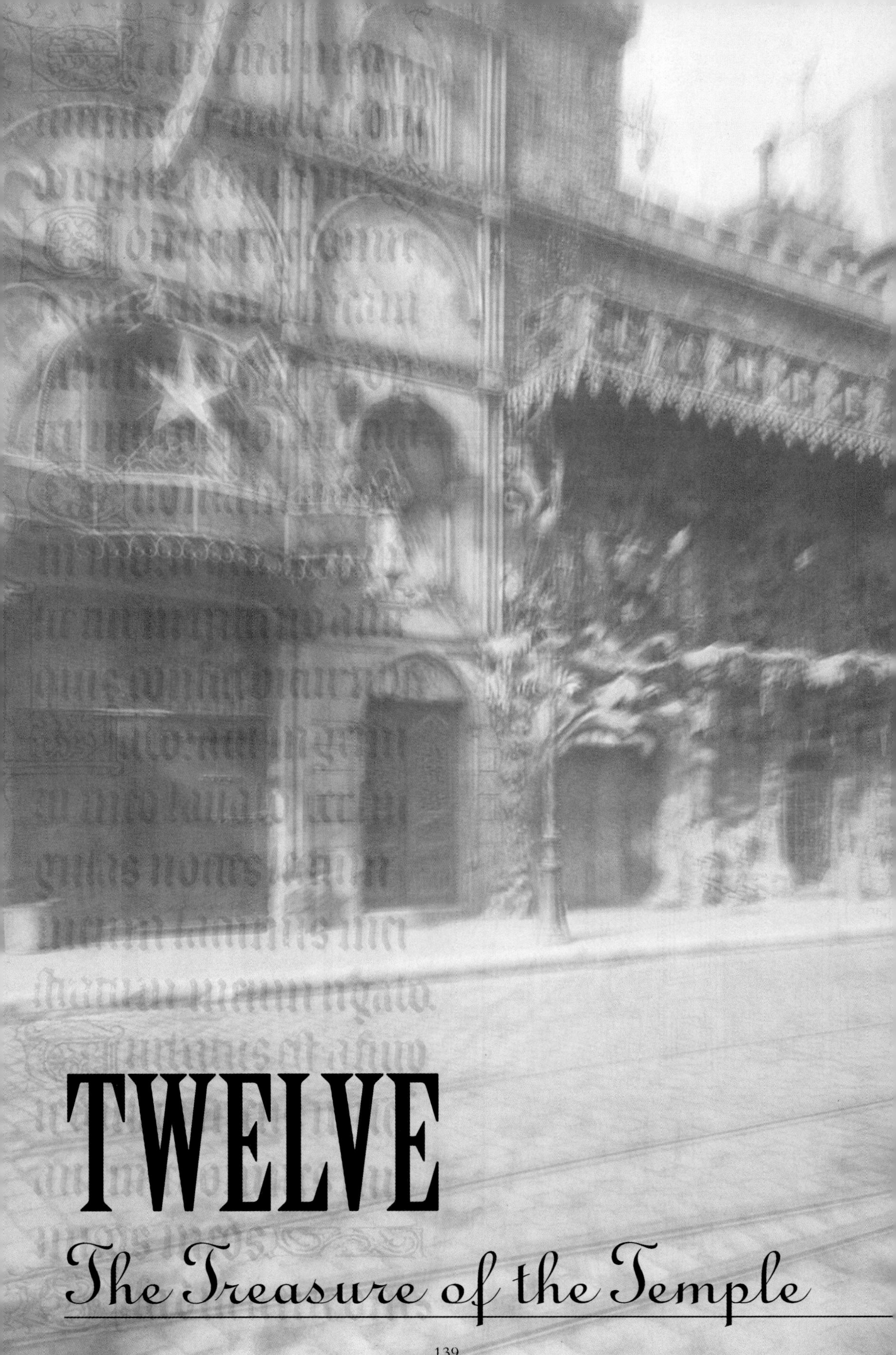

TWELVE

The Treasure of the Temple

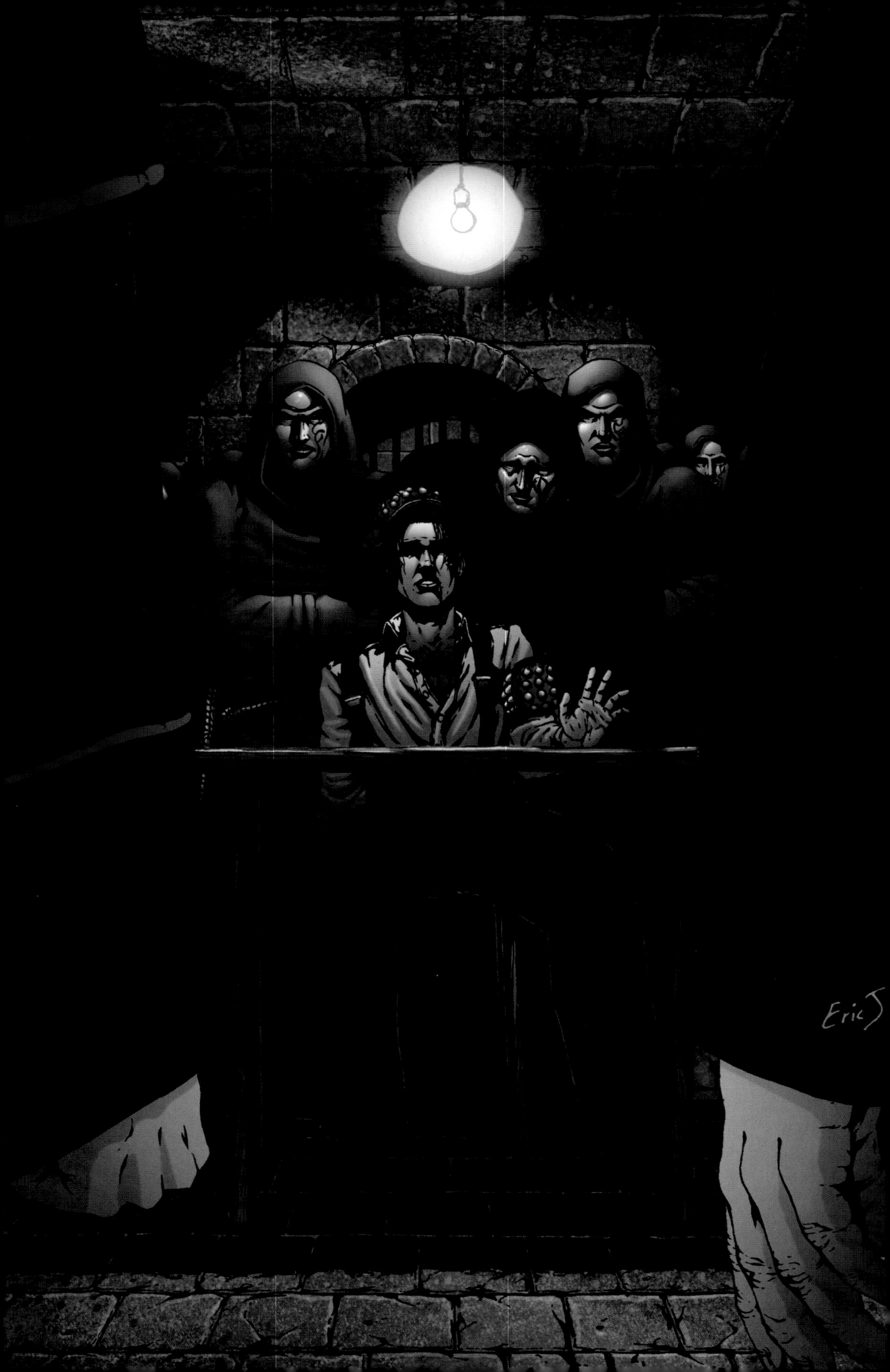
Eric J

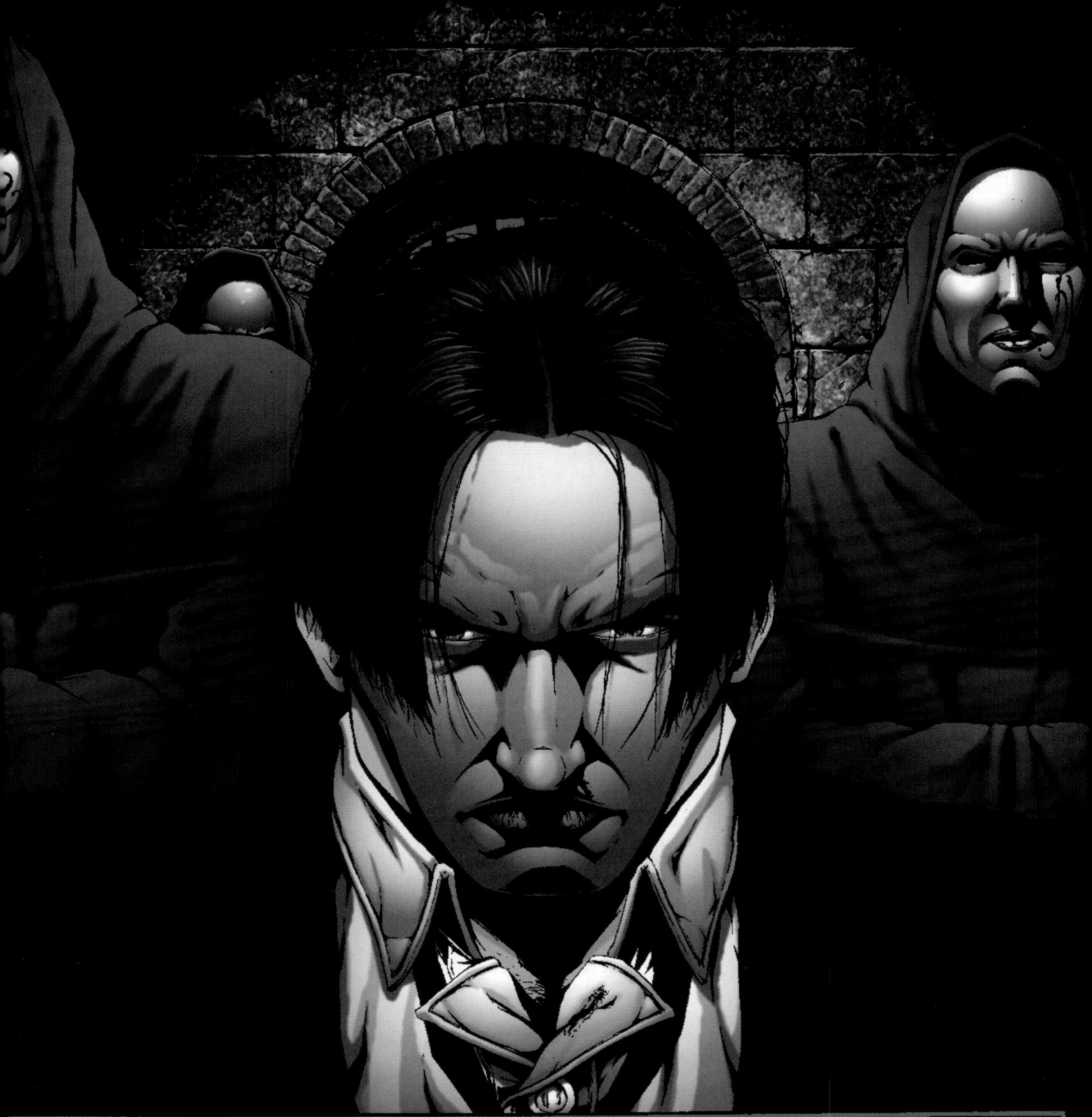

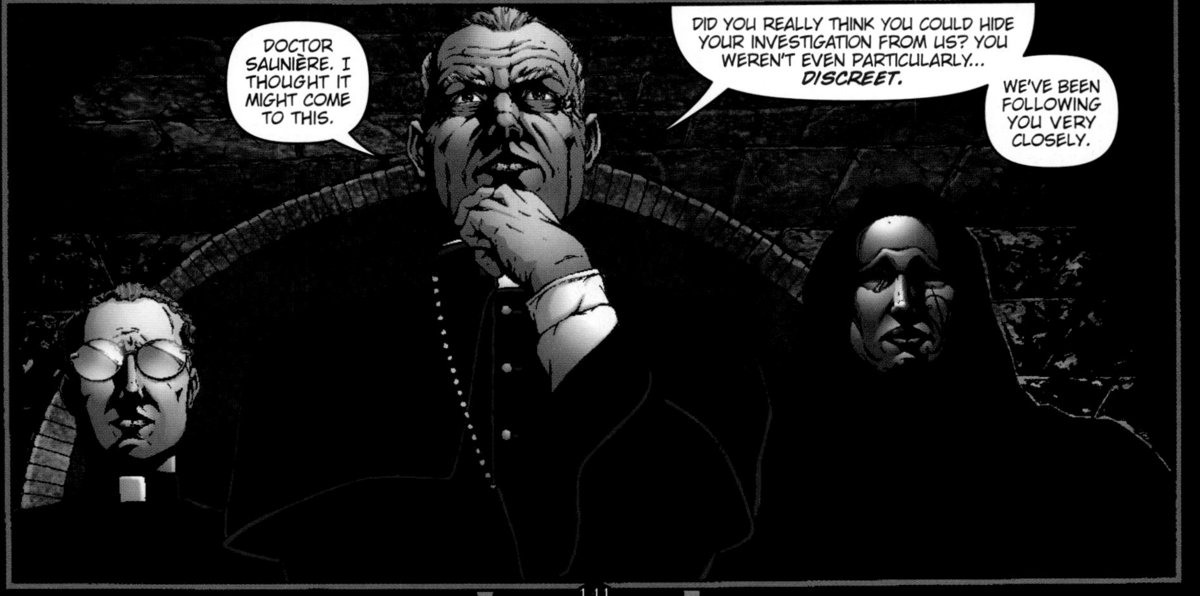
DOCTOR SAUNIÈRE. I THOUGHT IT MIGHT COME TO THIS.
DID YOU REALLY THINK YOU COULD HIDE YOUR INVESTIGATION FROM US? YOU WEREN'T EVEN PARTICULARLY... ***DISCREET.***
WE'VE BEEN FOLLOWING YOU VERY CLOSELY.

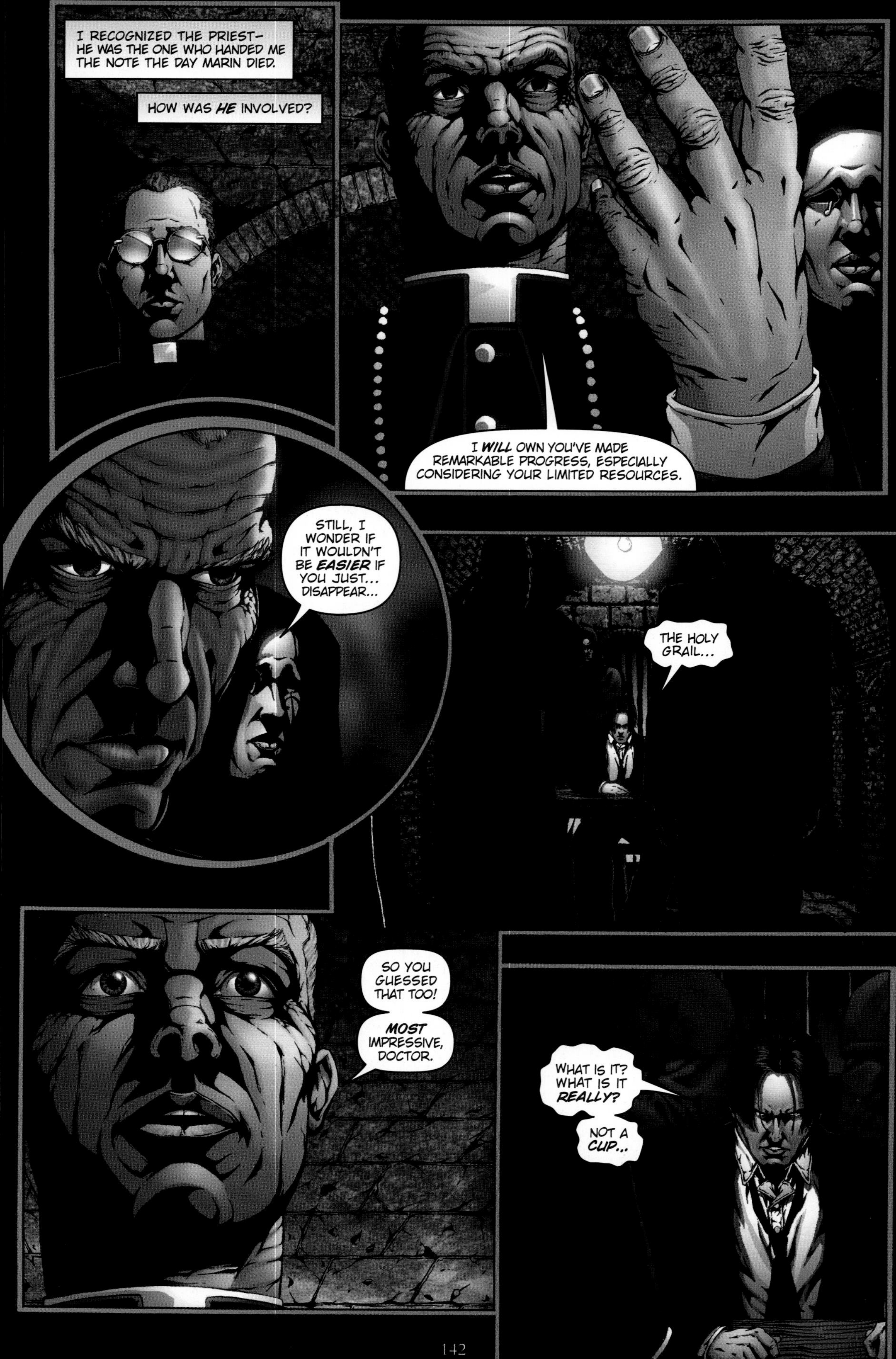

I RECOGNIZED THE PRIEST– HE WAS THE ONE WHO HANDED ME THE NOTE THE DAY MARIN DIED.
HOW WAS *HE* INVOLVED?
I *WILL* OWN YOU'VE MADE REMARKABLE PROGRESS, ESPECIALLY CONSIDERING YOUR LIMITED RESOURCES.
STILL, I WONDER IF IT WOULDN'T BE *EASIER* IF YOU JUST... DISAPPEAR...
THE HOLY GRAIL...
SO YOU GUESSED THAT TOO!
MOST IMPRESSIVE, DOCTOR.
WHAT IS IT? WHAT IS IT *REALLY*?
NOT A *CUP*...

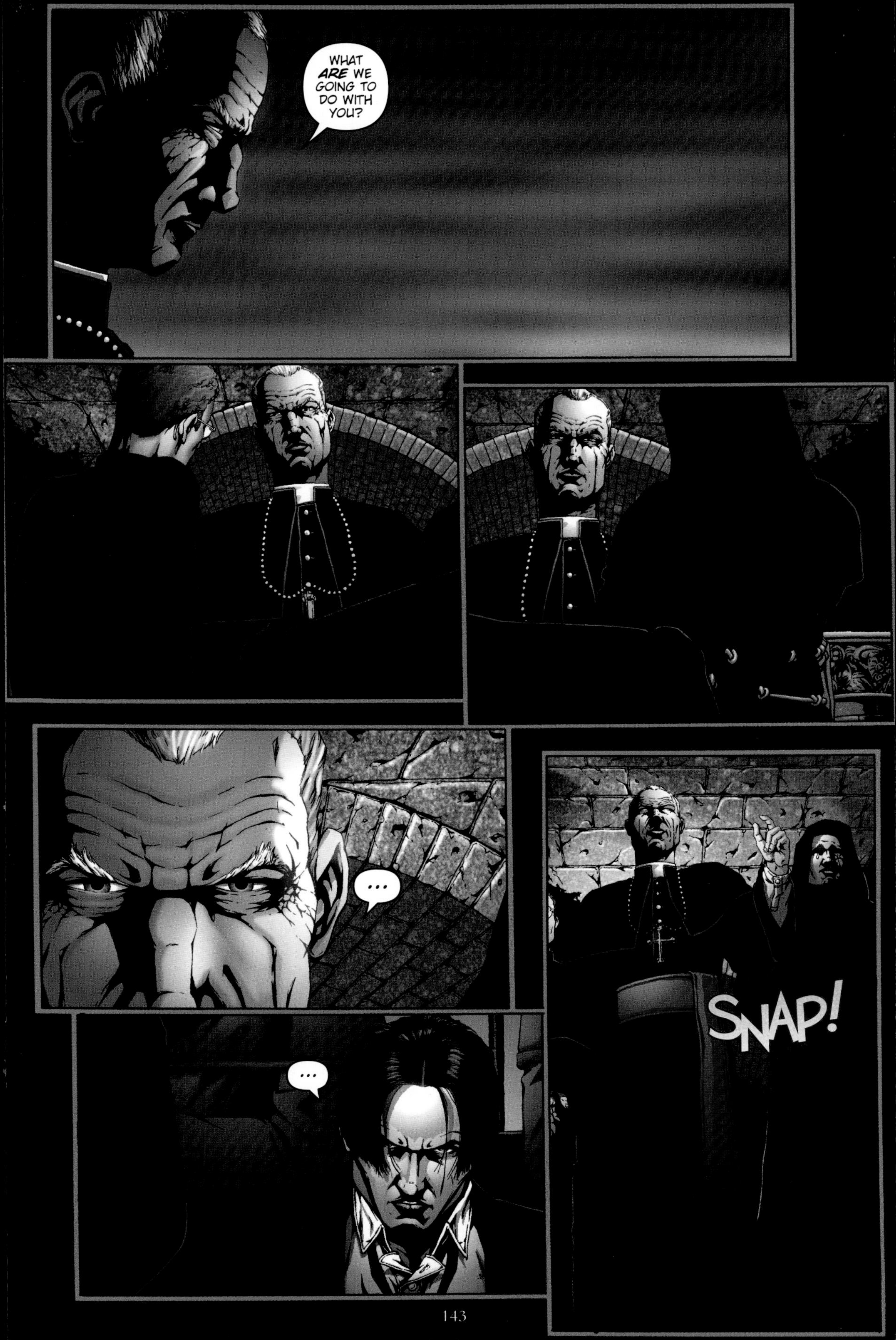
WHAT ARE WE GOING TO DO WITH YOU?
...
...
SNAP!

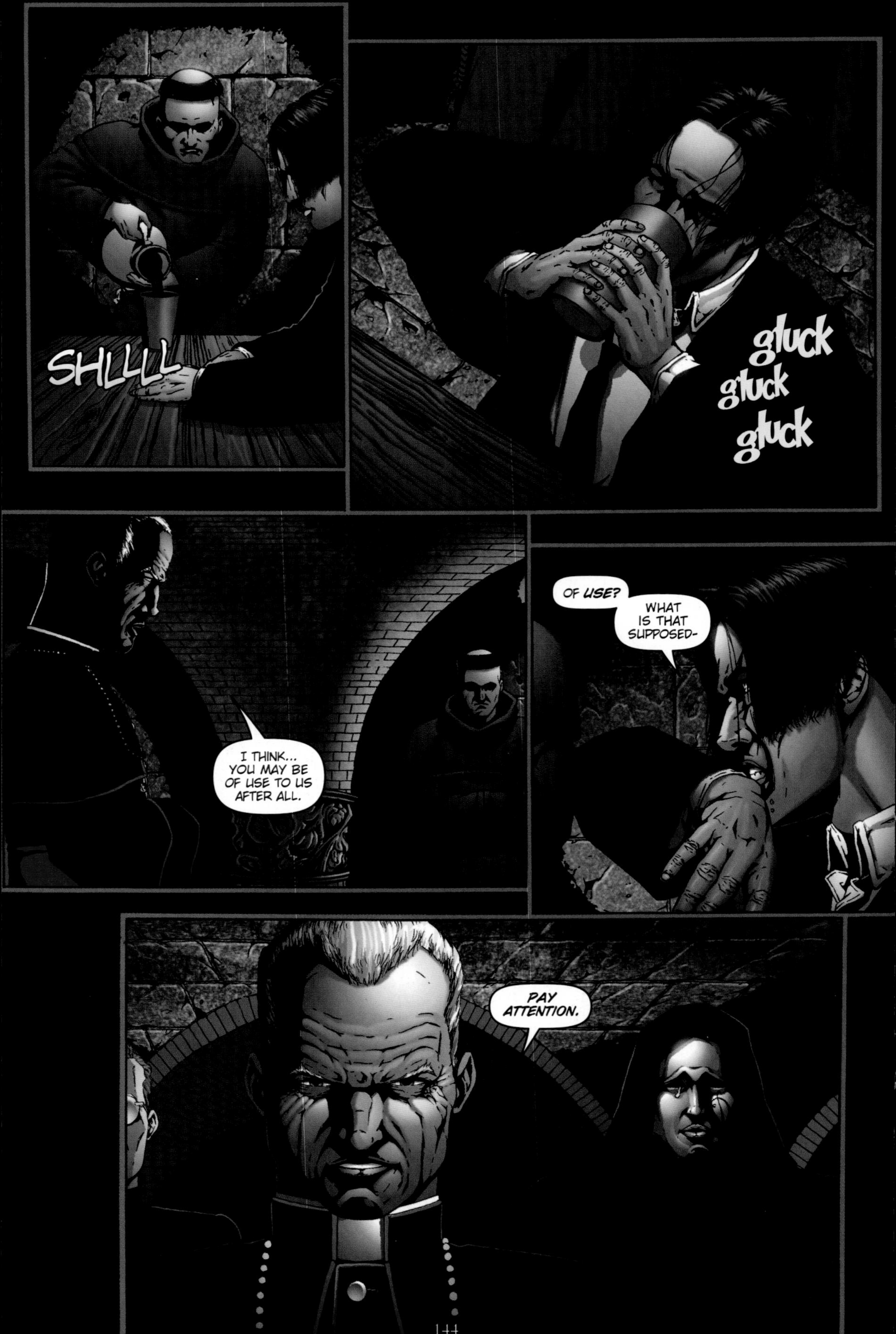
SHLLLL
gluck
gluck
gluck
I THINK... YOU MAY BE OF USE TO US AFTER ALL.
OF *USE?*
WHAT IS THAT SUPPOSED-
PAY ATTENTION.

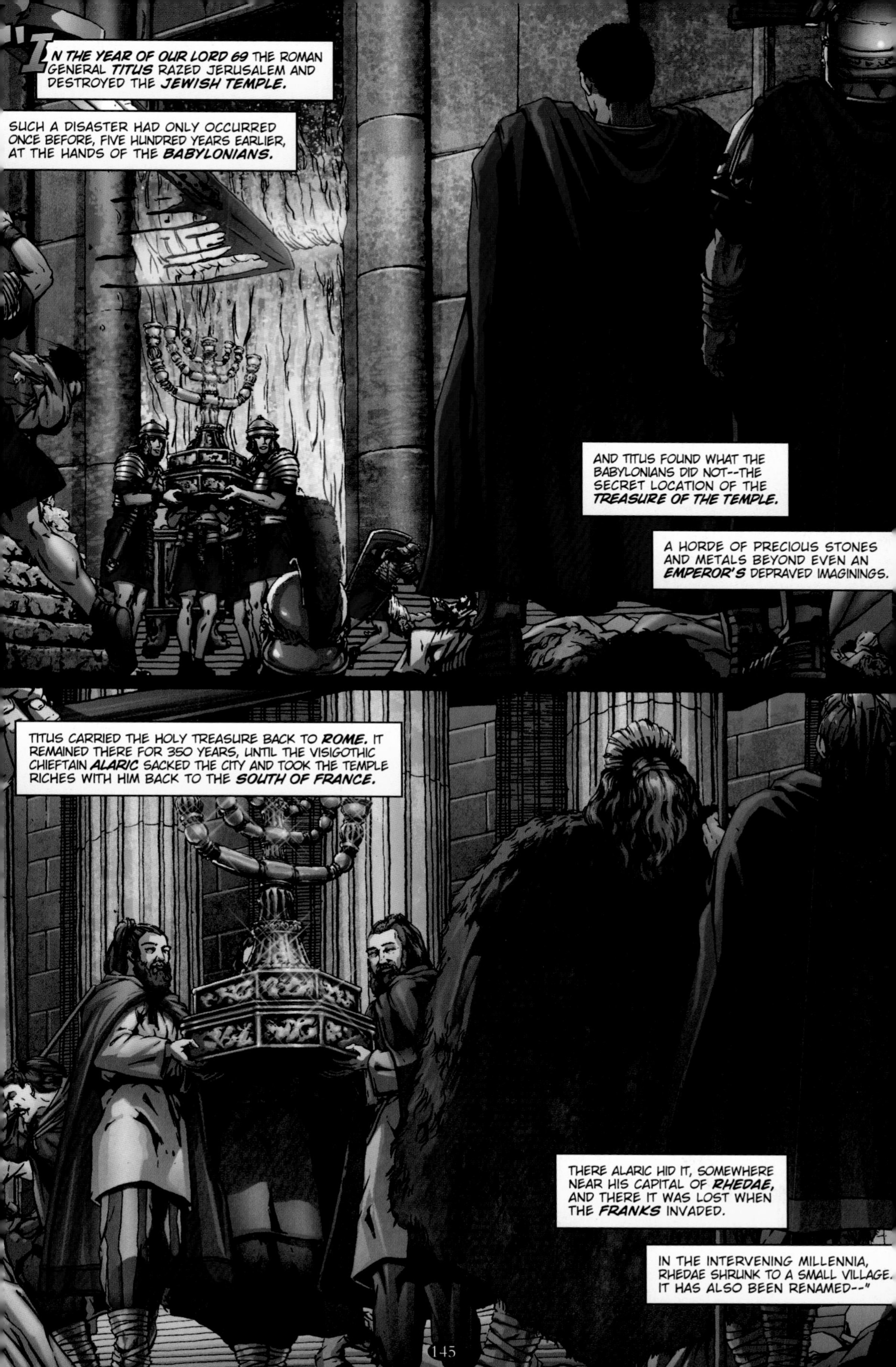
"IN THE YEAR OF OUR LORD 69 THE ROMAN GENERAL TITUS RAZED JERUSALEM AND DESTROYED THE JEWISH TEMPLE.
SUCH A DISASTER HAD ONLY OCCURRED ONCE BEFORE, FIVE HUNDRED YEARS EARLIER, AT THE HANDS OF THE BABYLONIANS.
AND TITUS FOUND WHAT THE BABYLONIANS DID NOT--THE SECRET LOCATION OF THE TREASURE OF THE TEMPLE.
A HORDE OF PRECIOUS STONES AND METALS BEYOND EVEN AN EMPEROR'S DEPRAVED IMAGININGS.
TITUS CARRIED THE HOLY TREASURE BACK TO ROME. IT REMAINED THERE FOR 350 YEARS, UNTIL THE VISIGOTHIC CHIEFTAIN ALARIC SACKED THE CITY AND TOOK THE TEMPLE RICHES WITH HIM BACK TO THE SOUTH OF FRANCE.
THERE ALARIC HID IT, SOMEWHERE NEAR HIS CAPITAL OF RHEDAE, AND THERE IT WAS LOST WHEN THE FRANKS INVADED.
IN THE INTERVENING MILLENNIA, RHEDAE SHRUNK TO A SMALL VILLAGE. IT HAS ALSO BEEN RENAMED--"

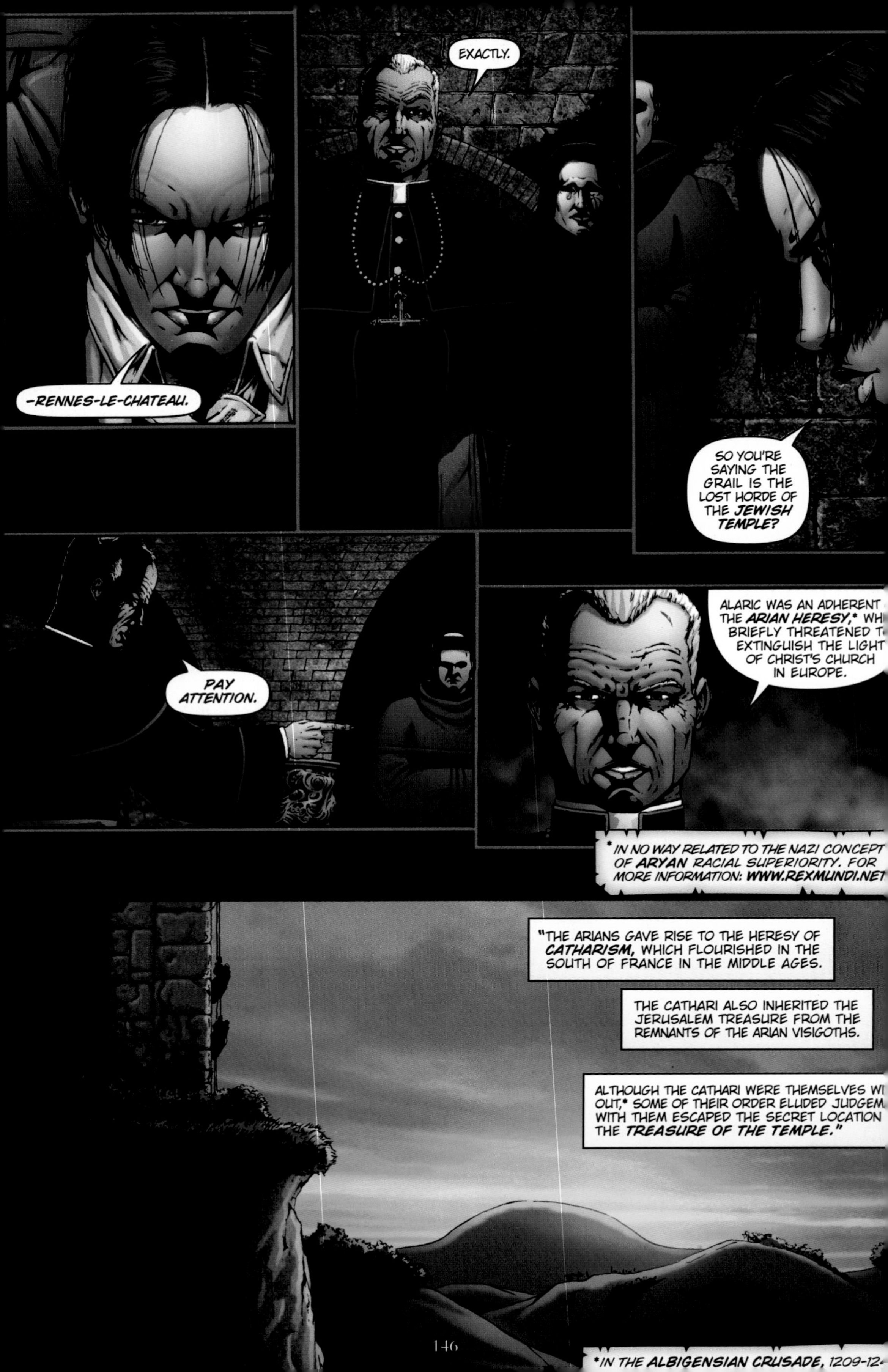
-RENNES-LE-CHATEAU.
EXACTLY.
SO YOU'RE SAYING THE GRAIL IS THE LOST HORDE OF THE JEWISH TEMPLE?
PAY ATTENTION.
ALARIC WAS AN ADHERENT THE ARIAN HERESY,* WH BRIEFLY THREATENED T EXTINGUISH THE LIGHT OF CHRIST'S CHURCH IN EUROPE.
*IN NO WAY RELATED TO THE NAZI CONCEPT OF ARYAN RACIAL SUPERIORITY. FOR MORE INFORMATION: WWW.REXMUNDI.NET
"THE ARIANS GAVE RISE TO THE HERESY OF CATHARISM, WHICH FLOURISHED IN THE SOUTH OF FRANCE IN THE MIDDLE AGES.
THE CATHARI ALSO INHERITED THE JERUSALEM TREASURE FROM THE REMNANTS OF THE ARIAN VISIGOTHS.
ALTHOUGH THE CATHARI WERE THEMSELVES WI OUT,* SOME OF THEIR ORDER ELUDED JUDGEM WITH THEM ESCAPED THE SECRET LOCATION THE TREASURE OF THE TEMPLE."
*IN THE ALBIGENSIAN CRUSADE, 1209-12

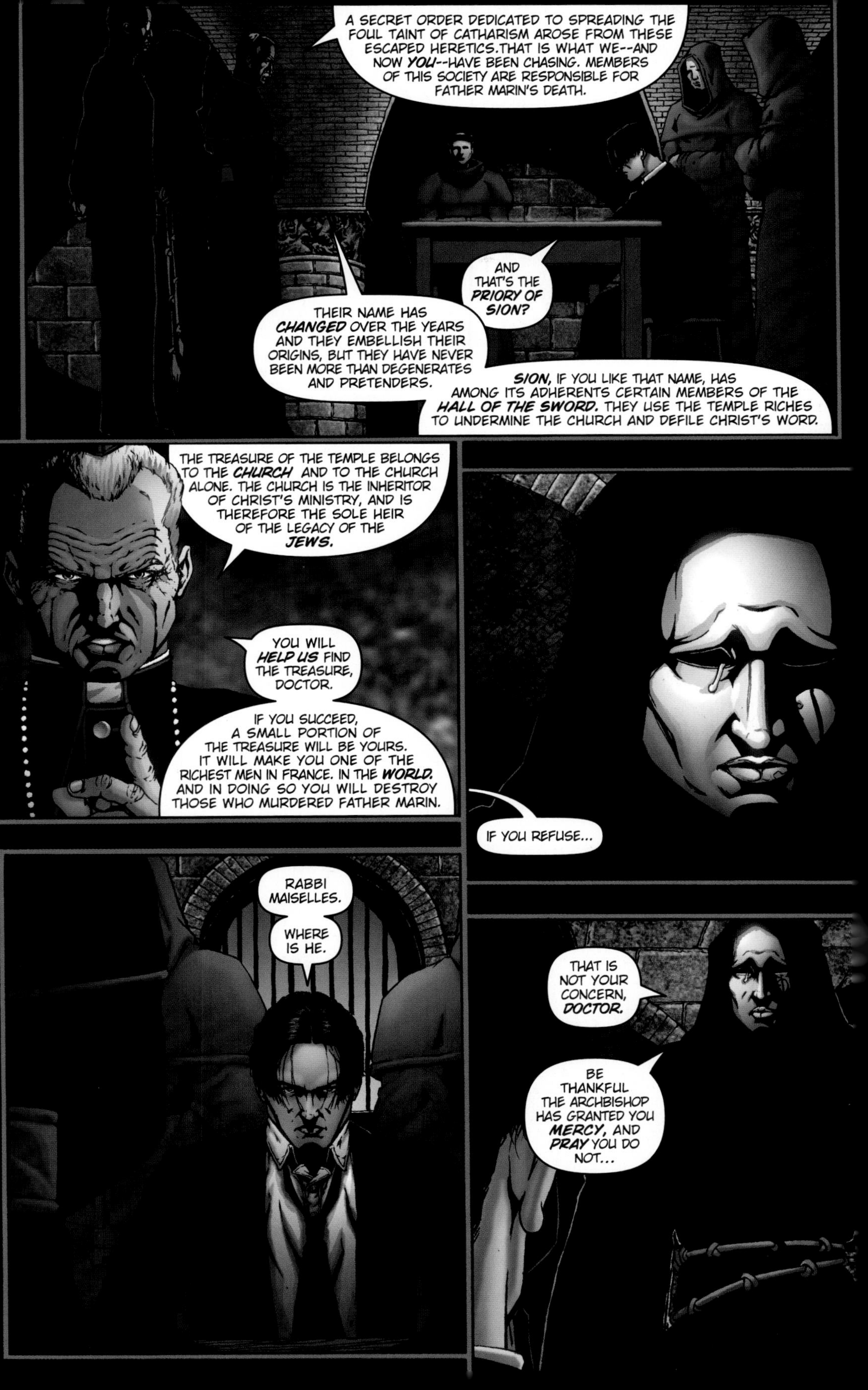
A SECRET ORDER DEDICATED TO SPREADING THE FOUL TAINT OF CATHARISM AROSE FROM THESE ESCAPED HERETICS.THAT IS WHAT WE--AND NOW YOU--HAVE BEEN CHASING. MEMBERS OF THIS SOCIETY ARE RESPONSIBLE FOR FATHER MARIN'S DEATH.
AND THAT'S THE PRIORY OF SION?
THEIR NAME HAS CHANGED OVER THE YEARS AND THEY EMBELLISH THEIR ORIGINS, BUT THEY HAVE NEVER BEEN MORE THAN DEGENERATES AND PRETENDERS.
SION, IF YOU LIKE THAT NAME, HAS AMONG ITS ADHERENTS CERTAIN MEMBERS OF THE HALL OF THE SWORD. THEY USE THE TEMPLE RICHES TO UNDERMINE THE CHURCH AND DEFILE CHRIST'S WORD.
THE TREASURE OF THE TEMPLE BELONGS TO THE CHURCH AND TO THE CHURCH ALONE. THE CHURCH IS THE INHERITOR OF CHRIST'S MINISTRY, AND IS THEREFORE THE SOLE HEIR OF THE LEGACY OF THE JEWS.
YOU WILL HELP US FIND THE TREASURE, DOCTOR.
IF YOU SUCCEED, A SMALL PORTION OF THE TREASURE WILL BE YOURS. IT WILL MAKE YOU ONE OF THE RICHEST MEN IN FRANCE. IN THE WORLD. AND IN DOING SO YOU WILL DESTROY THOSE WHO MURDERED FATHER MARIN.
IF YOU REFUSE...
RABBI MAISELLES.
WHERE IS HE.
THAT IS NOT YOUR CONCERN, DOCTOR.
BE THANKFUL THE ARCHBISHOP HAS GRANTED YOU MERCY, AND PRAY YOU DO NOT...

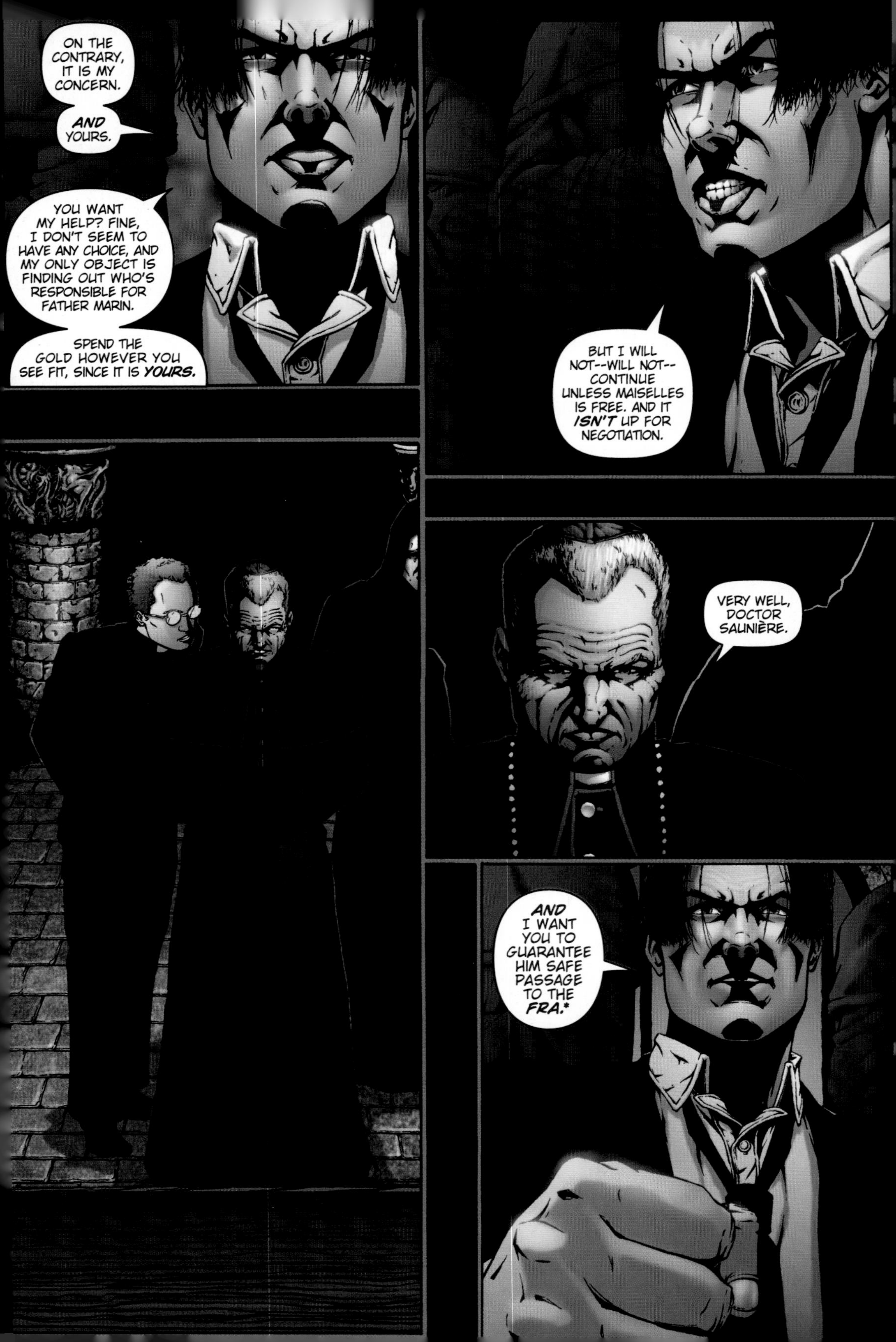
ON THE CONTRARY, IT IS MY CONCERN.
AND YOURS.
YOU WANT MY HELP? FINE, I DON'T SEEM TO HAVE ANY CHOICE, AND MY ONLY OBJECT IS FINDING OUT WHO'S RESPONSIBLE FOR FATHER MARIN.
SPEND THE GOLD HOWEVER YOU SEE FIT, SINCE IT IS YOURS.
BUT I WILL NOT--WILL NOT--CONTINUE UNLESS MAISELLES IS FREE. AND IT ISN'T UP FOR NEGOTIATION.
VERY WELL, DOCTOR SAUNIÈRE.
AND I WANT YOU TO GUARANTEE HIM SAFE PASSAGE TO THE FRA.*

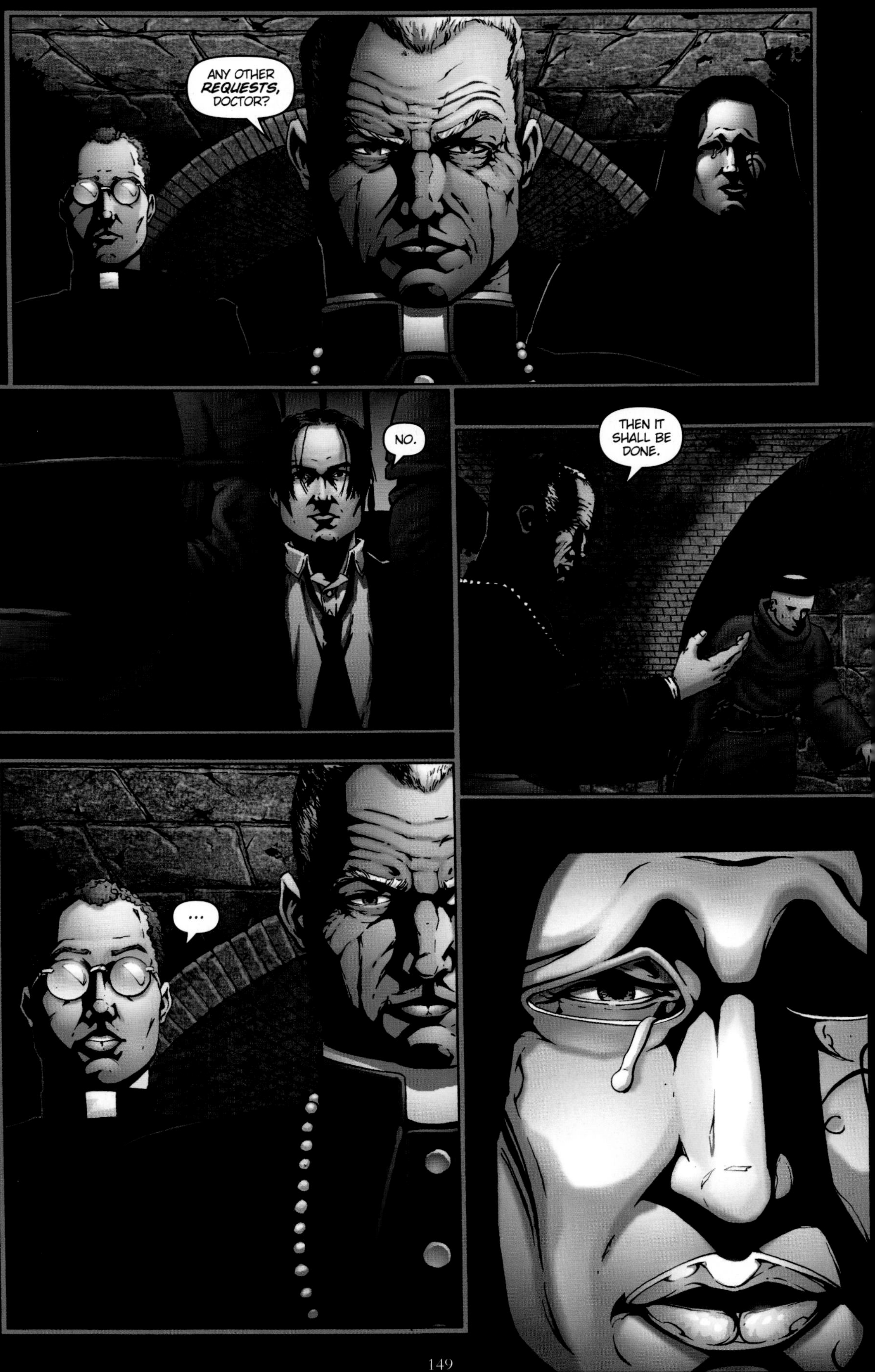
ANY OTHER REQUESTS, DOCTOR?
NO.
THEN IT SHALL BE DONE.
...

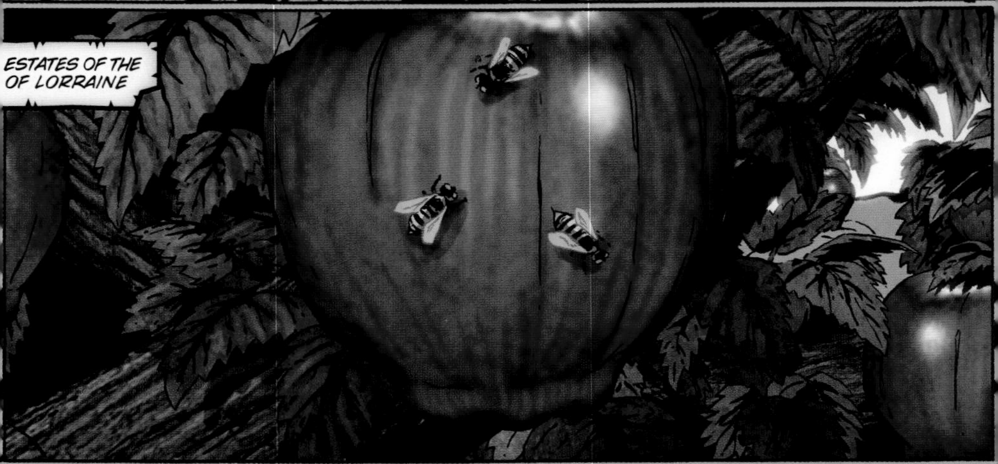
ESTATES OF THE
OF LORRAINE

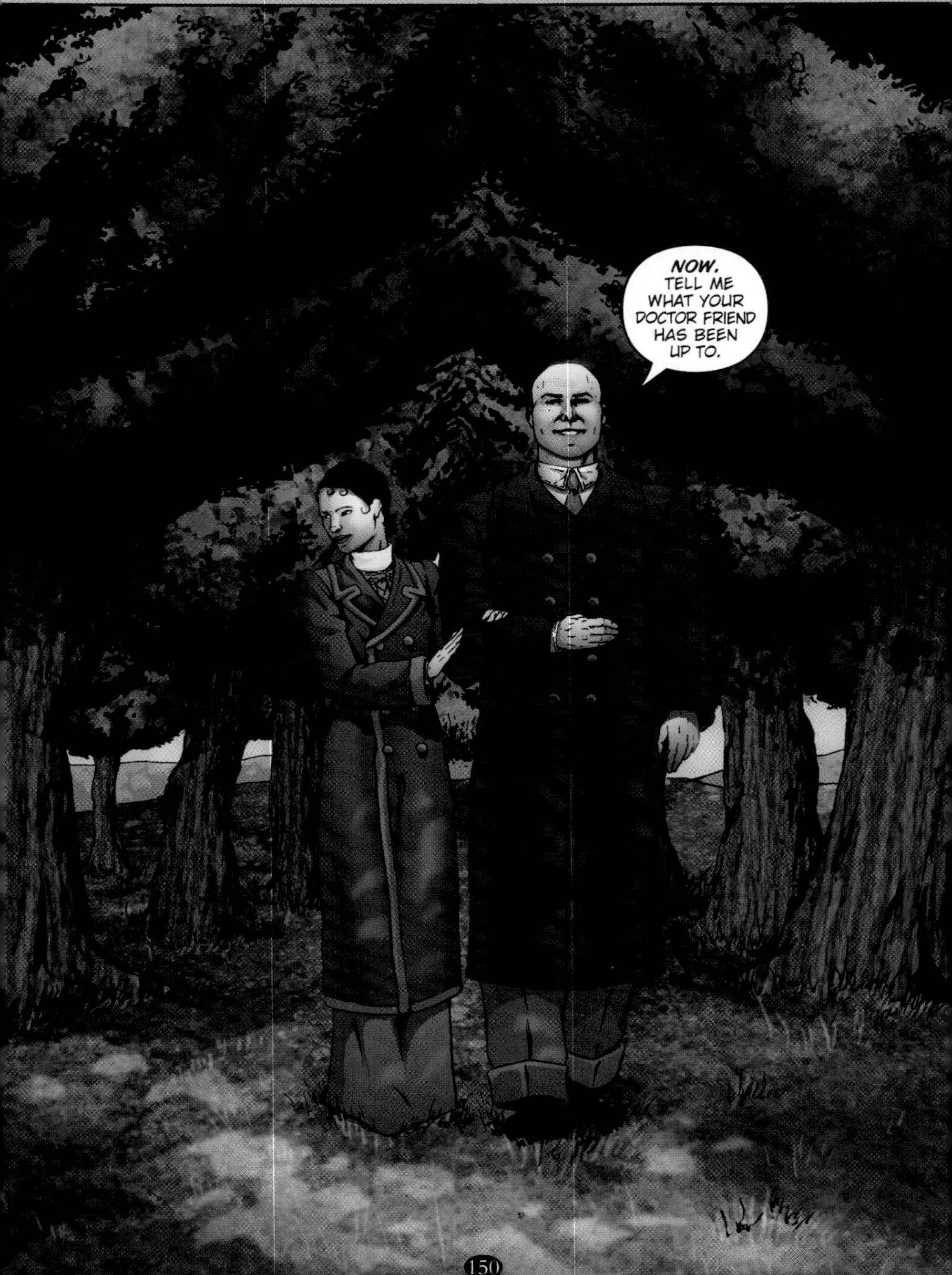
NOW. TELL ME WHAT YOUR DOCTOR FRIEND HAS BEEN UP TO.

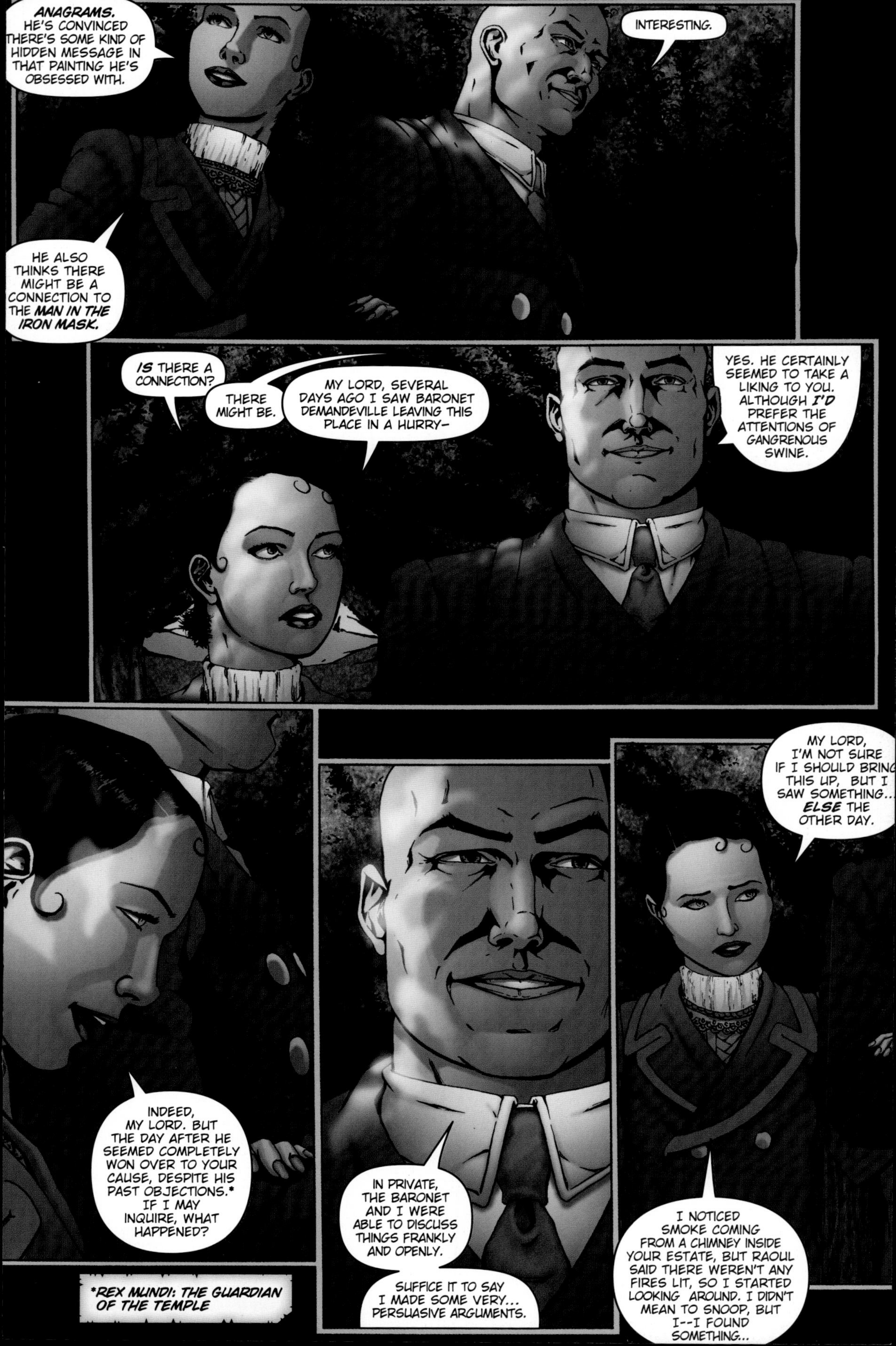
ANAGRAMS. HE'S CONVINCED THERE'S SOME KIND OF HIDDEN MESSAGE IN THAT PAINTING HE'S OBSESSED WITH.
INTERESTING.
HE ALSO THINKS THERE MIGHT BE A CONNECTION TO THE MAN IN THE IRON MASK.
IS THERE A CONNECTION?
THERE MIGHT BE.
MY LORD, SEVERAL DAYS AGO I SAW BARONET DEMANDEVILLE LEAVING THIS PLACE IN A HURRY–
YES. HE CERTAINLY SEEMED TO TAKE A LIKING TO YOU. ALTHOUGH I'D PREFER THE ATTENTIONS OF GANGRENOUS SWINE.
INDEED, MY LORD. BUT THE DAY AFTER HE SEEMED COMPLETELY WON OVER TO YOUR CAUSE, DESPITE HIS PAST OBJECTIONS.* IF I MAY INQUIRE, WHAT HAPPENED?
*REX MUNDI: THE GUARDIAN OF THE TEMPLE
IN PRIVATE, THE BARONET AND I WERE ABLE TO DISCUSS THINGS FRANKLY AND OPENLY.
SUFFICE IT TO SAY I MADE SOME VERY... PERSUASIVE ARGUMENTS.
MY LORD, I'M NOT SURE IF I SHOULD BRING THIS UP, BUT I SAW SOMETHING... ELSE THE OTHER DAY.
I NOTICED SMOKE COMING FROM A CHIMNEY INSIDE YOUR ESTATE, BUT RAOUL SAID THERE WEREN'T ANY FIRES LIT, SO I STARTED LOOKING AROUND. I DIDN'T MEAN TO SNOOP, BUT I--I FOUND SOMETHING...

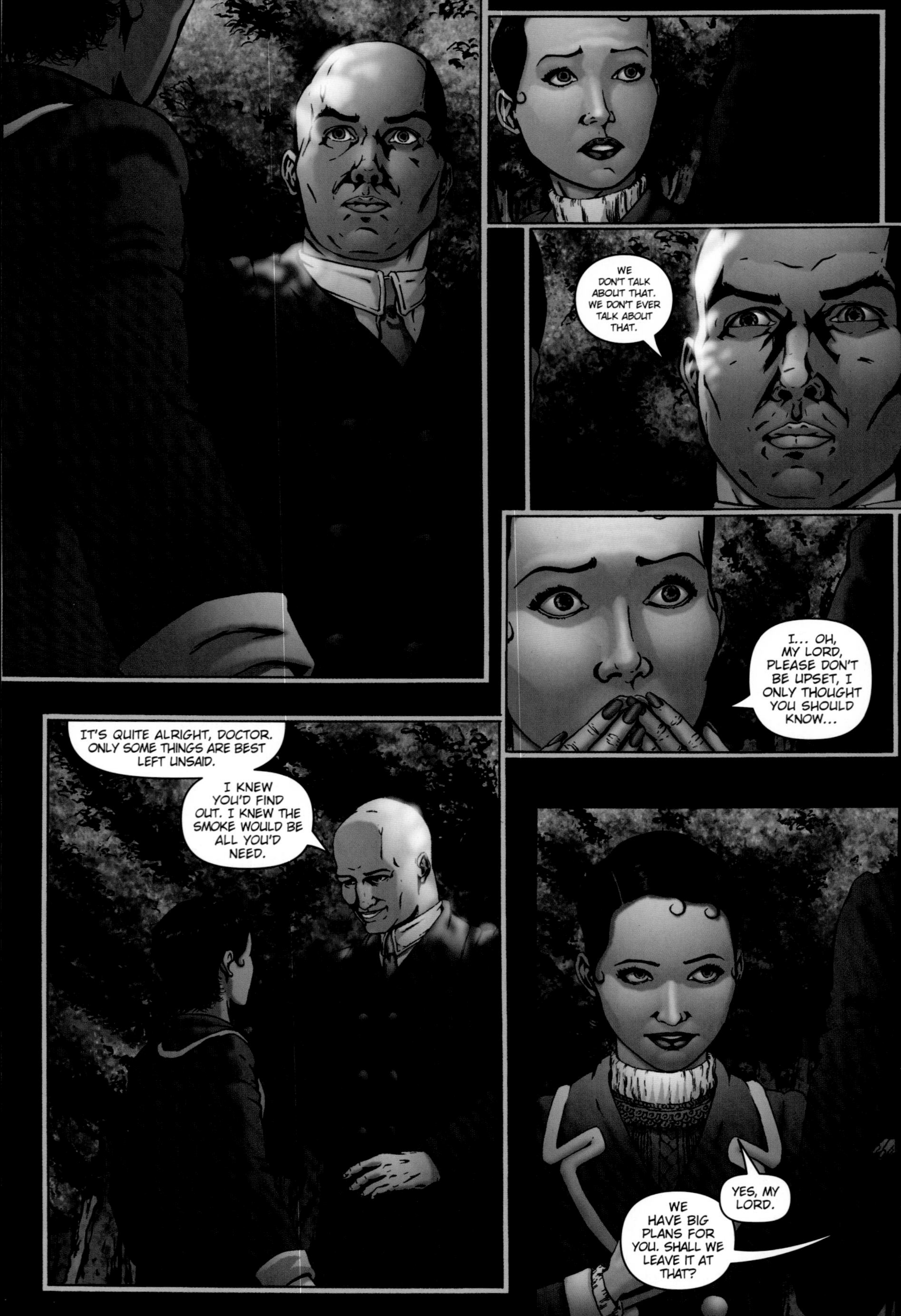
WE DON'T TALK ABOUT THAT. WE DON'T EVER TALK ABOUT THAT.
I... OH, MY LORD, PLEASE DON'T BE UPSET, I ONLY THOUGHT YOU SHOULD KNOW...
IT'S QUITE ALRIGHT, DOCTOR. ONLY SOME THINGS ARE BEST LEFT UNSAID.
I KNEW YOU'D FIND OUT. I KNEW THE SMOKE WOULD BE ALL YOU'D NEED.
WE HAVE BIG PLANS FOR YOU. SHALL WE LEAVE IT AT THAT?
YES, MY LORD.

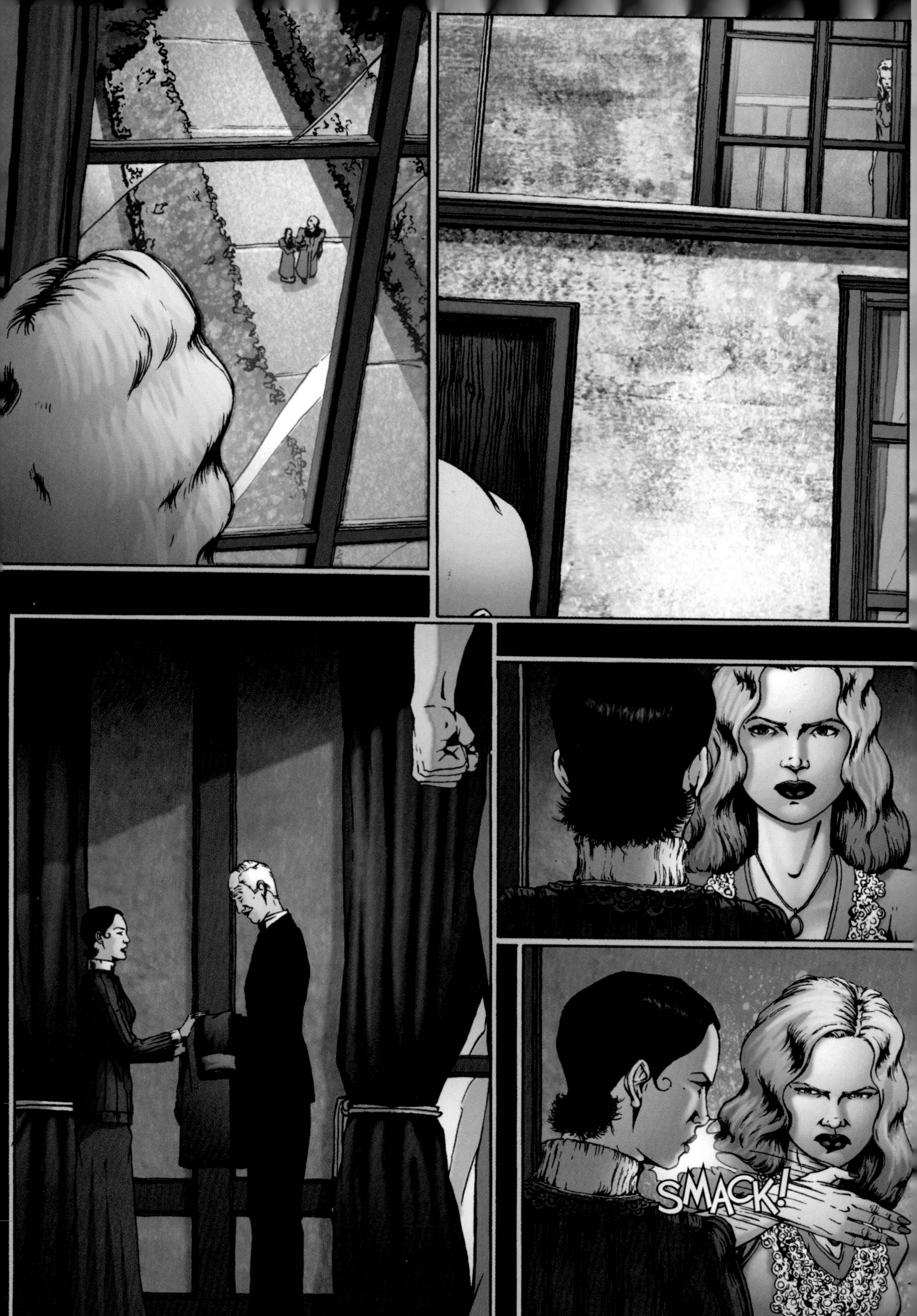
SMACK!

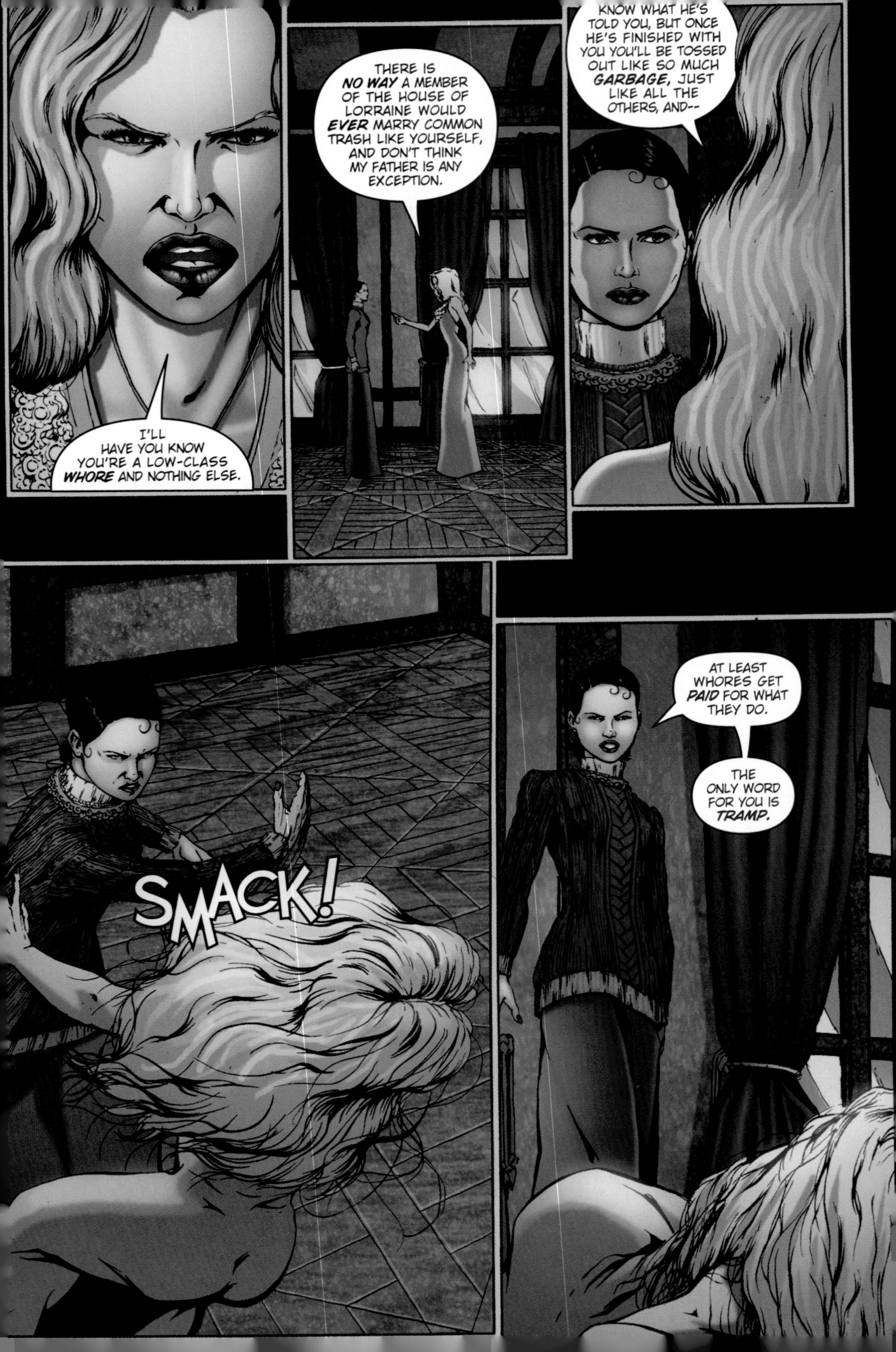
I'LL HAVE YOU KNOW YOU'RE A LOW-CLASS WHORE AND NOTHING ELSE.
THERE IS NO WAY A MEMBER OF THE HOUSE OF LORRAINE WOULD EVER MARRY COMMON TRASH LIKE YOURSELF, AND DON'T THINK MY FATHER IS ANY EXCEPTION.
KNOW WHAT HE'S TOLD YOU, BUT ONCE HE'S FINISHED WITH YOU YOU'LL BE TOSSED OUT LIKE SO MUCH GARBAGE, JUST LIKE ALL THE OTHERS, AND--
SMACK!
AT LEAST WHORES GET PAID FOR WHAT THEY DO.
THE ONLY WORD FOR YOU IS TRAMP.

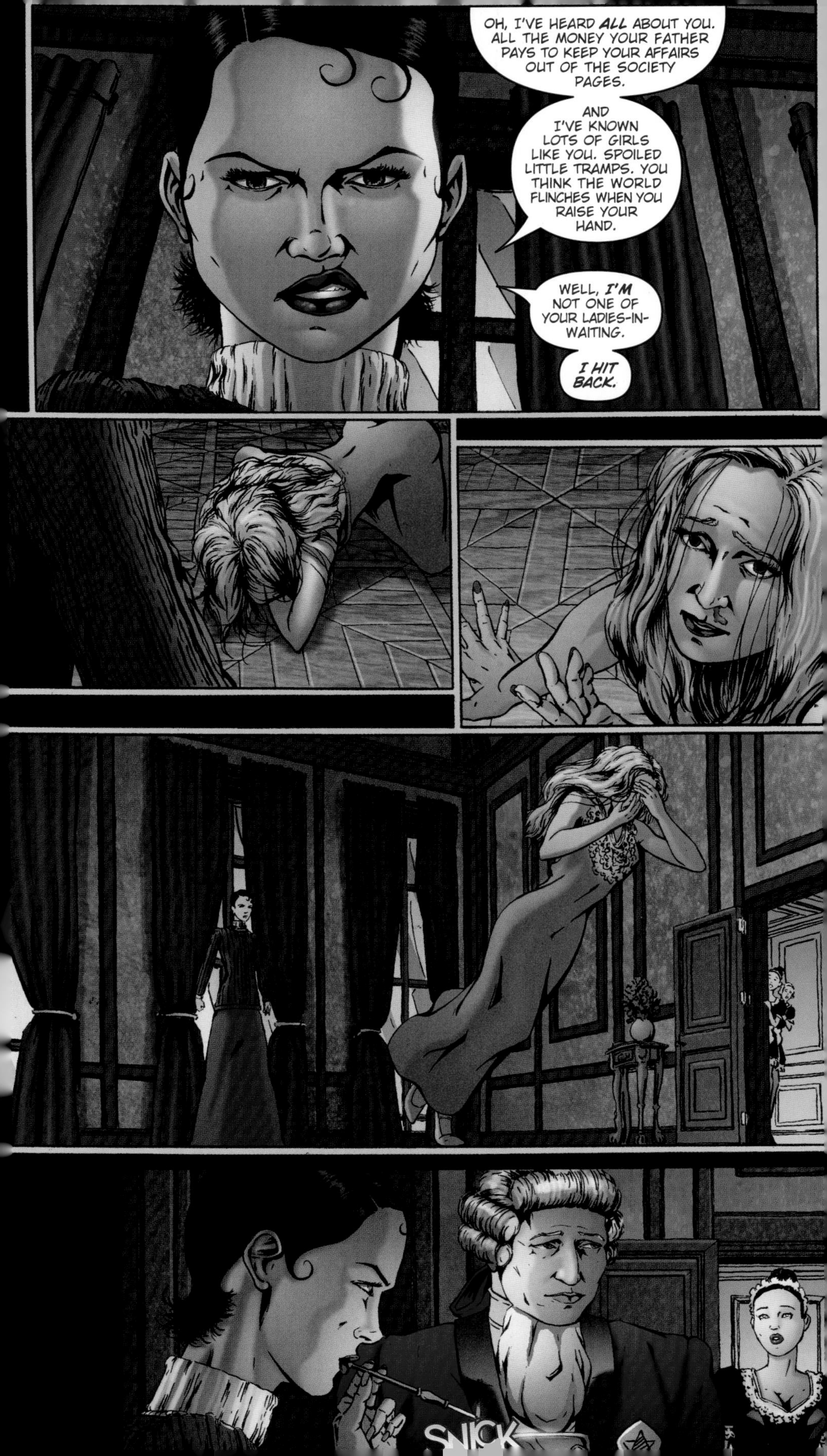
OH, I'VE HEARD ALL ABOUT YOU. ALL THE MONEY YOUR FATHER PAYS TO KEEP YOUR AFFAIRS OUT OF THE SOCIETY PAGES.
AND I'VE KNOWN LOTS OF GIRLS LIKE YOU. SPOILED LITTLE TRAMPS. YOU THINK THE WORLD FLINCHES WHEN YOU RAISE YOUR HAND.
WELL, I'M NOT ONE OF YOUR LADIES-IN-WAITING.
I HIT BACK.
SNICK

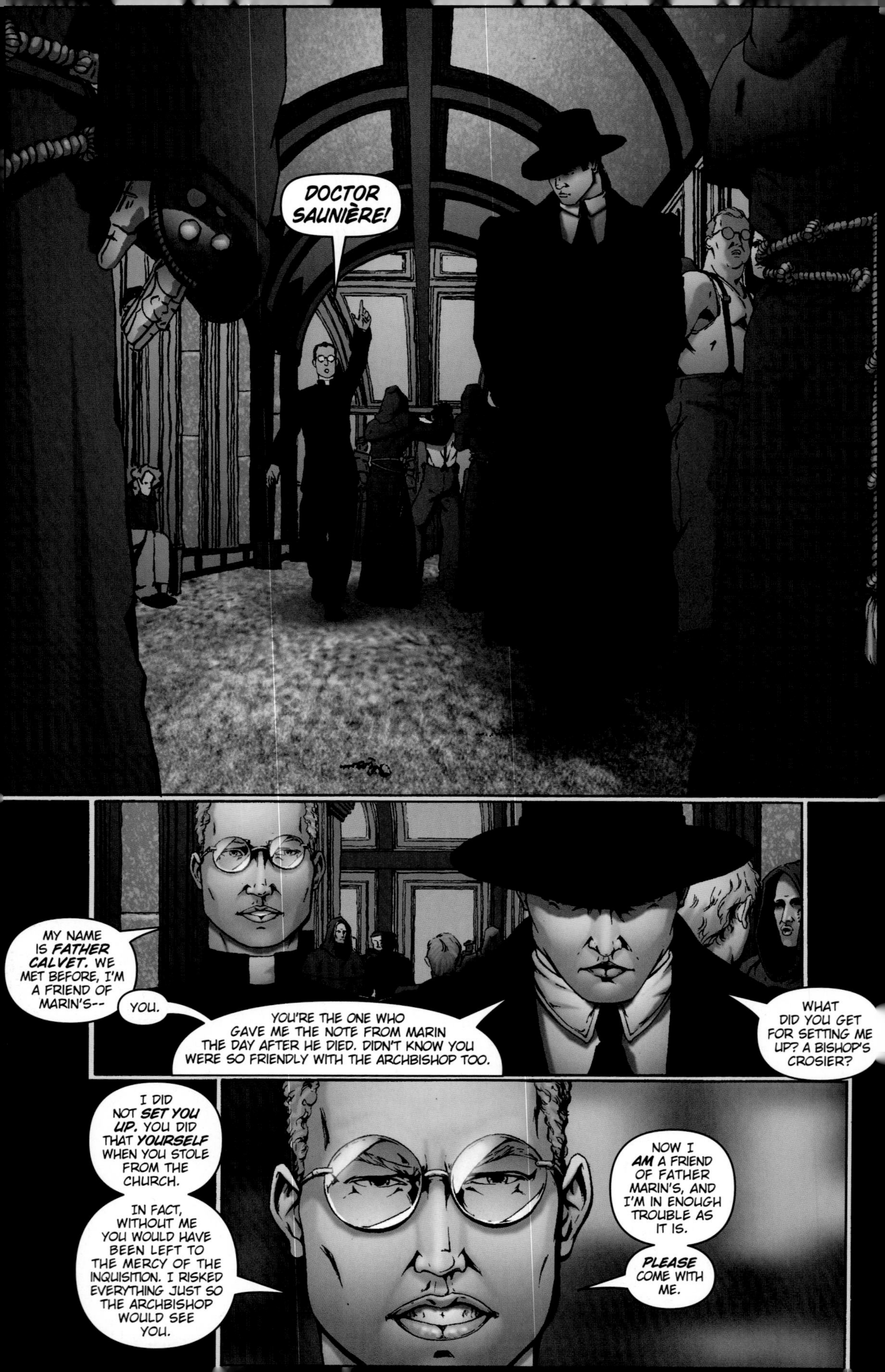
DOCTOR SAUNIÈRE!
MY NAME IS **FATHER CALVET.** WE MET BEFORE, I'M A FRIEND OF MARIN'S--
YOU.
YOU'RE THE ONE WHO GAVE ME THE NOTE FROM MARIN THE DAY AFTER HE DIED. DIDN'T KNOW YOU WERE SO FRIENDLY WITH THE ARCHBISHOP TOO.
WHAT DID YOU GET FOR SETTING ME UP? A BISHOP'S CROSIER?
I DID NOT **SET YOU UP.** YOU DID THAT **YOURSELF** WHEN YOU STOLE FROM THE CHURCH.
IN FACT, WITHOUT ME YOU WOULD HAVE BEEN LEFT TO THE MERCY OF THE INQUISITION. I RISKED EVERYTHING JUST SO THE ARCHBISHOP WOULD SEE YOU.
NOW I **AM** A FRIEND OF FATHER MARIN'S, AND I'M IN ENOUGH TROUBLE AS IT IS.
PLEASE COME WITH ME.

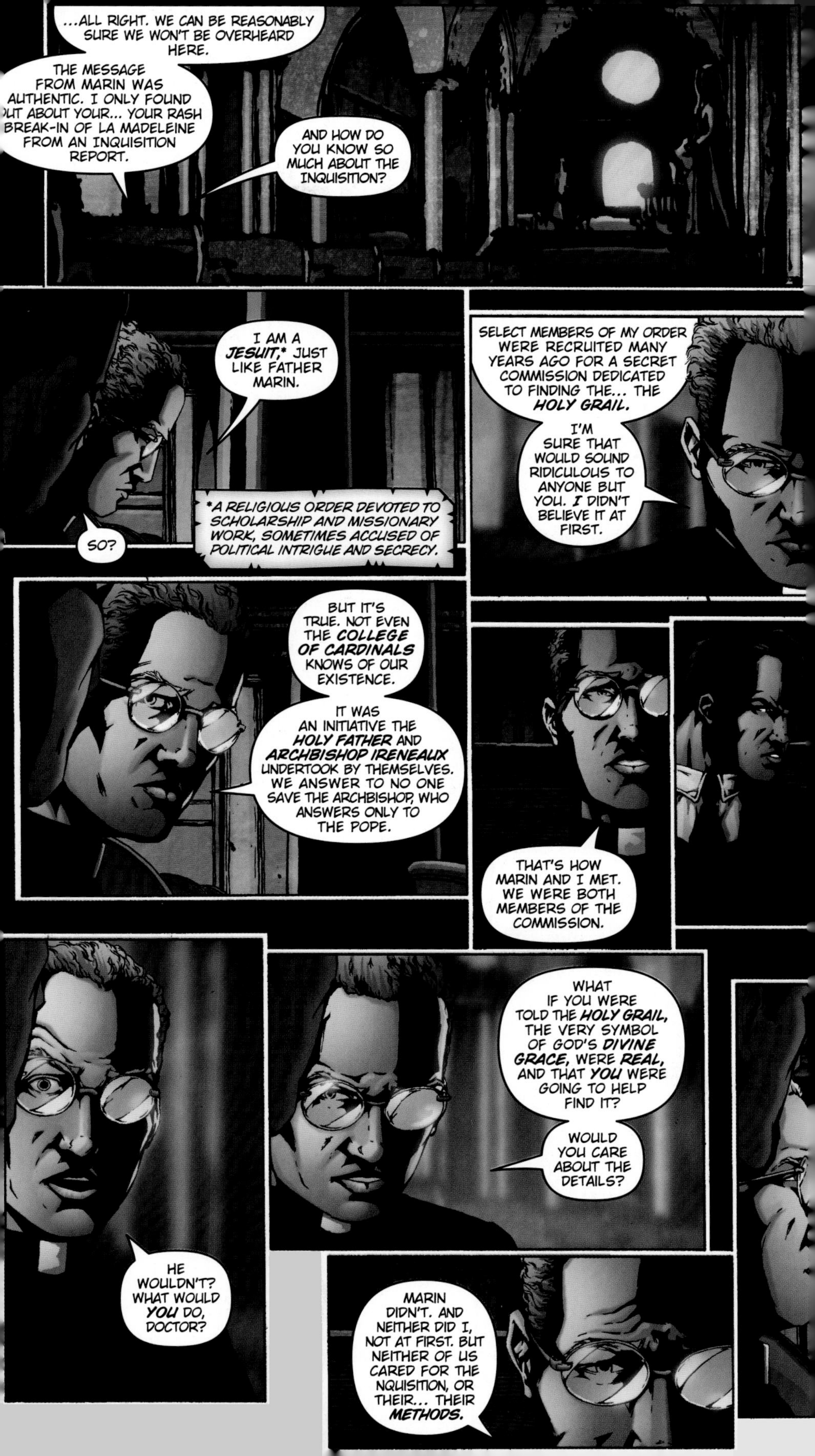

...ALL RIGHT. WE CAN BE REASONABLY SURE WE WON'T BE OVERHEARD HERE.
THE MESSAGE FROM MARIN WAS AUTHENTIC. I ONLY FOUND OUT ABOUT YOUR... YOUR RASH BREAK-IN OF LA MADELEINE FROM AN INQUISITION REPORT.
AND HOW DO YOU KNOW SO MUCH ABOUT THE INQUISITION?
I AM A ***JESUIT,**** JUST LIKE FATHER MARIN.
SO?
**A RELIGIOUS ORDER DEVOTED TO SCHOLARSHIP AND MISSIONARY WORK, SOMETIMES ACCUSED OF POLITICAL INTRIGUE AND SECRECY.*
SELECT MEMBERS OF MY ORDER WERE RECRUITED MANY YEARS AGO FOR A SECRET COMMISSION DEDICATED TO FINDING THE... THE ***HOLY GRAIL.***
I'M SURE THAT WOULD SOUND RIDICULOUS TO ANYONE BUT YOU. ***I*** DIDN'T BELIEVE IT AT FIRST.
BUT IT'S TRUE. NOT EVEN THE ***COLLEGE OF CARDINALS*** KNOWS OF OUR EXISTENCE.
IT WAS AN INITIATIVE THE ***HOLY FATHER*** AND ***ARCHBISHOP IRENEAUX*** UNDERTOOK BY THEMSELVES. WE ANSWER TO NO ONE SAVE THE ARCHBISHOP, WHO ANSWERS ONLY TO THE POPE.
THAT'S HOW MARIN AND I MET. WE WERE BOTH MEMBERS OF THE COMMISSION.
HE WOULDN'T? WHAT WOULD ***YOU*** DO, DOCTOR?
WHAT IF YOU WERE TOLD THE ***HOLY GRAIL,*** THE VERY SYMBOL OF GOD'S ***DIVINE GRACE,*** WERE ***REAL,*** AND THAT ***YOU*** WERE GOING TO HELP FIND IT?
WOULD YOU CARE ABOUT THE DETAILS?
MARIN DIDN'T. AND NEITHER DID I, NOT AT FIRST. BUT NEITHER OF US CARED FOR THE NQUISITION, OR THEIR... THEIR ***METHODS.***

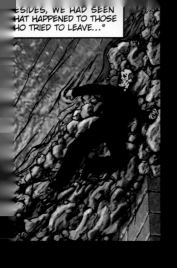

ESIDES, WE HAD SEEN HAT HAPPENED TO THOSE HO TRIED TO LEAVE..."

MARIN ESCAPED BY TAKING THE ASSIGNMENT GUARDING THE SCROLLS BENEATH LA MADELIENE.

WHY DIDN'T HE TELL ME THIS?

HE PROBABLY WANTED TO PROTECT YOU, DOCTOR.

I GUESS HE HAD SECRETS. I KNEW HIM MOST OF MY LIFE, AND I NEVER SUSPECTED *ANY* OF THIS. I WONDER WHAT ELSE THERE IS I DON'T KNOW...

OK. NOW WHAT'S THIS ABOUT THE GRAIL BEING THE LOST TREASURE OF JERUSALEM? AM I CORRECT IN ASSUMING IT'S PURE LIES?

NOT... *PURE* LIES, NO.

THE ARCHBISHOP TOLD YOU *HALF-TRUTHS* TO MISLEAD YOU THROUGH GREED.

AS TO THE *FULL* TRUTH, I ONLY KNOW BITS AND PIECES MYSELF.

FROM WHAT I CAN TELL, THE GRAIL DOESN'T HAVE ANYTHING TO DO WITH LOST JEWISH TREASURE, OR ANY KIND OF *MATERIAL* TREASURE, FOR THAT MATTER...

THEN WHAT IS IT? WHAT ABOUT THE *TEMPLARS*? WHAT ABOUT THE *HOUSE OF LORRAINE*?

LORRAINE... SWEET MARY MOTHER OF GOD... I CAN'T POSSIBLY GET INTO THAT NOW, I HAVE

A WORD OF ADVICE, DOCTOR.

YOU MIGHT BE IN *MORE* DANGER NOW THAT THE ARCHBISHOP HAS TAKEN AN INTEREST

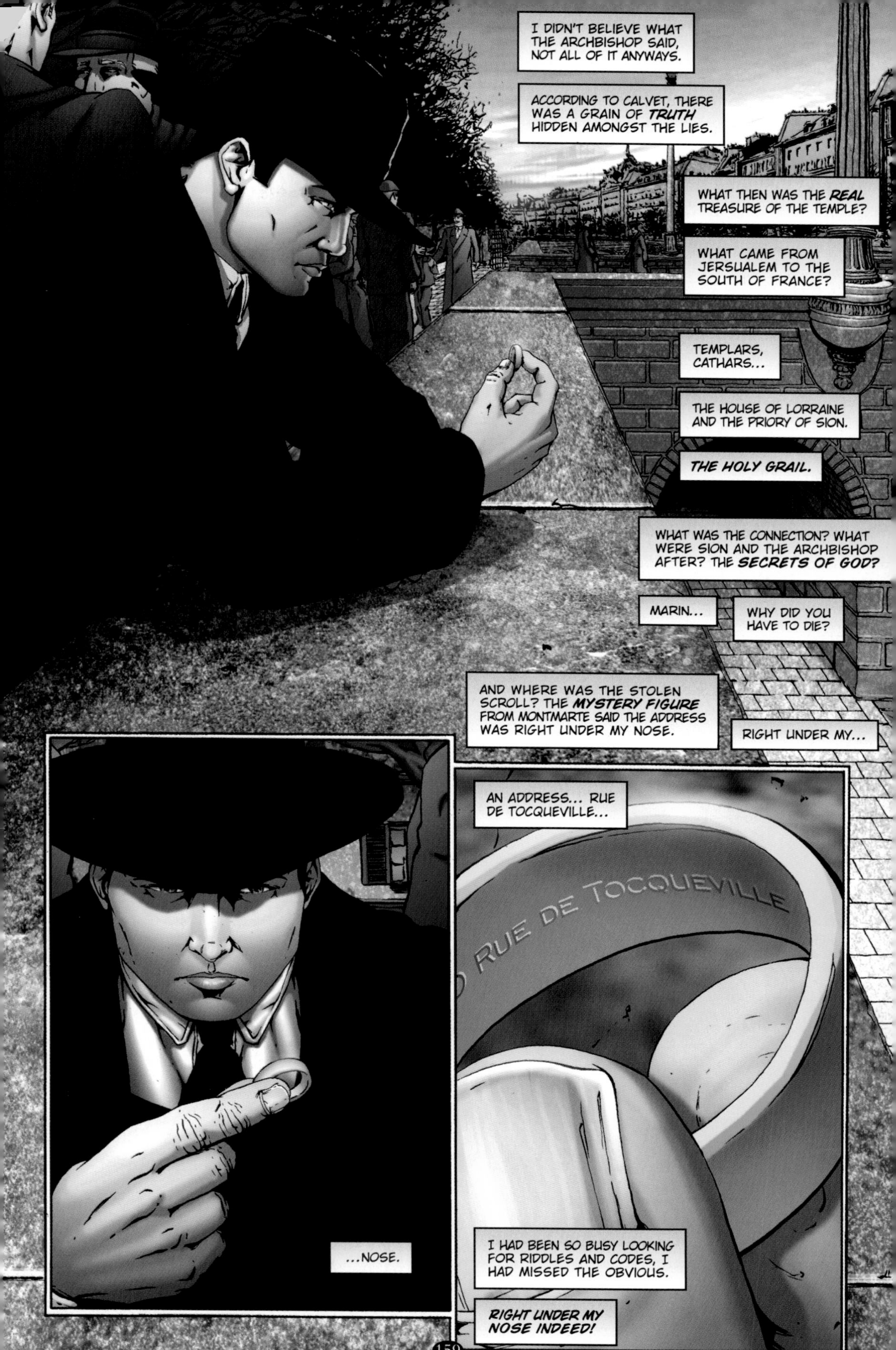
I DIDN'T BELIEVE WHAT THE ARCHBISHOP SAID, NOT ALL OF IT ANYWAYS.
ACCORDING TO CALVET, THERE WAS A GRAIN OF TRUTH HIDDEN AMONGST THE LIES.
WHAT THEN WAS THE REAL TREASURE OF THE TEMPLE?
WHAT CAME FROM JERSUALEM TO THE SOUTH OF FRANCE?
TEMPLARS, CATHARS...
THE HOUSE OF LORRAINE AND THE PRIORY OF SION.
THE HOLY GRAIL.
WHAT WAS THE CONNECTION? WHAT WERE SION AND THE ARCHBISHOP AFTER? THE SECRETS OF GOD?
MARIN...
WHY DID YOU HAVE TO DIE?
AND WHERE WAS THE STOLEN SCROLL? THE MYSTERY FIGURE FROM MONTMARTE SAID THE ADDRESS WAS RIGHT UNDER MY NOSE.
RIGHT UNDER MY...
...NOSE.
AN ADDRESS... RUE DE TOCQUEVILLE...
RUE DE TOCQUEVILLE
I HAD BEEN SO BUSY LOOKING FOR RIDDLES AND CODES, I HAD MISSED THE OBVIOUS.
RIGHT UNDER MY NOSE INDEED!

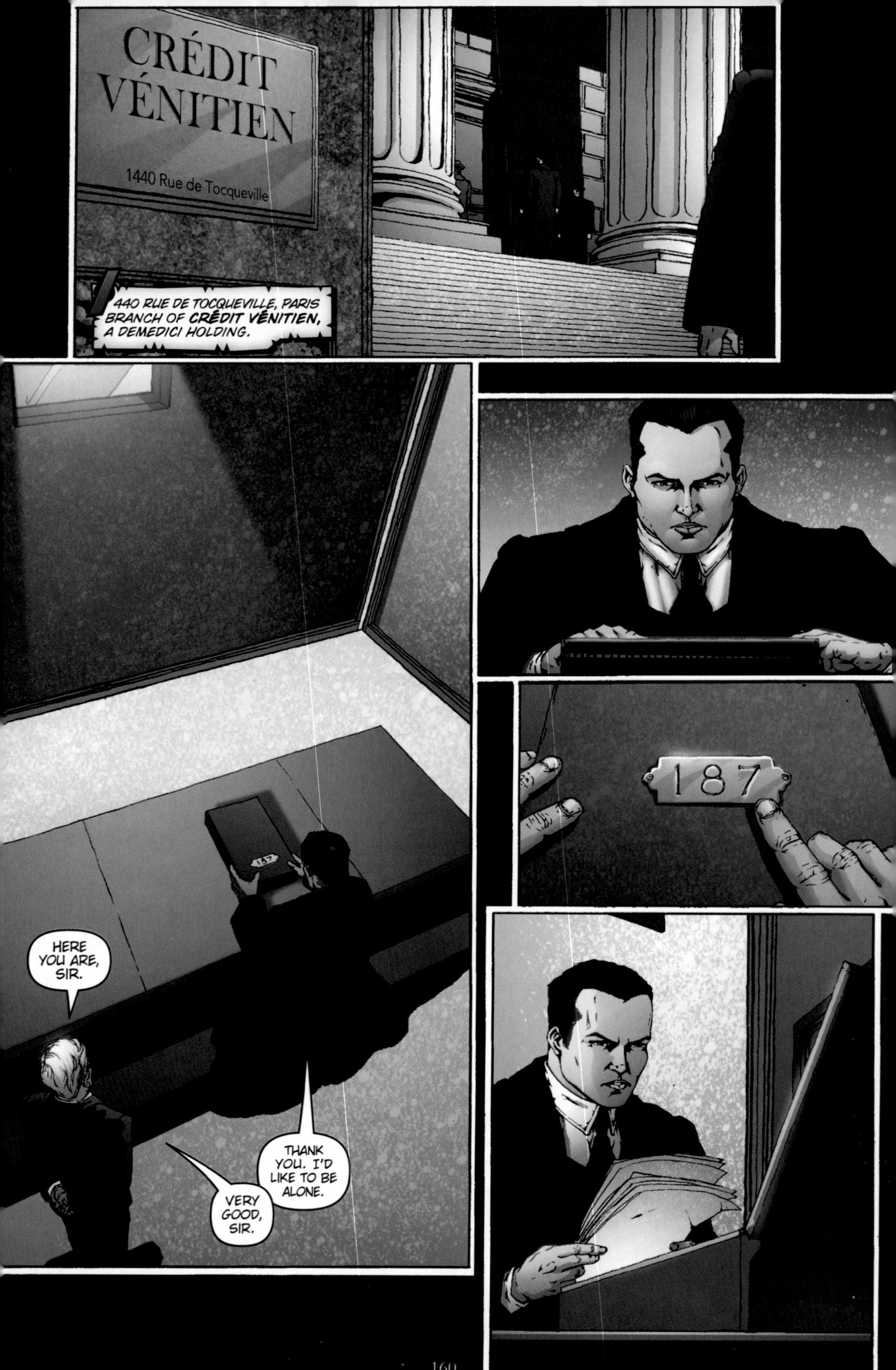
CRÉDIT VÉNITIEN
1440 Rue de Tocqueville
440 RUE DE TOCQUEVILLE, PARIS BRANCH OF **CRÉDIT VÉNITIEN**, A DEMEDICI HOLDING.
HERE YOU ARE, SIR.
THANK YOU. I'D LIKE TO BE ALONE.
VERY GOOD, SIR.
187

THE VENERABLE HOUSE OF DeMEDICI

This may be the last thing I ever write. I assumed the whore would die, but Dumont? The priest? If the Man in White can kill a priest, he can kill me just as easily. And there's nothing I can do about it, save hope someone finds the contents of this box.

I gave the scroll over to be destroyed, as ordered, but not before making this photostatic copy. I have no idea what to make of it, but it must be very important to have cost so many lives.

TO WHOMEVER FINDS THIS:
I hope you can make better use of it than I. And if I die, I hope you can bring down the bastards that do the dirty deed.

Hugo De Medici

REST IN *HELL*, DEMEDICI.

TTIKThRaMYNNGENTTJNaKaTPFTSTTCI
dpestervaetextejrsticaypTirTsnsuispep
plfTtaesteexungetnttodaekedtxalter
tsetvtxtvddxiscarjortisqviyekatcuhmtka
hen vtvmnonxvenvttgkecenpdtsdena
gentes?dixtnufemhoecnonqustadee
adcvtmsedquhinfykelktetloucvloshcah
nmtvrpotkabetedtxttejkgoiteshvsstn
epvlgtvkaemsedeservnetillqvdpavpsek
hemttsnohltiscumfmeavtetmnonses
viltekotzvkhamvqltaextmvdactstq
akvntnonnpkoteprtesvmetantvmmse
eh~tqvemksvsctaovitamoxktvtscpogt
kvtnctpejssacekcdotvmvmtetlazcak
lvtamylvttpropytektlhxvmahthgn
dehantTntesvm

MARIN. AT LAST.

BUT WHAT SECRETS DID IT HIDE?

AT LAST, I HAD THE SCROLL YOU DIED FOR.

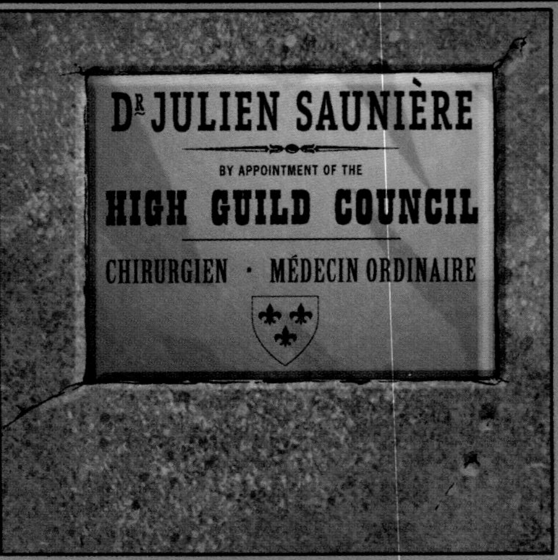
DR JULIEN SAUNIÈRE
BY APPOINTMENT OF THE
HIGH GUILD COUNCIL
CHIRURGIEN · MÉDECIN ORDINAIRE

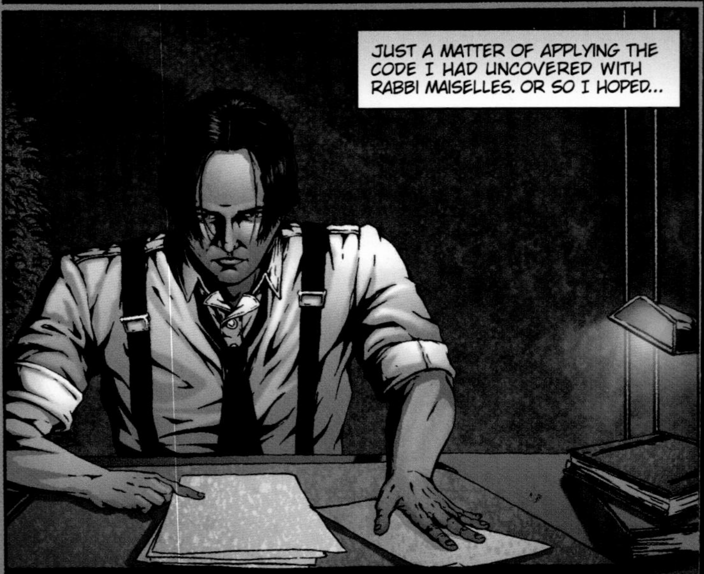
JUST A MATTER OF APPLYING THE CODE I HAD UNCOVERED WITH RABBI MAISELLES. OR SO I HOPED...

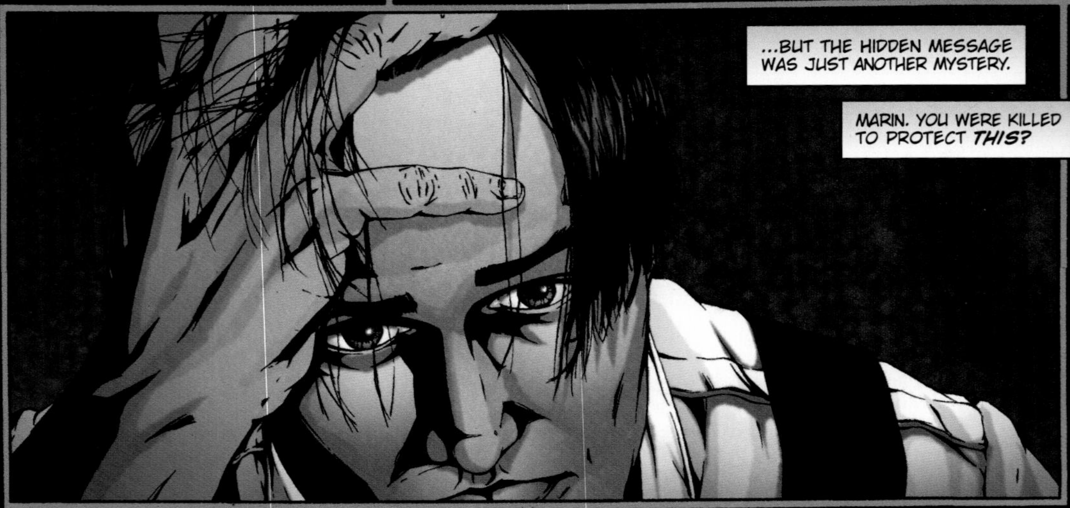
...BUT THE HIDDEN MESSAGE WAS JUST ANOTHER MYSTERY.
MARIN. YOU WERE KILLED TO PROTECT *THIS?*

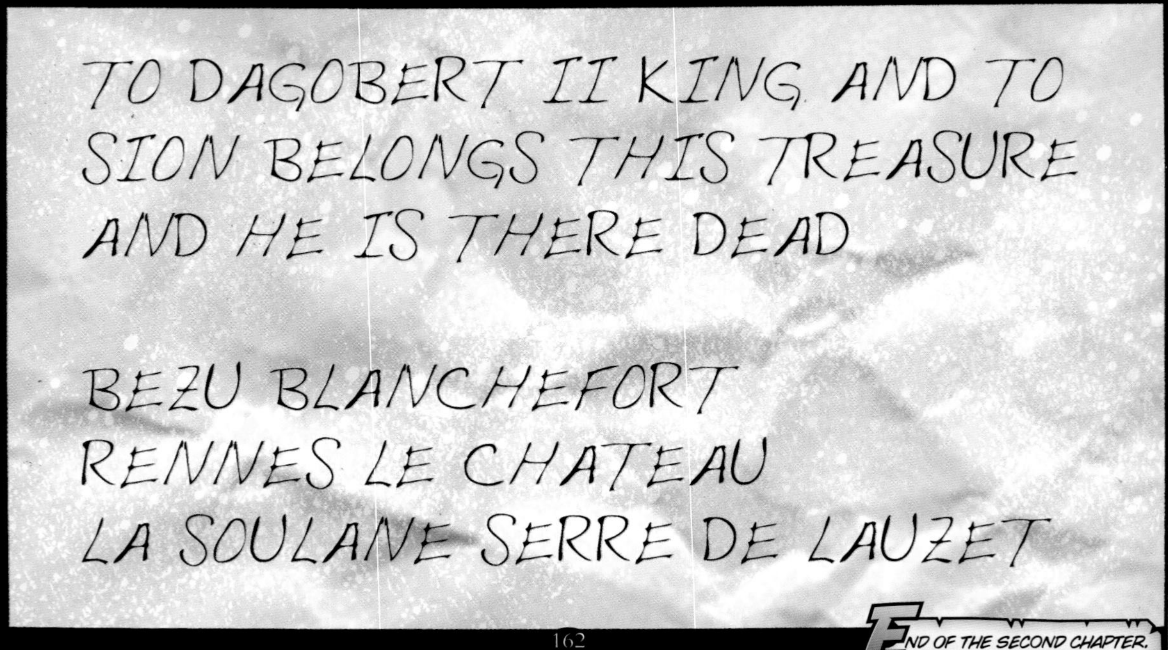
TO DAGOBERT II KING AND TO
SION BELONGS THIS TREASURE
AND HE IS THERE DEAD
BEZU BLANCHEFORT
RENNES LE CHATEAU
LA SOULANE SERRE DE LAUZET

END OF THE SECOND CHAPTER.

Le Journal de la Liberté

Paris' leading anglophone newspaper • vol. 205, no. 97 • Oct. 28, MCMXXXIII

Papal Seal

Editors in Chief: M. Tait Bergstrom, M. Matthew Pasteris. **Story Editor:** M. Arvid Nelson. **Art Editors:** M. EricJ, M. Jeromy Cox. **Photography Editor:** M. Alexander Waldman. **Layout Supervisor:** M. William Kartalopoulos. **Editors Emeritus:** M. Clark A. Smith, M. Howard P. Lovecraft, M. Robert E. Howard. Redacted by the Holy Parisian Inquisition under the direction of His Excellency Archbishop Emile-Jean Ireneaux. Le Journal de Liberté is printed under the benign auspices of his most puissant majesty KING LOUIS XXII of FRANCE.

GOD SAVE THE KING.

of Approval

INQUISITORS UNCOVER CHILD SMUGGLING RING

Destitute street waifs abducted and sold into slavery in Cordova and Asia Minor; "despicable" says Inquisitor.

Paris, 13ᵗʰ Arrondissement — six month-long Ecclesiastical [in]vestigation into a child smuggling [rin]g culminated in success the [ot]her day when Inquisitors raided [th]e offices of Mathieu Cancelier, a [pr]ominent Paris businessman.

Inquisitors discovered "around [tw]o dozen children, hog-tied and [ga]gged," in a secret compartment in [th]e basement of Cancelier's offices, [ac]cording to Church authorities. [T]he children were aged five to [tw]elve, mostly urchins from the [ne]arby Village d'Ivry shantytown.

"They were all in pitiful condi[ti]on. It was apparent they had not [ea]ten for days and had received [ve]ry little water. Some showed [si]gns of physical abuse," Brother [Jea]n-Pierre, lead Inquisitor on the [ca]se, said.

Cancelier was taken into cus[to]dy and has been charged with [m]ultiple counts of abduction of a [m]inor and intent to engage in [hu]man trafficking.

Father Antonio Dolcino, the [ca]non lawyer assigned to prosecute [th]e case, said the Church would [se]ek Cancelier's execution.

"Cancelier is a monster with[ou]t any regard for Christ's laws. We [fe]el we have a very strong case and [s]ay he will be swinging from a [ro]pe within a few months."

Cancelier was not made avail[ab]le to comment on the charges.

Cancelier's council, Pierre [M]odot, insists his client is not guilty.

"Mr. Cancelier has assured me [h]e is completely innocent of these [ch]arges," Modot said.

He offered no explanation for [th]e presence of the children or the [se]cret dungeon in Cancelier's office. [A] detailed and plausible vindica-tion is forthcoming, pending our own private investigation," he said. "My client may be the victim of a conspiracy by business rivals. He is a wealthy man. Why would he risk everything he has by taking part in illegal activities?"

Le Journal investigators have discovered Cancelier is in arrears for several years of taxes, and his textile manufacturing businesses are deeply in debt.

Inquisitors received a tip from an anonymous informant which lead to the discovery beneath Cancelier's office.

"In cases like this, we rely heavily on informants. It is impossible to predict when and where the fiends will strike," Brother Jean-Pierre said.

He believes the children were destined for a "fate worse than death" in the lands of the Ottomans and Cordovans.

"Most of these children would have ended up as slaves," he said. "It is not uncommon for the Mohammedans to castrate their boy slaves, or for children to end up working in brothels. This is the most despicable crime I can think of."

Cancelier probably captured the children by enticing them with promises of food or money, Dolcino said. "In some cases he opportunistically abducted them off the street," he said.

More arrests many be pending.

"We have uncovered the names of a number of people we are anxious to talk to," Dolcino said. "Mr. Cancelier could not have run this operation by himself. This is by its very nature an international, multi-party operation. We have only uncovered the tail of the serpent." Dolcino decline to speculate further.

Carmelite nuns are working to reunite the shaken children with their families. Orphans will be placed in the care of the Church.

"All things considered, they are in good condition," Sister Mary-Line, assigned to care for the children, said. "One only wonders how many children before them have been carted off to oriental brothels and harems like so much human cattle."

Saved from a fate worse than death." Joyous children reunited with parents after their harrowing ordeal. Photo: Eugène Atget, Senior Photographer.

RUMORS SPARK ANTI-JEWISH RIOTS IN PRAGUE

Prague, Holy Roman Empire — At least one hundred people died and many more were injured last night in a riot in the Jewish quarters in the Czech city of Prague. The riots also left dozens of Jewish businesses and homes destroyed.

The strife broke out when a four year-old boy was discovered missing. The child's father, Frantisek Uzelacová, suspected "certain Jews had kidnapped the child," according to city officials.

Uzelacová suspected the child's captors had killed the child and drank his blood, the so-called "blood libel."

Although the boy was found several hours later fishing on the Vltava River, widespread anger incited by the rumor had gained irresistible momentum.

"There was simply nothing we could do until the mob subsided," Vladimír Solnicka, mayor of Prague, said.

Inquisition officials said they were likewise incapacitated.

"Such things happen from time to time. It is regrettable, but we do not have the resources to confront mass disorder of this magnitude," a Church official said.

One priest, Father Vjaceslav Otcenásek, said he offered his church as a sanctuary. "The mob respected the sanctity of Christ's house, but there were not many who made it through the doors, no more than a few dozen," he said.

Emperor Rudolph expressed his "outrage" in an official response to the violence.

Despite the statement, the jews of Prague seemed despondent about reparations or trials for their attackers.

"Who would willingly confess to taking part in this?" Rabbi Slot-*continued on page A12*

Russian and Japanese Naval Vessels Exchange Bowshots

Northern Sea of Japan — Russian and Japanese naval officials each accused the other of territorial violations yesterday in a tense stand-off in the northern Sea of Japan.

A Russian fishing vessel was spotted in waters claimed by both nations. A Japanese warship arrived, "forcing our navy to respond in kind," Russian cruiser captain Nikolai Kuznetsov said.

Although the warships exchanged fire, neither side claims to have aimed for the other vessel.

"This was a demonstration only, but the Tzar will only tolerate so much impudence from these devils *continued on page A8*

❧ Inquisition Blotter ❧

Don't Eat the Pies!

Two young lads were caught "attempting to commit the sin of onanism" into a large batch of tarts in a Fifth Arrondissement pâtisserie, according to Inquisitors. The name of the pastry shop is being withheld "to protect the interests of the owner."

The two boys, Jean Duchamp and Guillaume Benet-Pantin, both aged 14, were remanded to the care of their parents.

"These miscreants did not complete their vile act, so we took no further action," said Brother Marcel, the Inquisitor on the scene. "But had they successfully cast their seed onto the pastries, we would have responded appropriately." Marcel said such a response could include "amputation of the offending member, as prescribed by scripture."

The owner of the pastry store was visibly shaken by the episode.

"Seems like every time I turn around someone is trying to use my baked goods for a purpose other than what G-d intended. Why can't these kids just go drill a hole in a watermelon?"

A Gladiatorial League of Sorcerers?

According to some Inquisition officials, it's possible. Early yesterday morning inquisitors and gendarmes responded to complaints of a disturbance deep within the Cimetière Montparnasse.

Gravedigger François St. Honoré reported the disturbance.

"There were explosions, flashing lights, all colors, and weird chanting it sounded like," St. Honoré said. "I didn't dare go near the place where it was going on."

Inquisitors on the scene found evidence of a "pitched battle involving the occult sciences." According to Brother Jean-Marc, the lead investigator, there were also signs the fight was part of a "coordinated spectacle."

"There's evidence a crowd numbering as many as one hundred individuals gathered to watch, almost like a tennis match," Brother Jean-Marc said.

But it doesn't mean the fight was a stage performance.

"There is physical evidence suggesting this was a serious melee, perhaps a fight to the death," a source within the Gendarmerie said. Brother Jean-Marc refused to comment further.

According to investigators, the scene is reminiscent of several others found over the past few weeks, in the Jardin des Tuilleries and the quays of the 12th Arrondissement,

amongst other places.

"We cannot rule out the possibility this is the work of morbid individuals who gather together by moonlight to observe and presumably gamble on violent sorcerous contests," Brother Jean-Marc said. "But it is impossible to say anything save they are exceedingly well-organized. They disperse very quickly and leave little behind in the way of physical evidence."

St. Honoré, the gravedigger, is convinced this theory is correct.

"I tell you, I saw shapes and shadows of people moving around the monuments and headstones a few minutes before the lights and noises started up," he said. "They were like ghosts. This job is creepy enough without crazies blasting up the grounds late at night."

Dope Fiends Using Catacombs to Smuggle Opiates

Inquisitors have uncovered a suspected network of "dope-runners" utilizing Paris' 18th century catacombs to transport and stash their merchandise.

Overcrowding in Paris graveyards became so acute in the late 1700s that corpses would overflow into people's wine cellars, and the noxious rainwater runoff from overcrowded burials poisoned drinking water.

City officials were forced to convert ancient Roman limestone quarries in catacombs, wherein were stacked hundreds of thousands of human bones, transported from gravesites above ground.

Transportation of a different sort is going on nowadays.

"We did not make any apprehensions, but we saw clear signs of traffic in certain catacombs in the Third Arrondissement," Brother Christof, the Inquisitor assigned to the case, said. "In addition, we located and destroyed a considerable quantity of laudanum, presumably stashed for sale or transportation at a later time."

The network of limestone tunnels beneath Paris is perfect for smugglers, Christof contends.

"It offers criminals and subversives the perfect medium through which to move from place to place quickly and undetected," he said.

Tracking down the elusive smugglers may be a gigantic undertaking.

"No one really knows exactly how big the network of catacombs is. Some people even think it continues all the way to Montmarte, but I doubt that," Anastasia Bourdain, chairwoman of the Paris Athenaeum, said. "Still, there are

certainly many unexplored passageways underground. It would be almost impossible to find someone who didn't want to be discovered."

Servant's Corpse Found Outside Hotel

Workers at the upscale Hôtel Duc de Berry discovered the mutilated corpse of a young woman, the servant of a visiting English dignitary, early yesterday morning.

Inquisitors who responded to the report confess they are puzzled by the crime.

"The body was discovered in an alley behind the hotel but seems to have been moved shortly after the commission of the crime," Brother Matthew, a novitiate Inquisitor on the scene, said. "But there's no indication of where the crime itself took place."

"There's something ritualistic about it. Three stab wounds to the neck, and any one would have been enough to kill. The last blow nearly decapitated her," Dr. Antoine Laborde, forensic attache from the Guild of Physicians, said.

Further details of the case are not forthcoming, as an investigation is underway. Hotel management declined to comment on the incident. The slain girl's master could not be reached.

Lower House Member Caught With His Pants Down (or Off)

Baron Georges Deleaval, standing member of the Hall of the Robe, was caught lying down yesterday—naked and handcuffed to a bed in an establishment known to Inquisitors as a "den of iniquity and habitation for women of ill repute".

Lord Deleaval's clothes and possessions, including money and jewelry, were "not present" according to Brother Eustache, who arrived in response to complaints from hotel occupants of shouting and thumping in Lord Deleaval's room.

"Looks like a shakedown," Eustache said.

Not so, according to Deleaval.

"It was simply awful," Deleaval said. "I happened on a young woman who told me her mother needed medical care beyond her means. I offered to help, as would any Christian gentleman. Imagine my surprise when, upon entering the building she claimed was her mother's residence, three young, muscular brutes jumped me and knocked me unconscious. The next thing I knew I was exposed and chained to a bed."

"There were no injuries anywhere on Lord Deleaval's body

that I could see," Eustache said.

Occupants of the building tell different story from the lord.

"I saw his lordship goin[g] upstairs with a young boy, I'd s[ay] about sixteen, with a few bottles [of] apricot oil, a pair of handcuffs, an[d] some hotsauce. Anyways, you ca[n] guess what they were up too," sa[id] a building resident who spoke o[n] the condition of anonymity.

Lord Deleaval was released [to] the care of his wife and children[.]

Watching the Detectives

Marchioness Philippa Ambro[se] deBouron was briefly detained [by] Inquisitors yesterday after s[he] physically assaulted a man she co[n]tends was a private investigat[or] whom her husband hired to "fo[l]low her every move."

Jacques Gittes, the man t[hat] flamboyant young marchione[ss] assaulted, is in fact a chartered pr[i]vate investigator, although it is n[ot] clear he was actually stalking La[dy] Philippa.

But the lady's opinion of hi[m] was quite apparent to those w[ho] overheard the scuffle.

"The lady called him a numb[er] of names I shall not repeat for t[he] sake of modesty," an umbre[lla] salesman who witnessed the inc[i]dent said.

Inquisitors on the scene d[id] not charge Gittes, as they dete[r]mined he was not responsible f[or] the disturbance.

"This is not Lady Philipp[a's] first run-in with the Inquisitio[n,] nor do we expect it to be her las[t,]" said Church officials on the scen[e.] "She has a history of vituperati[ve] and combative behavior."

Lady Philippa was released [to] the care of Lord deBouron, wh[o is] twice his wife's age.

Prominent Rabbi Taken into Custody

Inquisitors and Gendarmer[ie] officers stormed the home of Rab[bi] Albert Maiselles yesterday evening[.]

Eyewitnesses heard lou[d] thumping and shouting in th[e] rabbi's apartment, whereafter [he] and an unknown male companio[n] were directed into a black van.

Brother Moricant, the ranki[ng] Inquisitor on the scene, declin[ed] to comment on the abduction[.] Archbishop Ireneaux mov[ed] quickly to enjoin the matter, sea[l]ing it from public scrutiny.

The whereabouts of Rab[bi] Maiselles and his companion a[re] unknown. Maiselles was respecte[d] amongst the jews of Paris for h[is] extensive occult knowledge.

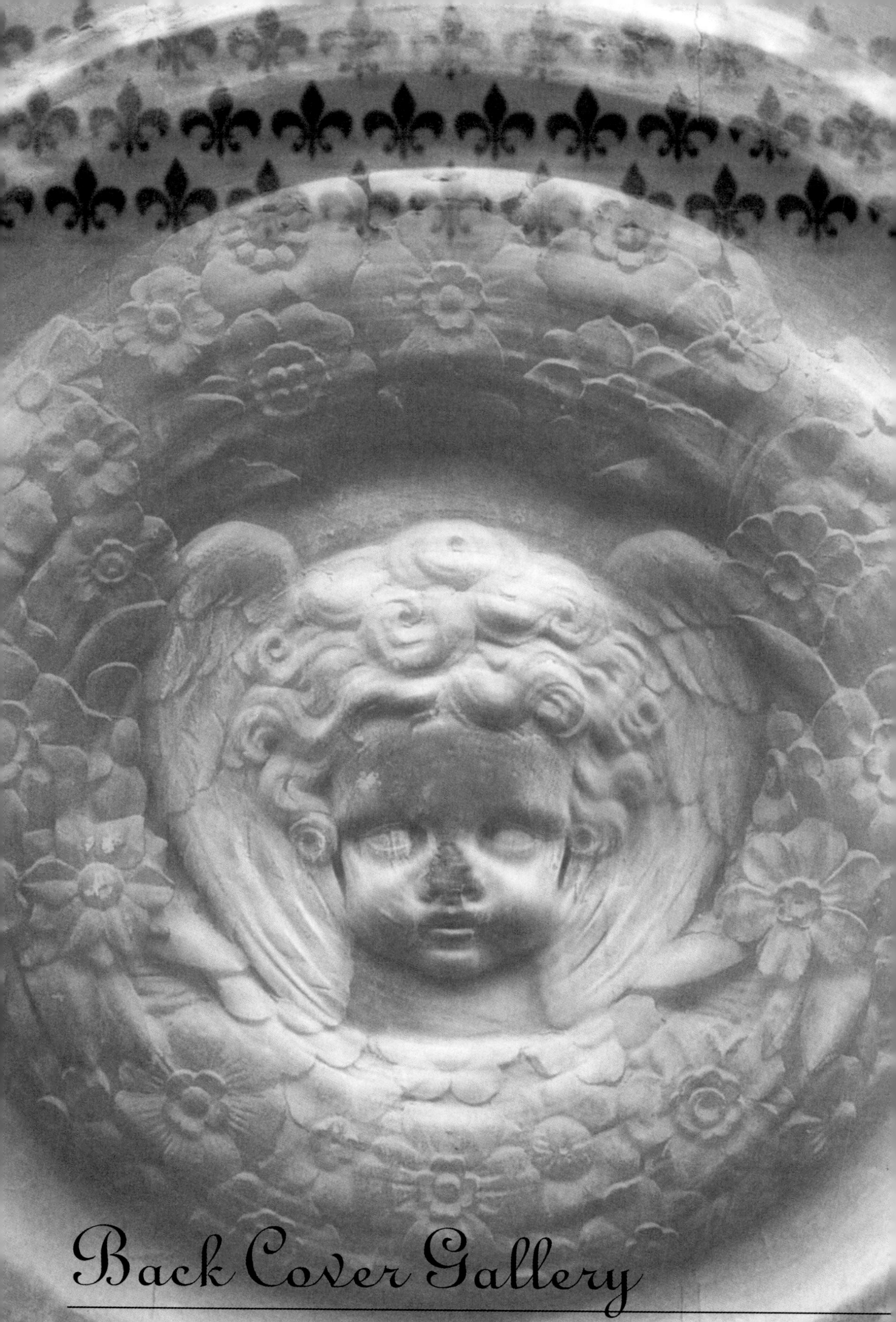

Back Cover Gallery

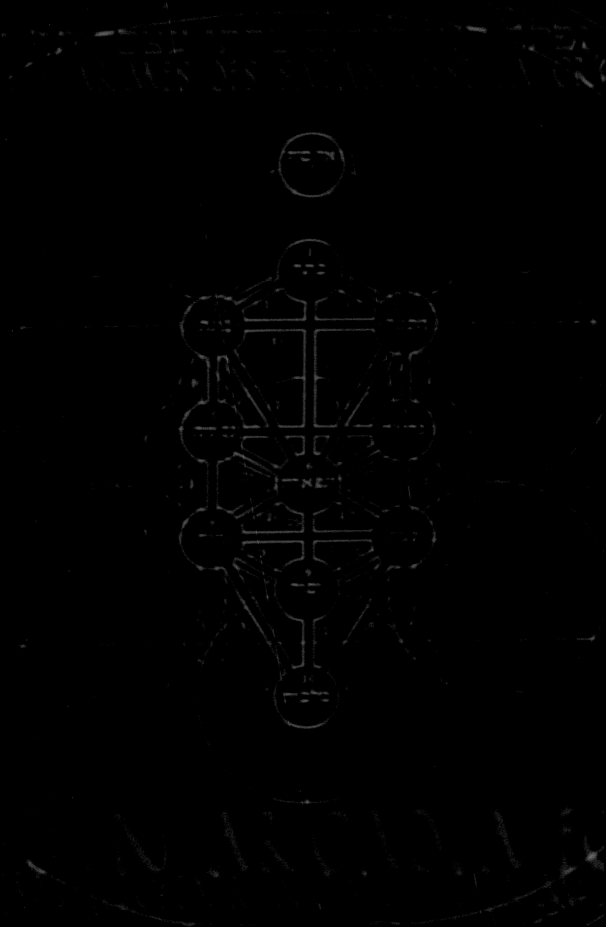

Tone Rodriguez

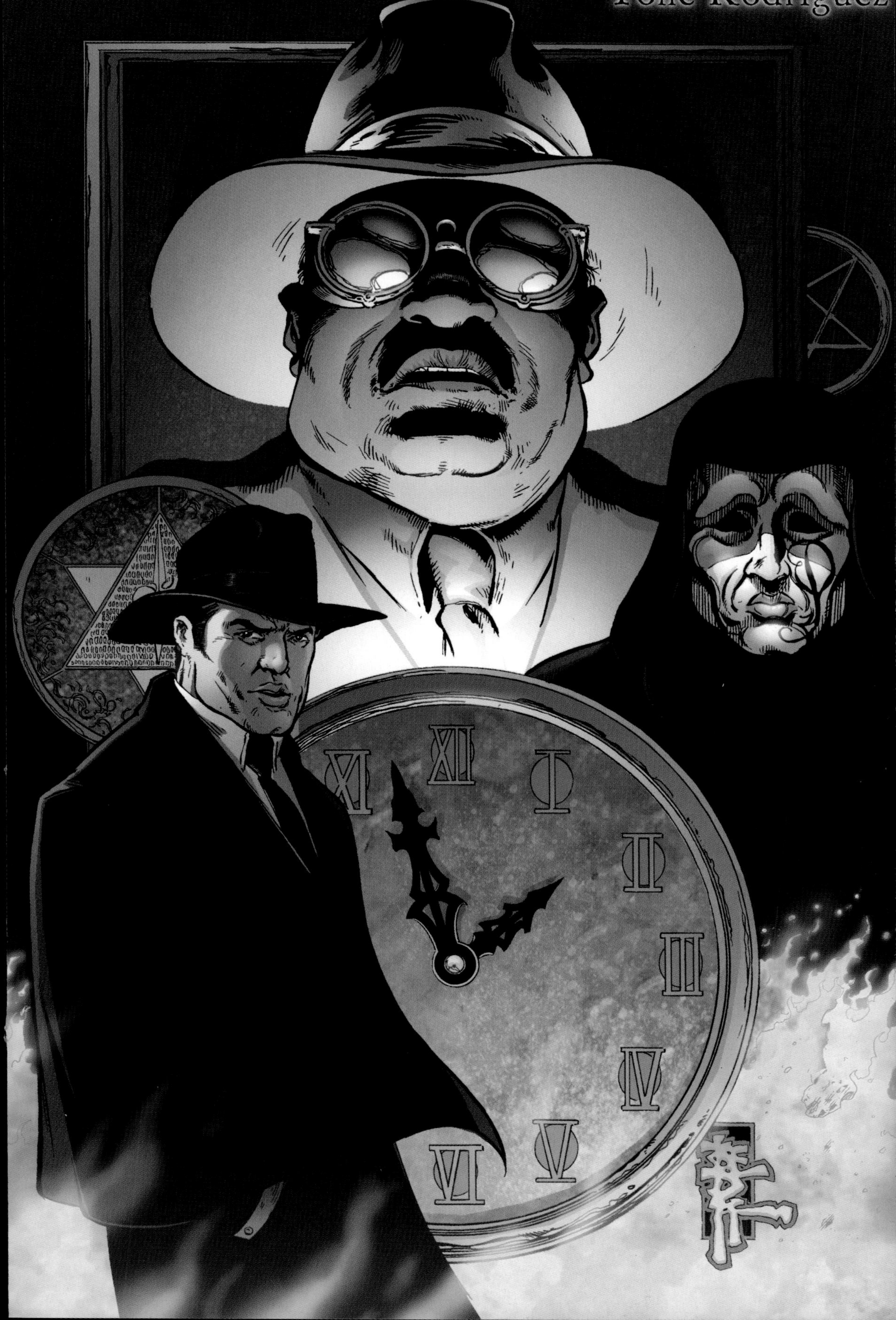

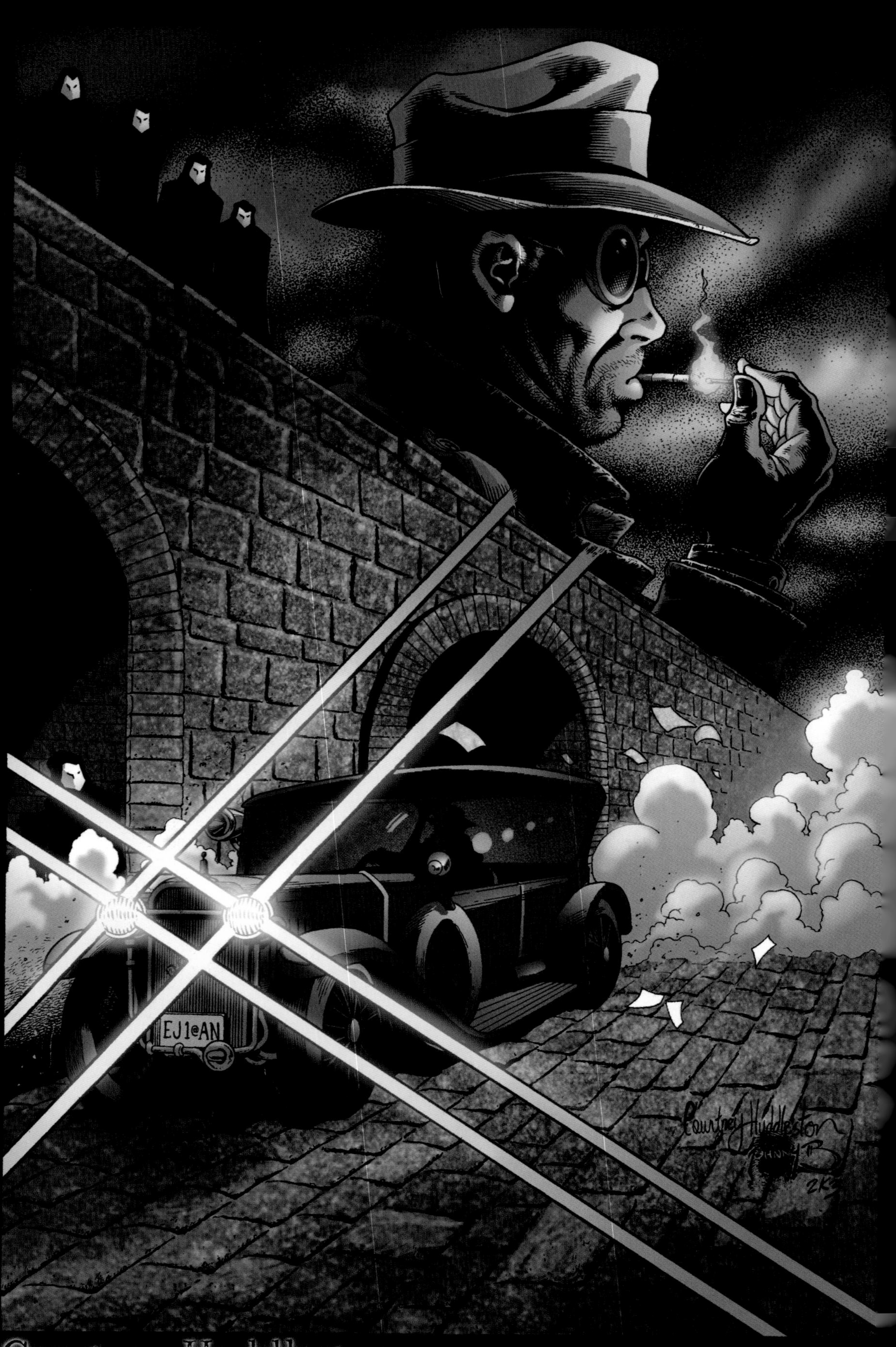
EJ1@AN
Courtney Huddleston

Courtney Huddleston

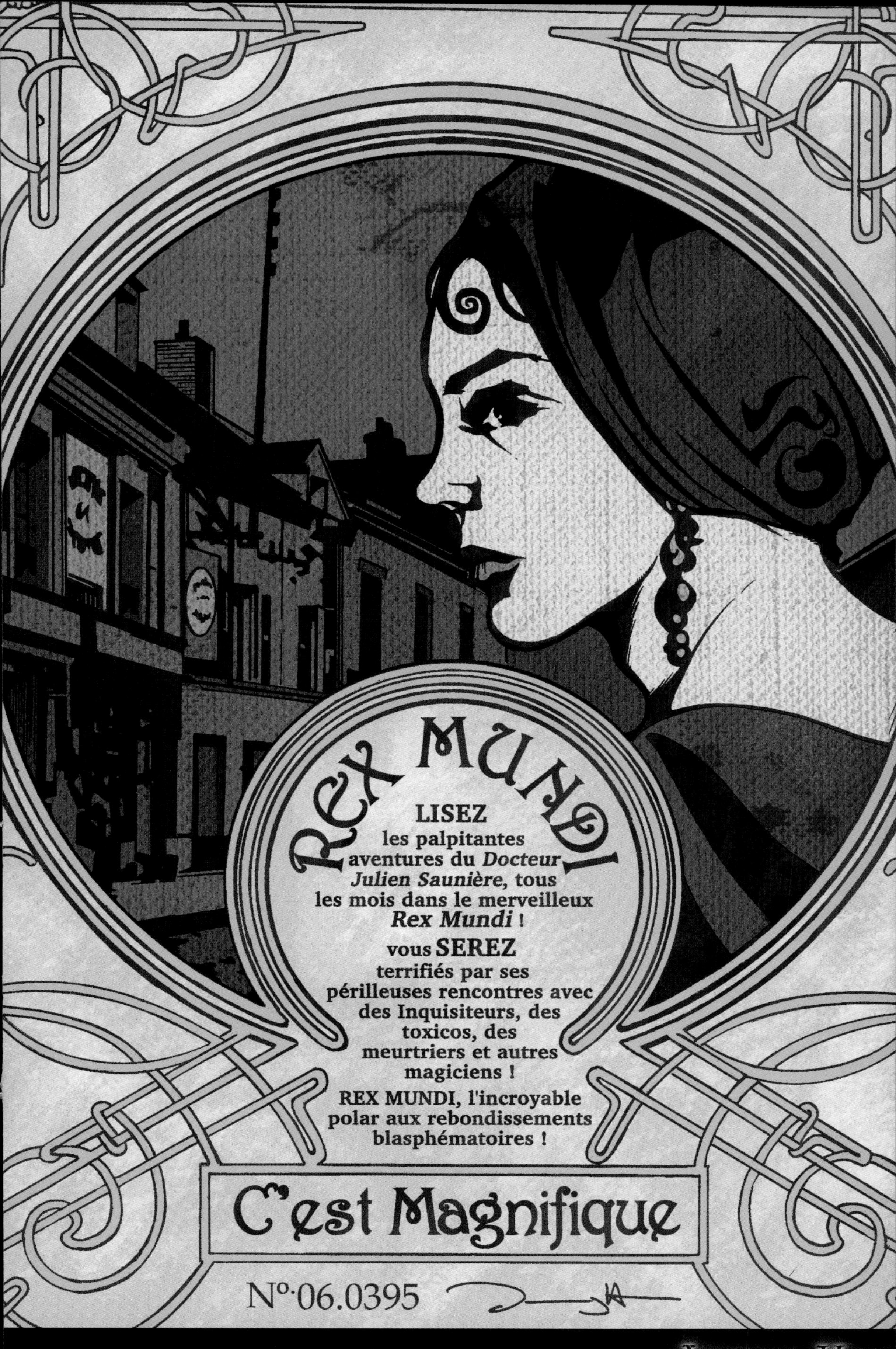
REX MUNDI
LISEZ
les palpitantes aventures du *Docteur Julien Saunière*, tous les mois dans le merveilleux *Rex Mundi* !
vous SEREZ
terrifiés par ses périlleuses rencontres avec des Inquisiteurs, des toxicos, des meurtriers et autres magiciens !
REX MUNDI, l'incroyable polar aux rebondissements blasphématoires !
C'est Magnifique
Nº·06.0395

Jeremy Haun

Toby Cypress

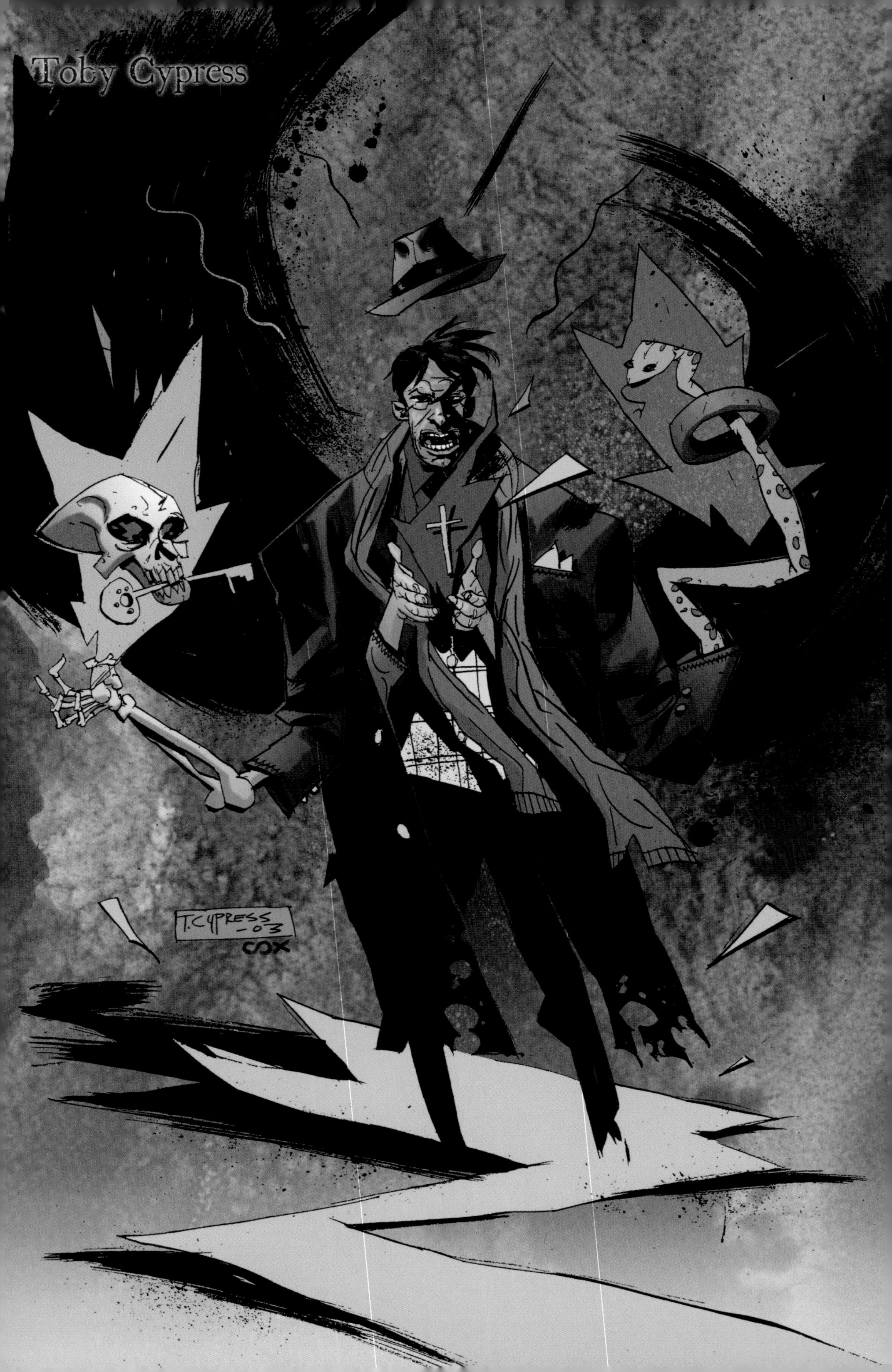
T. CYPRESS -03
COX

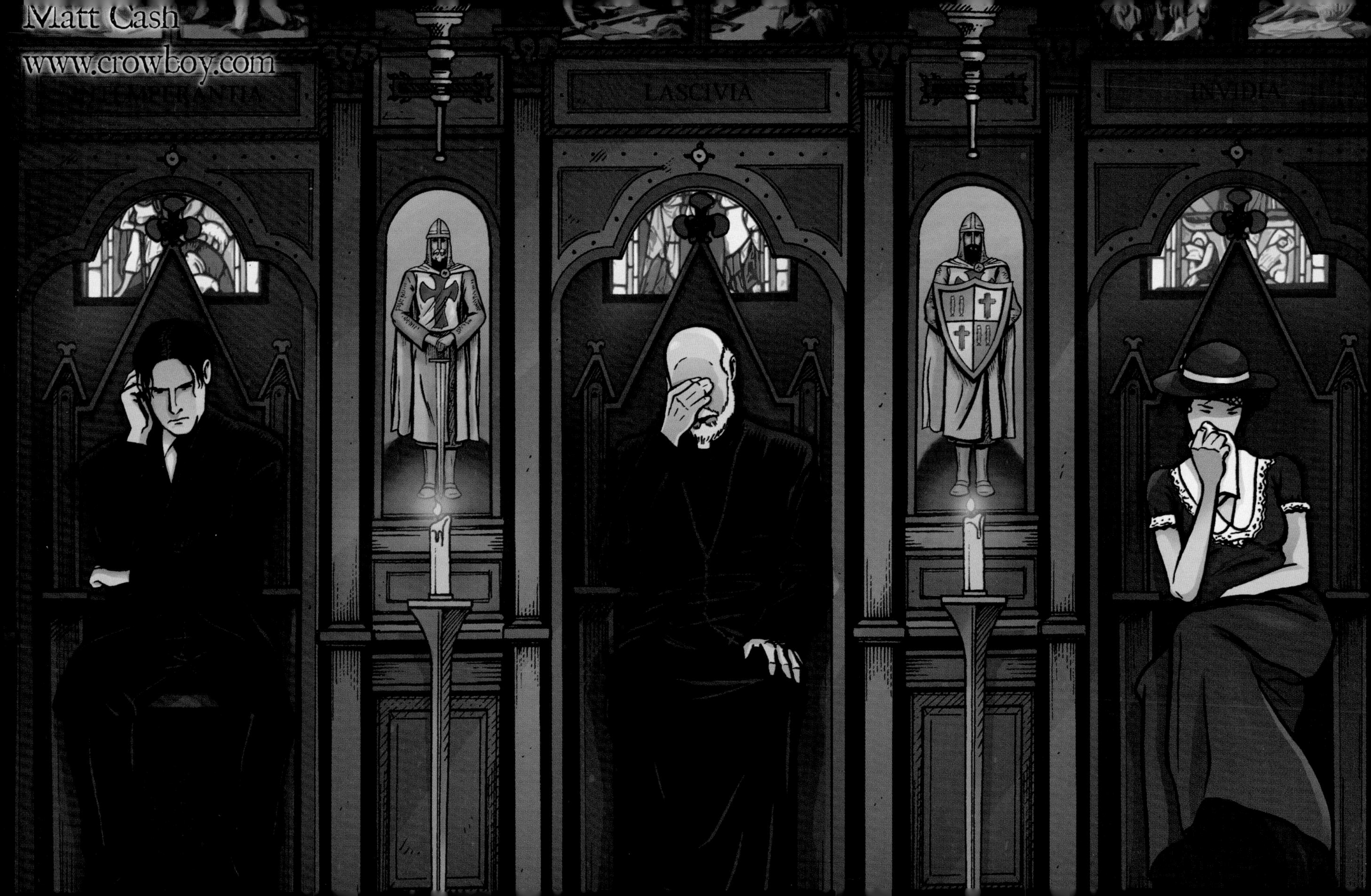
Matt Cash
www.crowboy.com
LASCIVIA
INVIDIA

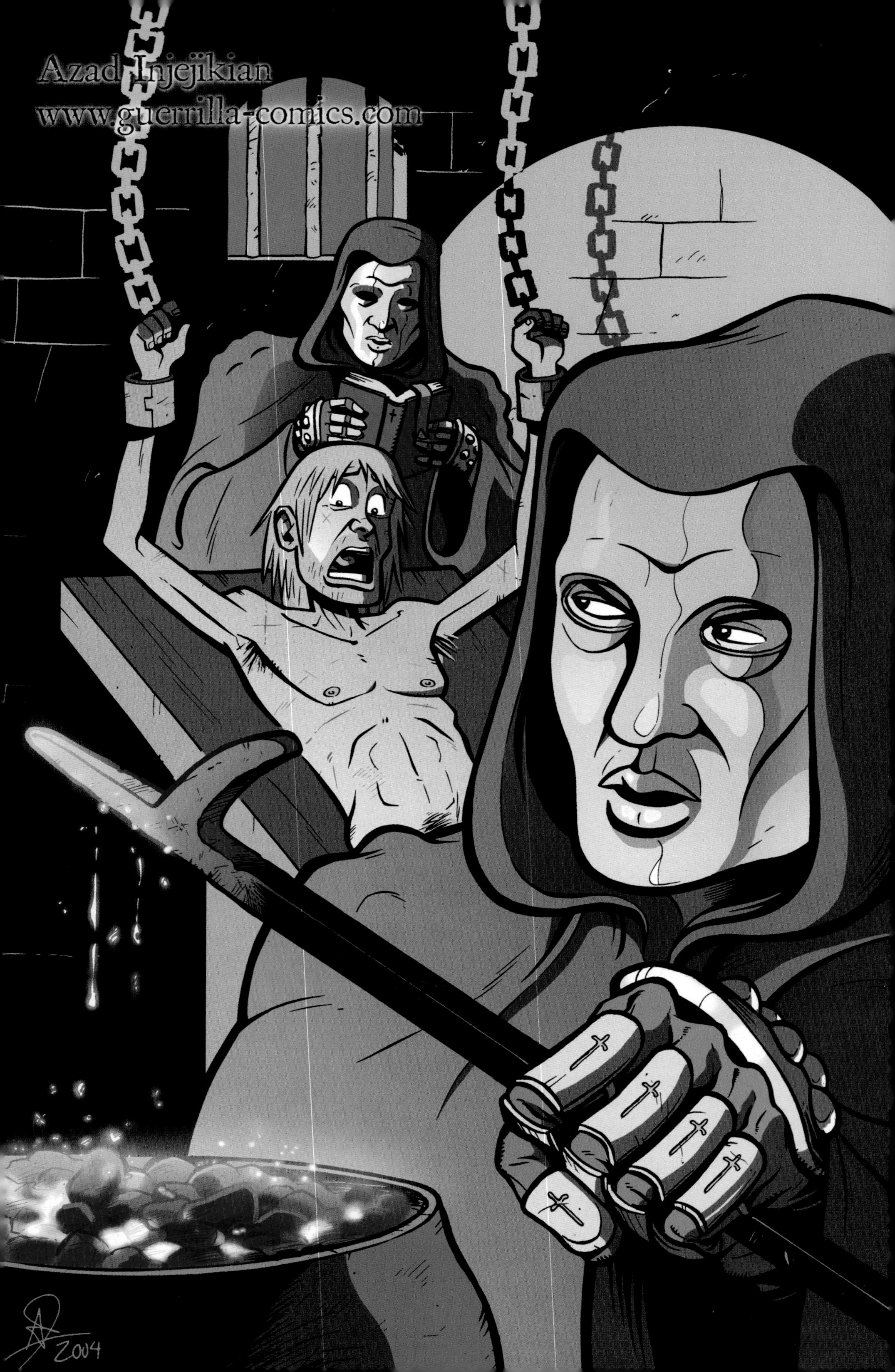
Azad Injejikian
www.guerrilla-comics.com
2004

IMAGE COMICS, INC.

Erik Larsen - *Publisher*
Todd McFarlane - *President*
Marc Silvestri - *CEO*
Jim Valentino - *Vice-President*

Eric Stephenson - *Executive Director*
Missie Miranda - *Controller*
Brett Evans - *Production Manager*
B. Clay Moore - *PR & Marketing Coordinator*
Allen Hui - *Production Artist*
Joe Keatinge - *Traffic Manager*
Mia MacHatton - *Administrative Assistant*
Jonathan Chan - *Production Assistant*
www.imagecomics.com

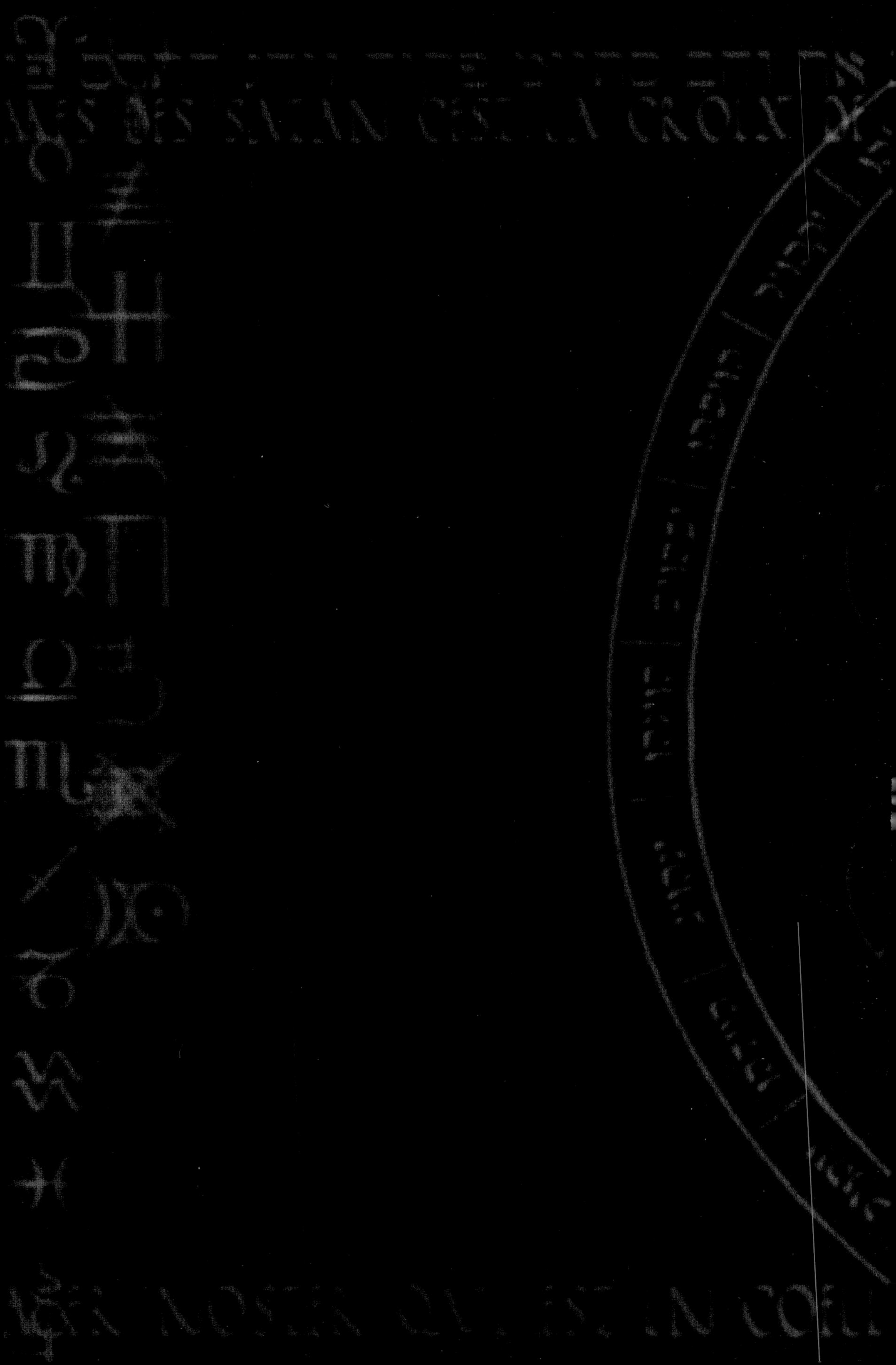
DES SATAN CEST LA CROIX
NOSTER QUI EST IN

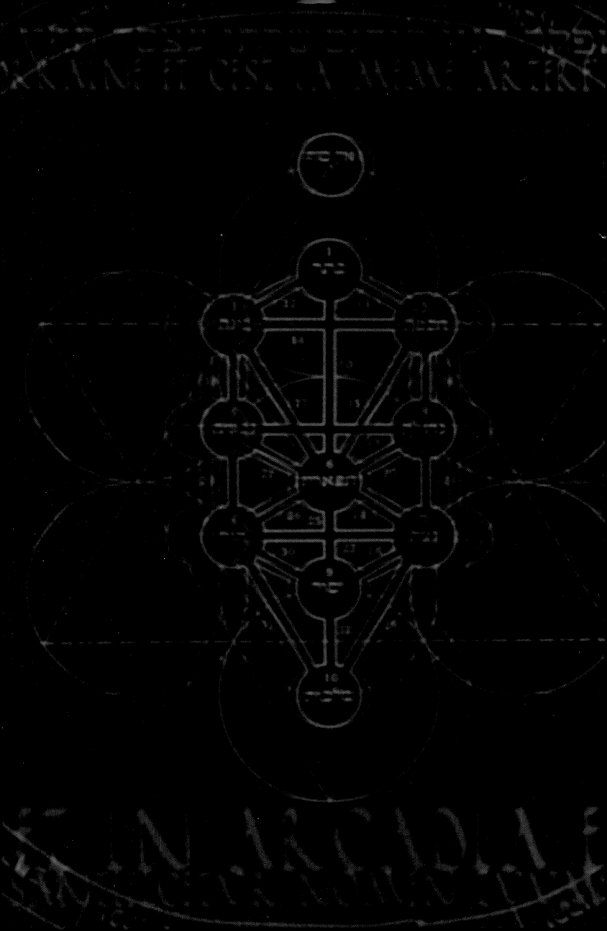

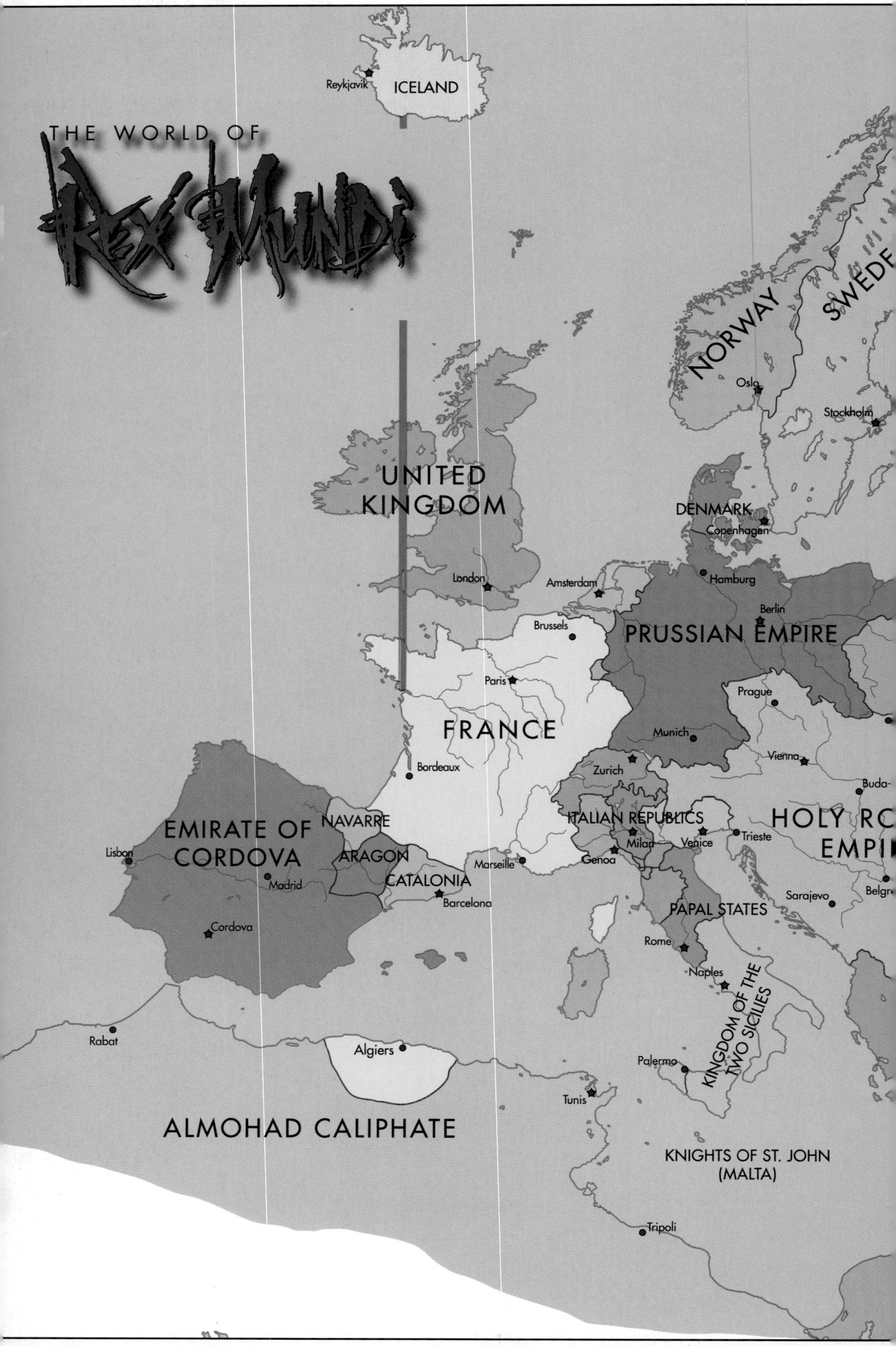
THE WORLD OF
REX MUNDI
ICELAND
Reykjavik
NORWAY
SWEDE
Oslo
Stockholm
UNITED KINGDOM
London
DENMARK
Copenhagen
Hamburg
Amsterdam
Brussels
Berlin
PRUSSIAN EMPIRE
Paris
Prague
FRANCE
Munich
Vienna
Bordeaux
Zurich
Buda-
EMIRATE OF CORDOVA
NAVARRE
ITALIAN REPUBLICS
HOLY RO
EMPI
Trieste
Lisbon
ARAGON
Milan
Venice
Marseille
Genoa
CATALONIA
Madrid
Barcelona
Sarajevo
Belgr
PAPAL STATES
Cordova
Rome
Naples
KINGDOM OF THE TWO SICILIES
Rabat
Algiers
Palermo
Tunis
ALMOHAD CALIPHATE
KNIGHTS OF ST. JOHN
(MALTA)
Tripoli